M000317417

THE "GREATEST PROBLEM"

HARVARD EAST ASIAN MONOGRAPHS 365

THE "GREATEST PROBLEM"

Religion and State Formation in Meiji Japan

Trent E. Maxey

Published by the Harvard University Asia Center
Distributed by Harvard University Press
Cambridge (Massachusetts) and London 2014

Printed in the United States of America

The Harvard University Asia Center publishes a monograph series and, in coordination with the Fairbank Center for Chinese Studies, the Korea Institute, the Reischauer Institute of Japanese Studies, and other facilities and institutes, administers research projects designed to further scholarly understanding of China, Japan, Vietnam, Korea, and other Asian countries. The Center also sponsors projects addressing multidisciplinary and regional issues in Asia.

Library of Congress Cataloging-in-Publication Data

Maxey, Trent Elliott.
The "greatest problem" : religion and state formation in Meiji Japan / Trent E. Maxey.
pages cm. — (Harvard East Asian monographs ; 365)
Includes bibliographical references and index.
ISBN 978-0-674-49199-1 (hardcover : alk. paper) 1. Japan—Politics and government—1868–1912. 2. Religion and state—Japan—History—19th century. 3. Japan—Religion—1868–1912. 4. Secularism—Japan—History—19th century. I. Harvard University. Asia Center, issuing body. II. Title.
DS881.95.M38 2014
322'.1095209034—dc23

2013032660

Index by Mary Mortensen

∞ Printed on acid-free paper

Last figure below indicates year of this printing

24 23 22 21 20 19 18 17 16 15 14

To Libby, for reasons beyond count—
"Let her works praise her in the gates"

Contents

Figures

Acknowledgments

This is not the book I set out to write. My plan was to produce a study of Protestant Christian intellectuals in Japan affiliated with Uchimura Kanzō's "churchless Christianity." I was interested in why these men had written compulsively about the topic of religion and the state in the first half of the twentieth century, but I was not happy about the prospect of producing what would amount to a collection of intellectual biographies. Just as I was preparing to spend fourteen months in Tokyo conducting research, a fellow graduate student introduced me to the work of Gauri Viswanathan. As a result, my interest shifted from studying the particular views of a few intellectuals to exploring the systemic origins of the concept of religion in relation to the state in modern Japan. When and how did people begin to grapple with the question of how best to configure the nation-state in relation to religion? How does the conceptual and historical deconstruction of religion that has progressed across a number of disciplines alter the way we understand the relationship between the modern Japanese state and religion? What follows is my attempt to answer these questions.

I have incurred countless debts in the years since my research began. It is with a sense of humility and futility that I endeavor to acknowledge those who have made this journey possible, bearable, and even enjoyable. A good acknowledgment, it seems, is written in narrative form, walking the reader through the stages of a book's production as though it had a clear origin and a foreordained conclusion. Like my chance introduction to Viswanathan's work, I owe a great deal to felicitous exchanges along the way, and chance does not lend itself to a tidy narrative. It is most honest, I think, to acknowledge those who have made this book possible and who, I hope, will find traces of their contributions in its pages.

Research for this book was supported generously by fellowships and grants from the Japan Foundation, the dean of the faculty at Amherst

College, and the Reischauer Institute for Japanese Studies at Harvard University. Librarians and archivists, including Fred Kotas, Sharon Domier, and the staffs of the National Diet Library, National Archives of Japan, and Tokyo University Meiji Newspaper Magazine Archive, patiently provided their expertise.

At Cornell University I learned a great deal about wrestling with theory and history from Naoki Sakai, and from Michael Steinberg I gained a nuanced understanding of religion within the cultural history of nineteenth-century Europe. Brett de Bary kindly served on my dissertation committee and provided penetrating readings of my work. My fellow graduate students—Tze May Loo, Ben Middleton, Aaron Moore, Vyjayanthi Ratnam, Seth Jacobwitz, and Daniel McKee, to name but a few—all contributed to a colloquy that I continue to draw upon.

The Reischauer Institute at Harvard University provided an invaluable postdoctoral fellowship during a sabbatical year that allowed me to delve into the arcane details of the Imperial Diet. I am particularly grateful to Helen Hardacre, Andrew Gordon, and Abe Ryuichi for reading an early version of the manuscript. Postdoctoral fellows Jun Uchida, Jon Abel, Jessamyn Abel, Chelsea Foxwell, and Todd Henry provided moral support and helpful feedback. Along the way, colleagues across the disciplines and across the world have responded to portions of this book as chapters, conference presentations, and declarations over coffee and beer. I am particularly grateful to Emily Anderson, Suga Koji, Hoshino Seiji, and Ian Miller for their encouragement and insight.

My colleagues at Amherst College have modeled how to combine teaching and scholarship in ways that I will always aspire to emulate. I thank Samuel Morse, Jerry Dennerline, Monica Ringer, Tim van Compernolle, Wako Tawa, Hilary Moss, Paola Zamperini, Rick Lopez, and Adam Sitze, in particular, for their unsurpassed collegiality.

I consider myself particularly fortunate to have been blessed with not one but two generous mentors who demonstrated the utmost of both scholarly rigor and human decency. My undergraduate adviser, Laura Hein, encouraged my interest in graduate work and demonstrated a level of care and moral purpose in her scholarship that I will continue to strive for. And J. Victor Koschmann was what every graduate student seeks in an adviser: incisive, nurturing, and open to questions and approaches beyond his immediate interest. I will always remain in their debt.

This book was helped immeasurably by the detailed suggestions provided by my two readers, Sarah Thal and John Breen. I doubt I have done justice to their input, but the book is certainly better for it.

Finally, I would like to thank my family. My parents, Walter and Mary, supported my pursuit of an academic career from the very beginning. My sister, Shelley, has provided a welcoming home at all stages along the way. I would not have survived my time in Tokyo without the good cheer and intellectual company of my uncle, Paul Axton; I trust he sees traces of our conversations in these pages. And last, and most emphatically, I thank Libby, my wife. She has tirelessly read countless drafts and used her considerable editorial talent to improve my often tiresome and difficult prose. Thank you for your faith and patience.

Note to the Reader

All Japanese names are given with surnames first, as is customary in Japan. Long vowels are indicated with macrons, except in the case of commonplace names and terms, such as Tokyo, Kyoto, and Shinto. Lunar calendar dates have been converted to Gregorian dates following Nojima Jūsaburō, *Nihon reki seireki gappi taishōhyō* (Tokyo: Nichigai asoshietsu, 1987).

Introduction

> The matter of religion is indeed the single greatest problem confronting political policy, and if not properly addressed it may produce unforeseeable problems in the future and lead to insurmountable complications. In light of the experience of nations through the ages, this appears a matter not to be taken lightly.
>
> —Inoue Kowashi, 1884

Defining the "Greatest Problem": Religion and State in Meiji Japan

By the close of the nineteenth century, the modern Japanese state projected a secular appearance. The Imperial Constitution guaranteed, albeit conditionally, the freedom of belief, and the imperial institution itself was kept aloof from sectarian identification or affiliation. Religious indoctrination and rituals were excluded from school curricula, public and private alike, and professional clerics were barred from running for public office. Ideological formulations and administrative practices were careful to define religion as distinct from the state. Yet many students of prewar Japan have taken these secular policies to be a thin disguise masking what was in fact a quasi-religious state.[1] As early as 1912, Basil Hall Chamberlain (1850–1935) described "Mikado-worship" and "Japan-worship" as a religion invented "to subserve practical worldly purposes."[2] Though Chamberlain categorized as religion the national holidays and civic rituals directed toward the veneration of imperial ancestors, few in Meiji-era Japan did so, including those who identified themselves as religious. At issue then, as now, was the signification of religion as a category of political recognition. To the extent that the state resisted characterizing something like "mikado-worship," or emperor worship, as religious, it closed off certain avenues of critique and contestation. The architects of the Meiji state were quick to identify those avenues, and in addressing them gave shape to the dominant political grammar of religion in modern Japan.

By a "grammar of religion," I refer to the conceptual and administrative rules that came to govern the articulation of state policies concerning religion. From the regulation of religious sects, clerics, and practices to the identification of civic duties and the determination of educational content, the state could play a decisive role in constructing the rules that governed not only the practice of religion but its discursive boundaries as well. When Catholic students from Sophia University hesitated to visit Yasukuni shrine as part of their Imperial Army Reserve Corps training in 1932, for example, the Ministry of Education formally declared that "their salutes involve nothing more than a demonstration of patriotism and loyalty." The Vatican accepted this official determination of the secular character of Yasukuni shrine and announced in 1936 that "since ceremonies of this kind are endowed with a purely civic value, it is permissible for Catholics to join in them." While admitting that the character of visits to Yasukuni was open to interpretation, Kevin Doak concludes, "The Vatican knew that the interpretation that ultimately mattered was that given it by those in positions of responsibility."[3] The formal authority of the Japanese state, affirmed in this instance by the Vatican, included the ability to designate certain actions, beliefs, and institutions religious or not. Implicit in this interpretive exercise was the existence of a positively defined domain of religion imagined as separable from other spheres of public life.

This was not always the case. The changes that swept Japan in the nineteenth century included a new way of understanding religion: specifically, as a generic category that could, in theory at least, stand distinct from other spheres of life. As Helen Hardacre observes in her study of Shinto and the modern Japanese state: "In pre-Meiji Japan there existed no concept of religion as a general phenomenon, of which there would be variants like Christianity, Buddhism, and Shinto. People spoke of having faith (*shinkō*) in particular *kami* and Buddhas, but no word existed to designate a separate sphere of life that could be called 'religious,' as opposed to the rest of one's existence."[4] There is a historical distance to be traveled here, from a political and social order that lacked the discursive grammar provided by a generic conception of religion to one organized, in part at least, around that grammar. The adoption of religion as a discursive means to isolate a sphere of life took place unevenly, across multiple constituencies and contexts, and generated conflict and negotiation, as a growing wealth of scholarly literature amply documents.[5] Nonetheless, the state, with its integrationist aspirations and diplomatic concerns, invested disproportionately in constructing the political grammar of religion, which others resisted, compromised with, or co-opted.

Inoue Kowashi (1843–1895), an influential member of the Meiji government who played a role in drafting the Imperial Constitution, the Imperial Household Law, and the Imperial Rescript on Education, placed a great deal of emphasis on the "matter of religion" when in 1884 he declared it "the first and greatest problem confronting political policy [*seiryakujō jitsuni daiichi no daimondai*]."[6] Inoue's invocation of religion as a problem, perhaps the greatest problem, presupposed new modes of governance and corollary imperatives, most notably defining all aspects of the imperial institution in opposition to religion. Those imperatives came as hard-won lessons for the fledgling state, as the Home Ministry admitted, also in 1884: "Many problems have already resulted from directly involving the government in religion. However, the benefits [of that involvement] are not yet apparent. . . . Religion is a category in which the government should not be deeply involved."[7] The historical distance between an absence of religion as an organizing category and the imperative to properly situate the state in relation to it marks a political distance as well. Hence, tracing the intellectual and political history of religion as a category leads to a relatively unexamined question: Why did the state, its oligarchy, the bureaucracy, and accompanying intellectual discourse come to see "religion" (*shūkyō*), a neologism in Japanese, to be a problem, perhaps even "the greatest problem"? The history of this concern, and the Meiji leadership's response to it, is also a history of state formation; it is the subject of this book.

The secular pretensions of the Meiji state grew out of this concern, rather than from a coherent secular*ist* project.[8] Efforts to shield the state from competition with Christianity, from Buddhist disaffection, from internecine conflict among Shinto priests, not to mention the rationalist claims of "civilization" and "enlightenment," led to the political construction of religion as a category to be rendered distinct from the state. For this reason, the chronological scope of this book corresponds to five so-called separations, each of which modified the institutional arrangements between the state and what came to be designated religion. These include the 1868 disassociation of Shinto *kami* from Buddhist deities, the separation of the Bureau of Rites from the Ministry of Doctrine in 1872, the 1882 separation of Shinto priests from doctrinal instructors, the constitutional separation of state and religion in 1889, and the administrative separation of the Home Ministry Bureau of Shrines from the Bureau of Religion in 1900. These separations not only marked moments of institutional and statutory adjustment within the Meiji state but they also bring into focus the conceptual and political stakes involved in the definition and regulation of religion. Primarily at stake was the defensive deployment of the imperial institution and diplomatic negotiations with the conceit of "Christian civilization." Running through both areas was a recurring conversation about the limits of power and the improvised pursuit of more mediated operations of state authority, operations that relied on concessions of liberty, especially religious liberty.

Functionally, the five separations both generated and attempted to resolve "the matter of religion." For example, the disassociation of Buddhist deities from Shinto *kami* in 1868 created a novel sectarian divide that existing administrative frameworks were ill-equipped to handle.[9] That administrative challenge was compounded by an epistemic question: What was the status of rituals and doctrines associated with Shinto shrines and *kami*? Did they constitute a sectarian framework in competition with Buddhism and Christianity? No longer melded into a doctrinal and institutional complex with Buddhism, the newly independent shrines and their priests stood alone but in proximate relation to the recently restored imperial institution. That newfound proximity rendered the possibility of disbelief and sectarian competition a new and pressing political concern, which was expressed in the 1872 separation of ritual from doctrine. The "matter of religion" came into focus for the early-Meiji state in confronting such newfound administrative and epistemic challenges. Religion marked an administrative site at which the state struggled to clarify and synchronize its regulation of and relations with the idiosyncratic traditions and institutions of Buddhism, Christianity, and what came to be called Shinto, not to mention the multitude of other faiths, movements, and practices later lumped together as "quasi-religions" (*ruiji shūkyō*). Epistemically, religion came to mark the boundary at which ritual and doctrinal formulations of imperial authority, and the integrationist aspirations of the modern state, appeared most vulnerable to contestation or even rejection.

The challenges posed by religion were animated by what I call a crisis of conversion. The political discourse of late-Tokugawa and Restoration-era Japan did not begin with an awareness of religion as an epistemic or administrative concern. Rather, the "internal woes and external threats" of the first half of the nineteenth century stimulated a novel interest in the boundaries of the realm and in the loyalties of a populace fragmented by region and status. In the influential vision of Aizawa Seishisai, the integrity of the Tokugawa realm was threatened from within by spiritual heterodoxy and from without by Christian conversion. Aizawa and others after him defined the cardinal concepts of *kokutai* (national polity) and *saisei itchi* (the unity of rite and rule) in response to the perceived threat of internal fragmentation and colonial encroachment. Peter van der Veer observes that "the colonial era makes new imaginations of community possible, and it is especially in the religious domain that these new imaginations take shape."[10] This applies to the role religion played in refracting new imaginations of national community as Japan confronted semicolonial pressures through much of the nineteenth century. Committed to generating a national community through rites, doctrine, and the imperial institution, the architects of the modern state came to recognize religion as a site of incessant competition among exchangeable forms of belief and practice. Constructed in this way, religion threatened to expose an ineradicable moment of contingency at the heart of a national community mediated by ritual practices and confessed beliefs concerning the imperial institution. Put differently, the unfolding process of state formation and nationalization in Meiji-era Japan entailed a trial-and-error process of distinguishing necessary and contingent identifications, and religion took on importance as a depository for contingent identifications that could not be criminalized but nonetheless needed to be subordinated. The Ministry of Education's declaration in 1932 that visits to Yasukuni shrine were "a demonstration of patriotism and loyalty," and hence necessary as opposed to contingent, expressed the institutionalized assumption that separating the realm of public obligation from religious commitments was both possible and desirable. Tracing the genealogy of that possibility and desire from the perspective of the state illuminates not only the history of religion in modern Japan but also the role religion played in foregrounding anxieties concerning the boundaries of the Japanese national community and the limits of direct state control.

State Shinto and the Religious Turn

The construct of State Shinto (*Kokka shintō*) continues to loom large over any consideration of state and religion in prewar Japan, and despite a wealth of empirical research that has modified prior generalizations, discussions of the state's relationship to Shinto tend to obscure the undercurrent of insecurity that shaped the Meiji government's approach to religion.[11] Beginning with D.C. Holtom's work published prior to and during the Pacific War, a number of prominent postwar studies examining religion and the modern Japanese state have focused on Shinto and its particularities to explain the essential character of state authority.[12] Influentially described by Murakami Shigeyoshi as the "religious foundation of state authority as part of the modern emperor system," the term "State Shinto" suggests that the special relationship between the state and Shinto shrines was the primary focus of ideological energies in prewar Japan.[13] Indeed the Meiji government quickly established the principle that Shinto shrines, newly purified of Buddhist elements, possessed an intimate connection to the imperial house, and hence the state (such as with the 1871 declaration that shrines conducted "rites of the state"). This principle, never formally rescinded prior to 1945, has made it easy to imagine the modern state pursuing a sequence of policies with the apparent intent to establish Shinto as a state religion.[14]

Yet, just as the once historiographically dominant emperor system has come under criticism as a monological explanation for prewar Japanese history, the idea of a coherent and consistent State Shinto has come in for significant revision.[15] The state's regulatory relationship with Shinto shrines underwent a series of substantive shifts before anything resembling State Shinto took shape in 1900, when a Home Ministry bureau dedicated to shrines was created. These shifts, often reductions in state support for shrines and priests, suggest a vexed and complicated relationship between the political leadership of the Meiji state and Shinto shrines.[16] In fact, a visible "trough" in state support for Shinto priests and shrines characterizes the state's relationship to Shinto through much of the Meiji period. At its inception in 1868, the new state pursued a set of policies that employed both rituals and doctrine to express in unmediated form the authority of the imperial institution. In the process, shrines and their priests were separated from Buddhism and given the opportunity to define Shinto as a distinct construct. From the early 1870s through the end of the nineteenth century, however, the government ceased actively promoting Shinto as an unmediated expression of state authority (measured in terms of funding for shrines and official status granted to the Shinto priesthood). Three of the most formative decades in modern Japan are thus characterized by a full-scale retreat from state sponsorship of Shinto.

This so-called trough marks a well-acknowledged but little-explained trajectory in state policy. Initial attempts to promote a direct relationship between Shinto and the state confronted "difficulties," "floundered," and "proved anachronistic in the new age."[17] The apparent anachronism of nativist ideologues and Shinto priests, famously depicted in Shimazaki Tōson's *Before the Dawn*, masks the broader political project that stood behind state policy. The Meiji government turned to the imperial institution because it provided the surest means to integrate an archipelago fragmented by a history of regional and status distinctions. Reflecting the integrationist aspirations of a fledgling state faced with a restive and fragmented populace, policy makers attempted to create an order that linked the emperor, as a ritual principal, with a network of shrines, to register the population through shrines and to disseminate a doctrine that connected the afterlife, rational civilization, and political loyalty. With its own institutional and conceptual definition ambiguous to begin with, Shinto was never the primary concern of the state. Rather, Shinto assumed its modern appearance as a result of state efforts to remove perceived obstacles to its project of effectively integrating the archipelago under its centralized authority; to the frustration and resentment of the priesthood, much of what it wanted to include in Shinto appeared to impede that project.

The state's treatment of Shinto occurred within a broader framework designated by the "matter of religion," a framework for debating issues such as how Buddhism would relate to the state, whether and how Christianity would be liberalized, and how state-directed moral education would avoid sectarian conflict. To capture this framework, Japanese scholars have taken what amounts to a religious turn, historicizing the concept of religion to more accurately situate Shinto in prewar Japan and, more generally, to consider the intersection of political power and religion.[18] In the case of Shinto, therefore, the emergence of a discursive order wherein the religious character of Shinto could be problematized in the first place needs to be explained, for it was in bifurcating Shinto into nonreligious and sectarian components that State Shinto achieved its clearest form. State Shinto is unthinkable in the absence of a divide, however tenuous, between the religious and nonreligious. And if the assertability of that divide relied on a construct of religion, the construction of religion in nineteenth-century Japan was part of a global conversation concerning the political disposition of religion within nation-states and colonial empires.

A Global Grammar of Religion

The Japanese word *shūkyō* acquired its modern lexical range by serving as a translation for the Latinate term "religion." The grammar of religion in Meiji Japan has thus been approached as a matter of translation and the adoption of Western norms. Clearly, *shūkyō* gained currency as a translation with traces of its foreign derivation never fully exorcized. At the same time, the significance of religion as a new discursive grammar cannot be reduced to its foreign derivation. That is to say, while the novel category of religion, conceived of as private, doctrinal assent, appeared incommensurate with existing forms of belief, ritual practice, and their place in Japanese daily life, that dissonance cannot be reduced to an assumed incommensurability between Japan and the West.

Religion nonetheless took on political salience in Meiji Japan within global crosscurrents. The semicolonial regime imposed by the so-called unequal treaties made religion a topic of debate, with Christianity informing the Meiji state's diplomatic calculations and its definition of religion. Historicizing critiques of the modern construction of religion commonly stress the privileging of private, individual belief (that is, Protestant Christianity) as the normative definition of religion and religiosity. The application of that definition of religion was intimately linked to the rise of Western imperialism and colonial administration. By emphasizing private, individual belief, the grammar of religion mapped the world in terms of temporal progress: primitive, natural religion at the periphery and progressive, rational Protestantism at the center.[19] The political and intellectual elite of Meiji Japan grew keenly aware of this hierarchy, and the language of "Christian civilization" accompanied the diplomatic interaction between the Meiji government and the dominant treaty powers. Religion constituted one site among many wherein Japan negotiated its place within a global hierarchy.

The grammar of religion within the West, at the same time, underwent noticeable change and produced considerable friction during the nineteenth century under the often-intertwined demands of integrating nation-states and administering colonial empires. Hence, while Japanese elites received a dominant institutional and conceptual vocabulary of religion from the "Christian West" and struggled to define themselves in relation to it, they also observed the ambivalences and tensions that shaped European and American conversations regarding the nature and boundaries of religion. Just as the image of a Japanese "nation" contained the shadows of the West against which it was co-figured, the modern vocabulary of religion in Japan reflected larger shifts taking place within an international order structured by sovereign nation-states, colonial empires, and capitalist exchange. It was in those shifts that the Meiji state found grounds of commensurability between its integrationist aspirations and similar projects in Europe and North America.

For example, the modern grammar of religion served to render religion discrete from other spheres of social and political life, a function that grew out of the particular history of Christian Europe. Post-Reformation realignments of individual belief, ecclesial institutions, and state authority resulted in the development of a political and intellectual vocabulary that celebrated private, individual faith and a "secular" social and political sphere liberated from competing claims of faith. The language of tolerance that emerged in the wake of religious conflict created, at the very least, a dominant social imagery that facilitated the transposition of Christian theology and institutions into universal appeals to humanity and progress.[20] Perhaps more significantly, the emergence of the language of tolerance and private belief corresponded to the development of capitalist modes of production and liberal legal systems that emphasized private property and contractual relations. As in the example of Moses Mendelssohn's *Jerusalem, or, On Religious Power and Judaism* (1783), the appeal for religious toleration on the basis of private belief entailed the surrender of "religious power"—that is, its retreat from public spheres, particularly the economic and political spheres. Put differently, positing religion as something private, superficial, or optional allowed social and political spheres to mobilize claims of rational and natural authority. "By constructing religion and religions," Timothy Fitzgerald observes, "the imagined secular world of objective facts, of societies and markets as the result of the free association of natural individuals, has also been constructed."[21] The central purpose of the line demarcating the religious and the secular was to mark off certain ideologies, institutions, and social configurations as rational, authoritative, and belonging to the realm of public duty and state regulation. By separating religion from the secular, incommensurable differences marked by sectarian affiliation, ritual practice, or cosmological imagination could be removed from markets and political systems. Defining and regulating religion, in short, provided one way for difference to be mapped and managed within nation-states and colonial empires.

In the process of developing an explicit divide between the religious and the secular, higher-order identities (citizenship, race, culture) theoretically superseded sectarian distinctions, and religion increasingly designated a benign yet useful complement to social order and moral improvement. Gauri Viswanathan, for instance, relates attempts to remove sectarian restrictions on citizenship in mid-nineteenth-century Britain to a fundamental reconfiguration of the relationship between political power and religion: "By the mid-nineteenth century, with criteria of doctrinal allegiance no longer determining Englishness, national identity increasingly required a differentiation between political and civil society. Civil society emerged as the privatized domain onto which were displaced a variety of religious distinctions that had no place in political society, or in what came to be construed as the more transcendent plane of secularism."[22] Nineteenth-century states—at both the colonial and the national level—increasingly positioned themselves above a diverse population, and religion came to designate the messy plurality that threatened the proper operation of political authority if it were not relegated to the realm of private belief. It was within this discursive arrangement that public conversions, as in the case of John Henry Newman's conversion to Catholicism, appeared particularly disruptive, because they reasserted the public and political relevance of religiously mediated identities. Conversion, "by undoing the concept of fixed, unalterable identities, . . . unsettles the boundaries by which selfhood, citizenship, nationhood, and community are defined, exposing these as permeable borders."[23] Religion, if it was to possess a public footprint in a modern nation-state, was expected to be either neutral or changeless in relation to the dominant national imagination. Hence, secularity and the freedom of religion relied on a construct of religion that displaced multiple and shifting identities to a private sphere.

Quick students of this history and the contemporary shifts it was producing in Europe, the architects of the modern Japanese state grasped the advantage to be gained from disassociating the imperial institution from the sphere of religion. In this sense, the Meiji-era concern to separate religion from the state can be described in terms of governmentality, a shift in modes of government from external forms of coercion ("technologies of power") to more internal and subjectified forms of mobilization ("technologies of the self").[24] In the context of nineteenth-century Japan, the concept helps describe how the state came to grips with its inability to directly coerce the populace into adopting certain goals and norms. The term *jinshin* (the hearts of the people) dominated Meiji-period political discourse, often expressed as the need to capture the people's hearts (*jinshin shūran*).[25] The political project to capture and control the peoples' hearts confronted a domestic and diplomatic environment that precluded the use of physical violence. The chief complication to initial post-Restoration efforts to enforce the ban against Christianity, for example, was the inability to carry it out by force. When hidden Christian communities in and around Nagasaki surfaced, the Meiji state faced a diplomatic environment that prohibited executing the wayward peasants. Instead the state attempted to "convert" the Christians, which then raised the question of what they were being converted *to*, as well as how that endeavor related to the sovereign prerogatives of the imperial institution. The need to secure the voluntary allegiance of Christian peasants without resorting to force led the Meiji state into murky waters in which educating and proselytizing, morality and religion, and national and spiritual identities were hardly distinguishable. Formalizing a grammar of religion and thus creating a boundary between the secular and the religious offered the state a way out—a way it shared with Western states.

To be certain, elements specific to the Japanese context did shape the modern conversation concerning religion in Japan. The complex and shifting relations between the traditions of Shinto and Buddhism, as well as between Shinto and the imperial institution, for example, resist simplistic analogies to sectarian and church-state relations in eighteenth- and nineteenth-century Europe. Nonetheless, the manner in which these relationships were deemed problematic in nineteenth-century Japan betrays the unavoidably global character of modernity.

Overview

In his introduction to a volume on religion and national identity in modern Japan, Klaus Antoni emphasizes the extent to which "political, cultural, and religious elements are closely interrelated in Japanese history as in most modern societies."[26] That these elements are always already interconnected in Meiji Japan, as elsewhere, seems self-evident. Why it might have appeared expedient to distinguish political and religious elements, however tenuous the distinction may have been, remains to be considered. The focus of this book, therefore, draws upon ideological treatises, policy debates, diplomatic negotiations, journalism, and parliamentary politics to trace the anxiety expressed by the political and intellectual elites as they came to recognize the desirability and difficulty of pursuing a "religious settlement." My aim is not to reassert a "top-down" approach to Meiji history but to examine how state actors, invested in the project of creating an integrated nation-state, imagined its relationship to a fragmented and potentially restive populace. As such, the focus remains on the domain of language and policy; the social history of "religious life" in Meiji Japan largely remains beyond the scope of this study.

The roughly three decades of political and intellectual history examined here are organized in reference to what the Home Ministry called the "religious settlement" (*shūkyō shobun*). The Japanese word *shobun* carries the connotation of disposal, and the bureaucratic pursuit of a religious settlement indeed amounted to an attempt to dispose of religion. As Kitagaki Kunimichi, the governor of Kyoto, described the Home Ministry's 1884 settlement to Buddhist leaders, "The foundation has been laid to prevent any religion from relating to national governance in the future."[27] The difficulty of achieving a permanent settlement provides the primary drama of this history.

The five chapters of the book span the years 1868 to 1900 and trace the genesis of the "greatest problem," the pursuit of a "religious settlement," and the adjustments of that settlement under the constitutional order of the 1890s. In the wake of the Meiji Restoration of 1868, the government pursued an interdependent set of policies in the absence of an articulated conception of religion. The operation of those policies resulted in a novel political imperative to separate the imperial institution from a realm of conversionary competition. Chapter 1 of this volume employs the trope of conversion to analyze both the motivation behind these policies and how the imperative to insulate the emperor from religion first arose within the state. A set of policies that collectively created and propagated a national doctrine as an expression of state authority during the first five years of the Meiji era gave rise to an unprecedented question: What were the consequences of placing the imperial institution in direct competition with Buddhism and Christianity? This question, first posed in late 1871, brought into focus a central concern of the oligarchic government—to insulate the prestige of the imperial institution from the possibility of failure—and marks the political generation of religion as a subject of debate.

The new imperative to segregate the imperial institution from religion also emerged against the backdrop of a global order dominated by the "Christian West." As the Japanese elite negotiated with treaty powers that self-identified as Christian nations, they also confronted a tension in the diplomatic posture of those powers. The treaty powers were caught between advocating both general religious tolerance and the adoption of "Christian civilization." Diplomatic negotiations prompted by Japan's attempt to maintain the prohibition against Christianity revolved around the Japanese concern to shield its fragile authority from Christian missions, while the treaty powers insisted on the vital connection between civilization and religious toleration. Chapter 2 considers how, within the asymmetrical power relations operating under the unequal treaties, appeals to religious toleration could not be separated from the specific advocacy of Christianity. For the Meiji government, Christianity posed a threat to stability. For the treaty powers, Christianity was inseparable from the universal metric of civilization. This apparent impasse found a measure of resolution in the Iwakura Embassy, which toured the United States and Europe between 1871 and 1873. Including some of the most influential members of the government, the embassy observed firsthand the shifting significance of Christianity and religion among the advanced Western nations. The Kulturkampf in Germany and the expansion of public education in Britain and France, for example, appeared to secure state authority over the public domain at the expense of Christian churches, particularly the Catholic church. Discovering a fundamental commensurability between their concern for stability and these developments, Japan's oligarchic leadership learned to place its authority in tension with religion more generally, rather than with Christianity specifically. At the same time, the conceit of Christian civilization remained an obstacle to parity with the West. The Meiji government had no choice but to adopt and adapt to the dominant discourse of religion found in the Christian West. That dominant discourse, however, proved a moving target, reflecting the shifting signification of "Christianity" and "religion" alike within the nation-states and colonial empires of nineteenth-century Europe and North America.

Discussions of religion following the Iwakura Embassy's travels thus carried a dual burden: to diffuse the potential for disruption that any accommodation of Christianity would likely produce and to simultaneously promote the proper form of religion in the name of progress. The intellectual discourse of the 1870s prominently featured the relationship of religion to the "enlightenment and civilization" pursued by the Meiji state. As evidenced in the influential debates of the Meiji Six Society, that discourse also struggled to separate the concept of imperial authority from the domain of religion. ("Theocracy" entered the public vocabulary of Japan as a clearly negative term at this time.) The conceptual difficulties encountered in that attempt were mirrored in the Meiji state's struggle to at once regulate and disassociate itself from the religious tensions of the 1870s. Chapter 3 traces the state's effort to implement the political imperative identified in Chapter 1. The demise of the Ministry of Doctrine in 1877 brought an end to the state's attempt to harness both Buddhism and Shinto in the service of a national doctrine and marked the beginning of Buddhist self-regulation. It also signaled the first articulation of an ideal of "subjectified" religion: private religious belief subordinated to state goals. In short, an authentic and self-determining religious identity stands apart from state power, but actually presumes that power and responds to its demands.

Applying this ideal of a discrete and subjectified religion to the regulation of Shinto proved difficult and contentious. Prompted in part by internecine conflict within the Shinto priesthood, the government attempted to split Shinto into religious and nonreligious entities in its ongoing attempt to insulate the imperial institution from religion. That bifurcation ran counter to how Shinto priests and organizations envisioned Shinto and its relation to the state. Chapter 4 examines how the government's growing concern to direct and control "the people's hearts" in the face of the Freedom and People's Rights Movement (Jiyū minken undō) accelerated its attempts to minimize the official role of Shinto. At the same time, the continuing project to revise the unequal treaties ensured that diplomatic calculations also shaped the conversation. The perceived need to win the "sympathy" of the treaty powers in order to revise the unequal treaties led to rumors that the Meiji government planned to convert to Christianity and adopt it as a state religion. Those rumors complicated the government's efforts to arrive at a "religious settlement" in the summer of 1884; they also reveal how the undercurrent of competition and conversion continued to drive the political concern with religion. The settlement, and the related reform of Shinto shrines, marked the bureaucratic and ideological attempt by the state to dispose of religion as a source of political concern. The settlement attempted to separate religion from the state, circumscribe the ritual role of the emperor, render Shinto shrines fiscally independent, and provide a measure of autonomy to religious sects.

The 1889 Imperial Constitution codified the religious settlement by explicitly rejecting religion as a component of national definition. It thus adopted the principle of religious freedom over toleration, implying the state would recognize no differences between religions. In addition, the conditional guarantee of the freedom of belief introduced an interpretive requirement to distinguish unfettered belief from what Inoue Kowashi called the "domain that governs all people." Chapter 5 traces the history of that interpretive requirement through the first decade of the Imperial Diet, culminating in the failure of the Religion Bill and the creation of a Shrine Bureau in 1900. The Imperial Diet provided a critical stage for negotiating the statutory and administrative boundaries of religion. The 1890s witnessed the potential for sectarian politics, as both shrine priests and Buddhist sects mobilized to use the representative function of the legislature to avoid the full application of the religious settlement. With the government promising a general religion law that would uniformly regulate Christianity, Buddhism, and Shinto, Shrine priests feared the majority of shrines at the prefectural level and below would be equated with temples and churches. Buddhist sects resented the prospect that the state would not differentiate between Christianity and Buddhism, despite Buddhism's long history in Japan and its claim to represent the majority of the nation. The shrine priests were successful in getting the Imperial Diet to validate their concerns as nonreligious, nonsectarian, and hence public concerns of national interest. Buddhist sects, in contrast, confronted the strategic consequences of embracing the category of religion, as their claim to majoritarian status was rejected as divisive sectarianism. In this way, constitutional government in Meiji Japan organized itself, in part, in relation to the requirement to distinguish the religious from the nonreligious, the contingent from the necessary. The apparent commencement of State Shinto in 1900 came as a result of this decade-long clarification of the grammar by which the state would relate to and regulate religion, not as an unambiguous endorsement of Shinto.

In the course of five separations spanning the first thirty years of the Meiji era, the modern Japanese state came to adopt a political grammar of religion that addressed the ineradicable moment of contingency that lies at the foundation of every nation-state. The challenge to secure, at least theoretically, the identification and loyalty of a socially and cognitively fractured populace brought the matter of religion into political focus. The new grammar of religion, expressed in political discourse and administrative practice, worked to displace sectarian difference from the national imagination. The concept of *shūkyō* may have been novel to modern Japan, but the modern Japanese state would be unthinkable in its absence.

Terminology

The analytical task of this book is complicated by the plurality of terms translated as "religion," and some explanation of how I have approached that plurality seems warranted. As noted above, *shūkyō* only gradually established itself as the principal translation for the Latinate word "religion"; into the second decade of Meiji, a number of terms competed to designate the religious.[28] The multiple Japanese translations initially applied to "religion" reflected not only the novelty of the category but also its slippery contours. Terms such as *shūshi* 宗旨 and *shūmon* 宗門 originally referred to sectarian boundaries within Buddhism and grew out of early-modern administrative arrangements. When employed more generically to include Shinto and Christianity, the terms accentuated the ecclesial institutions of ordained clerics, hierarchical organizations, and formalized adherents.[29] In contrast, compounds employing the character *kyō/oshie* 教 emphasized doctrinal content over organizations, as in *shinkyō* 神教, *hōkyō* 法教, and *kyōhō* 教法. Terms such as *kyōmon* 教門 and *shūkyō* 宗教 combined those emphases, designating formal sectarian organizations of doctrinal focus. Compounds employing the broadly suggestive *dō/michi* 道 worked to amplify the conceptual misalignment between Japanese practices, doctrines, and institutions and the Latinate category of religion. Containing the Japanese inflection of the *dao*, compounds such as *shintō* 神道, *taidō* 大道, and *seidō* 聖道 retained a broad range of signification that reached beyond organizations and doctrine to ritual and self-cultivating practices, cutting across the bifurcations of rite and doctrine, private belief and communal relevance.[30] For this reason, terms such as *shūyō* 修養 and *dōtoku* 道徳 often designated practices, ideologies, and associations that resisted being rendered private and contingent within the public space of Meiji-era Japan.[31]

Kyō, with its apparent emphasis on doctrine and private belief, was no less ambiguous, however. The early-Meiji period was, to borrow Tanigawa Yutaka's phrase, an "era of teaching" (*kyō/oshie no jidai*) during which activities and institutions associated with the ideogram 教 were ill-defined and overlapping.[32] For instance, the project of *kyōka* 教化, so central to the ideological programs of the early-Meiji state, designated both education in the simplest terms and an explicitly sectarian project of conversion. Buddhist and Shinto clergy were thus mobilized in the early Meiji years to teach (*oshieru*) a doctrine (*oshie*) in a discursive space that did not readily admit or necessarily require a demarcation of where religion or private belief ended and education and public orthodoxy began. Perhaps more difficult to translate is the term *kokkyō* 国教; literally, "national teaching," the compound could be rendered as national religion, state religion, state doctrine, or teachings for the nation. The apparent lack of semantic transparency is not merely a function of translation, however.[33] For the pragmatic leadership of the Meiji government—men such as Itō Hirobumi—*kokkyō* clearly suggested a sectarian orthodoxy ratified by the state. For conservative voices within the state, such as Motoda Nagazane, however, the term evoked sociopolitical precepts rooted in the moral idiom of Confucianism. As we will see in Chapter 4, within the Meiji state this indeterminacy drove a considerable amount of the debate concerning religion.

Though I translate many of these terms as "religion" for the sake of economy, I present the original Japanese terms in parentheses throughout the book in order to retain the multivalent character of the discourse as it developed in Japan. Within that space, the winnowing of terms employed to designate religion corresponded to the narrowing scope of legitimate activity available in the name of religion. The Meiji period began with an undifferentiated space for teaching in which Buddhist and Shinto clerics were called upon to participate in the educational programs of the state. By 1900, however, a Ministry of Education directive prohibited the inclusion of religious instruction and rites in public and private schools, signaling the state's intent to circumscribe religion and create a formal divide between the realm of public, necessary indoctrination and private, contingent confession of belief. At the same time, the narrowing of religion's signification also bestowed a certain degree of privilege on private belief and sectarian organizations. Religion was reified as a domain on which the state disclaimed any direct control. Recognized sects were granted a measure of institutional autonomy, and the freedom of belief, however conditional it may have been in practice, was valorized in the name of religion. In short, as it took shape the discursive operation of religion acquired a fundamental ambivalence: it designated a realm of unstable competition among a plurality of identities, loyalties, and practices, but it also provided the conceptual and regulative means by which to contain and mobilize that plurality in the service of a centralized nation-state. From the perspective of the state, a nascent conception of religion as a generic and discrete component of human society identified as "religious" those loyalties and activities that needed to be subsumed beneath a higher order of loyalties and activities.

CHAPTER 1

The Crisis of Conversion in Restoration Japan, 1868–1872

> If we do not transform them, they will transform us.
>
> —Aizawa Seishisai, 1825

> We fear that later generations will mistakenly understand the divine spirit of the imperial ancestor to be the founder of a doctrine.
>
> —Council of the Left, 1871

The deployment of the emperor by the fledgling Meiji government as the wellspring of legitimacy appeared predictable enough in late 1867, when it declared the "restoration of kingly rule [*ōsei fukko*]." How the imperial institution would become the nucleus of a new state, however, was as unpredictable as it was unprecedented. The conceit of "restoration" barely masked the dizzying sequence of experimentation and innovation undertaken by the Meiji government as it struggled to claim legitimacy and exert effective control over the Japanese archipelago. In a short span between 1868 and 1872 the new government pursued a series of policies that many have characterized as an attempt to establish Shinto as a state religion (the commonly used phrase is *shintō kokkyōka seisaku*).[1] The government declared *saisei itchi*, or the unity of rite and rule, to be the foundational principle of the state; revived the eighth-century Department of Divinities (Jingikan); disassociated Buddhism from Shinto; and created a Missionary Office (Senkyōshi) to promulgate a "Great Doctrine." Yet by early 1872 the Department of Divinities and the Missionary Office had been dismantled and an institutional separation between ritual and doctrinal expressions of imperial authority was introduced. The attempt to promote Shinto as a national creed had apparently failed, and the government moved on to a new experiment, the Ministry of Doctrine (Kyōbushō).

The institutional adjustments made in the early months of 1872 marked an incomplete but illustrative threshold in how the Meiji state would come to position the imperial institution. It is grossly inaccurate, however, to characterize policies pursued during the first four years of the Meiji era as an attempt to establish Shinto as a state religion. Subsequent debates over the proper relationship of state and religion, as well as whether Shinto could be considered a religion, have obscured the reality: that the so-called policy to establish Shinto as a national religion was pursued in the absence of a clear conceptual or institutional definition of either Shinto or religion. Shifting the focus away from Shinto as the organizing term, this chapter examines how those policies generated a novel imperative to shield the imperial institution from the possibility of failure.

The Meiji leadership began the task of defining imperial authority against the backdrop of an imagined crisis of conversion, a crisis that brought the ineradicably contingent nature of belief and identification into focus. Crucial formulations of imperial authority at this time—*saisei itchi*, in particular—were articulated and imagined in terms functionally commensurate to Christian conversion. The first four years of the Meiji period were thus spent attempting to construct a ritual and doctrinal apparatus around the imperial institution that would be capable of mimicking what Christianity was imagined to accomplish—attracting the affection of a listless populace—and hence counteracting it. The possibility of failure inherent in any conversionary project informed the decision to separate imperial ritual from doctrine, the first step toward a formal disavowal of the religious nature of the imperial institution and the Meiji state.

The effort to distinguish ritual from doctrine in 1872, however imperfectly realized, marked the beginning of the state's concern to place the imperial institution beyond the realm of contestable beliefs and sectarian identification. Ironically, the Restoration-era pursuit of ritual and ideological purity generated fissures that did not exist before, by creating a sectarian break between Buddhism and what came to be called Shinto. The disassociation of Shinto from Buddhism and the aggressive attempt to counter the imagined conversionary prowess of Christianity resulted, in short, in a new political imperative to separate state and religion. A diplomatic environment dominated by the unequal treaties and the new regime's reliance on foreign support contributed to this process by forcing the Meiji leadership to enforce the prohibition against Christianity through persuasion rather than violent punishment, including execution. This experiment in pastoral intervention provided what amounted to a trial run for the imperial institution—its mythology, rituals, and the charisma of the emperor—in securing the loyalty of the general population.

The perceived failure of that experiment introduced a crucial negative definition to imperial authority that informed subsequent policy debates concerning the character of Shinto, the regulation of religion, and the proper deployment of imperial authority as state ideology. The policy trajectory for separating religion and state, as well as granting the freedom of belief, emerged from this fundamental concern to use the imperial institution as an integrative resource.

Crisis and Conversion in Late-Tokugawa Japan

The specter of foreign encroachment haunted the political imagination of late-Tokugawa Japan. Famines, peasant unrest, and a general sense of decay compounded the palpable sense of crisis, expressed as "internal woes, external threats." This crucible of crisis heightened the ideological and pragmatic significance of the imperial institution for many, including Aizawa Seishisai (1782–1863). Aizawa's 1825 treatise, *New Theses* (*Shinron*), provided perhaps the most influential articulation of the vital importance of regenerating the emperor as the focal point of life on the Japanese archipelago.[2] Strikingly, it did so by placing the threat of Christian conversion in the foreground of the crisis confronting the Tokugawa polity. Though initially kept private, the *New Theses* was published in 1857, just one year before the Tokugawa shogunate signed the commercial treaties of 1858, opening the realm to foreign commerce and paving the path for the backlash that ushered in the Meiji Restoration. To a generation of loyalists who fought to replace the shogunate with a restored imperial government, Aizawa's treatise provided a powerful prism through which to view the world and Japan's place in it. What they saw was a world colored by a competition to convert.

Aizawa was a scholar-official serving the Mito domain, one of the three Tokugawa collateral houses that was known for its loyalist thought, often referred to as Mito Learning (Mitogaku). That school of thought drew on the eighth-century imperial "mythistories," the *Kojiki* and *Nihon shoki*, and interpreted them through a Confucian lens, calling for the rectification of society, or "the rectification of names," by restoring hierarchies of loyalty.[3] In his *New Theses*, Aizawa wedded this emphasis on the proper arrangement of the sociopolitical order to his diagnosis of the external threat confronting the Tokugawa realm. Hence the *kokutai*, the national polity organized around the heavenly mandate of the emperor and his sacerdotal role, provided both a template for an ideal sociopolitical order and a means to respond to the foreign threat, notably Christian conversion. Expressed as *saisei itchi*, the unity of rite and rule, the political salience of the imperial office came to be linked to the priestly character of the emperor. Aizawa defined, in short, the *kokutai* and *saisei itchi* in terms opposed but functionally commensurate with Christian conversion.[4]

Christian conversion became Aizawa's focus in part because of how he interpreted the foreign threat confronting the Tokugawa realm. Prior to writing his treatise, Aizawa interrogated English sailors who had been shipwrecked off the Mito coast. The information Aizawa gleaned from the English sailors, combined with his awareness of Russian movement into the vaguely defined Ezo territories to the north, painted a picture of a world increasingly controlled by "barbarians" who employed Christianity as their most effective means to subjugate populations. Russian movement across Siberia into Ezo troubled Aizawa and his contemporaries because between the Russians and Tokugawa authorities stood the Ainu, a population indigenous to the northern islands and largely unassimilated into the sociocultural world of Tokugawa Japan. By the mid-eighteenth century, the Russians had secured footholds in the Kurile Islands and begun Russifying the local Ainu population, who adopted Russian names and dress, and Russian Orthodox Christianity. In Aizawa's view, the foreign powers succeeded in expanding their sway, as in the case of Russia and the Ainu, because Christianity allowed them to conscript their subjects into service. Christianity provided the means for the Russians to unite and mobilize both their own subjects and the peoples they conquered: "They rely upon Christianity as the sole source of their strength. This so-called doctrine [*kyōhō*] is evil and shallow, not worth discussing. Its essence, however, is easy to comprehend and its words are calculated to easily entice the ignorant commoners." Once the commoners are enticed, Aizawa wrote, "nothing can undo their confusion. This is the secret of the method employed by the barbarians."[5] Vulnerable to conversion, the Tokugawa realm faced inevitable encroachment. The rather fabulous prowess of Christianity that Aizawa invokes, to convert "ignorant commoners" en masse into agents of foreign conquest, owed a great deal to the anti-Christian polemics of the mid-seventeenth century and their exaggerated portrayals of Catholic missionaries as sorcerers intent on bewitching the people. At the inception of the Tokugawa shogunate, demonizing the foreign faith provided authorities with the best means to instill a fear and loathing among the educated and common classes alike.[6] At the same time, mass conversions appeared a credible threat in Aizawa's eyes, less because of the specific character of Christian doctrine and practice than because of the actual fragmentation he witnessed within the Tokugawa realm. Put another way, the specter of Christian conversion reflected how Aizawa imagined the state of the Japanese polity, more than it did an accurate grasp of the actual method of colonization practiced by foreign powers. While the "barbarians" used Christianity to convert, unite, and mobilize those they conquered, he believed the Tokugawa realm lacked unity and hence could not be mobilized in defense. In response to this absence of integration, Aizawa put forward what has been described as a "theology of the national body," an essential politico-spiritual community that could be "regenerated by ritual practice."[7]

The *kokutai,* according to Aizawa's account, was established by the founding emperor, Jinmu, when he acknowledged the debt owed to his divine ancestor, Amaterasu, by ritually expressing filial devotion. The ideal of *saisei itchi* was thus located in the ancient founding of the Japanese polity, when the emperor served as both political and sacerdotal principal, leading the realm in rites of devotion to imperial and common ancestors alike. The centralized ritual order that arose from this foundational moment deteriorated through the centuries owing to the proliferation of numerous heresies and evil doctrines that led the commoners astray. As Aizawa put it, because the "people's natural sentiments cannot avoid favoring profit and fearing spirits," countless heresies have entered the realm to draw them away from the Way of the *kami* (*shintō*) that in ancient times had "captured the hearts of the people (*minshin wo shūshū*)."[8] Aizawa called for the revival of a centralized ritual order, with the emperor and his court at its center, to once again capture the hearts of the people.

According to this vision of the *kokutai* and *saisei itchi*, Christianity was not the only enemy of stable integration under the imperial institution. Aizawa's call to reintegrate the national body through the unity of rite and rule also identified as obstacles a wide array of institutions as well as popular beliefs and practices. These included Buddhism, "perverse" forms of Confucianism, folk beliefs, and practices such as shamanism.[9] Aizawa was by no means unusual among Confucian intellectuals in denigrating popular beliefs and practices, or in calling Buddhism corrupt and wasteful. In what is considered a "paradigmatic" form of anti-Buddhist reform, in the 1840s the Mito domain forcibly abolished at least 190 temples and laicized the monks attached to them. Bells and other implements at the temples were recast as cannons.[10] Ironically, it was the privileged role Buddhism came to play in enforcing the anti-Christian edicts that gave rise to much of the anti-Buddhist polemics of the early-modern period.[11] With very few exceptions, all within the Tokugawa realm were required to register with a Buddhist temple, and priests were to certify their parishioners were not Christian. Aizawa blamed the resulting Buddhist monopoly on funeral rites for accelerating the decline of imperial rituals and for the spread of doctrines concerning judgment and salvation in the afterlife. The Ikkōshū (Shin sect) in particular, with its exclusivist doctrines and promise of salvation, "forbade worshiping at the shrines" and instead venerated a foreign god. More generally, the doctrine of "original reality, manifest traces" (*honji suijaku*) defined the Shintō *kami* to be mere manifestations of Buddhas and "betrayed Heaven and deceived man," thus undermining the *kokutai* from within.[12] In effect, Buddhism, like the other heresies Aizawa identified, stood in competition with the national body and its rituals for the hearts of the people, or *minshin*.

At the heart of Aizawa's treatise lay a clear recognition of the contingent nature of identification and loyalty. The potential for mass conversion to Christianity and the actual erosion of the *kokutai* by "heresies" (*itan*) arose from the mutable nature of the human heart, a heart that those in authority had to capture and retain. When Aizawa advocated regenerating the *kokutai* through a ritual order, therefore, the *kokutai* did not refer to an original linguistic, racial, or ethnic unity that had only been lost or contaminated. Aizawa imagined the national polity to have originally been a mechanism to convert and assimilate alien populations into the imperial realm. Thus, he declared the *kokutai* to be a revival of the ancient "Way" that allowed Emperor Jinmu and his descendants to "control the barbarians."[13] Because the barbarians "desire to transform the middle kingdom by *turning against us* the method used by past emperors to transform them," an immutable means to unify the peoples' hearts had to be established.[14] Whether the *kokutai* or Christian conversion, the stratagem was the same: to capture and assimilate alterable identities. The contest between the "middle kingdom" of Japan and the barbaric periphery was not, in the long term, to be military or economic; rather, it was to be a contest to decide who would transform, and thereby assimilate, the other, according to Aizawa: "If we do not transform them, they will transform us."[15] By framing Tokugawa Japan as the "middle kingdom," Aizawa subjected Wajin commoners and the Ainu alike to the logic of conversion and assimilation.[16] The seemingly self-evident assertion that both Ainu and commoners were vulnerable to conversion translated the threat of foreign encroachment into a crisis of conversion. The absence of a populace that reliably self-identified with the ruling order rendered the specter of Christian conversion threatening to Aizawa and his contemporaries.

The political and social turmoil of the mid-nineteenth century that culminated in the Meiji Restoration set the stage for a rapid and radical reconfiguration of nearly all aspects of society on the Japanese archipelago. That reconfiguration was guided by the Meiji state's attempt to forge the archipelago into a cohesive unit of administration under a sovereign emperor, in whose name the state could undertake the radical reforms deemed necessary to achieve parity with the treaty powers. The ideological tropes employed to define the "restored" authority of the emperor were not manufactured ex nihilo, nor were they given concrete definition by some unbroken tradition. Concepts such as the *kokutai* and *saisei itchi* grew out of the "internal woes and external threats" that plagued the final decades of Tokugawa rule.[17] The new regime's initial pursuit of a series of policies intended to realize the unity of rite and rule—linking the imperial institution to shrines, rites, and a pantheon of *kami*—can easily appear benighted and anachronistic.[18] However, in view of Aizawa's diagnosis of the crisis confronting the Japanese polity, a crisis of potential conversion, those policies can be read as rational and purposeful attempts to integrate a populace.[19] Through *saisei itchi*, the *kokutai* was imagined in commensurate opposition to Christian conversion, Buddhism, and countless other heresies, with the hearts of the people up for grabs. As a result, the claim of the imperial institution to be the divinely ordained and inevitable locus of authority of the polity confronted a question: what if the hearts of the people were drawn to "profit and fear of spirits"? Christianity was the primary threat, but preparing to confront it required removing the "heresies" that corrupted the ritual order that should have directly linked the populace to the imperial institution.

Aizawa's ideological vision as articulated in 1825, despite its emphasis on the imperial institution, presumed the continuation of the Tokugawa polity. By the time the Tokugawa *bakufu* collapsed in late 1867 and the new government claimed to rule in the name of the emperor, the concepts of *kokutai* and *saisei itchi* assumed even greater ideological weight, providing the means to articulate the basis for and operation of imperial sovereignty.[20] What Aizawa envisioned as a mode of reform became a revolutionary program, one that fundamentally altered the character of the imperial institution. At the same time, post-Restoration articulations of s*aisei itchi* retained its clear opposition to the threat of Christian conversion, sustained by the broad reach of anti-Christian discourse from the late-Tokugawa into the Meiji period.[21] Shinto and Buddhist clerics, nativist scholars, and many among of the loyalist samurai were united in viewing Christianity as the principal manifestation of foreign encroachment.[22]

Restoring Unity and Creating Division

Saisei itchi surfaced immediately as a guiding principle for the Meiji state after the "restoration of kingly [imperial] rule" was declared at the end of 1867.[23] From the outset the new government, a coalition of pro-imperial activists, courtiers, and daimyo, faced division internally and an obvious deficit in legitimacy externally.[24] Dominated by the domains of Satsuma and Chōshū and locked in a civil war against forces loyal to the Tokugawa *bakufu*, the Meiji government relied on the imperial institution to buttress its claim to legitimate authority. Compounding its perceived lack of legitimacy, the new government had inherited a poorly integrated polity organized around the semiautonomous daimyo domains; initially, the new regime could directly administer only those regions surrendered by the Tokugawa. The possibility of effective governance by the new state, not to mention its very survival, depended on gradually establishing administrative control over the domains. In the face of these demands, the government formally declared the restoration of the "unity of rite and rule" in April 1868.[25] Imperial rituals offered the best means by which to demonstrate the legitimacy of the Meiji state and to begin establishing the preeminence of the court over the domains and their feudal privileges.

Despite its relevance to pressing political demands, as a guiding principle *saisei itchi* lacked a precise institutional definition. Like many concepts that structured political discourse following the Restoration, the unity of rite and rule was pursued in the name of restoration, as exemplified in the revival of the Jingikan, the eighth-century Department of Divinities. The listless position of this department, as well as its shifting designations, during the early months of 1868 reflected the unsettled role of rituals within the state.[26] The past provided merely the raw material for devising and adapting a ritual order best suited to the demands of the day. Those demands, as John Breen observes, required the simultaneous "politicization" and "ritualization" of the emperor.[27] The fledgling government staked its legitimacy on the interdependent conceits of the emperor ruling in person (*tennō shinsei*) and conducting rituals in person (*tennō shinsai*). Initially, at least, the "conceptual vacuum" at the center of *saisei itchi* accommodated multiple visions of what the principle meant in practice, allowing those committed to the ideal of restoring pure, ancient precedents and those interested in pragmatically constructing a centralized nation-state to converge in emphasizing the ritual character of the imperial institution.[28] That convergence did not last, however, in large measure because the pursuit of *saisei itchi* generated its own excess. Simultaneously politicizing and ritualizing the emperor did more than provide a means for using the imperial institution; it generated new friction that threatened the very stability and integration sought by the government.

Saisei itchi created a framework for implementing two central strategies for employing the imperial institution as an integrative resource. The first was to ritually reinforce the source of imperial sovereignty: the ancestral bequest of the eternal mandate to rule the Japanese realm (*tenjō mukyū no shinchoku*).[29] The divine and unbroken lineage of the imperial house and the ethical imperative of filial devotion formed an ideological complex that was ritually employed both within the state and externally, toward the general populace. The second strategy aimed to facilitate an immediate connection between the emperor and the Japanese realm as a whole, expressed in terms of the emperor's "single gaze, equal benevolence" (*isshi dōjin*). These two approaches took shape through 1868, beginning with the Charter Oath Ceremony in April and ending in the anniversary of Emperor Kōmei's death in February 1869.

The Charter Oath Ceremony took place on the day following the declaration of *saisei itchi* and famously employed the sacerdotal character of the emperor to identify the executive members of the government with the emperor and to confirm the ancestral investment of imperial sovereignty.[30] The emperor personally swore an oath to the *kami* of heaven and earth (*tenshin chigi*) and was assisted not by the courtiers who traditionally served as ritual intermediaries, but by Sanjō Sanetomi (1837–1891), a representative of the executive Council of State (Dajōkan). Though a courtier himself, by virtue of his position as vice president (*fukusōsai*) of the government, Sanjō's participation in the ceremony directly identified the executive members of the government with the emperor and his heavenly mandate.[31] This helped lay the groundwork for diminishing the role of courtiers, who were intent on reinvigorating their hereditary claims to influence within the imperial court, as well as the daimyo, who had reason to expect a council of daimyo would form the center the new state. The final version of the five articles of the oath removed any explicit mention of a council of daimyo, promising ambiguously instead to decide all matters by public discussion (*kōron*).[32] The ceremony concluded with the assembled daimyo and courtiers signing an oath of loyalty; their loyal devotion to the emperor was to mirror the emperor's loyal devotion to his divine ancestors. The ritual in effect employed the emperor's sacerdotal authority to address the lack of cohesion within the government by identifying the executive members with the emperor, and it set the stage for curtailing the role of the daimyo and courtiers within the new government.[33] When the so-called Seitaisho constitution issued in June reduced the number of senior and junior councilors (*gijō* and *sanyo*) in the government from 126 to 42, most of those removed were daimyo and courtiers.[34]

The Charter Oath Ceremony leveraged the imperial institution to reconfigure the internal composition of the government. Yet, while the order of the ceremony and content of the oath were published, it is doubtful that the ritual echoed beyond the immediate confines of the court.[35] It was the content of the oath, especially the promise that all matters would be determined by public discussion, that was subsequently invoked by the Freedom and People's Rights Movement, which demanded popular representation.[36] Whatever function the ritual played in ordering the government, the emperor remained a distant and largely unknown presence for the majority of the population. In fact, members of the government recognized quickly the need to free the young sovereign from the confines of the court and create a more direct identification of him with the Japanese realm as a whole. As early as May 1868, Ōkubo Toshimichi (1830–1878) railed against the courtiers who wanted to sequester the emperor within the palace, out of sight. The only way to ensure the Restoration would succeed, he argued, was to remove the divide between the court and the government, and render the emperor the singular lord of the realm. To that end, Ōkubo suggested designating Osaka the new capital of Japan.[37] Conservative courtiers successfully scuttled that proposal, but a precedent for imperial progresses (*gyōkō*) outside of Kyoto was set with a forty-day sojourn in Osaka during the spring of 1868.

Moving the emperor beyond the confines of the court took on greater urgency following the surrender of Edo castle in May of the same year. Ongoing resistance by the pro-Tokugawa alliance in the northeast made bringing the Kanto plains firmly under imperial control a strategic necessity, resulting in a movement within the government to designate the former seat of the Tokugawa *bakufu* an eastern capital. Edo was accordingly renamed Tokyo, "the capital of the east," in September, and the young emperor journeyed east in November, symbolically reenacting Emperor Jinmu's fabled eastern conquest that led to the establishment of Yamato. As the emperor progressed toward the Kanto plains, the government used imperial connections to prominent shrines along the way to emphasize the emperor's claim to rule the entire realm. For instance, the emperor stopped to worship at Atsuta shrine in Nagoya, closely associated with Prince Yamatotakeru's mythic subjugation of the restive east and the putative resting place of the Kusanagi sword, one of the three imperial regalia. On arriving in Tokyo, an edict was issued declaring the emperor "viewed east and west equally" and would personally oversee all affairs of government (*banki shinsai*). To complement this promise of imperial attention to the eastern provinces, a second edict reiterated the revival of *saisei itchi*, named Hikawa shrine of Ōmiya to be the guardian shrine (*chinju*) of the Kanto region, and promised imperial support for its rituals.[38] The political intent of the young sovereign's visit to Tokyo in the fall of 1868 was given full expression through the sacerdotal character of the imperial office.[39]

These two strategies proved useful for the government well beyond 1868 as it deployed imperial authority in the service of nation building. The great imperial progresses of the 1870s and 1880s and the Imperial Rescript on Education of 1890 both continued these early strategies for integrating the archipelago.[40] Transforming the sovereign into a political and ritual principal, however, also occasioned a radical reconfiguration of institutional and discursive arrangements best characterized as combinatory. For ardent proponents of *saisei itchi*, restoring the sacerdotal prerogatives of the emperor required removing adulterating elements, the heterodoxies that Aizawa blamed for contaminating the national body and its ritual focus on the imperial institution. The observance of the *niiname* rite, announced in late-1868, provides an example. The autumn harvest ritual had been revived at court since 1688, but this time the government attempted to communicate its significance beyond the confines of the court. Commoners were encouraged to visit shrines on the day of the rite, synchronizing their worship with the emperor's worship. The pronouncement also forbade reciting Buddhist sutras or ringing bells at temples in Kyoto and its vicinity. In the language of the pronouncement, the ancient rituals were to be "pure" (*junsui*), unadulterated by foreign influences.[41] Unifying rite and rule provided a compelling pretext for undoing the combinatory tradition that had characterized the ritual landscape of the archipelago for so long.

As indicated by the proscription against ringing bells and reciting sutras during the *niiname* rite, Buddhism was perceived to be the most prominent impurity that needed to be removed from imperial rituals, a point made very clear when Emperor Meiji returned to Kyoto in February 1869 to memorialize the anniversary of his father's death. Because filial devotion was to be the cornerstone of the ritual order, the manner in which the young emperor would memorialize his father bore considerable weight. Emperor Kōmei was memorialized employing rites invoking *kami*, not Buddhist deities.[42] The removal of Buddhism from the last significant rite of 1868 capped a series of regulations that matched the ritual deployment of the emperor with a radical disestablishment of Buddhism. Beginning in the spring, and paralleling the pursuit of *saisei itchi*, the Restoration government had issued a series of orders intended to disassociate Buddhist and Shinto deities.

Although couched in terms of "restoring" and "clarifying," these orders marked nothing short of a cultural revolution, given the millennium of doctrinal and institutional affiliation between the two traditions, especially within the imperial court.[43] Just four days after the restoration of the unity of rite and rule was declared in April, all Buddhist monks serving at shrines were ordered to laicize. The series of orders that followed through May built on and clarified the fundamental intent behind this initial order: to ensure that the imperial institution, and the ritual order associated with it, stood alone, purified of foreign elements. To that end, shrines, with their *kami* and priests, were disassociated from Buddhist temples and monks. Buddhist titles for the *kami*, such as *gongen*, or avatar, were forbidden, and all Buddhist implements were to be removed from shrines.[44] Furthermore, symbiotic ties between the imperial family and Buddhist monasteries were severed when offspring of the imperial family and courtiers were no longer allowed to take the tonsure and become Buddhist monks and nuns, and imperial princes and princesses who had become heads of temples and monasteries (*monzeki*) were ordered to laicize.[45]

As indicated by Aizawa's polemic, the attempt to radically disassociate Buddhism from shrines came with ample precedent. Tokugawa-era ideologues often considered Buddhism a decadent waste of resources at best, and a corrupting influence on the commoners at worst.[46] Reforms that reduced the number of Buddhist temples within a domain and created Shinto alternatives for funerals and the sectarian registration of the populace, however, often failed to outlive the daimyo pursuing them and were limited by the Tokugawa *bakufu*'s basic reliance on Buddhist institutions to regulate sectarian affiliation and register the population.[47] By comparison, the thoroughness with which Buddhism was removed from the imperial court following the Restoration, and the prominent position of anti-Buddhist reformers within the government, suggested to contemporaries, especially Buddhist clerics, that disestablishment might be permanent and complete. While the phrase *haibutsu kishaku*, or "eliminating the Buddha and destroying the Shākyamuni," circulated to describe government policy toward Buddhism, no one could predict the outcome of the separation orders. The deeply entrenched role of Buddhism and the fundamentally tenuous nature of state authority at the time precluded eradicating it entirely. At the same time, the separation orders unleashed anti-Buddhist sentiments to significant effect, with more than 40,000 Buddhist temples closed or destroyed by 1872.[48] In many instances, enforcement of the separation orders resulted in violent confrontations at shrines under Buddhist control, most famously the Hiyoshi shrine at the foot of Mount Hiei.[49] Such incidents and the scope of the separation orders fueled the perception that the new government was setting out to eradicate Buddhism, a perception that the Council of State sought to dispel. In response to violent confrontations between Buddhist monks and shrine priests in May, the Council of State sought to blame the conflict on the long-standing enmity between the two groups. When the council declared in October that it did not intend the "elimination of Buddhism," it was as much an acknowledgment of the widespread perception as it was an effective denial.[50]

The belief that the imperial government intended to eradicate Buddhism threatened to undermine efforts to subdue the restive northeastern provinces, where imperial forces battled a pro-Tokugawa alliance into the fall of 1868. A pamphlet addressing Shin-sect Buddhist adherents that was circulated in the north, for example, accused the government not only of eliminating Buddhism but also of accepting "the evil teaching of Christianity from the foreigners." Adherents of the Buddhist dharma were exhorted to resist the new government.[51] For the government, the pamphlet bore witness to the potential of Buddhist affiliations to challenge the imperial government's claims to loyalty and affiliation.[52] Acknowledging the sect's potential for mobilizing its adherents, the Council of State issued a directive to the abbots of the five head Shin-sect temples in August. The directive reiterated the assurance that the government was not engaging in *haibutsu kishaku* and admonished the abbots to properly instruct their branch temples and adherents to recognize the legitimacy of the new government.[53]

In reality the Restoration government had much to risk if it attempted to eradicate Buddhism. The regime relied on fiscal contributions from the two Honganji temples, and many so-called loyalist Buddhist priests (*kinnōsō*) maintained significant contacts within the government, especially among the Chōshū faction.[54] Nonetheless, adopting *saisei itchi* as a founding principle of the new state required substantially reducing official ties between Buddhism and the state. The most drastic of the disestablishment measures came between 1869 and 1873. All Buddhist temples, as well as Shinto shrines, were ordered to surrender their land to the state in 1871. The following year, the state declared it would no longer police the Buddhist clergy's adherence to the precepts of ordination, including eating meat, marrying, and growing hair.[55] These changes, as Richard Jaffe notes, forced substantial changes in how Buddhist sects organized themselves and how ordinations and main-branch relations among temples were policed.[56] Abandoning its predecessor's role as the enforcer of clerical precepts and the direct arbiter of sect administration meant the Restoration government was confronted with an unavoidable question: How would a state founded on rituals that exclude Buddhism be able to regulate it? *Saisei itchi* had opened an unprecedented divide between Buddhism and the state, and in the immediate future, at least, there were no discursive or institutional means to manage that divide.

For some within the government, displacing Buddhism from the ritual center of the state implied simultaneously installing a "restored Shinto" in its place. As executives within the Department of Divinities, Kamei Koremi (1825–1885), the lord of Tsuwano, and his retainer, Fukuba Bisei (1831–1907) played leading roles in shaping policy concerning *saisei itchi* and "restored Shinto."[57] Kamei was a devoted student of Kokugaku nativism and a disciple of Ōkuni Takamasa (1793–1871), and many of his retainers, Fukuba included, served the loyalist cause and the new government.[58] Kokugaku was primarily an eighteenth-century philological movement dedicated to restoring a pristine Japanese community by resurrecting linguistic and ritual practices presumed to have existed prior to contamination by continental influences from China.[59] In the decades prior to the Restoration, the philological project took on strong political tones and produced reformist efforts by its adherents. Hence, prior to the Restoration, Kamei and Fukuba had declared in Tsuwano that "there is a distinction between the way of the *kami* and the way of the Buddha," and once appointed to the Department of Divinities, they recommended a "pronouncement ordering the people of the realm to revere the shrines" and obey the laws of the imperial nation. Such a pronouncement would "declare restored Shinto [*fukko shintō*] to be the sect [*shūmon*] of the imperial nation."[60] Although the proposal included the caveat that "Buddhist adherents who practice their faith in private [*watakushi*] will be tolerated," the use of the term *shūmon* to categorize "restored Shinto" announced an ambitious vision for what Shinto could become under the principle of *saisei itchi*.[61]

In the context of disassociating Shinto from Buddhism, the term *shūmon*, translated here as "sect," possessed a distinct institutional referent: the early-modern system of inspecting sectarian affiliation, known as *shūmon aratame*. As part of its anti-Christian campaign from the mid-seventeenth century onward, the Tokugawa *bakufu* required subjects to register as parishioners (*danka*) at a Buddhist temple and to record births, deaths, marriages, and changes of residence with the parish monk. This system functioned to ensure the eradication of Christianity through annual inspections of sectarian affiliation and the compilation of sectarian registers (*shūmon ninbetsuchō*).[62] Not only were Buddhist temples given a monopoly over funerary rites and the power to certify the sectarian affiliation of their parishioners, but converting between Buddhist sects was also restricted.[63] Some shrine priests, assisted by a Kokugaku movement concerned with clarifying the native in opposition to the foreign in the late eighteenth and early nineteenth centuries, petitioned for the right to disaffiliate from their Buddhist parish temple and conduct their own funeral and memorial rites.[64] Officials permitted Shinto funerals in some cases, but with the common precondition that parish temples give permission as well. This requirement, combined with the restriction that only the priest and his designated heir could receive Shinto burial, meant that nativist priests and their sympathizers were nursing considerable frustration and resentment through the end of the Tokugawa period.[65] Designating restored Shinto a *shūmon* in its own right thus promised to realize the dream of alternative sectarian affiliation and funerary practice. It also meant expanding the scope of *saisei itchi* significantly, beyond rituals associated with the imperial court, to include doctrine and ritual practices that reached into the everyday lives of the populace.

The Restoration government never formally declared a "restored Shinto" the *shūmon* of the state. Nonetheless, the disestablishment of Buddhism and the emphasis placed on imperial rituals left no doubt that the primary ideological idiom of the state would draw from something called Shinto, however it was to be defined. Thus, when the government decided that it could counter the threat of Christian conversion only with a competing doctrine, an ambitious but ill-defined "Shinto" was the sole tool at its immediate disposal. The so-called Great Promulgation Campaign combined the innovative use of imperial ritual with a project to enforce the ban on Christianity through the persuasive force of doctrine, not physical violence. The conceptual and practical difficulties that accompanied that project resulted in a narrowed definition of *saisei itchi*, a definition based on separating doctrine from ritual.

The Great Promulgation Campaign

Emperor Meiji visited the Department of Divinities in February 1870 and delivered an edict that inaugurated what came to be known as the Great Promulgation Campaign (Taikyō senpu undō). The edict drew on the premise of *saisei itchi*, stressed what the divine ancestors had bequeathed to the imperial line, and called for the clarification of a governing doctrine (*chikyō*) that would "unite the hearts of the masses."[66] As the edict's title, "The Edict Proclaiming the Great Teaching," makes clear, the weight of the document rested less on ritual (*sai*) and more on the idea of teaching (*kyō*), as both noun and verb. The short document identified the content of the "Great Teaching" rather vaguely with Shinto (*kannagara no michi*) and charged the Missionary Office with the task of spreading the teaching (*fukyō*) to all. This was ostensibly the beginning of a grand project to ensure that all subjects would loyally identify with the imperial government, and to prevent the feared spread of Christianity. In reality, the initial phase of the promulgation campaign undertaken by the Missionary Office was short-lived and patently ineffective. The campaign nonetheless reflected an abiding fear of Christianity, and the evident failure of the Missionary Office exposed vulnerabilities in the use of *saisei itchi* as a founding principle of the state.

Although the threat of Christian conversion Aizawa invoked had been largely imaginary, Christianity did pose a tangible problem in the final months of Tokugawa rule. In 1867, more than three thousand "hidden Christians" from the village of Urakami identified themselves to French Catholic missionaries who had built a church in the treaty port of Nagasaki. The presence of French priests encouraged the villagers to practice their faith more openly and to end their outward compliance with the Temple Registry System, most notably by refusing to support their parish temple and to conduct Buddhist funeral rites for their dead. Though the local magistrate arrested the leaders of the Christian community and some were tortured, the *bakufu* refrained from executing the Christians, bowing to pressure from the treaty powers, especially France. This flagrant violation of the long-standing prohibition of Christianity, and the shogun's apparent inability to enforce his own law in the face of foreign pressure, provided ample ammunition for loyalists critical of Edo's weak posture toward the foreign powers. Armed with Aizawa's rhetoric of a "national body" unadulterated by foreign heresies, pro-imperial activists assumed that a restored imperial state would vigorously enforce the ban on Christianity.

Ironically, the very circumstances that motivated the vigorous enforcement of the ban on Christianity prevented the overt use of physical force. The 1867 incident was not the first time underground Christians were exposed in Urakami. In fact, the events that began in 1867 are counted as the last of four "collapses" (*kuzure*) of the underground community, dating back to the eighteenth century. The Nagasaki magistrate had refused to pursue prior allegations, largely because the Christians were content to remain underground and there was little institutional incentive to admit the presence of so many crypto-Christians two centuries after the prohibition was instituted.[67] The fourth exposure of the Urakami community forced the authorities to respond with vigor because of the foreign presence at Nagasaki's treaty port. Not only did the French priests encourage the Urakami Christians to overtly challenge the Temple Registry System, but the diplomatic representatives of the treaty powers also heightened the perceived stakes of treating the Christians leniently. When the Tokugawa *bakufu* ceased to exist in late 1867, the Urakami Christians, while nominally under village arrest, were traveling freely between villages and prompting other communities of hidden Christians to openly seek the instruction of the Catholic missionaries.[68] Such was the state of affairs the Meiji government inherited when it assumed control of Nagasaki.

The new government had little choice but to reaffirm the prohibition, and little initial interest in doing otherwise, in part because overtly accommodating Christian practice outside the treaty ports would have provided an excuse for xenophobic radicals to undermine its fragile rule. With the slogan of "revere the emperor, expel the barbarians" (*sonnō jōi*) still echoing in the volatile post-Restoration political environment, the leadership had good reason to fear that any concessions, real or perceived, would undermine its legitimacy and threaten the personal safety of its members. In a famous example, Yokoi Shōnan (1809–1869) was assassinated in the streets of Kyoto in February 1869 because he was rumored to be promoting the adoption of Christianity. At the same time, the pragmatic decision to take up the treaty obligations of the *bakufu* also meant that diplomatic calculations limited the Restoration government's options in enforcing the prohibition.[69]

The consequences of this double bind became abundantly clear to the Restoration government in the spring of 1868. Sawa Nobuyoshi (1835–1873), a particularly zealous loyalist courtier, was dispatched to Nagasaki as the new government's magistrate in March 1868.[70] His staff included Inoue Kaoru (1835–1915), Ōkuma Shigenobu (1838–1922), Sasaki Takayuki (1830–1910), and Matsukata Masayoshi (1835–1924). With the exception of Sasaki, all of these men later assumed positions of oligarchic leadership within the Meiji state. The disposition of the Urakami Christians proved one of the first challenges confronted by these future oligarchs.[71] Sawa feared that leaving the Christians unchecked might even lead to a second uprising like the Shimabara Rebellion, the seventeenth-century peasant rebellion that cemented the image of Christianity as a destabilizing element. The Nagasaki magistrate's office arrested the leaders of the Christians and lectured them to repent (*kaigo*) of their faith.[72] When they refused, Sawa dispatched Ōkuma and Inoue to obtain permission from the central government to execute the leaders and exile the rest of the Urakami Christians.[73] This request prompted a debate at the highest levels of the government on the disposition of the underground Christians .

Sanjō Sanetomi, Kido Takayoshi (1833–1877), and Gotō Shōjirō (1838–1897) convened a conference to discuss the Urakami matter on May 15 at the West Honganji temple in Kyoto, where the emperor temporarily held court. Kido was "deeply disturbed" by the matter, while Ōkubo Toshimichi feared radicals in Nagasaki might use the Christians as a pretext to attack foreigners and thus provoke foreign intervention.[74] The so-called Kobe and Sakai incidents in the spring of 1868 that involved violent clashes between xenophobic samurai and foreigners, both civilians and soldiers, had already proven costly for the Meiji government. Harry S. Parkes (1828–1885), the British minister, was attacked on March 23 as he made his way to the imperial palace for an audience with the young emperor.[75] He escaped uninjured, but the government had every reason to fear the diplomatic fallout from further attacks by samurai disgruntled by the government's pragmatic decision not to close the treaty ports, as many in the anti-Tokugawa camp had long demanded under the slogan "Revere the emperor, expel the barbarians." The presence of samurai activists in Nagasaki who had threatened direct action over the Urakami issue merely underscored the impossibility of lifting the prohibition against Christianity.[76]

In an admission of the delicate nature of the Urakami matter, the leadership solicited proposals from all members of the government.[77] Kokugaku nativists, Ōkuni Takamasa chief among them, seized the opportunity to clamor for the propagation of a "Great Doctrine" (*taikyō*), distinct from Buddhism and capable of countering the inherent allure of Christianity. Ōkuni sympathized with Sawa's desire to punish the Urakami Christians and agreed "with the magistrate's proposal that the state establish teachings of the Great Way for all to see." In the absence of a "single doctrine [*kyōhō*] for the entire imperial nation," however, "the opposing doctrine cannot be overwhelmed." The need to provide the wayward villagers of Urakami with something to convert to became the recurring theme of Ōkuni's proposals. The problem for Ōkuni was the contemporary state of Shinto; he complained that the schools of Shinto found in mid-nineteenth-century Japan were mere lamps, incapable of illuminating very far. To compete with and subsume the doctrine of foreign nations (*ikoku no kyōhō*), the state would have to assemble scholars and officials to determine the grand and true form of Shinto.[78]

Ōkuni's grand and true form of Shinto was to consist of a "sacred Shinto" (*seigyō shintō*) and a "simple Shinto" (*igyō shintō*), each with its own instructors. Sacred Shinto would explain the *Kojiki* and *Nihon shoki*, and also draw from Chinese Confucianism, Indian Brahmanism, Buddhism, and Western doctrine. Astronomy, geography, and physical sciences were also to be included. Such a Japanese doctrine, Ōkuni promised, could instruct and direct foreign regions.[79] Simple Shinto, devised for the ignorant and superstitious masses, would stand beneath sacred Shinto and provide clear and simple instruction in virtue (that is, obedience to authorities). The primary concern for Ōkuni was to ensure the superior position of Japan within the global order.[80] This meant he would interpret Shinto and the imperial myths in a universal mode that subsumed all other discursive forms, including international law.[81] Although the bifurcated form of Shinto that Ōkuni envisioned at this early date appears to anticipate later attempts to distinguish between a "nonreligious" shrine Shinto and a "religious" sect Shinto, Ōkuni does not recognize any boundary between religious and other discourses; the only boundary that matters is one between the learned and the ignorant.[82] The revived Department of Divinities was the natural state organ to determine and disseminate the comprehensive and universal Shinto that Ōkuni envisioned. Writing to Kamei Koremi, his erstwhile patron and student who served in the Department of Divinities, Ōkuni linked the renewal of imperial rule with the renewal of Shinto: "Along with the renewal of government, Shinto should also be renewed, defined, and promulgated throughout Japan."[83]

Although many, including Kido, argued for sentencing the Urakami Christian leaders to "severe punishment" and the rest to exile, the government decided to temper Sawa's request by first attempting to admonish the Christians to recant (*kaishin*), and to execute their leaders only after that attempt had been exhausted.[84] This reluctance to use violence allowed Ōkuni and his disciples within the government, Kamei and Fukuba, to successfully press for a project to convert by persuasion.[85] The Restoration government's hesitation to execute the Urakami Christians and eradicate the prohibited faith with force resulted in a search for a solution that offered the Christians a functional equivalent to their faith. If the violent eradication of Christianity during the seventeenth century and the subsequent regime of temple registration characterized a clear technology of domination, the post-Restoration concern to provide the

Christians with a doctrine to embrace can be seen as an attempt to use what might be described as a form of pastoral power. By proposing to offer a doctrine that would replace Christianity, the governed assumed, in effect, the responsibility of directing individuals toward beliefs and practices that would assure happiness in life and in death.

Political authority admonishing the common classes to adopt proper sociopolitical ethics was nothing new to post-Restoration Japan. The Edict Proclaiming the Great Teaching employed the term *chikyō*, which can be translated as "governing doctrine" or "governance and teaching," to express a long-held and uncontroversial belief in the inherent interdependence of stable political rule and inculcating ethical standards in the masses. In fact the Restoration government repeatedly employed public allocution (*jinmin kokuyu*) as a means to convey its ideological legitimacy. The Kyoto prefecture, for example, issued a lengthy declaration of the new imperial government's claim to legitimacy in December 1868 and called on all subjects to respond to the debt they owed to the emperor. This document was reprinted and distributed to all local governments in March 1869, marking an early attempt to communicate a concise ideological basis for the new regime. The notice accompanying the copies of this document declared, "The essentials of shepherding the people [*bokumin*] lie in conducting governance and teaching together."[86] The teachings contained in the Kyoto prefecture's document stressed the loyalty and filial devotion owed to the emperor, who as the son of heaven (*tenshi*) inherited an unbroken mandate to rule the divine land. These ideas, in turn, were based in reason (*dōri*) and custom (*fūgi*); they did not, however, appeal to soteriological questions of reward and punishment in the hereafter or to the specifics of a Shinto pantheon and rituals. What set the Great Promulgation Campaign apart was the explicit intersection of the project to combine governance and teaching with the emperor's sacerdotal prerogative under the unity of rite and rule, a nascent definition of Shinto as a sectarian identity, and the specter of Christian conversion that motivated the campaign in the first place. Prior to the pursuit of *saisei itchi* and the disassociation of Shinto and Buddhism, Buddhism had assumed the burden of ministering to the spiritual fate of the people. Under the *saisei itchi* regime, a "restored Shinto," directly associated with the imperial institution, would assume that burden.

Exile and persuasion were to be the primary means of dealing with the formerly hidden Christians of the Nagasaki region. The government announced in June 1868 that more than four thousand Christians from Urakami were to be exiled to thirty-four domains, and Kido Takayoshi was dispatched to Nagasaki to "take charge of the matter."[87] It was hoped that, by dispersing the villagers and separating them from the foreign priests, they could be better coaxed to abandon their Christian faith. The domains ordered to host the exiles were instructed to "teach them gently and attentively, treating them well so that they may become good folk [*ryōmin*] again."[88] Few of the domains were eager to assume the fiscal and administrative burden of hosting these potentially troublesome exiles, however, and some even feared the spread of Christianity to their domain.[89] Lacking leverage and resources to overrule the domains, the government postponed fully implementing the exile plan and eventually scaled it back to eighteen domains. In June, Kido managed to oversee the exile of 114 men, considered leaders within the Urakami community, to the three domains of Chōshū, Tsuwano, and Fukuyama.[90] The remaining villagers were not exiled from Urakami until early 1870; nearly three thousand Christians were shipped out of Nagasaki a few days after the emperor inaugurated the Great Promulgation Campaign on February 3, 1870.

The practical question of how to deal with several thousand Japanese Christians, filtered through the ideological prism of *saisei itchi*, furnished the rationale for the Great Promulgation Campaign. The call for a uniform national doctrine, repeatedly advanced by ideologues like Ōkuni Takamasa, converged with the pragmatic pursuit of an integrated national population under diplomatic conditions imposed by the unequal-treaty regime. The primary state organ to undertake this promulgation campaign was the Missionary Office. An embryonic version of the office had been created in early 1869 and it began operating in earnest in November when it was attached to the Department of Divinities, giving the revived department the unprecedented mandate to determine and propagate a national doctrine.[91] Ono Nobuzane (1823–1910) is credited with shaping the initial vision for the Missionary Office.[92] A Confucian scholar, Ono had worked to convert the Urakami Christians initially exiled to his domain of Chōshū in 1868. He claimed to have achieved significant success there and offered his services to the Restoration government. Tokoyo Nagatane (1838–1886), a Kokugaku scholar serving in the Department of Divinities, credits Ono with impressing upon the government the need "erect our national doctrine and thus prevent the people from desiring their doctrine (i.e., Christianity)."[93]

As an executive within the Missionary Office, Ono worked to formulate a national doctrine that mirrored the basic contours of Christianity as he understood it: a single, omnipotent deity and the promise of reward and judgment in the afterlife. He condensed this doctrine into a short pamphlet entitled *The Essence of the Divine Doctrine* (*Shinkyō yōshi*) in which he elevated the imperial ancestor to a supreme deity, declaring that all things were made and sustained by Amaterasu, the sovereign of heaven and earth. Since all souls originated in Amaterasu, in death they returned to their source to rest in peace. Worshiping Amaterasu alone, therefore, was sufficient to secure the happy repose of one's soul.[94] Ono tied this vision of salvation, via Confucian language, to a stable sociopolitical order maintained by the five ethical relations between lord and subject, husband and wife, father and child, elder and younger sibling, and friends.[95] By grounding ethical relations in an explicit theology of creation, divine sovereignty, ritual worship, and soteriology, Ono's doctrine placed the imperial institution at the center of a doctrine intended to compete with Christianity. Ono's elevation of Amaterasu had the added benefit of complementing efforts by Fukuba and others to consolidate Shinto around an axis linking the Grand Shrines of Ise and the imperial palace.[96]

Despite the clarity of Ono's vision, or perhaps because of it, debilitating theological disputes beset the Missionary Office almost from its inception.[97] Scholars belonging to the Hirata school of Kokugaku nativism in particular charged Ono and the Tsuwano faction, represented by Fukuba, with heterodoxy. Founded by Hirata Atsutane (1776–1843), the Hirata school was noted for its focus on the "hidden realm" (*kakuriyo*) and the destiny of the human soul.[98] Interwoven questions concerning cosmogony, the proper hierarchy of the Shinto pantheon, and the location and character of the afterlife stood at the center of these debates. At issue was the definition of Shinto as it would be promulgated under state aegis. Kokugaku nativists, for instance, opposed attempts to consolidate the pantheon and doctrine around Amaterasu, the imperial progenitress. They were committed to a more diversified pantheon that emphasized the "three *kami* of creation" (*zōka sanshin*) who preceded Amaterasu. In the partisan words of Tokoyo, a member of the Hirata school:

> Ono's accomplishment in creating an unprecedented office is without parallel. However, because his doctrine was thought up from Confucian views, it was not based upon the three *kami* of creation, and it venerated Amaterasu alone. Its theory concerning the destination of the soul, moreover, put forward Ono's personal view that good souls will rise to the Plains of High Heaven [*takamagahara*] and evil souls will descend to the Land of the Dead [*yomi no kuni*]. The teachings of the missionaries were warped as a result, and the officials of the Office suffered from this illness.[99]

The Hirata school stressed the dispersed and delegated authority of the *kami*.[100] Consequently, the imperial ancestor was not the only *kami* that demanded the attention, doctrinally and ritually, of the Department of

Divinities.[101] This view also affirmed the critical role of the department and, by extension, the priests who, as ritual intermediaries, assisted imperial rule by presiding over the rituals for their respective shrines and *kami*. The Hirata school's approach, as we will see, clashed with the more radical conception of *saisei itchi* and *tennō shinsai* that Fukuba promoted.

The status of the Deity Hall (Shinden) within the Department of Divinities reflected this tension. At the center of the eighth-century precedent for the Department of Divinities stood the Hall of Eight Deities (Hasshinden), where the eight tutelary deities who protected the emperor and state were ritually worshiped. Officials of the Meiji Department of Divinities, especially those belonging to the Hirata school, sought to resurrect the hall, and a temporary version was built in January 1870 after a number of delays; the Great Promulgation Campaign was announced at the formal inauguration of the hall at the beginning of 1870.[102] The hall, however, was designated provisional (*karishinden*), in part because in addition to the eight tutelary deities, the spirits of the imperial ancestors that had been removed from the Buddhist memorial hall in the palace were also enshrined in the hall. This created a situation in which the officials of the Department of Divinities served as the ritualists for the tutelary deities and imperial ancestors, not the emperor, a situation that contradicted the principle of the emperor personally conducting all rituals (*tennō shinsai*). Hence, along with emphasizing the ancestral link between the emperor and Amaterasu, Fukuba and his allies sought to move the spirits of imperial ancestors out of the Department of Divinities and into the palace, where the emperor could venerate them in person.[103] The theological disputes, prompted by the promulgation campaign, thus exposed significant fault lines in implementing unity of rite and rule as the founding principle of the state.

The theological disputes triggered by the Missionary Office's unprecedented mandate to determine and promulgate a national doctrine also exposed the easily contested character of "restored Shinto," and by extension the state's teachings themselves. In September 1870, members of the Hirata school serving in the Department of Divinities and the Missionary Office were told to assemble at the residence of Hirata Nobutane (1828–1872). The assembled disciples were told that some in their official capacities had signed off on heterodox doctrines (*isetsu*) concerning the location of *yomi*, the land of the dead.[104] This was denounced as an unbearable insult to the teachings of Hirata Atsutane, and to the master's heir and grandson, Nobutane. The six disciples accused of this crime, including Tokoyo Nagatane, were forced to sign a formal apology as members of the Hirata school. In his retrospective account, Tokoyo claimed to have had qualms about apologizing privately for actions conducted in an official capacity: "It was not a shame for me personally, it was a shame for the office." His concern appears to have been born out, as Fukuba and others used the incident to accuse the Hirata school of adjudicating the official business of the Department of Divinities and the Missionary Office as a private academy (*shijuku*).[105] Tokoyo lamented that the incident appeared to furnish an excuse to remove the majority of Hirata disciples from the two offices, when a reduction of staff was announced in January 1871. The Missionary Office and the Department of Divinities both being formal organs of the state and staffed by state officials, it did not take long for the ongoing theological debates in such a politically immediate space to be regarded a liability.

Not surprisingly, there is ample evidence that a significant amount of skepticism concerning the capacity of "restored Shinto" existed within the Restoration government from an early point. In the spring of 1869, for example, the Foreign Ministry (Gaikokukan) submitted the following query to the Kōgisho assembly for deliberation: "Can we in reality employ Shinto to teach and direct (*kyōdō*) all the people of Japan at this time?"[106] The resulting discussions were not recorded in the official minutes of the assembly, but the skepticism expressed by the query is self-evident. The crux for most members of the assembly, composed primarily of samurai representing daimyō domains, remained the assumed threat of mass conversions to Christianity and the inability to respond to such an eventuality with force. A related proposal was submitted from within the Kōgisho assembly the following month: "Although the daily spread of Christianity is supposed to be countered with admonition [*setsuyu*]," it held, the stubborn nature of the populace called for strict punishment. Unless violent means were employed in enforcing the prohibition of Christianity, the proposal concluded, those who were lost to the evil doctrine would "surely come to harm the nation." In the vote taken in response to the proposed use of force to counter Christianity, 20 voted in favor of force while 164 voted against it; the assembly was unanimous, however, in insisting that the spread of Christianity be countered. A minority called for banishing Buddhism at the same time, but the most common recommendation was to establish a "doctrine" (*kyōhō*) that the common people could rely on instead of Christianity.[107]

Despite the theological stalemate that took hold of the Missionary Office by the middle of 1870, the persistent demand to respond to the Urakami matter and the broader threat of Christianity it represented produced a modest amount of action. Six members of the Missionary

Office, including Ono, traveled to Nagasaki in the spring of that year.[108] The office's efforts in Nagasaki, the only area beyond its Tokyo headquarters in which it operated with any consequence, indicates what Ono and his colleagues sought to realize in practice. The missionaries began their work in Nagasaki with the express purpose of stamping out any potential vestiges of Christianity and preventing it from spreading further. The chief tools at their disposal consisted of shrine parishioner registration (*ujiko shirabe*) and Shinto funerals. Shrine parishioner registration was first provisionally implemented in July 1870 in the eight jurisdictions considered most vulnerable to the influence of Christianity, including Nagasaki.[109] All births were to be reported to the local village or ward head for certification, and then newborns were to be taken to the local shrine with the certificate to receive a shrine amulet. Unregistered adults were also required to register as parishioners (*ujiko*). The village or ward head was to inspect the amulets every six years when registration records were reviewed, and parishioners' amulets were to be returned to the shrine at the time of their death. Implementing this system throughout the archipelago required designating one shrine per district a tutelary shrine (*ubusuna jinja*). This designation was not put in place until August 1871, when regulations for rural district shrines were issued as part of an effort to categorize and standardize shrines throughout the archipelago.[110] There is some debate as to whether shrine parishioner registration was intended to replicate Tokugawa-era temple registration. As it was formally announced in 1871, shrine registration differed from its Buddhist antecedent in that the process remained in the hands of local officials, not the shrine priests, and funerary rites were not required; that is, registration as a shrine parishioner did not preclude Buddhist funeral and memorial rites.[111] The shrine registry system, moreover, was quickly superseded and rendered redundant by the civil registry system (*koseki seido*) that was announced in May 1871. The fact that its initial implementation was focused on Nagasaki and the treaty ports, where the spread of Christianity was feared most, nonetheless indicates that the registration was part of the larger move to replace Buddhism with Shinto as the primary means to banish the foreign creed. A requirement that Buddhist priests and nuns register as shrine parishioners, included in the provisional system of shrine registration announced in 1870, illustrated the dramatic reversal from the temple registration system.[112]

The account of the Missionary Office's activities in Nagasaki left by Nishikawa Yoshisuke (1816–1880), a member of the Hirata school who served in the office, indicates that shrine parishioner registration was central to the office's efforts.[113] He writes in a letter sent home: "There isn't a person, from the prefectural governor down to the poor and children, who does not have an amulet from their tutelary [*ubusuna*] shrine hanging from their necks. If anyone is found without one, they will be captured as a follower of the evil teaching."[114] In addition to registering the population of Nagasaki as parishioners of local tutelary shrines, the missionaries also made sure to direct local veneration toward the imperial center. They built a branch shrine of Ise in the village of Urakami, and instructed the remaining villagers to venerate Amaterasu, the divine ancestor of the emperor enshrined therein. The missionaries also organized regular lectures with the aid of local officials. Children attending private academies (*terakoya*) were brought to these lectures, as were adults. They were instructed to adhere to the "Great Way" (*taidō*) and to register as shrine parishioners. Nishikawa records with some satisfaction that these efforts were bearing fruit in the form of Shinto funerals: "We began lecturing at our residence and they are quite successful, with at least 100 in attendance each time. The evil followers in Urakami village are disappearing, and over 40 people have requested Shinto funerals. An evil place is truly becoming a divine place."[115] The conduct of Shinto funerals, a significant innovation, considering the strict proscriptions against defilement that Shinto priests adhered to, marked one of the clearest attempts to substitute Buddhism with a new faith capable of stemming the feared tide of Christian conversions.[116]

The Missionary Office's efforts in Nagasaki continued to meet with some success through 1871. The missionaries designated the first of every month as a day to worship at local shrines and reported that the majority of residents visited the shrines.[117] Those activities were undercut, however, by political realities in the capital. Reinforcements were not dispatched to Nagasaki, and the plan to recruit and train missionaries failed because domains refused to send staff members, on the grounds that none was qualified.[118] What ultimately robbed the Missionary Office's efforts of full support from the Restoration government, however, was a growing awareness that emphasizing the immediate and direct role of the emperor should not be connected to a project of pastoral intervention that dealt overtly with the soteriological concerns of the populace. Employing a "restored Shinto" to counter Christianity, in other words, took on the appearance of placing the emperor personally in competition with Christianity.

Traces of this concern can be found in the difficulties officials faced when attempting to convert the Christians exiled from Urakami village. When the foreign press began reporting rumors that the Christians exiled to the domains of Ōmura, Kanazawa, Daishōji, and Toyama suffered from poor treatment in late 1870, the Meiji government was compelled to allow the British consul in Niigata to visit the exiled Christians.[119] His inspection revealed generally poor living conditions for the exiled Christians.[120] Embarrassed, and seeking to head off further diplomatic complications, the government ordered all domains hosting the exiles to improve the conditions under which they were kept. To oversee these improvements, Tokyo dispatched Nakano Takeaki (1844–1898) and Kusumoto Masataka (1838–1902) from the Foreign Ministry to inspect seventeen domains hosting exiled Christians.[121] The resulting reports submitted by Nakano and Kusumoto provide a picture of local officials struggling to implement Tokyo's order to "educate" or "instruct" (*kyōyu/oshie statosu*) the Christians and thus induce them to convert.[122] In fact, the reports highlight how the very project to persuade and convert the exiles lacked a clear discursive script.

The improvements Nakano and Kusumoto implemented were intended to treat the Christians less as prisoners and more like guests in order to avoid diplomatic criticism. This shift from prisoner to guest also reaffirmed the emphasis on conversion by words (*kyōyu*) as opposed to physical torture, and the reports reveal how this emphasis forced regional officials to combine doctrinal and legal language in dealing with the exiles. The Christians were told they were being punished as criminals for breaking the law but were also admonished to recant their faith and convert to Buddhism or Shinto. The result was an awkward intersection of claims to legal and spiritual authority, the conflation of political and spiritual loyalty, and assertions regarding the afterlife (especially in relation to funeral rites). Accounts of these attempts to convert the Christians on the part of the domain officials, and the changes suggested by Kusumoto and Nakano's reports, indicate the frustration of the regional officials as they attempted to discharge their duty. How and to what the Christians were to be converted was a continued source of confusion. Kusumoto and Nakano both strove to achieve a degree of uniformity among the domains, not only in how they treated the exiled believers but also in how they sought to convert them. Kusumoto's repeated instructions concerning the burial of Christians who died in custody, for example, point to a key characteristic of this attempt at consistency: the use of newly formulated Shinto rituals. In eleven out of the twelve prefectures he inspected, Kusumoto instructed officials to bury according to Shinto funeral rites (*shinsōsai*) deceased exiles who had converted from Christianity[123] Even if the believers had converted or had expressed an interest in doing so, Kusumoto insisted that efforts to "instruct" (*kyōyu*) them should continue. Those who did convert were to recite an oath before the local tutelary *kami*, receive purification (*oharai*), and sign an oath in blood. He also stipulated that those who were converted with the divine texts (*shinten*)—the imperial mythistories—should be buried according to Shinto funeral rites, while those who converted to Buddhism (*buppō*) should be given Buddhist funerals upon their death. Despite the caveat acknowledging the possibility of Buddhist conversion, Kusumoto's report mentions only Nagoya and Hiroshima employing Buddhist priests to convert the Christians. Even in those domains, the desirability of eschewing Buddhism and employing Shinto texts appears to have been understood by the local officials: "Because they are ignorant of Buddhism, they have stated that from now on they will employ the divine texts [i.e., the *Kojiki* and *Nihon shoki*] and select an official to be charged with instructing [the Christians]."[124] The clear preference for using the imperial mythistories to convert the Christians corresponded to the basic framework of *saisei itchi* and the separation of Buddhism from Shinto.

While many of the domains were less than enthusiastic in their efforts to convert the Urakami exiles, Kusumoto and Nakano insisted on observing their efforts and left detailed accounts of some of those sessions.[125] An official in Fukuyama, for example, impressed upon the believers both the need to be loyal to the emperor and the proposition that Deus and Ame-no-minakanushi-no-kami were one and the same (an argument employed by Ōkuni Takamasa): "Because [their reverence for the Lord of Heaven] appears to be the root of all of their misapprehensions, we have instructed them to exclusively revere [*sennen sonsū*] the sovereign of all things and great ancestor of the imperial nation, Minakanushi-no-kami, in exchange for their reverence for the Lord of Heaven."[126] Rather than reject belief itself, the project to secure political loyalty and obedience led to improvised discussions of doctrine and the proper object of belief. In its manual for converting the Christians, the domain of Tsuwano explicitly stressed the soteriological equivalence of the imperial Great Way to Christianity; the punishment or salvation of the soul was guaranteed by the workings of the *kami*.[127]

It was, in fact, the exiled Christians who asserted a distinction between political and spiritual loyalty. Their response to being reprimanded for believing in the Lord of Heaven at the cost of disobeying the emperor is recorded as follows: "Born in this country, we will render any service to the emperor [*tenshi-sama*], the lord of this country; we will not consider it too much to give our bodies and our lives. Our souls [*tamashii*], however, cannot obey the emperor; we intend to surrender them to the Lord of Heaven." This distinction between temporal service and transcendent loyalty, likely imparted to the Christians by their

French priests, clashed with the expansive notion of "doctrine" and the pastoral claims of the imperial government that the official was charged to impart. Arguing that the word "Deus" was simply a foreign name for Minaka-nushi, he pressed the Christians to "call it Minaka-nushi in Japanese; it is not necessary to call it Deus." The Christians, astute enough to turn this logic of equivalences on its head, responded that if they are indeed the same thing, "there should be no harm in not calling it Minaka-nushi but Deus instead." Still, the possibility of "converting" to an equivalent faith appears to have appealed enough to some of the Christians to prompt them to pose the following query: "If we change our hearts and believe in the Minaka-nushi, will we be permitted to not worship the various other gods? Also, will we be allowed to not join any sect [*nanishū e mo*]? Naturally, if we must join another temple, we cannot change our hearts. . . . If we can worship the Minaka-nushi alone, some of us will change their hearts." They would only convert, in other words, by moving into an empty sectarian space wherein no Buddhist temple or Shinto shrine could claim them as parishioners. The logic of the Great Promulgation Campaign did not envision and thus could not accommodate this plea to render sectarian affiliation irrelevant to questions of political loyalty. The reports conclude, pessimistically, with the observation that those who expressed a desire to convert quickly changed their minds, but the officials vowed to continue their efforts to "instruct" them.[128] The failure to convert the exiled Christians was not merely a result of limited resources. Blending demands for loyal obedience to the emperor with theological debates concerning the proper name of a supreme deity exposed the weakness of the logic underlying the campaign.

Despite mounting difficulties, the Missionary Office clung to the logic that supported its mandate to determine a doctrinal expression of imperial rule that could be used to repel Christianity. The office attempted to escape its theological paralysis by submitting a proposal to the Council of State in the summer of 1871. The proposal included a doctrinal statement, "A Summary of the Great Doctrine" ("Taikyō yōshi"), which in significant respects mirrored Ono's theology summarized in his "Essence of the Divine Doctrine" ("Shinkyō yōshi") and called for the worship of Amaterasu as the sovereign deity of heaven and earth.[129] This was submitted to the Council of State with the explicit request that it be promulgated in the emperor's name. Doing so would have demonstrated his theocratic authority to determine orthodox doctrine, an authority implied in the declarations of the unity of rite and rule. The Council of State, however, issued a different document, the "Essence of the Great Doctrine" ("Taikyō shiyō"), not as a public edict but as an official communication to the regional governors (*chihōkan*).[130] This difference is significant, for the Council of State clearly chose not to issue an official doctrine in the name of the emperor, an act that, as Haga Shōji observes, would have clearly established the theocratic character of the imperial institution.[131] Instead, the notice addressed regional officials and instructed them to guide the people in the Great Doctrine. Even though the pronouncement laments the fact that the Great Doctrine has yet to spread through the nation and unite the hearts of the people (*jinshin*), its call to "revere the *kami*" and "clarify human ethics" makes no mention of a sovereign creator or of life after death. The doctrine, in other words, did not concern itself with judgment and reward in the afterlife, nor in determining the divine agency behind creation. The emphasis, instead, returned to the first of the two central strategies for utilizing the imperial institution: claiming the ancestral mandate to rule, and claiming the ethical leadership of the emperor in embodying the virtue of filial devotion.[132] The scope of pastoral authority claimed by the promulgation campaign was receding.

The Council of State's doctrinal adjustment in the summer of 1871 was subtle, but its timing was significant. Ten days after the "Essence of the Great Doctrine" was announced to the governors, the Council of State declared the abolition of domains and the creation of prefectures, thereby eliminating the last vestiges of the semiautonomous daimyō domains.[133] The stability afforded by this successful assertion of central authority prompted a broad reorganization of the state, and many policies came under review, including the Great Promulgation Campaign. By rejecting the Missionary Office's formulation of doctrine in August, the Council of State signaled a desire to move beyond the debilitating theological debates that had plagued the office from its inception. The conversionary prowess of Christianity and its subversive potential remained a concern for most within the government, but the campaign to counter it with a national doctrine appeared destined to fail. The campaign had to continue, but in a fashion that would minimize the state's risk of failure.

Separating Doctrine from Ritual

The persistent fear of Christianity and the Missionary Office's inability to mount a viable response to it presented Buddhist clerics with an opportunity to reassert their utility to the state and demand an administrative framework that included temples and sects.[134] Disestablished by the separation edicts, the Buddhist sects had lost most of their formal ties to the state and the imperial court, ties they were keen to reestablish.

Shimaji Mokurai (1838–1911), a priest of the Nishi-Honganji Shin sect with close ties to Kido Takayoshi and the Chōshū faction within the government, for example, petitioned in 1871 for the creation of a state department dedicated to the regulation of Buddhism.[135] Even members of the government feared that continuing to disadvantage Buddhism would only create a disaffected populace ripe for Christian conversion.[136] Such concerns, combined with the apparent shortcomings of the Missionary Office, resulted in calls for a new government ministry, one that would mobilize not only a "restored Shinto" in opposition to Christianity, but also Buddhism and Confucianism. By including Buddhism and Confucianism, any national doctrine promulgated in opposition to Christianity would cease to be narrowly coextensive with "restored Shinto."

Recommendations issued in late 1871 by the Sain, or the Council of the Left, led by Gotō Shōjirō and Etō Shinpei (1834–1874), illustrate the calculus that informed the move to include Buddhism and Confucianism in the campaign to counter Christianity.[137] Etō's draft recommendation to establish a Ministry of Doctrine questioned the wisdom of competing with Christianity in the name of a divine doctrine linked directly to the imperial institution:

> Now in terms of the Learning of the Way [*dōgaku*], Shinto [*jingi*] is now being propagated [*senkyō*] throughout [the realm]. . . . Hence now the intrusion of the Christian doctrine [*kyōhō*] approaches each day, and when we compare it to the doctrines of Confucianism and Buddhism, its harm is profound and its force [*ikioi*] is truly difficult to resist. . . . I ask that you consider what state of affairs awaits the empire in thirty years. There will be the divine doctrine [*shinkyō*], Confucianism, and several forms of Buddhism; add to this the three teachings of Jesus, and amongst its many teachings the argument for republican government will arise. The various doctrines will view each other with enmity and seek to sway the hearts of the people, thus leading to upheaval. Most dreadful troubles will confront the state. We must think far ahead and prevent this eventuality. The court has already created an office of missions in order to bring the hearts of the people to believe one doctrine by spreading it throughout the realm. This Missionary Office preaches the divine doctrine. Whoever preaches the divine doctrine represents the *kami* [*kami no myōdai*], and must take the *kami*'s heart as his own and be one with the *kami*. If this missionary were to debate with a foreign teacher and fail [*oyoba zaru koto aru toki wa*], where will the fault lie? The failure of the divine doctrine will thus be the failure of the *kami*. The Western doctrine will gain

> ever greater force, and missions will be unable to prevent it. If Confucianism and Buddhism cannot prevent it, it may, in the end, result in the slighting of the imperial family. What then will our national polity stand upon?[138]

Etō emphasized the potential for failure inherent in the project to respond in kind to Christian conversion; precisely because Christian proselytizing was so potent a threat, the likelihood of failure and thus injury to the prestige of the imperial institution was high. Any failure on their part would be the state's failure. Etō's observation that any plurality of doctrines would necessarily "view each other with enmity and seek to sway the hearts of the people" accentuated this possibility of failure. The imperial institution, he warned, must not be placed in the same category as, and hence in competition with, that plurality.

The formal recommendation submitted to the Council of State by the Sain in January 1872 rendered Etō's logic more explicit. It called for creating a ministry charged with overseeing shrine priests, Buddhist sects, and Confucian scholars. In calling for a clear adjustment to the promulgation campaign, the chamber made clear what it feared most: "We fear that later generations will mistakenly understand the divine spirit of the imperial ancestor [*soshū no shinrei*] to be founder of a doctrine [*kyōhō*]. This is why a department in charge of doctrine must be established."[139] This fear of misapprehending the imperial ancestor, presumably Amaterasu herself, to be the originator of a doctrine that competes with other doctrines for the faith and adherence of the populace is best understood in light of the crisis of conversion that served as the backdrop of the Great Promulgation Campaign. As Gauri Viswanathan observes, referring to the nineteenth-century British Empire, "Conversion ranks among the most destabilizing activities in modern society."[140] The act of conversion exposes as porous and unstable communal boundaries, identifications, and loyalties imagined or desired to be secure. *Sasei itchi* was supposed to secure the sociopolitical boundary of the Japanese realm by deploying the combined political and ritual prerogatives of the emperor, not to exacerbate differences by placing the state in direct competition with established doctrines and their constituents, namely Buddhism. In its recommendation, the Sain first articulated what would become a guiding and consistent imperative of Meiji state policy.[141] The imperial institution was not to be placed in conversionary competition; that is, loyal identification with the emperor's ancestral mandate to rule the archipelago must not be exposed to an explicit moment of contingent choice. The separation of imperial rituals from doctrine marked the beginning of a consistent imperative to disavow the sectarian character of the imperial institution. Although it remained ill-defined discursively and institutionally, "religion" began to come into focus at this time as something inherently competitive and therefore unstable and cofigured in opposition to the political claims of the state.

To be sure, multiple agendas shaped the institutional reforms concerning ritual and doctrine undertaken in late 1871 through early 1872, not just the logic expressed by Etō Shinpei and the Sain assembly. Buddhist clerics were naturally eager to be included in the state-directed doctrinal project, and many within the government feared the destabilizing potential of further antagonizing Buddhist sectarians. An uprising by Shin sect adherents in Mikawa in the early months of 1871 only confirmed the potential for disturbances if state policies were taken to be anti-Buddhist.[142] Some within the Ministry of Divinities, including Fukuba Bisei, understood the elimination of the ministry as necessary for fully realizing *saisei itchi* in the form of the emperor personally conducting imperial rites. Others, particularly within the Sain, simply demanded a more effective means of preventing the spread of Christianity. Running through and outlasting these agendas, however, was the new imperative to segregate the imperial institution from the unstable realm of doctrinal competition. The reforms undertaken in late 1871 and early 1872 cumulatively reaffirmed the conceit of *saisei itchi* while simultaneously initiating an increasingly mediated relationship between the imperial institution and doctrinal professionals. A direct identification of the emperor and his rituals with a doctrinally articulated Shinto and its missionaries was replaced with what Miyachi Masato characterizes as the imperfect mediation of multiple doctrines, including Buddhism, Shinto, and Confucianism.[143] In short, the *kokutai* was to be situated above a plurality, demanding their conformity but refusing to confront them on the same terms. In doing so, the government began to address the problem of how to relate the state to Buddhism. Separating doctrine from rites, and using doctrine as a potentially generic category that could subsume multiple sectarian identities, the government groped its way toward a mediated relationship between the state and Buddhism. As we will see, it was for this reason that Buddhist clerics led the way in formalizing a distinction between religion qua doctrine and ritual through the 1870s.

The principle of *saisei itchi* was reaffirmed by further consolidating state rituals around the person of the emperor, removing intermediary institutions and ritualists. The Department of Divinities was reconfigured as the Ministry of Divinities (Jingishō) in September 1871 to bring it directly under the executive center of the government, the Seiin, or Central Council. Members of the Department of Divinities argued that the ideal of uniting rite and rule would be better realized if the ritual organ of the state was actually brought into the political center, rather than left at the margins of the state, an arrangement partially realized when Sanjō Sanetomi briefly occupied the head posts in both the Central Council and the Ministry of Divinities.[144] This was quickly followed by the announcement that the spirits of the imperial ancestors and imperial regalia housed within the provisional Deity Hall of the Ministry of Divinities would be moved into the imperial palace. The decision to abolish the Ministry of Divinities and the Missionary Office in April 1872 and create the Bureau of Rites (Shikiburyō) to administer imperial rites was a natural extension of this attempt to consolidate *saisei itchi* around the personal ritual role of emperor. With the dismantling of the Ministry of Divinities, the remaining deities of heaven and earth (*tenshin chigi*) were also moved into the palace, creating the three deity halls (*kyūchū sanden*) that, still today, constitute the site for all primary imperial rituals.[145]

Seemingly radical calls made at this time to move the Ise and Atsuta shrines into the imperial palace indicate the extent to which imperial rituals were being consolidated around the person of the emperor.[146] Ise was not moved, although the official character of it and all other Shinto shrines had been affirmed when shrines were declared "sites for conducting state rites" in June 1871.[147] The hereditary appointments of shrine priests were replaced with official appointments because treating shrines as extensions of private houses "went against the political structure of *saisei itchi*." An accompanying order introduced a centralized ranking system for all shrines.[148] Imperial shrines (*kanpeisha*) and national shrines (*kokuheisha*) stood at the top of these ranks, and they were in turn classified into major, middle, and minor grades. Shrines dedicated to apotheosized exemplars, including Toyotomi Hideyoshi and Tokugawa Ieyasu, as well as recently created shrines for those who died for the loyalist cause, including what became Yasukuni shrine, were ranked as special shrines (*bekkakusha*). All other shrines, the vast majority, in fact, were grouped as "various shrines" (*shosha*) and ranked according to their jurisdictional affiliation; prefectural, district, town/village shrines (*kensha, gōsha, chōsha, sonsha*) were identified with local units of government and the rest were designated unranked shrines (*mukakusha*). The initial rankings announced in 1871 placed a great deal of emphasis on the imperial and national shrines and indicate a preliminary bifurcation between shrines deemed essentially linked to the imperial institution and those only tenuously connected. Funding and official recognition granted to shrines differed greatly according to the ranking system, and policy makers steadily decreased the scope of state support for the majority of shrines and their priests. By 1879 there were thirty major imperial shrines, twelve middle imperial shrines, two minor imperial shrines, and twenty special shrines. Beneath these, there were 176,722 civic shrines. Though the number of elite shrines increased incrementally, to 108 by 1929, the vast majority of shrines—111,699 in 1929—remained civic.[149] The Grand Shrines of Ise continued to receive unquestioned state ritual patronage outside the confines of the imperial palace, but how the full range of shrines would relate to the imperial institution was left undetermined when the Ministry of Divinities was replaced by the Ministry of Doctrine in April 1872.[150]

At the same time that the principle of *saisei itchi* was being institutionally consolidated around the person of the emperor, the creation of the Ministry of Doctrine separated an increasingly circumscribed set of rituals from an expanding conception of doctrine. Shrine priests, however, were brought under the jurisdiction of the new ministry and were endowed with a dual character that straddled the ritual-doctrine divide. This meant the ritual expression of imperial authority could not be coextensive with Shinto so long as some components of Shinto were involved in the doctrinal project. A state organ that together administered imperial rituals and promulgated a doctrine disappeared, cutting short the ambitions of many Kokugaku ideologues and shrine priests to create a "restored Shinto." The imperfect separation of the ritual and the doctrinal, anticipating the later bifurcation of Shinto into shrine Shinto and sect Shinto, also meant that the Ministry of Doctrine did not bring into effect a secure disassociation of the imperial institution and "religion." The dream of a "restored Shinto" subsuming Buddhism and other creeds died hard among Shinto partisans who moved from the Ministry of Divinities and Missionary Office into the Ministry of Doctrine. Still, by formally including all Buddhist sects alongside shrine priests in the "Doctrinal Instructor" (*kyōdōshoku*) system, the new ministry gave form, in principle at least, to a generic category of "doctrine" within which multiple doctrines coexisted. Through the Ministry of Doctrine, the Meiji government retained full and direct control over all Shinto shrines and Buddhist sects, including clerical ordination and appointments.[151] Yet by reintegrating Buddhism into its doctrinal program, the ministry did introduce a mediating term in the relationship between the emperor and indoctrination: Buddhism could never be confused for a doctrine founded by the imperial ancestor.

The connection between shrines (belonging to the ranked system of imperial rituals) and priests (belonging to the doctrinal supervision of the Ministry of Doctrine) meant the disassociation of state and doctrine-cum-religion was less than complete. The way in which this continued association would be deemed problematic, however, was clearly articulated within the government at this time. The relationship of shrines and priests to the nascent regulatory space of "religion" was not directly addressed until 1882, as will be examined in Chapter 4. However, the fundamental trajectory of placing the emperor beyond the realm of choice, and hence outside of religion, was already firmly mapped with the establishment of the Ministry of Doctrine and the accompanying separation of ritual and doctrine.

Conclusion

Talal Asad observes that hegemonic power does not operate by creating uniformity. Rather, it functions best by classifying difference: "The claim of many radical critics that hegemonic power necessarily suppresses difference in favor of unity is quite mistaken. Just as mistaken is their claim that power always abhors ambiguity. To secure its unity—to make its own history—dominant power has worked best through differentiating and classifying practices."[152] To the extent that the Meiji government sought to assert the hegemonic authority of the state through the imperial institution, it discovered the limits of enforcing uniformity, or erasing difference. Doctrine, rendered increasingly distinct from the imperial institution, came to provide a means to differentiate and classify practices and identifications—Shinto, Buddhist, even Christian—beneath the hegemonic authority of the state. That doctrine, rendered distinct from ritual, came to function in this way is hinted at by the inclusion of the recommendation to tolerate Christian belief in the collection of reform recommendations circulated within the government in late 1871.[153] If, as James Ketelaar suggests, the pursuit of *saisei itchi* marked an attempt to produce "a purportedly closed ideological order wherein the present place, as the unity of past and present, of seen and unseen worlds, could recognize no Other, no 'outside' of itself," the separation of rite from doctrine marked a significant amendment to that closed ideological order.[154] For the imperial institution to secure a uniform relationship to a heterogeneous population, an ability to sequester difference based on ritual affiliation and doctrinal belief was required.

Conversion, in this analysis, foregrounds the intense political concern directed toward the project of assimilating and integrating the populace of the Japanese archipelago. The dissonance between the specifically sectarian valence of conversion and its broader application here draws attention to how the perceived threat of Christian conversion, and the response to it, came from a sociopolitical imagination that could not initially imagine religion as a discreet sphere of human belief and activity. Christian conversion appeared likely and threatening precisely because religious identities and practices were imagined to be inseparable from political and communal loyalties. The concept of conversion focuses our attention on the ineradicable moment of contingency that underlies all imaginations of boundaries, communities, and identities. The imperative to distinguish imperial authority from religion in early Meiji Japan arose from the attempt to contain that moment of contingency and to limit its role in defining the "nation's" relationship to the emperor.

CHAPTER 2

Religion and Diplomacy in a Semicolonial World, 1853–1873

> And, from all time, the Christian nations have alone inspired this confidence, for there only where there exists an identity of religion, is there identity of manners, and there only, justice and love.
>
> —"The Christian Question," *Japan Weekly Mail*, 1872

> It is the independence of this power within a State, this *Imperium in Imperio*, which the rulers of China and Japan alike object to, as fatal to their own authority and supremacy; and they resist its encroachment within their territories as the Emperor of Germany and the Queen of England resist similar pretensions to the assertion of a power above the law.
>
> —Rutherford Alcock, *Times* (London), 1873

As they sailed from Yokohama for the United States in late 1871, the members of the Iwakura Embassy carried with them the documentary record of diplomatic negotiations, accumulated since the arrival in Japan of Commodore Perry in 1853, concerning the status of Christianity in Japan. Diplomatic relations between the Meiji government and the treaty powers covered a broad range of issues, many of them economic, but the issue of Christianity proved particularly thorny and intractable during the first decades. The fact that the Japanese leadership embarked on an ambitious tour of the United States and Europe with these "Christian Documents" (*yaso shorui*) in hand underscores the diplomatic significance of Christianity for the early-Meiji government.

The diplomatic significance of Christianity appears to arise from how it motivated treaty powers to pressure the Meiji government to adopt a policy of religious freedom.[1] The powers did bring considerable pressure to bear on the Japanese leaders, preventing them from enforcing the ban on Christianity with violent suppression, for example. By the time the Iwakura Embassy returned from its lengthy tour of the West, the public notice boards in Japan prohibiting the practice of Christianity had been removed and the Urakami Christians had been released from exile. The correlation between the embassy's experience and the beginning of the so-called silent toleration of Christianity is deceptively simple, however, and can lead one to miss the larger significance of the lessons learned by the embassy. The diplomatic arena shaped state policy toward "religion" in complex ways.

In its effort to rehabilitate and reinvent the imperial institution, the Meiji government was forced to negotiate its ritual and doctrinal configuration, resulting in the first attempts to distinguish state authority from a nascent concept of religion. The potential reintroduction of Christianity, backed by the might of the treaty powers, marked another critical site where Meiji elites learned to define and contest the boundaries of religion. Christianity, especially its pietistic Protestant forms, for example, played a dominant role in shaping conceptions of religion among Japanese elites.[2] Private, doctrinal belief compatible with the universal progress of rational civilization provided the benchmark for gauging authentic religion. Whatever failed to reach that benchmark could be, and frequently was, deemed superstition or simply primitive. However, this emphasis on the dominant template provided by Christianity and the West misses the fact that the image of Christianity fluctuated within the hegemonic discourse of the modern West. Japanese elites, in other words, grappled with Christianity as the normative standard of religion at a time when the public position of religion was undergoing significant contestation in North America and Europe. The diplomatic crosscurrents that shaped the definition and treatment of religion in mid-nineteenth-century Japan, to borrow Gauri Viswanathan's phrase, reveal "discordances where there might be a will to hear only tonality and harmony."[3] The imagined crisis of conversion revealed a Japanese polity in political and social flux. In a similar fashion, negotiating Christianity's status within Japan exposed discordances surrounding the place of Christianity and religion within the nation-states and empires of the West. Diplomatic interventions on behalf of the Urakami Christians did not convey a settled and clear message to the Japanese government. And as a partner to diplomatic negotiations, the Meiji government's own attempts to clarify the boundary between religion and its political authority were not merely exercises in "catching up" or accepting settled norms. They were, rather, attempts to navigate the complex and often treacherous waters of nineteenth-century diplomacy and nation building.

In short, the Iwakura Embassy, which toured the United States and Europe between 1871 and 1873, did more than simply convince Japanese leaders of the need to accommodate foreign demands to legalize the practice of Christianity within Japan.[4] Consisting of the core of leadership that would steer the government through the difficult and formative years of the late 1870s, including Iwakura Tomomi (1825–1883), Kido Takayoshi, and Ōkubo Toshimichi, the embassy observed firsthand the shifting disposition of Christianity and its institutions among the treaty powers. Protestant anti-Catholicism, stoked by the Roman Catholic Relief Act of 1829, still resonated in 1870s Britain, while on the Continent, Bismarck's Kulturkampf and the expansion of public education appeared to expand state authority at the expense of Christian churches, particularly the Catholic Church.[5] The growth of urban, industrial societies and the accompanying formation of nation-states produced the drive toward state-directed popular education. While the increased availability of public education heightened literacy rates, it also brought states face to face with the sectarian passions of their populations, and the early 1870s witnessed tensions over the place of religion within education in the United States, Britain, France, and Germany. In each of these cases, the conception and practice of religious liberty confronted the question of whether public education could or should be neutral toward private belief. The debate over public education, conducted primarily around the role of the Roman Catholic Church within the European nation-states, illustrates the inherent conflict in the process of creating a public sphere independent of religion during the nineteenth century.

Iwakura and his companions found much in common between these developments in North America and Europe and their concern to establish and protect the prerogatives of the state in Japan. They also discovered the utility of employing the generic category of religion, not Christianity specifically, as the term to place in opposition to assertions of state authority and prerogative. The contact zone of their semicolonial encounters provided the treaty powers and Japan with a historical moment in which the boundary of "religion" proved a shared political and intellectual concern. At the same time, recurring appeals to "Christian civilization" reflected the asymmetrical nature of the encounter and reinforced the lesson that Japan would not achieve parity with the West until it adopted a liberal if not positive posture toward the Christian faith, in particular. Under the relations of power imposed by the unequal treaties, the Meiji government had no choice but to adopt and adapt to the dominant discourse of religion found in the Christian West. That dominant discourse, however, proved a moving target, reflecting the shifting significations of "Christianity" and "religion" alike.

Spreading Amity and Commerce, or Christendom?

Shūkyō made its first appearance in the Japanese lexicon as a translation for "religion" in the diplomatic exchanges inaugurated by Commodore Matthew Perry (1794–1858) and which culminated in the treaties of amity and commerce concluded between Japan and the treaty powers.[6] Religion, in these negotiations, did not designate a generic or neutral category; it referred primarily to Christianity. The ambiguity of negotiating the place of Christianity in Japan through the generic category of religion introduced an abiding tension to the diplomatic exchanges between Japanese authorities and Western diplomats. Perry's first expedition in 1853 immediately exposed this tension between the promise of religious neutrality and an avowed identification with Christianity. The letter from U.S. president Millard Fillmore (1800–1874) that the commodore delivered to Tokugawa authorities contained the following the assurance: "The Constitution and laws of the United States forbid all interference with the religious or political concerns of other nations. I have particularly charged Commodore Perry to abstain from every act which could possibly disturb the tranquility of your imperial majesty's dominions."[7] Phillip Franz von Siebold (1796–1866), the German physician who had once served the Dutch factory in Deshima, had warned a member of Perry's expedition that unless the United States promised not to overturn the current political and religious order in Japan, the *bakufu* would be sure to refuse any treaties.[8] Well aware of the long-standing prohibition of Christianity in Japan, the Fillmore administration emphasized its religious neutrality in the hope of convincing the Tokugawa *bakufu* to end its policy of isolation.

Despite Fillmore's assurances and Siebold's warning, appeals to Christian civilization were quick to surface in Perry's exchanges with Tokugawa officials. In one instance, Perry explained the demand for a guarantee that American sailors shipwrecked on Japanese shores would receive aid in the following terms: "With the Americans, as indeed with all Christian people, it is considered a sacred duty to receive with kindness, and to succor and protect all, of whatever nation, who may be cast upon their shores, and such has been the course of the Americans with respect to all Japanese subjects who have fallen under their protection."[9] If discussing "sacred" duties with a military representative of a "Christian people"—backed by the technological might of the "Black Ships"—did not alarm *bakufu* officials, the inclusion of a Bible and Christian literature among scientific and technical books presented to the shogun the following year certainly did: "The Christian sect is prohibited by national decree [*gokokkin no gi*]; moreover, the letter we received from your President last year states that you will not spread the doctrine [*kyōhō*]. What do you mean by including these texts? They should be burned immediately."[10] Perry's response to this astute criticism did nothing to resolve the tension in having a Christian representative profess religious neutrality. He reiterated President Fillmore's assurances of noninterference but also threatened to travel to Edo in person to demand the return of the Christian literature, lest it be burned. Burning the scriptures of a faith venerated by most Americans, Perry declared, would constitute a grave offense.[11] His bold Christian identification combined with the thinly veiled threat of force undercut any claim to religious neutrality in the eyes of Tokugawa officials and merely reaffirmed the association of Christian proselytizing with the aggressive diplomacy of Western powers. Christianity, in short, appeared part and parcel of the amity and commerce Perry professed to seek.

The 1854 Treaty of Kanagawa, a result of Perry's second expedition to Japan, opened a new era of diplomacy for Japan, one in which the Japanese authorities committed to ongoing engagement and negotiation with foreign powers. First the Tokugawa then the Meiji authorities adapted to this new culture of negotiation wherein "nothing superseded defending the ideological, intellectual, and physical boundaries between themselves and Westerners."[12] Among the boundaries the Japanese authorities sought to defend, none was more significant than the prohibition of Christianity. When Perry sought to include language in the 1854 treaty guaranteeing the right of American citizens to build churches and to worship, the *bakufu* refused to accept it, citing earlier assurances that the United States would not interfere in the religious affairs of their realm.[13] Townsend Harris (1804–1878), the first consul and minister of the United States to Japan following Perry's treaty, repeated the demand for an explicit guarantee of religious liberty in the commercial treaty he was appointed to negotiate. His diary entry of December 6, 1857, conveys his resolve:

> The first blow is now struck against the cruel persecution of Christianity by the Japanese; and, by the blessing of God, if I succeed in establishing negotiations at this time with the Japanese, I mean to boldly demand for Americans the free exercise of their religion in Japan with the right to build churches, and I will also demand the abolition of the custom of trampling on the cross or crucifix, which the Dutch have basely witnessed for nearly two hundred and thirty years without a word of remonstrance.[14]

For their part, Tokugawa officials prioritized the maintenance of a physical boundary between foreigners and the Japanese populace by limiting concessions to the physically confined space of Yokohama (and subsequently other treaty ports). The Treaty of Amity and Commerce concluded on July 29, 1858, between the United States and the Tokugawa *bakufu* thus granted the right of religious liberty to American nationals, but firmly rejected Harris's request to permit Christian missions among the Japanese.[15] Tokugawa authorities kept concessions to a minimum, hoping that the presence of foreign nationals in the treaty ports would not translate into the rapid spread of Christianity.

The 1858 Treaty of Amity and Commerce formed the basis for all subsequent treaties the Tokugawa *bakufu* signed with the treaty powers (initially the United States, Britain, Russia, France, and Holland). Article VII stipulates:

> Americans in Japan shall be allowed the free exercise of their religion, and for this purpose shall have the right to erect suitable places of worship. No injury shall be done to such buildings, nor any insult be offered to the religious worship of the Americans. American citizens shall not injure any Japanese temple or *mia*, or offer any insult or injury to Japanese religious ceremonies, or to the objects of their worship. Americans and Japanese shall not do anything that may be calculated to excite religious animosity. The Government of Japan has already abolished the practice of trampling on religious emblems.[16]

This and similar articles provided the formal basis for negotiating all subsequent questions related to the practice of Christianity in Japan.[17] The article crucially limits religious liberty to foreign nationals and emphasizes the need to avoid "any insult or injury" and "religious animosity" between foreigners and the Japanese populace.[18] These commercial treaties also famously included extraterritorial jurisdiction for the treaty powers and curtailed Japanese tariff autonomy. Extraterritoriality, at least, did not appear to Tokugawa officials to be a significant concession, since it erected a clear legal boundary between Japanese subjects and foreign nationals—the free practice of Christianity could be permitted within the confined physical and legal space of the treaty ports, distinct from the prohibition left in place everywhere else.[19]

The amity and commerce into which the Tokugawa *bakufu* entered from 1858 onward was undeniably based on an inequality of power, an inequality that made the defense of any boundaries a difficult task.[20] Commercial interests, and the corollary interest in political stability, animated the treaty powers' approach to Japan from the beginning—

hence the repeated promises of religious neutrality and noninterference.[21] The entrenched cultural attitude that Christian civilization stood at the vanguard of progress undercut those promises, however, and resulted in repeated demands for the introduction of religious liberty. Harris, while negotiating the 1858 treaty, pressed his Tokugawa counterparts to permit the Japanese populace to practice Christianity by appealing to the inherent connection between progress and religious liberty. Nations such as Spain and Italy, he argued, remained poor and underdeveloped because those governments restricted their subjects' religious beliefs.[22] Religious liberty, Christianity, and the progress of civilization formed a triad of mutually reinforcing terms that the Tokugawa and, subsequently, Meiji authorities had to contend with. Negotiating the status of Christianity within Japan, in short, implied negotiating Japan's status vis-à-vis the civilized West.

The Diplomatic Negotiation of Belief

This tension between religious neutrality, codified in the language of the treaties, and the celebration of "Christian civilization" runs through the diplomatic negotiations prompted by what became known as the Urakami Incident. Straddling the political divide of the Meiji Restoration, and thus involving both the Tokugawa *bakufu* and the Meiji state, the discovery in 1865 of communities of hidden Christians in the environs of Nagasaki proved a diplomatic headache not just for the Japanese authorities but for the representatives of the treaty powers as well. They were caught between the pragmatic desire to uphold the terms of the treaties and thus ensure the stable commercial operation of the treaty ports, on the one hand, and the ideological celebration of Christian identity and the corollary support for Christian missions, on the other. This ambivalence played out as a series of intractable diplomatic negotiations between 1865 and the Iwakura Embassy's departure in 1871.

In the first place, diplomatic representatives were caught between irreconcilable constituencies within the treaty ports. Merchants, diplomats, and missionaries quickly populated the ports opened by the commercial treaties.[23] Missionaries, in particular, arrived expecting that as a natural consequence of the foreign presence in Japan, the prohibition would be lifted and proselytizing among the Japanese would be permitted. The zeal with which the missionaries identified the foreign presence with the Christian mission stood in stark contrast to the lukewarm or even hostile attitude of the merchants and members of the diplomatic corps. The interests and priorities of the merchant community, the diplomatic corps, and the missionaries, as well as foreigners hired by the Japanese, naturally differed. Missionaries often complained of lax morals and poor church attendance on the part of fellow treaty port residents, and churches were often poorly supported.[24] For their part, the merchant community feared missionary activities would provoke antiforeign sentiment and violent attacks, which were already intense during the final years of Tokugawa rule. Diplomats were caught in the middle and attempted to balance the pragmatic pursuit of stability in the interest of commerce with their sense of duty as representatives of "Christian nations."

The so-called Yokohama Incident brought the tensions within the foreign community to the fore. In 1862, Prudence S. B. Girard (1821–1867), a French Catholic missionary, began to address groups of curious Japanese who came to see the new "French temple" (*furansu dera*) built in Yokohama.[25] Sensitive to any breach in the boundary between the foreign settlements and the Japanese populace, *bakufu* authorities arrested fifty-five of those present during one of Girard's sermons. They were quickly condemned to be executed for violating the prohibition against Christianity. The French minister, Gustave Duchesne de Bellecourt (1817–1881), protested to the Tokugawa authorities along with his British counterpart, Rutherford Alcock (1809–1897). At the time of his appointment, de Bellecourt had received ambivalent instructions from Paris regarding the issue of Catholic missionary activity in Japan. He was instructed that the French government's interests in Japan were purely secular in nature.[26] At the same time, he was given to understand that even if missionary activity was not to be supported, converts were to be defended:

> If the government of the Emperor is resolved in conformity with the conduct it has already followed in China, of in no way provoking Japan by Catholic propaganda, it cannot, however, envisage its indifference were it to succeed in reaching the hearts of the population having so far remained inaccessible to the light and blessings of Christianity; above all it could not countenance abandoning the right of protecting the missionaries under any circumstance.

The tortured emphasis of these instructions propelled the French minister to accept a compromise with the Tokugawa authorities: the French missionaries were ordered to cease preaching in Japanese and to bar any Japanese citizen from entering the church; in exchange, those who had been arrested were released without further punishment. In his report to the French foreign minister, de Bellecourt expressed the difficulty with which he balanced "the duty which humanity imposes on me with the not less imperious duty of the prudence which is necessary to ensure the maintenance of our relations here, and of the dignity and future of the Christian religion in this country."[27]

Though minor, the incident illustrates the oppositions sustained within the diplomatic negotiation of Christianity's status within Japan. The Tokugawa *bakufu* indicated no inclination to relax the prohibition, if only because of the increasing pressure generated by an imperial court bent on expelling the foreigners. Christian missionaries refused to allow diplomatic pragmatism to fundamentally curtail their activities.[28] Christianity transcended any consideration for the national interests of their respective governments. For their part, the diplomatic representatives of the treaty powers—by no means consistent or unanimous in their priorities—struggled to balance the premise of formal religious neutrality with their defense of religious liberty.

The Urakami Incident of 1865, though far more dramatic than the preceding incident in Yokohama, nonetheless followed similar diplomatic dynamics. In 1862, Pope Pius IX canonized the twenty-six martyrs who had been executed outside of Nagasaki in 1597. The Catholics' focus on the southwestern port was natural enough, given its history as the site of successful missionary activity and, later, martyrdom in the sixteenth century. When the Church of the Twenty-Six Martyrs was completed in the foreign district of Ōura in 1865, the French missionaries hoped it would help them discover the descendants of earlier believers. On March 17, just one month following its completion, representatives of a hidden community of Christians identified themselves to the missionaries at the church. Prompted by reports that a statue of Mary stood within the church, a group from the village of Urakami approached Benard T. Petitjean (1829–1884), the resident priest, and reportedly confessed, "Our hearts are the same as your heart" (*warera no mune, anata no mune to onaji*).[29] Satisfied that the French missionaries venerated Mary, were celibate, and represented the pope in Rome, the villagers eagerly sought instruction and the sacraments from the priests.[30] Though thrilled by the emergence of a community of believers willing to identify themselves as Catholics, Petitjean expressed concern over their apparent lack of caution in the face of the prohibition.[31] In fact, the boldness demonstrated by the Urakami Christians may have reflected their confidence in the presence of the treaty powers in Nagasaki.[32]

Tokugawa authorities were well aware of the clandestine interaction between the French missionaries and the villagers. Urakami had already been the site of three prior "collapses" (*kuzure*) in which villagers had been accused of or prosecuted for heterodox beliefs and practices.[33] The first two instances had been met with lenience on the part of the Nagasaki magistrate, who lacked any incentive to "discover" the persistence of a faith outlawed for nearly two centuries and believed to have been annihilated.[34] Increased foreign contact during the first half of the nineteenth century, along with a heightened sense of political and social crisis, altered the light in which the presence of underground Christian communities was viewed. Consequently, the third *kuzure* of 1856, in the wake of Perry's expeditions, resulted in the deaths of a majority of the Urakami community's leadership.[35] The opening of a treaty port in Nagasaki, and mounting criticism for opening the ports in the first place, prompted Tokugawa authorities to respond decisively in 1865. On July 15, four temporary chapels where the missionaries conducted Mass in secret were raided, and more than eighty men and women were arrested, of whom sixty-eight were imprisoned.[36]

These arrests marked the fourth Urakami *kuzure* and the start of six years of tense diplomatic exchanges with the treaty powers. As his predecessor had done in Yokohama, the French minister Leon Roches (1809–1900) immediately intervened on behalf of the arrested Christians.[37] As an ally to the Tokugawa *bakufu*, Roches was able to secure meetings with Tokugawa Yoshinobu in Osaka on August 24, and he invited the shogun aboard a French warship the following day. Aboard that ship, an accompanying Tokugawa official learned from a French naval officer that France had severed Annam's (Vietnam's) tributary ties to China and secured control over several of its "counties" (*gun*) as a result of conflict stemming from the activities of Catholic missionaries (*sōkan*).[38]

Contrary to the impression given by such unguarded disclosures, the treaty powers feared further destabilizing the Tokugawa regime and strengthening the hand of antiforeign factions then coalescing around the imperial court. Their diplomatic protests, therefore, struck a cautious note, and interventions frequently took the form of private, unofficial advice that emphasized the universal and humanitarian basis for religious liberty, while avoiding any discussion of the specificities of Christianity.[39] The diplomats attempted to establish a distinction between the illegality of missionary activity and the potential legitimacy of Christian belief itself.

Roches employed this distinction to achieve a compromise with the *bakufu*. He accepted the culpability of the missionaries for violating the terms of the treaties and ordered them to remain within the foreign district of Nagasaki, to cease visiting villages such as Urakami, and to discourage the villagers from visiting the church in Ōura. In exchange, the arrested Christians were to be released but confined to their village (*mura azuke*).[40]

Roches explained the settlement to Petitjean, by then consecrated as bishop of the Catholic Church in Japan, in a letter dated August 8, 1867. Pointing out how moderate and tolerant the attitude of the *bakufu* appeared to be, Roches suggested Petitjean cease active ministry (i.e., conferring the sacraments) to the Japanese Christians, at least for the time being. As an ally, he explained, France had reason to be concerned that the *bakufu* remained vulnerable to criticism on this issue, and the status of Christianity was likely be resolved with the future revision of the treaties. Moreover, Roches suggested, the Christians were arrested for violating laws that demand outward compliance with rituals, and the acceptance of "certain external formalities" (*de certaines formalités extérieurs*) should not annul their faith.[41] Roches's suggestion that religious belief should not be annulled by external practices clearly disregarded core tenets of the Catholic faith, especially the significance of the sacraments. Pressing the distinction between internal belief and external ritual was expedient for Roches in balancing the French state's diplomatic interests against its desire to defend the "future of the Christian religion."[42] It also illuminated the divide between purely Catholic and secular French concerns as they played out in a semicolonial context.

The distinction that Roches proposed additionally ignored the crucial importance of "external formalities" to the Urakami Christians themselves. It was precisely their refusal to obey the ritual requirements of the prohibition that prompted the Nagasaki magistrate to raid the community.[43] Moreover, despite the compromise with Roches, the *bakufu* refused to release the arrested villagers until they recanted their faith (*kaishin*).[44] Weakened by its struggle with the imperial court over the opening of the port of Hyōgo to the treaty powers, the *bakufu* could ill afford to appear weak in enforcing the requirements of its own prohibition.[45] Nagasaki officials interrogated and tortured the imprisoned Christians from September through October. Although only six of the prisoners were tortured, the effect on the others was immediate. Of the eighty-three imprisoned, all but one were released after signing an oath recanting their faith.[46] The community in Urakami responded by ostracizing those who had recanted, and many were barred from their own homes. Faced with this communal pressure, thirty-eight of them informed the village headman of their desire to retract their oaths (*kaishin modoshi*). External formalities, not internal belief, remained crucial to the cohesion of the Urakami community.

By the time the Tokugawa *bakufu* formally ceased to exist on November 9, 1867, the Urakami Christians, while nominally under village arrest, were traveling freely between villages, prompting other communities of hidden Christians to openly seek the instruction of the missionaries.[47] When the fledgling Meiji government declared the restoration of imperial rule, it was faced with these activities and the abiding assumption within the foreign community that the free propagation of the Christian faith would inevitably come to Japan. The Meiji leadership pragmatically accepted the legitimacy of the treaty regime negotiated by the Tokugawa, but it also attempted to reinforce the prohibition against Christianity. Compelled to seek amicable relations with the treaty powers but unwilling to permit the free practice of Christianity, the Meiji government's actions ensured that the diplomatic negotiation of belief continued beyond 1868.

Nonetheless, the fall of the *bakufu* gave diplomats, missionaries, and the Urakami Christians the impression that the worst might be over. The new government was eager to secure the recognition of the treaty powers while it worked to quell armed resistance from pro-*bakufu* forces and consolidate its authority. On February 8, 1868, the vice minister for foreign affairs, Higashikuze Michitomi (1833–1912), met with the representatives of the treaty powers to announce that the new government would exercise sovereignty over the domestic and foreign affairs of Japan. Two days later, the government sent a letter to the representatives promising to "faithfully execute all foreign treaties."[48] Further reinforcing this pragmatic embrace of the "open country" policy, the Charter Oath, issued by the young Emperor Meiji in April, declared that the "evil customs of the past shall be broken off," and that "knowledge shall be sought throughout the world so as to strengthen the foundations of imperial rule."[49]

Beyond these gestures the new government was no more willing nor in any better position to lift the prohibition against Christianity. Although attacks on foreigners had created considerable headaches for the government, the fear of violence against foreigners cannot alone account for the decision to maintain the prohibition. As discussed in the previous chapter, members of the Meiji government were themselves keenly afraid of the potential spread of Christianity. An unsteady combination of zealous nativism, pragmatic concerns about antiforeign violence, and genuine fears within the government about the spread of Christianity informed the initial constellation of ritual and doctrinal policies meant to secure the prestige of the imperial institution and counter the potential spread of Christianity. The unresolved problem of Urakami stood at the center of many of these policies, especially the creation and operation of the Missionary Office. These initial policies as they were applied to the Urakami Christians kept Christianity alive as a source of diplomatic friction.

On April 7, 1868, the Meiji government reaffirmed the public notice boards (*kōsatsu*) that the Tokugawa *bakufu* had used to publish laws and decrees.[50] Five permanent notice boards were to be kept in public view, one of which declared: "The evil sect of *Kirishitan* [*kirishitan jashūmon*, or Christianity] is strictly forbidden. A reward will be given for informing the authorities of suspicious persons." When their tacit expectation that the Tokugawa-era prohibition would be lifted was betrayed, representatives of the treaty powers protested the publication of these notices. Robert van Valkenburgh (1821–1888), the U.S. minister resident in Japan, warned Foreign Minister Higashikuze and Vice Minister Nabeshima Naohiro (1846–1921) of the negative effects that the notice boards might produce. Disclaiming any intention of interfering in the "internal affairs of Japan," van Valkenburgh said he nonetheless deemed it his "duty to call Your Excellencies [*sic*] attention to the fact that the Christian religion is the religion of the Country I have the honor to represent," and that the edict against Christianity would "necessarily tend to affect the relations between the United States and Japan." "As the Representative of a Christian Nation," he urged his Japanese counterparts to reconsider "this important matter."[51]

These were not the sentiments of van Valkenburgh alone. Secretary of State William H. Seward (1801–1872) took the matter of the notice boards quite seriously, ordering van Valkenburgh to "proceed in the matter with firmness and without practicing any injurious hesitation or accepting any abasing compromise." Should the Japanese refuse to rectify the situation, Seward warned in a subsequent communication, it would "only prepare the way for fearful and bloody and political convulsions, which will not cease until Christianity shall have established its claim to be recognized and maintained by the Government, and shall be universally accepted and adopted throughout the Empire. Humanity indeed demands and expects a continually expanding sway for Christianity."[52] Though Seward's strident rhetoric stands out among the diplomatic voices, the triangle he drew linking Christianity with civilization (progress) and religious liberty was by no means unique to him.

No evidence suggests van Valkenburgh conveyed Seward's aggressive message to the Meiji government, and the other treaty powers did not echo such extreme rhetoric. Yet the foreign representatives did uniformly protest the notice boards, prompting the Japanese to revise the language of their anti-Christian edict, separating "evil sects" and "*kirishitan*."[53] This linguistic sleight of hand went some way toward mollifying the diplomats, who were intent on preventing any insult to the "Christian civilization" they represented. In fact, Ernest Satow (1843–1929), the noted British diplomat then serving under Harry S. Parkes (1828–1885), British minister plenipotentiary to Japan, had privately suggested to a Japanese contact "that instead of specifically mentioning Christianity the decree should merely forbid 'pernicious sects' in general."[54] Satow's advice contained an important lesson: so long as the conversation was about generalities (pernicious sects) and not about Christianity in particular, the Japanese government could expect greater latitude from the treaty powers.

That latitude was quickly exhausted, however, when, on June 7, the Meiji government ordered the exile of up to four thousand Urakami Christians to thirty-four daimyo domains (*han*). Citing the villagers' persistent adherence to the prohibited faith, the order declared that their exile was determined with "exceptional lenience" (*kakubetsu no gojihi*).[55] Although the order was unpublished, rumors of it quickly reached the foreign representatives, and on July 13 the foreign consuls in Nagasaki sent a joint letter to Sawa Nobuyoshi, governor of Nagasaki, asking where the Urakami Christians were being sent, how they were to be treated, and on what basis they were being exiled. As in all previous diplomatic protests, the letter expressly denied any intent to interfere in the internal affairs of Japan. The consuls insisted, nonetheless, that to persecute the villagers for the sole reason that they believe in the Christian religion was unreasonable and would only harm the reputation of the Japanese government. In response, Sawa's office explained that the villagers were being exiled for violating the laws of the land (*kokuritsu wo okashi sōrō*).[56]

In practice, the authorities in Nagasaki managed to exile only 114 men, considered leaders within the community, to the three domains of Yamaguchi, Tsuwano, and Fukuyama.[57] The plan to exile all Christian villagers was delayed by fiscal constraints and resistance from the domains ordered to host the exiles. The relatively small scale of this initial exile and the Meiji authorities' insistence that the villagers were receiving lenient treatment for their civil disobedience blunted diplomatic protests for a time.

The Meiji government could not prevent news of the exile from traveling to the United States and Europe, however, where it was strongly condemned. An October 18 *New York Times* editorial decried the "banishment of two shiploads of Christians from (Nagasaki) under peculiarly painful circumstances." Although "it may seem useless for any foreign Government to protest against these persecutions," the editorial continued, "We think . . . that a joint protest from the Christian Governments of the world—a protest headed by the Mighty and Awful Republic of

America—might penetrate the ears even of the Mikado." The call for protest addressed to Secretary of State Seward concluded with, "Men should not be persecuted for being Christians in the Nineteenth Century."[58] The international press maintained pressure on the foreign representatives to engage the Japanese government on the issue of Christianity and the treatment of Japanese Christians.

Bolstered by the broad condemnation at home, British minister to Japan Harry Parkes assumed the lead in pressing the Meiji government to relax its treatment of the Japanese Christians.[59] The intensity of diplomatic concern escalated in November 1869 when the remaining Urakami Christians were ordered into exile. This was, in fact, merely a reiteration of the original June 7, 1868, order. When the Christian villagers were ordered to present themselves to authorities in early January 1870, they requested, and received, a delay, in the hope that it would provide enough time for the foreign diplomats to intervene on their behalf.[60] Protests lodged by Parkes and other representatives, however, failed to forestall the removal of 700 men on January 5 and the removal of the remaining villagers between January 6 and 11. Nearly 3,100 villagers were exiled from Urakami.

Parkes demanded a conference with the government in Tokyo, resulting in a meeting between the representatives of the treaty powers and the Japanese leadership on January 19, 1870. Representing the treaty powers were Harry Parkes (Britain), Maxime Outrey (d. 1898; France), Charles E. De Long (d. 1876; United States), and Max August von Brandt (1835–1920; Prussia). From the Meiji government, Minister of the Right Sanjō Sanetomi, Senior Councilor Iwakura Tomomi, Foreign Minister Sawa Nobuyoshi, and Vice Foreign Minister Terashima Munenori (1832–1893) were present. The most direct diplomatic exchanges concerning Christianity and the place of religion in Japan occurred at this conference. At issue were the questions of why Christians were singled out for persecution and what constituted lenient treatment, and the legal stipulations of the treaties. Both sides, to varying degrees of success, attempted to frame the negotiations in terms that avoided a direct discussion of Christianity itself. The Japanese insisted the villagers were being prosecuted—in a lenient fashion, at that—for criminal offenses, not for the content of their belief. The foreign representatives couched their intervention in humanitarian terms, arguing that religious liberty was a universal value that had nothing to do with an exclusive endorsement of the Christian religion. Despite these attempts, the Yokohama conference unavoidably turned to the specific character of Christianity as it related to the authority of the Japanese state.

In fact, Parkes attempted to gain leverage by threatening to place the character of Christianity at the center of the discussion. During an interview with Terashima two days prior to the conference, British chargé d'affaires Francis O. Adams (1825–1889) warned that the Meiji government's policy could force the British government to pursue a religious debate. He threatened, in other words, to debate the merits of Christianity itself, rather than questions of civil law and treaty provisions. To add further pressure, Adams also informed Terashima that Britain would postpone the promised withdrawal of its soldiers garrisoned in Yokohama.[61] Tellingly, Sanjō began the conference on the nineteenth by insisting that the authorities "do not move these people on account of their religious professions," and that they did not wish to debate the correctness of their religion (*shūshi*).[62] Parkes insisted, in response, on the singular importance of Christianity: the "only reason assigned [for the exile] being that these people professed the Christian religion, and that is the religion of my countrymen." Iwakura countered that the Urakami Christians were responsible for causing civil disturbances as the result of their faith. The treaty powers had to understand, he said, that "in Japan, where all the people believe in one religion . . . a sudden change or the sudden introduction of a new religion would produce great and constant political disturbances." Pressed by Outrey on this point, Iwakura conceded that Christianity rivaled the imperial institution itself, and that the exiled villagers would be allowed to return home only "if they follow the religion of their emperor, and obey the authority of the government." Terashima elaborated, explaining that "Christianity teaches our people to despise and disbelieve (the divine origin of the Mikado), and thus it brings this sacred thing into contempt." Terashima attempted to draw back from this statement later by distinguishing between the public behavior of the Christians and their private beliefs: "The government will not go so far as to try and find out the sentiments of a man's heart, and punish him for that; but these men are seditious and we cannot tolerate them."[63]

His caveat not withstanding, Terashima's initial declaration of the theological incompatibility between Christianity and the imperial institution appears to have been an honest indication of his views. He and Sawa were among those within the government most concerned with the specter of Christian conversion. They had jointly submitted a memorandum to Sanjō requesting that a clear set of doctrinal instructions (*kyōki*) be established so that the populace could easily put into practice the ideal of uniting rite and rule. They also expressed the intention to negotiate with the treaty powers to explicitly prevent the spread of Christianity.[64] John

Breen observes that the Meiji leaders were not "ideologically" opposed to Christianity but were concerned with safeguarding their own legitimacy.[65] Indeed, the Meiji leadership repeatedly insisted that precipitously legalizing Christianity would provoke a populace long taught to fear the foreign faith as evil. It cannot be denied, however, that the Department of Divinities and the Missionary Office were working to devise and disseminate a national doctrine at this time, and Terashima's statements placed the ideological, if not theological, character of Christianity at the center of the government's refusal to desist from exiling the Urakami Christians.

For all their bluster, Parkes and his colleagues could not press this line of discussion very far, largely because of the religious neutrality stipulated by the treaty regime.[66] Yet they made sure to repeatedly link demands for the humane treatment of the exiled believers and for the universal value of religious liberty to an endorsement of Christianity. De Long, the U.S. minister in residence, made this link explicit when he warned the Japanese that "such action as this on the part your government will send a thrill of horror throughout the United States, where freedom of religious belief is granted to all, and yet where the Christian religion is almost universally professed."[67] To persecute the Urakami villagers for their Christian faith alone, De Long concluded, would not only violate the universal right to the freedom of conscience but would also gravely offend the Christian sensibilities of the United States. It was precisely this connection between the endorsement of religious liberty and the presumed success of Christianity—indicated by the "yet" in De Long's declaration—that appeared most problematic to the Meiji leadership. In the midst of the Great Promulgation Campaign aimed at securing the imperial institution against challenges from Christianity, the diplomats merely reinforced the associative link between religious liberty and inevitable Christian triumph.

The Japanese officials did grant one concession to the treaty powers, promising to order officials in Nagasaki to suspend further deportations of Urakami Christians. Tokyo in fact did order Nagasaki to cease exiling the villagers until consultations with the foreign representatives were completed. That same order, however, reiterated the government's intent to insist on the legitimacy of the exile because it "fears its [i.e., Christianity's] spread" (*sono man'en o osoruru nari*). Sawa, by then promoted to foreign minister, notified the foreign representatives just two days after the conference that 2,810 Christians had already been removed from Urakami to nineteen different domains.[68] The diplomatic protests were, in sum, unable to alter the Meiji government's view that the open practice of Christianity threatened its legitimacy and stability.

Charles de Montblanc (1833–1894), a French aristocrat contracted to serve as consul general for the Japanese government in Paris, was asked in November 1869 to provide the government in Tokyo with an opinion on the diplomatic tensions arising from the Urakami situation.[69] His response schematized two diverging perspectives on this "very complex question": that of the foreigners and that of the Japanese. The foreigners accept the freedom of conscience, he said, since "religious belief is one thing that is only the business of each one in particular." Morality, political constitution, compliance with laws, and religion are all separate matters for the foreigners. From the Japanese perspective, in contrast, morality, religion, and political constitution are inseparable. Japan is referred to as a divine nation (*shinkoku*) and the emperor is designated the divine descendant (*shinson*). Any loss of belief in this divinity would only diminish respect for the political constitution. "Consequently, the religious question, which is very easy in Europe, is not much so in Japan."[70] In the actual negotiations of January 1870, however, the diplomatic representatives of the treaty powers struggled to disentangle the "religious question" of Christian belief from general appeals for the humane treatment of the Urakami Christians. If the diplomatic rhetoric had not already suggested as much, the Iwakura Embassy's travels through the United States and Europe from late 1871 quickly demonstrated that boundaries between morality, political structures, loyalty, and matters of religion were anything but clear and distinct in the "Christian West."

The Iwakura Embassy

While the treaty powers maintained pressure over the exile of the Urakami Christians and the continued prohibition of Christianity, the Meiji government consolidated its domestic authority with the abolishment of domains and the establishment of prefectures (*haihan chiken*) in August 1871.[71] Building on that stability, and seeking to gain a more direct understanding of the institutions that characterized modern civilization, the government sent an embassy to the United States and Europe. Notably, the embassy included members of the government who would later come to dominate policy discussions within the Meiji government, including Kido Takayoshi, Ōkubo Toshimichi, and Itō Hirobumi (1841–1909). The influence that the embassy's travels had on the priorities and policies pursued by the Meiji government through the 1870s and 1880s is difficult to quantify, but it was undeniably significant.[72]

The primary purpose of the embassy was to begin laying the groundwork for the eventual revision of the unequal treaties and to observe the institutions and technology of the industrializing "West." Regardless of the primary purpose, however, Christianity and religion ineluctably found their way onto the embassy's agenda. The very idea of sending an embassy is credited to Guido Verbeck (1830–1898), an American Dutch Reformed missionary who served as a consultant to the Meiji government. He first suggested to Ōkuma Shigenobu in 1869 that Japanese leaders should view firsthand the institutions of America and Europe, a suggestion that naturally included studying the role of religion and religious liberty.[73] Though Verbeck's suggestion was not explicitly acknowledged, members of the embassy had every reason to anticipate the topic of Christianity and religious liberty would be raised during their travels.[74] In a meeting with F. O. Adams less than a month before departing for America, Iwakura asked the British diplomat whether the embassy would encounter calls to legalize Christianity in Japan. Adams replied in the affirmative and warned Iwakura that the treaty powers would not agree to revise the treaties while the religion they practiced continued to be prohibited. Iwakura, a patron of many of the Kokugaku scholars then serving within the government, remained adamant that the political stability of Japan depended on the populace's belief in the divine ancestry of the emperor, something Christianity inevitably undermined.[75] The embassy also included many in the government who had been directly involved in the Urakami affair, including Kido, Yamaguchi Naoyoshi (1842–1894), and Nakano Takeaki, and they embarked anticipating a repetition of prior debates.

The embassy's travels through the United States and Europe did not fundamentally alter its members' views of Christianity as undesirable for Japan. At the same time, in observing the religious geography of the West, and the tensions that cut across that terrain, members of the embassy came to see an important congruence between their concerns and the political treatment of religion in the United States and Europe. This nascent sense of commonality, however, did not lessen the equally clear awareness that Japan's diplomatic status vis-à-vis the treaty powers depended in large part on how it dealt with Christianity.

Religious conversation accompanied the embassy from the very beginning of its travels. According to Kume Kunitake (1839–1931), the embassy's official chronicler, as the group traveled across the Pacific to San Francisco in December 1871, members anticipated being asked by their American hosts what "religion" they professed. Answering that they professed no religion was deemed risky, since it was understood that to declare oneself to be without religion was tantamount to admitting one was amoral and untrustworthy. Yet it seemed that declaring oneself Buddhist, Shinto, or Confucian would invite needless misapprehensions, since Americans were likely not to recognize any of those as proper religions.[76]

This concern was overshadowed by the criticism directed toward the prohibition of Christianity. Even before arriving in San Francisco, the embassy was forced to discuss the matter when Jonathan Goble (1827–1896), who had sailed with Perry in 1853 and later returned to Japan as a Baptist missionary, asked to speak with members of the embassy appointed to deal with matters of religion. Though the embassy did not include staff specifically appointed to discuss religion, Kume Kunitake, the chief secretary to Iwakura, and Tanaka Fujimaro (1845–1909), commissioner and deputy minister of education, were directed to talk to Goble.[77] It is unclear what Kume and Tanaka promised Goble, but on their arrival in San Francisco on January 19, 1872, he published an open letter to fellow Christians in the San Francisco papers, claiming he had been assured by members of the embassy that "at no distant day all restrictions against Christianity in their country would be removed and entire freedom of conscience in matters of religion would prevail."[78] Whatever effect this letter might have had on deflecting criticism of the Meiji government's policies toward Christianity, however, was immediately erased by the news of a new round of arrests. The small prefecture of Imari, adjacent to Nagasaki, made international headlines when its officials arrested sixty-seven Christians and transported them to Saga prefecture in December, ostensibly without notifying the government in Tokyo.[79] Fearing further diplomatic hindrances to the embassy, the caretaker government in Tokyo ordered the Christians released in late January. The embassy did not learn of the arrests until it had reached Salt Lake City.[80]

Held up in Salt Lake City for two weeks owing to heavy snows, members of the embassy debated how best to handle the complications arising from the prohibition of Christianity in Japan. Itō Hirobumi, vice ambassador and senior councilor of public works, along with Yamaguchi Naoyoshi, vice ambassador and junior councilor for foreign affairs, advocated lifting the prohibition as soon as the embassy returned to Japan. They attempted to win over Sasaki Takayuki, commissioner for the Ministry of Justice, to their point of view. Sasaki rebuffed them, pointing out that internal stability required a gradual approach and that precipitously adopting religious liberty would outstrip the populace's ability to comprehend such a policy. Put simply, he believed the populace would not grasp the proposition that religion (*shūshi*) stood outside the bounds of government authority.[81] Any talk of liberalizing religious belief, in Sasaki's view, had to wait for the thorough reform and enlightenment of the populace. Iwakura himself later reassured Sasaki that there was no official talk of lifting the ban on Christianity. This and subsequent debates among the Meiji leadership consistently pitted diplomatic expedience against fears of internal instability. The perceived need to appease the treaty powers by liberalizing Christianity and thus secure favorable conditions for treaty revision competed with the imperative to secure the state's domestic legitimacy. Itō remained the foremost proponent of lifting the ban in order to give an advantage to diplomatic negotiations, but as Sasaki cautioned him, the embassy was unlikely to resolve an issue that remained divisive in Tokyo.[82]

Salt Lake City also offered members of the embassy a glimpse of the religious divisions then present in the United States. Sasaki met Brigham Young, an "old priest" who had seven wives, and observed that the United States government greatly disapproved of the Mormon sect.[83] Kume also took note of the limited nature of religious liberty in the United States evidenced by the treatment of Mormonism. The Mormons were forbidden to spread their teachings and Young was placed under house arrest, yet the U.S. Constitution, Kume noted, did not grant the government the right to prohibit a religion. "Here the freedom of belief faces its limit. No one can provide a clear answer to my questions [regarding this matter]."[84] So long as polygamy could claim to be a religious doctrine, the absolute application of religious liberty should protect its practice, and yet that practice furnished the rationale for the persecution of the Mormon faith.

The embassy observed more than the limits of religious freedom in Salt Lake City. Sasaki also recorded a conversation he had with a scientist (*kyūrigakusha*) who asked him to explain the historical basis for prohibiting Christianity in Japan. On hearing Sasaki's explanation, the man declared that it seemed perfectly reasonable for the Japanese authorities to have banned Christianity, and suggested that progress would eventually remove all religions anyway. Sasaki expressed great satisfaction that the scientist did not advocate Christianity and approvingly observed that, "among scientists, religious debate [*shūshiron*] is anathema."[85] The presence of rational secularists in the United States encouraged Sasaki and confirmed his suspicion that religion functioned more as a tool to discipline and control the populace. He wrote in his diary that Japan should likewise use Shinto as a foundation and Confucianism as a support. Expressing his conservative sentiments, Sasaki lamented that members of the government most interested in the latest developments, however, considered Shinto to be benighted and that the populace remained selfish and undisciplined. On the point of using religion as a tool to maintain social discipline, Sasaki granted that the policies of the United States were clever.[86]

The Iwakura Embassy reached Washington, D.C., on February 29 and commenced a busy itinerary of formal visits to the White House, numerous banquets, and tours of inspection throughout the northeastern United States. The central preoccupation of the embassy became the unanticipated negotiations it entered into with Secretary of State Hamilton Fish (1808–1893), aimed toward revising the 1858 Treaty of Amity and Commerce. Although the original purpose of the embassy was to discuss the outline of future revisions to the treaty, Mori Arinori (1847–1889), the chargé d'affaires in Washington, encouraged Iwakura to open negotiations in the belief that the American government was willing to conclude a revised treaty on terms favorable to Japan.[87] The negotiations faltered from the outset, however, as it became immediately evident that the embassy did not comprehend the distinction the Americans drew between informal discussions and negotiations intended to produce a formal protocol.[88] As Marlene Mayo aptly observes, the Iwakura Embassy faced a "catechism of Western diplomacy."[89] This catechism imparted not only a working knowledge of Western diplomatic protocol but also a clear awareness of what the Meiji government would be expected to provide in exchange for equal treaties with the treaty powers.

Provisions for the freedom of religion naturally figured in the negotiations with Secretary of State Fish. Although Fish was primarily concerned with the commercial interests of the United States, he also demanded that the Japanese government guarantee the freedom of belief.[90] Fish presented Iwakura with a twelve-article counterproposal on March 13 in which the eleventh article guaranteed the freedoms of expression, publication, and belief. At their next meeting, on March 16, consistent with his previous position on the matter, Iwakura strongly resisted the inclusion of an explicit guarantee of religious liberty in a revised treaty. He insisted to Fish that his government did not "force religion [*kyōshū*] upon our people" but rather merely sought to restrict the sources of conflict between them and foreigners. Fish, fully informed by De Long of the Urakami affair, refused to accept any verbal assurances given by Iwakura and pressed for a written guarantee of the same rights enjoyed by U.S. citizens. Iwakura perceived Fish to be advocating the liberalization of policy toward Christianity in Japan, but Fish disavowed speaking on behalf of any specific religion.[91]

Kido returned to the question of religion in a conversation with Fish two days later. He asked him bluntly, "Why must an article on religion [*kyōhō*] be included in the revised treaty? This is a very troublesome matter [*meiwaku itashi ori sōrō*]." Fish reminded Kido of the Urakami Incident and the continuing exile of the Christians. While Kido protested that the matter did not involve foreigners nor concern religion, he also attempted to assuage Fish by assuring him that the Meiji government intended to ensure the "right to the thoughts of the heart [*shinsō no ken*]."[92] This promise of eventual liberalization did little to alter Fish's demand that any revised treaty include an explicit guarantee of religious freedom.

Members of the embassy recognized that religious liberty and its corollary, lifting the prohibition against Christianity, constituted unavoidable prerequisites for treaty revision. Informed by Fish that the embassy lacked explicit credentials from the government in Tokyo to conclude a formal treaty in Washington, Itō and Ōkubo Toshimichi were dispatched to Tokyo to receive the requisite credentials. Both men had been present at the conference between Kido and Fish on March 20 and were keenly aware that religion and the status of Christianity had factored into the negotiations.[93] On May 2, they presented the caretaker government in Tokyo with an outline of the negotiations. The outline identified the explicit goal of ending extraterritorial jurisdiction but also stated that the embassy was not yet willing to allow foreign residence outside of the treaty ports. In fact, the embassy was attempting to renegotiate the commercial treaties without fundamentally abandoning the Tokugawa-era objective of maintaining boundaries between foreigners and the Japanese populace. As Michael Auslin points out, the "Meiji leaders clearly were no more ready than their Tokugawa predecessors had been to demolish all remaining boundaries between Japanese and Westerners."[94] Interestingly, the outline that Ōkubo and Itō submitted concluded with a request that the notice boards prohibiting Christianity be removed: "Although no explicit prohibition against the foreign teaching (*gaikyō*) exists within Japanese laws, because the notice boards (*kōsatsu*) continue to proclaim that prohibition, the foreigners view us to be a barbaric nation that prevents the freedom of belief and refuses to grant us equal rights. For this reason, the notice boards should be removed."[95] Ōkubo and Itō pragmatically understood the metric of civilization against which Japan was being judged to be barbaric. The freedom of religion and the free practice of Christianity were necessary to satisfy the treaty powers that Japan was worthy of a more equal relationship. Their outline did not propose, however, a radical change in policy; they merely suggested removing the visible reminder of the prohibition and emphasized the absence of any other formal decree prohibiting Christianity. Yamazaki Minako suggests that the government in Tokyo had no intention of immediately proclaiming an end to the Christianity prohibition, citing the draft treaty that Terashima Munenori carried with him when he accompanied Ōkubo and Itō back to Washington. The draft did include a provision for the freedom of belief, but it also demanded the immediate end of extraterritoriality and the recovery of tariff autonomy—both of which had little chance of acceptance.[96]

By the time the draft reached Washington, the remaining members of the embassy had been informed that the "most favored nation" clause in the unequal treaties made it meaningless to attempt revision through bilateral negotiations; no single treaty would go into effect until all treaty powers signed equivalent treaties. When Fish declined to dispatch a U.S. envoy to a conference between the treaty powers and Japan to be convened in Europe, negotiations in Washington came to an effective end on July 22. Notably, the working draft of the revised treaty that had been exchanged by this date included the explicit guarantee of religious liberty.[97] The Iwakura Embassy abandoned all formal efforts to negotiate revisions to the existing commercial treaties for the remainder of its travels, but it clearly grasped that the freedom of belief would be a necessary, if insufficient, requirement for success in the future.

Perhaps reflecting this lesson, Iwakura's response to subsequent queries about the treatment of Christianity grew more flexible. In his first meeting with Lord Granville (1815–1891), the British foreign secretary, Iwakura declined to discuss the topic of Christianity in Japan but suggested that it be discussed at a later date. Granville broached the subject again five days later, observing that the greatest single difference between the political structures of Britain and Japan was the prohibition of religion. He explained to Iwakura that he had received many letters requesting that he discuss the matter with the Japanese ambassador. Even though Iwakura repeated his earlier explanation that an abrupt legalization of Christianity might provoke the populace, he also assured Granville that toleration would eventually be granted, and that until then, adherents of the faith would be treated leniently, assuming that they did not hinder political stability.[98] So long as they could be given in informal settings, Iwakura appears to have been willing to provide assurances, though he did believe in them himself. When representatives of the Council of the Evangelical Alliance visited the embassy to request the lifting of the prohibition against Christianity, Iwakura delivered a note assuring the council members that the prohibition against Christianity had not been reissued.[99]

Even as the Iwakura Embassy promised the eventual adoption of religious freedom in Japan, members continued to debate the political and social function of religion in the West. During his stay in London, Kido

Takayoshi arranged to meet students from Chōshū who were studying in Europe, most notably Aoki Shūzō (1844–1914), who was studying in Berlin. Shimaji Mokurai, the Shin sect cleric who had lobbied for the creation of the Ministry of Doctrine, also visited Kido numerous times to discuss the government's policies toward Buddhism. These conversations proved influential in shaping Kido's attitude about religion, and, as John Breen points out, this attitude did not include a softening approach to Christianity.[100]

In his meeting with Aoki, Kido asked why "Westerners" were so fervent in their religion. Aoki responded by drawing a direct relationship between Christianity and the achievements of the nineteenth-century West. He said Christianity provided the morality (*dōtokushugi*) that the Roman Empire lacked when it collapsed, and thus furnished the basis for civilization and enlightenment (*bunmei kaika*). Aoki then presented Kido with a Hegelian comparison between Christianity and Buddhism. Buddhism, he argued, began as a profound philosophical system but was corrupted by the Brahmanic doctrine of reincarnation. Compared with Christianity, this corrupted form of Buddhism encourages passivity instead of activity. If this is the case, Kido wondered, should the Japanese also believe in Christianity? Aoki responded by explaining religion as the "Way" (*michi*): "How can one discipline oneself, order a household [*ie*], and rule a country without relying on this Way? If we desire to correct hearts and discipline bodies, we cannot do so without relying on the power of sacred teachings [*shinsei naru kyōshi*]. This is why I believe religion is necessary."[101] Kido pressed the point, referring to the negotiations undertaken in the United States and the recommendation that Japan adopt Christianity as its principal religion. Aoki pointed to the history of political strife that engulfed England following Henry VIII's rejection of the Roman Catholic Church; any attempt to convert the nation out of political expedience would likely result in significant turmoil and violence. On hearing this, Kido reportedly turned to Itō Hirobumi and rebuked him for shortsightedly advocating that the entire government convert to Christianity.[102] Kido could accept the need for religion to provide the basic disciplinary force behind civilization and enlightenment, yet the wholesale adoption of Christianity appeared neither viable nor desirable. On his return to Japan, Kido emerged within the government as an advocate for rehabilitating Buddhism in order to discipline and mobilize the populace in a manner similar to the way Christianity functioned in the West. In his view, the lessons of religion in the West were more applicable to the Meiji government's treatment of Shinto and Buddhism than to the treatment of Christianity within Japan.

The Iwakura Embassy encountered sporadic protests organized by the Catholic Church and Protestant mission societies as it traveled through Europe in the spring of 1873. Iwakura repeated his promise of an eventual end to the prohibition against Christianity, and members of the embassy grew accustomed to distinguishing between the Christian and political leadership of the countries they visited.[103] Itō, for example, wrote to Inoue Kaoru explaining that foreign governments were forced to raise the matter of religious liberty because of the pressure applied by clergy and believers.[104] Whatever additional pressure the Catholic Church and others planned to apply to the Iwakura Embassy in the spring of 1873 was suddenly undercut, however, by reports from Japan that the exiled Christians were to be released and the prohibition would be lifted. The protests and pressure appeared to have borne fruit.

Given that the embassy had already decided to postpone attempts to revise the unequal treaties, and that diplomatic protests in Europe were relatively weak, it is doubtful that the embassy directly influenced the release of the exiled Urakami Christians.[105] The government had been debating since at least late 1870 whether exiled Christians who had recanted or converted should be allowed to return to Urakami.[106] The actual order from Tokyo to release villagers who had disavowed their Christian faith was not issued until March 15, 1872, and the remaining unconverted Christians were not released until a year later.[107] Informing those decisions were the collapse of the Missionary Office discussed in Chapter 1, the related failure to convert a significant number of the exiled Christians, the severe fiscal constraints of the state's budget, and diplomatic pressure. There were abundant reasons independent of the embassy's experience abroad to convince the government in Tokyo to abandon its policy of converting the Christians in exile. The Ministry of Doctrine had been established in 1872 without fully consulting the members of the Iwakura Embassy, suggesting the caretaker government was willing to act independently on matters related to ritual, doctrine, and Christianity.[108]

News of the Urakami Christians' release from exile was quickly followed by the removal of the notice boards proclaiming the continued prohibition of Christianity. The order for their removal was issued on March 22 on the grounds that "all know their contents well." Combined with the release of the exiled villagers, the representatives of the treaty powers and especially the missionary community in Japan interpreted the order as signaling the de facto end of the prohibition. Guido Verbeck, in a letter to a supporter, claimed these developments were clearly connected to the embassy's experience of Christian civilization: "One of the first results of the embassy was the opening of the eyes of these men . . .

to the fact that Christianity was the force of forces in true civilizations. With reflection came action. To make a long story short, the imperial ministers abroad telegraphed back to the government of Japan their impressions. The result was that the anti-Christian edicts hung up on the notice boards disappeared like magic."[109] This sanguine interpretation of affairs was quickly contradicted, however, as the government insisted that the prohibition had never been officially rescinded.[110] In June, the *New York Times* relayed Charles De Long's communication to the State Department indicating religious toleration had not in fact been granted in Japan.[111] There is some suggestion that the government merely removed the notice boards because of the cost associated with their upkeep and the spread of print-based methods of communicating laws and ordinances.[112] Whatever the motivation, the release of the exiled villagers and the removal of the notice boards produced a "silent toleration" (*mokkyo*), wherein the government could maintain the formality of the prohibition while it abandoned most direct efforts to enforce it. As a result, Christianity was placed in a legal and administrative limbo reflected in numerous "prohibited faith incidents" (*kinkyō jiken*) throughout the 1870s. As open conversions to Christianity occurred with greater frequency, panicked local officials sought guidance from the central government, often receiving little encouragement to enforce the prohibition.[113] In effect, the silent toleration of Christianity did not come to an end until private funerals (i.e., those not conducted by Buddhist or Shinto clerics) were legalized in 1884.

Whatever influence the Iwakura Embassy had over the developments in Japan in the spring of 1873, it certainly did not take the form of an unambiguous endorsement of religious freedom or Christianity. Embassy members, especially Itō, understood that achieving parity with the treaty powers would require accommodating the premise of Christian civilization in some manner, at least in the form of religious liberty. More significantly, the embassy had observed in the Christian West the complex and often tense interaction of religion and political authority, an interaction that confirmed their desire to place the state above and beyond the realm of religion.

Historicizing Christianity, Religion, and Civilization

The Iwakura Embassy is best known for the firsthand information about the United States and Europe that it brought back to Japan. With the effort to negotiate a treaty revision abandoned in the United States, the energies of the embassy were subsequently directed entirely toward acquiring as much understanding as possible of the institutions and ideas that animated the West. Kume Kunitake's official chronicle of the embassy's travels, *Beiō kairan jikki*, contains numerous accounts of visits to factories, government offices, schools, and churches. Members of the embassy marveled at the scale of industrial production and the wealth mobilized by capitalist societies. They took note of the recent character of many developments, both technological and political, and returned to Japan with an urgent sense of the need for and, more important, the possibility of emulating the advances of the West.[114]

The embassy also returned to Japan with lessons concerning the place of Christianity and religion within modern civilization. Key to those lessons were an increasingly nuanced understanding of Christianity as a marker of difference within the West and a functional conception of religion within modern civilization. In particular, Mori Arinori, Tanaka Fujimaro, and Kume Kunitake perceived the importance of the state's role in separating public education from religion, especially the clergy. These men shifted the focus from a concern with the compatibility of Christianity with the imperial state to a concern with the proper configuration of state, education, and religion to ensure a successful process of modernization.

Prior to the Iwakura Embassy's arrival in Washington, Mori Arinori had already begun to digest the contemporary understanding of religion in the United States and attempt to apply it to Japan. He submitted a memorial to the government in Tokyo in the summer of 1871, just after the exile of the Urakami villagers caused an outcry in the United States. In it he criticized the government for adopting inconsistent policies, namely exiling the Christian villagers while hiring Christian missionaries as consultants. As a result, he complained, it was difficult to direct Japanese students in the United States when they expressed an interest in Christianity. Because religious sects would invariably compete with one another, the government, Mori argued, had little to gain and much to lose from competing directly with religion (*shūmon*). The Japanese government should adopt a policy of complete religious neutrality, he proposed, providing no recognition or financial support to any religion. As a corollary, Mori suggested officials serving in the government should renounce any affiliation with a religious sect. Above all, increasing knowledge through general education was the best way to counter the ignorance that religion could foster. The greatest priority for the Meiji government, Mori concluded, was to establish schools.[115] To the extent that the Meiji leadership had any reason to fear the content of religious belief, education promised the most efficient means to address it.

Mori repeated this call for a decisive solution to the problem posed by the Christian prohibition in a subsequent memorial published in November 1872, after the embassy had passed through Washington, D.C. Entitled "Religious Freedom in Japan: A Memorial and Draft Charter," it was addressed to Sanjō Sanetomi, prime minister of the caretaker government in Tokyo, but written entirely in English.[116] Mori distributed this memorial to friends in Japan but did not intend it to be read widely, fearing possible reprisals from anti-Christian elements. The primary function of the text was to demonstrate to an American audience Japan's ability to digest and adopt enlightened and progressive thought.[117] This memorial has been called an exemplar of liberal thought in early-Meiji intellectual history, and the text does employ the primary elements of modern religious discourse: the inviolability of individual conscience or belief, the distinction between mere superstition and religion, and the view of Christianity as the vehicle of progress.[118]

Mori developed his argument in three stages; first, he appealed to the liberty of conscience to criticize the Meiji government's attempt to "impose upon our people a religion of its creation"; second, he refuted arguments against the introduction of Christianity into Japan; finally, Mori emphasized the need for a modern, national education system to cultivate individuals capable of exercising their freedom of conscience in a productive manner. Although Mori was later criticized in Japan for being pro-Western and pro-Christian, his take on Christianity and its place in Japan stopped well short of the radical endorsement provided by Nakamura Keiu (1832–1901), a contemporary known for his translation of Samuel Smiles and who called on the emperor to lead the nation in converting to Christianity.[119] Nonetheless, Mori did identify Christianity with progress: "It is fact, demonstrated by the history of the nations of the earth, among which none have so grandly advanced to the head of civilization as those whose religion has been Christianity."[120] While Mori conceded that the introduction of Christianity might well result in "revolution" and "discord," he claimed that no progress could occur without some degree of instability.

While Mori's memorial clearly privileged Christianity, one can also find in it subtle subversions of the discourse of religious freedom that undercut the identification of Christianity with civilization and progress. While he affirmed the primacy of the individual's freedom of conscience, Mori was also quick to affirm the plurality of religious faiths: "The array of religious faiths is one of the most interesting and edifying spectacles that can be presented to the mind of man."[121] Not only were religions varied, they were themselves variable. Christianity, as a religion proper, was in effect placed within a series of other religions and invested with historical variability. Perhaps more significantly, Christianity was relegated to the realm of private belief, a realm subject to the higher claims of education.

Education, specifically "popular education," Mori emphasized, provided the best means to secure the freedom of conscience: "While the laws are the best protection for our liberty, its greatest security depends wholly upon the character and potency of our popular education." The "entire absence of any particular religious influence" marked the "principle characteristic" of this education. Education led by the state, therefore, provided the basis for peace and stability: "It [the State] can best discharge its obligations by assisting in the diffusion of a knowledge of facts in science and art, thus it shall establish peace upon a solid foundation of enlightenment, and let the base influences of ignorance . . . perish through its own weakness as speedily as possible."[122] The rhetoric of enlightenment's power to purge benighted ignorance from the populace operated in conjunction with the concept of religion as private belief to promote the stability and progress that the Meiji government desired. Mori grasped the promise of rational education as a means to expel sectarian concerns from the public realm and place the state in control. He would not be alone within the government in advocating state control over education as a means to contain the destabilizing potential of religion.

The primary task of Tanaka Fujimaro, one of the two embassy members appointed to talk with Jonathan Goble on the voyage to the United States, was to observe educational systems in the West, and he played a central role in drafting the 1879 Education Ordinance (Kyōikurei) on his return to Japan. The official report on his study of educational systems in the United States and Europe was published in 1874, and it included observations concerning the relation of religion to education. For example, Tanaka declared at the outset his general conclusion regarding the role of religion in education: "Countries that leave the method of education in the hands of commoners and priests [*heimin sōryo*], leaving the government outside of it, have lost the primary path to developing human knowledge, speeding the progress of civilization, and placing their country ahead of others."[123] Tanaka underscored the lesson that clergy impeded the proper purpose of education—advancing knowledge in the service of progress—by citing specific examples he observed in the United States and Europe. In the New England states, for example, the administration of schools was placed in the hands of the government, as a result of which the schools helped the region, in Tanaka's words, progress beyond the "shame of slavery." British education, in contrast, had been held back by the dominance of the clergy and divisions based on sectarian affiliation. Hence, the 1870 Elementary Education Act introduced fundamental changes intended to strengthen nonclerical control over education. Tanaka noted that while Christian instruction remained in British primary schools, it was kept separate from the elementary curriculum itself. Religious instruction occurred only before or after curricular instruction, and a desire to avoid religious instruction had no bearing on a student's access to education.[124] These observations not only echoed Mori's emphasis on a secularized education but also emphasized the fact that the project of increasing state control over education and removing religious influence was a contemporary one in the West.[125]

The connection between public education, anticlericalism, and the containment of religion surfaced repeatedly in the Iwakura Embassy's observations. Bismarck's Kulturkampf, in particular, made a powerful impression on all members of the embassy, precisely because it pitted the Catholic Church against the German state. Helmut Smith characterizes the Kulturkampf as "a strategy of nation-building, supported by the state and centered on an attempt to create a common high culture in which national values, largely synonymous with those of enlightened Protestantism, would be shared."[126] Bismarck's primary concern was to secure the loyalty of Roman Catholics to the newly created German empire (centered as it was on Protestant Prussia), and consolidating state authority over matters of education constituted both the means and the end of restricting the influence of the Catholic Church. The Jesuit order, the most heavily involved in education, was expelled from Germany in 1872, just prior to the Iwakura Embassy's visit. To be clear, Bismarck sought not a radical separation of church and state with these measures but, rather, "a new, heightened state authority over the churches and a more carefully regulated relationship between government and religion."[127] It was in this Germany that Aoki Shūzō did his studies, and where he formed his attitude toward religion. When the embassy reached Germany in 1873, members were quick to note the similarities between Bismarck's concerns and their own. Iwakura wrote to Sanjō explaining the significance of the Kulturkampf:

> Within the empire [Germany], the Jesuits among the Catholic faith have been abolished and the priests have been sent beyond the national borders because they are a great harm to the government (this sect [*shūshi*] is the same as that which came to Nagasaki). Although the national custom has been that these priests are necessarily involved in

> the schools, this has now been quickly abolished. Many are praising Bismarck for pursuing this policy, saying he has accomplished more with this than in defeating France.[128]

Iwakura drew a clear parallel between his own government's efforts to contain the activities of Catholic missionaries and Bismarck's efforts to secure state control over education. Kume Kunitake echoed the lesson in his chronicle of the visit to Germany, noting that the "Church's involvement in school affairs is viewed as exerting a most negative influence through the harmful effect it has on the hearts and minds of the people." Breaking the hold of the Catholic Church over German society did not stop with education; Kume also credited Bismarck with instituting civil marriage. In his official chronicle, Kume suggestively followed his brief survey of the contemporary struggle between the German state and the Catholic Church with an account of Germany's recent ascent as a power within Europe, emphasizing to his Japanese audience that the importance of Germany would only increase in the future. The embassy received Bismarck's advice on the world of realpolitik as "significant words indeed, and we relished our chance to learn from the prince's eloquent words, knowing full well what a master tactician he is in the world of politics."[129] Those masterful tactics extended to the treatment of religion.

It was their consistently functional analysis of religion's place in the United States and Europe that allowed members of the Iwakura Embassy to discover significant convergence between their concerns and the political developments they observed in the West. This analysis paid scant attention to the doctrinal details of the various Christian sects found in Europe and focused on the apparent importance of religion as a disciplinary force in society, the relationship of religious identity to communal cohesion, and the role of the clergy and ecclesial institutions in impeding progress. Kume's chronicle of the embassy's progress through the United States and Europe, when it took note of religion, consistently maintained this functional approach. "In the West," he observed, "religion underpins culture and is of vital importance in encouraging industriousness. Whether a people have religious faith or not bears no small influence on their manners and morals." Religion also accounted for communal cohesion and explained the source and ferocity of conflict in Europe. This ability to foster cohesion explained the political utility of religion in Kume's eyes: "The upper classes of European society appear outwardly to treat the Church with the greatest devotion, but when one looks into their real feelings, it seems rather as if they are treating it as a tool to make the people follow them and their laws and thus are using it for their own ends."[130]

Yet the utility of religion appeared contingent on limiting the authority of the established churches, especially the Roman Catholic Church. Kume repeatedly condemned the clergy for exploiting the ignorant masses, extracting wealth to construct ornate churches, and resisting progressive education.[131] The regressive character of the clergy was confirmed by the correspondence between the less developed regions of Europe and spheres of Catholic and Orthodox Christian dominance. Not only did those churches hinder popular enlightenment, they also competed with political authority. It was in this vein that Kume highlighted the significance of Bismarck's reforms in Germany and Garibaldi's triumph in Italy. The unification of Italy had required defeating the Catholic Church's claims to temporal authority and staking a higher political claim over the land and populace of Italy. Even constitutionalism, Kume explained, which spread through Europe as a means to secure monarchies against the tide of revolution unleashed in France, also worked to fundamentally weaken the political strength of the Catholic Church and laid the foundation for contemporary progress.[132]

Underlying this functional approach was a keen awareness of the variety of religious configurations in the West. Kume noted a distinct decrease in religious fervor as the embassy traveled from the United States to Britain, and again from Britain to continental Europe. He also catalogued the existence of established state churches in Europe and the distinction between religious freedom and toleration. The United States had adopted the principle of religious freedom, disavowing any formal relationship between the state and a religion. Most other states possessed a formal state church and tolerated other religions; formal religious neutrality on the part of the state was not a common feature in Europe. The possibility of adopting a state religion while granting religious toleration provided a possible template for the Meiji government.[133] As a matter of fact, Kido, who had focused his attention on studying constitutional government, ordered Aoki Shūzō to draft a constitution for Japan in 1872 while the embassy was still in Europe. This document, the *Dai nihon seiki*, declared Buddhism to be the national religion of Japan; it also prohibited Christianity.[134] Whether the Meiji state would adopt freedom or toleration (premised on a formally adopted state religion) would remain an open question until the promulgation of the Meiji Constitution in 1889.

Kume interpreted the religious variety he catalogued to be a function of historical progress. Protestant regions were more advanced in their political and material civilization than Catholic regions, and Orthodox regions were particularly backward. Apparently referring to the Urakami affair and the activities of Russian Orthodox missionaries in Hakodate, Kume expressed concern that only Roman Catholicism and Eastern

Orthodoxy, religions "rejected by the advanced countries," appeared to be spreading eastward. Moreover, the yardstick of progress provided by religious difference could be applied within Japan as well. In Japan, for example, Buddhism resembled Eastern Orthodoxy and was a "feeble and idle religion." In Kume's view, in Japan the closest in function to Protestantism was Confucianism. The most advanced form of Protestantism advocated by contemporary scholars in Europe was "moral philosophy," and Confucianism was also a form a moral philosophy. Western intellectuals had begun to translate and study the Confucian classics, he noted, and they "think that in clarity and goodness the two teachings [Christianity and Confucianism] have much in common and that other teachings cannot rival them."[135] Confucianism, in Kume's eyes, had the potential to serve as a functional equivalent of the most evolved form of Protestantism, possibly placing Japan at the leading edge of civilization and progress.

The key, to Mori, Tanaka, and Kume, in identifying the proper configuration of state authority and religion was a generic and functional conception of religion. As Kume observed: "There are a great many religions in the world. Some are beautiful, some ugly, but in all it is essential to revere some divinity and defend oneself against greed and lust. That is to say, people worthy of respect are those who actually behave morally and are faithful and sincere, not those who proclaim high-flown theories about religion and morality."[136] While the diplomatic negotiations concerning Christianity and the freedom of religion in Japan had unavoidably revolved around the particular compatibility of Christianity with the imperial institution, the abstracted discourse of "religion" facilitated claims of essential commonality and commensurability. At the same time, if a functional and generic understanding of religion facilitated the articulation of convergence between Japanese and Western interests, the persistent rhetoric of "Christian civilization" marked the limit of that convergence. When Kume looked beyond a general discussion of religion to the particulars of Christian theology, he explained it in relationship to racial theory. Theological differences between the Christian West and the East, according to him, arose from racial differences. The "white race" was prone to violent passions that were difficult to control, hence a theology that stressed original sin and the fallibility of humanity arose to account for the struggle for self-control. The "yellow race," in contrast, was passive and could control its passions with relative ease. Moral teachings that emphasize the essentially good nature of humanity and perfectibility, such as Confucianism, arose in accordance with those racial characteristics.

Members of the Iwakura Embassy were not alone in identifying a fundamental convergence between the interests of the Meiji government and contemporary European governments in their approach to religion. A series of letters submitted to the *Times* of London in early 1873, for example, placed the debate concerning the status of Christianity in Japan squarely within contemporary European concerns regarding national sovereignty, religious identification, and education. The debate began with a January 15 letter signed by "A Japanese Student." In it, the anonymous writer criticized attempts to convert the Japanese to Christianity on the familiar grounds that the national religion provided the basis for political loyalty: "The national religion of Japan differs from every form of Christianity in this essential particular—that its tenets form the basis of allegiance due from the subject to the Sovereign." Leaving the specifics of the "native religion" unaddressed, the student drove home the fundamental claim that in Japan civil and religious authority remain one and the same: "With you 'Church and State' is a phrase; with us it is a living reality."[137] The following issue of the *Times* carried a response, signed by "A Resident in Japan," that questioned the identity of the purportedly uniform and unanimous native religion: "But when 'A Japanese Student' says that the native religion is one to which the Japanese people are profoundly attached, I would ask, what is the native religion?" Buddhism possessed a better historical claim to be "the religion of people" and had been tolerated "on the implied condition that its members should obey the law and should refrain from insulting the religion of the State," even though it did not give allegiance to the emperor. Why, then, could not Christianity be introduced on the same grounds?[138]

Rutherford Alcock, Harry Parkes's predecessor as British minister plenipotentiary to Japan, joined this editorial discussion on January 29 and placed the question of the Japanese government's treatment of Christianity in direct relation to contemporary European concerns. Specifically, Alcock argued that the highly contentious debate concerning Catholicism's place within the nation-states of Europe was analogous to the Japanese government's hesitance to legalize Christianity. The question of "the relation of the Roman Church and Catholic subjects towards the State has a direct and important bearing on Christian missions in the East." Regarding the difficulties Christian missions face in China and Japan, Alcock declared he was

> convinced that religion has very little or nothing to do with it. It springs exclusively from other sources, and those of an Ultramontane character, and taking their rise from very similar feelings and motives

> as the opposition manifested in so many countries, Roman Catholic and Protestant alike, at the present moment. Its real cause is jealousy of a foreign rival to the allegiance of the people, and a power which claims authority higher than any Sovereign's, and inimical to the free exercise of any power independent of the asserted spiritual dominion of a Church.[139]

The Iwakura Embassy could have found no more eloquent defense of its government's response to the Urakami Incident and attitude toward Christianity. Alcock went on to connect tolerance and education within the contentious discussion of state sovereignty and religious authority. "The question of education—a subject of equal agitation here—in France and Germany at the present moment, and the toleration of diverse creeds and forms of doctrine are both matters of such essential importance," he wrote, that too much compromise in favor of Rome might result in rebellion and civil war. The political leadership of Japan was not alone in facing the challenge of rendering a political order immune to a "religious" challenge to its authority: "It is the independence of this power within a State, this *Imperium in Imperio*, which the rulers of China and Japan alike object to, as fatal to their own authority and supremacy; and they resist its encroachment within their territories as the Emperor of Germany and the Queen of England resist similar pretensions to the assertion of a power above the law."[140] As the example of India instructs, Alcock concluded, the treaty powers would do well to disassociate themselves from any explicit missionary activity that disturbed political rule, as the French had mistakenly done by advocating on behalf of Catholic missionaries in Japan.

Conclusion

The diplomatic climate of the mid-nineteenth century played a crucial role in shaping the political conversation concerning religion in Japan. The character of that diplomacy, however, was more complex than a simple model of translation or imposition can capture. The accumulated lessons gleaned from negotiating the disposition of Christianity in late-Tokugawa and early-Meiji Japan taught the Japanese leadership the utility of employing religion as a generic term of commensurability and comparison. At the same time, the language of "Christian civilization" reflected the abiding asymmetry of power between Japan and the treaty powers. Revising the unequal treaties, a project that guided and justified a broad range of state-directed initiatives through the mid-1890s, continued to drive the Meiji government's attempt to settle its relationship with religion. Hence, the diplomatic negotiation of belief and the political utilization of the imperial institution formed the two fundamental parameters that dominated policy debates concerning the relationship of state and religion through the 1880s and into the 1890s.

The direct effects that the Iwakura Embassy's observations had on religious discourse and policy in Japan will be taken up in the following chapter. In general terms, the Meiji leaders' struggle to come to terms with the definition and place of "religion" within the nation-state they were striving to create was informed by similar shifts in Europe and the United States. Christianity remained a crucial component of the self-image of the treaty powers, yet its public role, as represented by increasingly private mission organizations and centralizing national governments, remained in significant flux. Bismarck's Kulturkampf marks a clear example of this flux. In Germany, the apparent rejection of Catholicism as antinational had the effect of mobilizing Catholics into organizations that sought to demonstrate their "German-ness." The same process can be discerned among Christians, both Protestant and Catholic, in Japan through the Meiji period. Japan and the treaty powers came to share the same key principles concerning religious freedom and toleration. Religious liberty could be bestowed only in proportion to the establishment of state authority above faith and ecclesial power. The private faith brought under that authority of the state, moreover, had to be articulated in service of the national good.

As the Meiji government's response to the Urakami Christians indicates, its concerns were initially directed toward Christianity specifically. In summary, the diplomatic negotiation of belief arising from the Urakami Incident and the Iwakura Embassy provided the Meiji leadership with an opportunity to transpose its concern from Christianity, specifically, to "religion" as it was more generally understood. That change brought into focus the shifting status of religion within Europe and America, exposing the contemporaneous nature of the question—how does "religion" figure into centralizing nation-states? In short, contemporary political concerns in Europe directed toward Catholicism, education, and consolidating national governments provided the Iwakura Embassy with a problematic Japan held in common with the West: how does a nation-state secure uncontested loyalty when a "national" population can be so easily fragmented by religion?

How that question would be addressed and resolved in early Meiji Japan remained far from clear when the Iwakura Embassy returned to Japan in 1873. The silent toleration of Christianity was by then offset by the Ministry of Doctrine, created during the embassy's absence. The following chapter examines the result of transposing the problem of Christianity into a problem of religion in general. As the Meiroku Society produced a public discourse focused on religion in general, for example, the question of how a discrete but generic religion would contribute to the nation-state came into sharper focus, and along with it the problematic nature of a "theocratic" imperial institution.

CHAPTER 3

Civilizing Faith and Subjectified Religion, 1872–1877

> Faith [*shin*] . . . is the source for all virtue and the origin of all conduct. It is the foundation for managing oneself and ruling others. The safety and health of our bodies, as well as the peace and prosperity of our country, begin by establishing great faith [*daishin*].
>
> —Nishi Amane, 1874

> If we allow the ritual veneration of the emperor's ancestors to be a religion, we would render the sacred spirits of all our emperors the same as the hidden and indeterminate gods of the various religions, gods who are believed by those who believe and are mocked by those who do not believe.
>
> —*Kyōgi shinbun*, 1874

Kume Kunitake, recalling the gulf separating the first half of his life from the second, observed that the Meiji period began with the need to distinguish between superstition (*meishin*) and religion (*shūkyō*), a need driven by the belief that while religion was necessary for civilization and progress, superstition was an impediment: "Still, the boundary [separating the two] was unclear. Pushed to its limit, to believe in things that are not scientifically or philosophically grounded would be superstitious; yet, religion could be considered superstitious as well."[1] Kume's recollection indicates how applying the category of religion to Meiji Japan was a taxonomical exercise that generated its own measure of anxiety. Not only had the Iwakura Embassy discovered the diplomatic expedience of discussing religion in the abstract, but applying the taxonomy of religion at home allowed officials and intellectuals committed to the enlightening and civilizing project of *bunmei kaika* to attack popular customs and beliefs as superstition and ignorance. At the same time, attacking superstition in the name of rationality and progress carried with it the potential of rendering religion vulnerable to the tides of enlightened progress.

The taxonomical project that accompanied the introduction of religion as an organizing category forced state officials, public intellectuals, and those directly engaged in the contested domains of religion and superstition into negotiations that sustained the concern to distinguish the imperial institution from the realm of contestable belief. These negotiations in the early 1870s were facilitated, in part, by a factional shift within the government. Disagreement over diplomatic relations with Korea split the government after the Iwakura Embassy's return and left Kido Takayoshi, Ōkubo Toshimichi, and others from the embassy in positions of significant influence.[2] Saigō Takamori (1827–1877), Etō Shinpei, and Gotō Shōjirō, who had remained in the caretaker government and retained a strong aversion to Christianity, resigned, removing powerful backing for the Kokugaku ideologues and Shinto priests within the Ministry of Doctrine.[3] This factional shift within the government, culminating in the 1877 Satsuma Rebellion, accelerated the retreat from a narrow pursuit of *saisei itchi* as the ideological cornerstone of the state and encouraged discussions of how the state should best relate to religion more generally.

The Meiroku Society (Meirokusha) and its journal, founded to promote enlightened debate at the invitation of Mori Arinori, provided the first extensive and public venue for this discussion. The society, though hardly a single voice, associated *shūkyō*—via Protestantism—with private, individual belief and contrasted it with what the members of the society deemed ignorant superstition. This shift to a broader question of the functional utility of religion, as opposed to how best to counter Christianity, unavoidably returned to the concern that the foundation of state authority—the imperial institution—should not be rendered an object of private, and thus contestable, belief. Hence, as the Meiroku Society framed its discussion of religion in relation to conversations regarding theocracy, international law, and morality, a basic dilemma emerged: the state had to disassociate itself from the unstable realm of private belief (religion) in the interest of effective governance, but it also had to retain some sort of claim over inner beliefs if the "unenlightened" majority was to be effectively molded into a body of civilized, national subjects.

The practical implications of this dilemma, rendered conceptually clear by the Meiroku Society's debates, played out in the operation of the Ministry of Doctrine. A legacy of the first attempt to separate imperial rituals from the precarious project of indoctrination in early 1872, the ministry attempted to mediate the relationship between the state and the doctrinal project by enlisting Buddhist clerics along with shrine priests, Confucian scholars, and even performing artists, such as Rakugo raconteurs and Kabuki actors, to disseminate a broadly formulated doctrine. In practice, however, Shinto partisans dominated the ministry and continued to marginalize Buddhist sects and their clerics.[4] Shimaji Mokurai, a Shin sect Buddhist cleric, embraced the category of religion in order to criticize this state of affairs and break free from the strictures of the ministry. In the process, he articulated a "subjectified" posture for religion—autonomous religious belief articulated in response to the demands of state power—that conformed to the interests of the Meiji government.[5] The Shin Buddhist criticisms of the Ministry of Doctrine and assertion of its autonomy as a religion in effect embraced the identification of Buddhism with the category of religion. The subsequent demise of the Ministry of Doctrine in 1877, then, left in its wake the first general outline of terms on which the avowedly religious might relate to the state.

Unsettling Enlightenment: The *Meiroku Journal* Debates Religion

The *Meiroku zasshi* (*Meiroku Journal*), published by the Meiroku Society between March 1874 and November 1875, set the intellectual agenda of the mid-1870s.[6] Of the ten founding members of the debate society, only two, Fukuzawa Yukichi (1835–1901) and Mitsukuri Shūhei (1826–1886) did not occupy positions within the Meiji government.[7] Subscribing members included Kamei Koremi, Tanaka Fujimaro, Maejima Hisoka (1835–1919), and Shimaji Mokurai, all of whom had close ties to the state and were intent on shaping its policies.[8] Among its better-known discussions of language reform, economics, and the role of intellectuals—all concerned with the advancement of civilization and enlightenment (*bunmei kaika*)—the journal also printed a number of essays on the subject of religion and how it should relate to state authority, individual liberty, and progress. A close reading of those essays reveals the chief discursive pressures bearing on the discussion of religion in early-Meiji Japan. The pressure to adapt and respond to the interwoven discourses of Christian civilization and international law, along with the pressure to shield the state (and the imperial institution) from competition, can be discerned in the nebulous intersection of belief, ritual, morality, and governance within these essays. By no means a unified voice, the fissures and tensions present in the Meiroku Society's debates bring to light the conceptual difficulties that accompanied efforts to define and settle the boundary of religion in the early 1870s. The discussions shared the proposition that such a category needed to be defined and settled as part of the effort to introduce enlightenment and progress to Japan.

With Mori Arinori as its likely conduit, the Meiroku Society adopted the functional approach of the Iwakura Embassy and discussed religion in the abstract, avoiding any overt sectarian affiliation of the sort that characterized the Kokugaku-inspired polemics of the Department of Divinities. The society promoted the premise that universal civilization and progress resulted from rational enlightenment, and rejected the idea that a specific form of ritual practice or doctrinal belief was essential to the unity of the Japanese nation. Treating religion instead as a distinct but general category of human life, isolable from other social and political spheres, these advocates of rational enlightenment weighed the relative utility of religion in securing the progress and improvement of the nation. Religion in effect came to be treated as a potentially neutral category in relation to the state, so long as it was confined to the realm of private, individual belief. Nonetheless, the normative image of Protestant Christianity lurked behind the supposedly neutral and unspecific category of religion and its universal applicability to progress.

One conspicuous symptom of this normative discourse on religion was the increasing marginalization of any public practice—prayer healing, divination, and ascetic wandering, for example—that did not mirror the image of Protestant faith. Popular spiritual practices and cosmologies, diffuse and often lacking clear ecclesial and doctrinal organization, were largely excluded from this emerging grammar of religion.[9] To be sure, there was nothing new, as Aizawa's 1825 thesis demonstrates, about elites belittling the putatively misguided beliefs and practices of the common masses and distrusting practitioners who catered to those masses. The phrases *inshi jakyō* (heretical worship and evil teachings) and *kōtō mukei* (preposterous matters) were frequently invoked by early-modern rationalists to criticize and reject popular practices and teachings.[10] At the same time, the conceits of civilization and enlightenment, linked as they were to the project of creating a nation, endowed the task of rescuing the masses from their benighted ways with greater urgency. For the early-Meiji philosophes, marginalizing those external practices and superstitious beliefs expressed the basic conviction that the "ignorant" commoners required some form of rational enlightenment, and the pursuit of an enlightened form of religious belief figured prominently in their discourse.

From the outset, therefore, the Meiroku Society's discussions centered on what form of religion would best improve the nation. Moreover, mindful of the government's move to separate doctrine from imperial ritual in 1871, the society also pursued a sharp distinction between religion and government. The ease with which these two concerns intersected—intervening in the interior lives of the populace while separating religion and political authority—explains why the boundary of religion and its place within early-Meiji Japan was difficult to define, even at the conceptual level.

Tsuda Mamichi (1829–1903), a legal scholar who had studied in Europe at the University of Leiden in the early 1860s, first raised the matter of religion (*kyōhō*) in the *Meiroku Journal* in relation to the question of how best to "advance enlightenment." Although he noted signs of increasing enlightenment throughout the country, Tsuda despaired at the thought of how long it would take to fully civilize Japan without selecting some means to actively educate the people: "What will advance the civilization [*kaiku*] of the nation in general [*kokumin ippan*] which has yet to advance? It is religion [*hōkyō*]. The purpose of religion, generally, is to guide the uncivilized to a good path." Not all religions were equally adept in fostering civilization, however, and Tsuda identified Protestantism as the best, especially its "new forms, which are liberal and closest to civilized thinking." As in all other aspects of human life, among religions the superior overcomes the inferior and the new replaces the old; for this reason, according to Tsuda, "considering the current state of things, the Christian invasion of our country is a natural progression that cannot be prevented, like the torrent of a river." For him, religion as a universal human phenomenon provided a temporal hierarchy that assumed a constant competition among creeds, a competition that identified the winner as the most modern and superior form. Inherent competition among religions both produced and reflected the universal progress of civilization.[11] His proposition to "adopt" the "most advanced" form of religion presumed a deciding subject that stood outside of religion and was capable of gauging relative degrees of advancement. Religion was thus made the object of rational, utilitarian selection by intellectuals, who acted on behalf of the nation in the interest of its progress. According to this schema, Protestant Christianity, representing self-reforming religion, stood head and shoulders above both Buddhism and Shinto, which represented the stagnant past that Japan had to leave behind if it was to compete on equal footing with the treaty powers.

Tsuda's essay sketched a rational and utilitarian concern with religion—in particular, its contribution to the civilization and enlightenment of Japan. It also retained the premise that authorities played a direct role in selecting a suitable "religion" for the nation. Nishi Amane (1829–1897), in contrast, introduced a confident distinction between faith (*shin*) and knowledge (*chi*), and the necessary separation of government (*seifu*) from religion (*kyōmon*), in a series of essays entitled "Theses on Religion."[12] Like Tsuda, Nishi had studied at the University of Leiden, and he would play a significant role in translating European philosophy into Japanese; he also later helped formulate state ideology, most famously the 1882 Imperial Rescript for Soldiers (Gunjin chokuyu). In his essays on the topic of religion, Nishi tackled the still-unsettled matter of what liberties would be granted to the practice of religion, and how state authority would police the boundary between free belief and controlled practice. Nishi's approach was built on three basic maxims: faith was universal; faith was based on assumptions of truth that can and do change; and superior and vulgar forms of belief existed. The first two claims resulted in his admonition that "even the brave cannot rob others of their faith with force. The wise cannot force belief upon others with argument." Therefore, because belief cannot be forced or controlled, the state should grant the freedom of belief (*hitobito no shinzuru tokoro ni makasu beshi*). Questioning Tsuda's assertion of rational autonomy, Nishi refused to place intellectuals or political leaders outside the realm of belief: "Being men, even though they are wise and erudite, surpassing the ignorant commoners, they also believe in the unknown." Belief, however eminent and erudite, could not serve as the basis of governance since it was inherently unstable: "When the falseness [of belief] is perceived, faith ceases."[13] In short, although all people possessed belief in the "unknown," because that belief was unstable, liable to change, and impossible to control, the state was best served by avoiding regulating it in any way.

Nishi anticipated possible objections to this bold call for the freedom of belief, especially as it related to the *kokutai*, or the national polity, with the emperor at its head: "If the government abandons the right to judge religion [*kyōmon wo zehi suru ken*] and thus leaves religion to the preference of the people, will it not come to injure the *kokutai*?" Nishi answered with the confident assertion that "the authority of government and the way of religion do not share the same source." Religion concerned matters that were unknown, while the state was interested only in compliance with laws and the preservation of peace. If religion and government thus occupied separate spheres, Nishi asked, how could the two conflict? He could not ignore the state's direct involvement in matters of belief through the Ministry of Doctrine, however, and conceded that the theocratic (*teokurashii*) character of the current government posed considerable risks: "Once the people grasp its [i.e., theocracy's] speciousness, that country will assuredly decline and nothing can change its fate." Only by severing ties between government and religion could injury to the state by "the evil in religion" be prevented.[14]

Nishi's audience, particularly those serving in the government, could not have missed the message of his argument: the state was gambling the very foundation of its authority by closely associating itself with easily contestable matters of belief. When people no longer believed in the imperial myths, what would prevent them from questioning the imperial institution's claim to sovereignty? At the same time, Nishi's attempt to disassociate belief from the *kokutai* by asserting a fundamental distinction between religion and government failed to explain how the ritual and ideological expressions of the "national body," elements crucial to the imperial institution's claim to sovereignty, could be distinguished from "religion."

Privileging *belief* by granting it liberty, Nishi proposed regulating only those outward religious *practices* that might lead to social and political disturbances. "There is no need to question whether people believe in foxes, badgers, Buddhas, or heavenly beings," he declared, since "matters within the heart" cannot be controlled. Instead, the government should "prohibit only outward contradiction of the nation's . . . rule without regard to what the people believe in their hearts."[15] Regulating potentially disturbing practices not only privileged private, individual belief but also betrayed a clear prejudice against the diffuse spiritual practices of the commoners that did not fall under the organizing frameworks of Buddhism, Shinto, or Christianity. As already seen, given Tsuda's argument, Nishi was not alone in belittling the folk beliefs of the "ignorant people," and the *Meiroku Journal* carried multiple essays decrying the irrational superstitions that continued to plague the backward population of Japan.[16] For state bureaucrats, Buddhist and Christian clergy, and an emerging class of medical and scientific experts, superstition became a cudgel to wield against the practices of the majority of the Japanese population, who appeared to cling stubbornly to a past and discredited way of life.[17] Likewise, Nishi affirmed the freedom to worship in the privacy of a home, but insisted that "building even small shrines outside of homes should be forbidden," meetings "of ten or more people in homes or outside officially permitted shrines and temples should be barred," and "assembling believers in mountains, forests, and uninhabited areas should be prohibited."[18] The right to private, individual belief, combined with the prerogative to maintain the peace, in Nishi's view, allowed the state to criminalize any practice that could deceive the gullible and foment public disturbances. In affirming the ongoing proscription of practices such as fortune-telling and faith healing, along with the strict regulation of the *shugendō* mountain ascetics, Nishi's liberal definition of religion explicitly retained the prerogative to brand certain practices superstitious and to intervene accordingly.[19]

Even if the state restricted itself to regulating only outward religious practices, Nishi admitted, it would still have to "clarify the great basis upon which government is established and thus destroy traces of contact" between religion and the state. By fundamentals on which the government stands, Nishi meant the *kokutai*, with its accompanying ritual and mythic articulations of imperial authority. Yet any formulation of imperial authority that appeared to deify the emperor not only would be false but would smack of Chinese precedents. To avoid that inconvenient appearance, Nishi suggested adopting a derivation of imperial sovereignty, such as "by the grace of Heaven" (*tenshoku*), that could apply to monarchs of all nations.[20] By appealing to "Heaven"—ambiguously applicable to both Confucian and Christian formulations of monarchical sovereignty—as the basis for imperial sovereignty, Nishi hoped to replace particular references to imperial myths with the same formulation of divine authority employed by monarchs in the Christian West.

The ease with which the imperial institution and religion could be sharply disassociated was quickly contested, however. Katō Hiroyuki (1836–1916), a strict materialist who would later champion social Darwinism, challenged Nishi's essay, questioning whether Nishi had in fact clarified a nonreligious foundation for state authority. Katō observed, "The phrase by the grace of Heaven [*tenshoku*] uses words from semicivilized China [*shina hankai*], and easily approximates theocracy."[21] This simple but incisive critique exposed the difficulty in rendering any formulation of foundational authority in purely immanent terms. As Jacques Derrida observes, any "purely rational analysis" of authority exposes the following paradox:

> The foundation of law—law of the law, institution of the institution, origin of the constitution—is a "performative" event that cannot belong to the set that it founds, inaugurates or justifies. Such an event is unjustifiable within the logic of what it will have opened. It is the decision of the other in the undecidable. Henceforth reason ought to recognize there what Montaigne and Pascal call an undeniably "mystical foundation of authority."[22]

Nishi's attempt to place the state and the *kokutai* outside belief in the unknown, or "religion," encountered just this unavoidably mystical foundation of authority. Put another way, Nishi could not define state authority in terms that made no claims on belief. His central concern to insulate the foundation of state authority from the inherent instability and competition of belief fell short of the demand to secure that authority in terms that permit no outside to itself. This inherent structure to foundational authority rendered impossible, at the conceptual level, all attempts to securely disassociate religion and the *kokutai*. Nishi never answered directly Katō's critique; rather, he spent the next three installments of his "Theses on Religion" discussing the rational derivation of theism and the metaphysical underpinnings of morality. The future author of the Imperial Rescript for Soldiers could not fully mask the mystical foundation of authority that lay beneath the *kokutai* and the emperor, though he recognized the need to do so.

Katō revisited the issue of "theocracy" in his 1875 *Kokutai shinron* (New Theory of the National Polity), wherein he rejected as theocracy all formulations that connected political authority to "heaven" (*ten*). In his view, only uncivilized (*mikai*) societies and states appealed to the will of heaven, divine edicts, or deities (*tenjin*) as a means to rule ignorant and unenlightened populations. Katō indicted Kokugaku nativists for attempting to do the same in post-Restoration Japan. Like Nishi, Katō anticipated the criticism his discussion was likely to provoke, that he risked undermining the *kokutai* by rejecting the emperor's status as a heavenly descendant and calling into question the sacred imperial texts. He attempted to preempt such critiques by distinguishing between the imperial texts themselves and the interpretations of those texts by Kokugaku scholars such as Motoori Norinaga and Hirata Atsutane. Because the texts describe what stands beyond human knowledge, they could never serve as the basis for government. Government belonged to the "human realm" (*ningenkai*), and thus any discussion of government had nothing to say about the sacred texts.[23] Although Katō faulted Nishi for failing to successfully disassociate the *kokutai* and the emperor from theocratic underpinnings, he shared the underlying anxiety that any distinction would be unstable in the face of an increasingly educated and politically mobilized population. Katō's subsequent "conversion" to social Darwinism and disavowal of the liberal political theories he espoused in the *Kokutai shinron* should be considered in light of this desire to find secure, nontheocratic ground for the *kokutai*. The "scientific" discourse of organic sociopolitical units may have provided Katō with an appealing alternative to ritually and doctrinally mediated constructions of such units.

While both Nishi and Katō inadvertently highlighted the difficulty of disclaiming the "theocratic" nature of the *kokutai* and state authority, they also indicated the extent to which Meiji discussions of religion looked toward contemporary European and American conversations, particularly legal discourse, concerning the regulation of religion and the freedom of belief. Appealing to the experience of the West provided the Meiroku Society, as well as most intellectuals of this period, with a narrative strategy that lent a considerable degree of authority, not to mention utility, to their discussions. Katō began running a translation of Joseph Parrish Thompson's *Kirche und Staat in den Vereignigten Staaten von Amerika* (*Church and State in the United States of America*) in the fifth issue of the *Meiroku Journal*.[24] Thompson, an American Congregational minister, authored the book in 1873 following a visit to Germany, in the hope of introducing an American solution to the Kulturkampf. Katō cited Thompson to explain that "if the enlightenment of human intellect and the stability of one's nation are desired, this [American] system must be adopted."[25] Thompson's text clearly formulated the distinction between tolerance and the freedom of belief, a distinction introduced to the Iwakura Embassy during its travels through the United States and Europe.[26] Tolerance referred to an arrangement in which "a government, which actually stands above the church and holds the power to administer and control the church, abandons part of this power of its own accord." Religious liberty, on the other hand, relied on no prior sanction and did not permit the government to retain the prerogative to establish a national religion. The precedent of toleration under European monarchies later provided Buddhists with an important precedent in calling on the Meiji state to formally adopt an established state religion (*kokkyō*). In the 1870s the competing legal logics of religious toleration and religious freedom provided Japanese intellectuals with divergent ways to imagine the relations among individuals, the state, and religion, mirroring the choice confronting policy makers.

The significance of the choice between a policy of religious tolerance and one of religious freedom has been easy to overlook. In his discussion of how the idea of religious liberty was translated and understood by the Meiroku Society, for example, Douglas Howland does not take into account this distinction between tolerance and freedom. As Howland observes, the Meiroku Society members, Katō included, did in fact render "absolute" the individual's right to private belief and affirmed the state's prerogative to regulate public expressions of belief in the interest of maintaining order.[27] Yet an open question stood behind that apparent consensus: Should a national religion be formally established or should the state pursue religious neutrality? Either choice, expressed in the legal terminology of tolerance or freedom, carried significant implications in early-Meiji Japan. Choosing something other than Christianity as a national creed threatened to undermine attempts to gain parity with the treaty powers, while establishing Christianity as a state creed confronted tremendous internal impracticalities and risks.[28] Yet legally adopting religious freedom, with the accompanying presumption of religious neutrality on the part of the state, would place the imperial institution in potential conflict with that freedom, or at the very least it might allow "religious" identifications to provide a basis for open critique and resistance.

Mori Arinori, the former chargé d'affaires to the United States and organizer of the Meiroku Society, also joined the debate with a translation of a foundational European legal text. Given his previous call for "religious liberty" in Japan, it was little surprise that Mori supported Nishi's call to strictly separate individual belief and government regulation, in contrast to Tsuda's call to officially adopt the religion (*isshū*) most conducive to progress. Mori affirmed the necessity of regulating religious practices that threaten the stability of the state and he appealed to European legal theory to support his position, presenting in his own work translated selections of Emmerich de Vattel's 1758 *Le droit des gens, ou principes de la loi naturelle appliqués á la conduite et aux affaires des nations et des souverains* (*The Law of Nations, or, Principles of the Law of Nature Applied to the Conduct and Affairs of Nations and Sovereigns*).[29] This eighteenth-century articulation of international law, still influential in the nineteenth century, reflected the European Enlightenment's concern to regulate and control religion (understood as Christianity) through appeals to natural law.[30] Private belief, so long as it remained private, did not concern the state, but religion, "once established publically in the open, becomes the administrative concern of the state." Individuals, in other words, did not possess the "the right to conduct themselves as they please and disrupt society." Not only did the public establishment and conduct of religion invite state regulation, it also shifted the believing subject from the level of the individual to the level of the "nation." That is to say, according to Vattel the nation was the subject that chose a religion, and a nation was in turn identified by the religion it chose: "When the majority of a nation adopts a single religion, this can be declared the state religion." This privileged position of the nation served to check the individual's right to religious declaration: "Individuals should not spread new religions. Any person with differing views of religion should always submit to the direction of the national authorities."[31]

Vattel's legal discourse contained not only the nascent national imaginary of eighteenth-century Europe but also the concomitant anti-Catholicism that would color much of the intellectual and political discussion of religion through the nineteenth century. "A country, if it does not possess the authority to control its religious affairs," Vattel warned, "is not independent and free." That fear, of course, was directed toward the imagined influence of Catholic priests over people whose "intelligence is not developed and who are easily manipulated." The fact that the priests were ordained and appointed by the Vatican "violates the inherent rights of the nation and contradicts the basic law of governance."[32] Mori's selection of Vattel's text brought into stark relief how the privileging of individual, private belief (Protestantism) over and against ritual, communal observances (Catholicism) accompanied the consolidation and assertion of political sovereignty over a "nationalized" population in Europe: "Religion, apart from its external manifestations, is never the administrative concern of government. Religion of the heart is the concern of each individual. So long as it does not disrupt society, no one can control or punish individual belief. Nor should individuals be punished for expressing their own thoughts unless these incite others or create parties."[33] Granting liberty to private belief while retaining the state's prerogative to regulate all forms of external practice and expression of belief exposed the bounded logic of liberalism that emerged from the eighteenth-century Enlightenment. Religious belief could not register in the public realm as difference (sectarianism) that would fracture or reach beyond the national imaginary and state authority. The definition of modern state sovereignty went hand in hand with the reduction of religion to individual, private belief. In this way, the articulation of the right to private belief was linked to the emergence of modern forms of sovereignty, a fact also evident in Meiji discussions of religion and its relation to the state, as well as in Mori's decision to translate Vattel.

Although Mori introduced Vattel by rejecting Tsuda's call for the adoption of a state religion most conducive to civilization and progress, Vattel's justification of a national religion undercut that rejection. Implicitly, at least, Mori's silence on the question of a national creed admitted the semicolonial curtailment of Japanese sovereignty. The Japanese intellectual and political elite, many of whom congregated around the Meiroku Society, recognized the need to win the recognition ("sympathy," in their words) of the treaty powers if they were to succeed in revising the unequal treaties and regain full sovereignty. Were the Meiji government to follow Vattel's advice and adopt a "national faith" based on majority identification, Buddhism would have been the most likely candidate.[34] Such an assertion of Japanese sovereignty would have hampered the effort for treaty revision, given the prevailing association of Christianity with Western civilization and progress. At the same time, adopting Christianity as the national creed ran the risk of inciting significant opposition within Japan. This dilemma, while only implicit here, was explicit in the eyes of the government. The Council of State had ordered its translation bureau to compile and translate European and American laws regulating the relationship of church and state, and the unpublished 1874 translation, *Kyōkai ritsuryō*, recommended that the Japanese state adopt the legal policy of the United States—religious freedom rather than toleration—likely in order to avoid the diplomatic liabilities of a non-Christian state religion.[35] The government's dilemma would only grow more pressing and consequential in the early 1880s as it set about drafting a constitution.

Both legal approaches to religion, toleration and the freedom of belief, privileged private belief as the dominant definition of what counts as religious. This did not mean, however, that members of the Meiroku Society understood outward practices, especially state rituals, to be inherently or obviously distinguishable from matters of belief. The preponderance of court rituals devoted to the veneration of imperial ancestors and deities, combined with the nationalization of shrines, most notably the Grand Shrines of Ise, made it difficult to assert the neutrality of the imperial institution and the state.[36] Nishi attempted to circumvent this problem by suggesting that court rituals and ceremonies, including the "veneration of royal ancestors," be designated "the affairs of the royal house" and made "unrelated to government."[37] The imperial rituals would, in effect, be rendered private in relation to the public operation of the state. Strikingly, this is the logic employed by the post-1945 constitution in Japan, allowing for the public maintenance of imperial rituals in accordance with the constitutional separation of state and religion (*seikyō bunri*). Nishi proposed solving the incomplete separation between outward ritual practices and private belief by in effect rendering private the emperor's sacerdotal function. Tsuda, in turn, argued for a strict separation between government and rituals on the grounds that all civilized nations had learned to separate the two: "In countries that have divided government and religion, rites (*saishi*) are no longer state affairs." Modern governments retained oversight of merely the enthronements, marriages, and funerals of monarchs, along with the opening of parliamentary sessions, as "great affairs of the state." Japan, Tsuda had to admit, faced significant difficulties in realizing a similar separation of ritual and government: "The imperial line has, for over 2,500 years, continued unbroken. As a result, many rituals of the state have been inherited unchanged from the divine age. This is what we call the unity of rite and rule and united governance and teaching. Thus none of our national ceremonies are more important than rites."[38] To Tsuda, because the imperial rituals stressed the ancestral veneration of a sun goddess, a normative definition of religion that privileged private individual belief could not secure the state's neutrality vis-à-vis that private domain. However, he could offer no suggestion as to how this state of affairs might be remedied, except for a vague hope for change in the future. The creation of a Bureau of Rites and Ministry of Doctrine in 1872 evidently failed to convince Tsuda that a significant separation had occurred. The boundary between religion and state authority remained both unsettled and unsettling.

Even as they sought to distance the imperial institution from the taint of religion, members of the Meiroku Society unanimously called for improving what they deemed to be "ignorant commoners" by helping them shed customs considered backward and superstitious. Education and morality provided the primary idiom of this discussion, and both terms became focal points for debates concerning what constituted acceptable religious belief and how the state would lay claim to the interior lives of the populace. The demand for education, especially as a vehicle to stamp out superstition, complicated efforts to separate private belief from the purview of public governance. Elites like those in the Meiroku Society took for granted the need for moral education to produce a civilized and disciplined population. What that morality should be grounded in and whether it was to be religious or neutral toward religion, however, was the topic of considerable debate through the early-Meiji period. Efforts by Confucianists such as Motoda Nagazane (1818–1891) to place morality (*dōtoku*) at the center of national education, for example, were accompanied by a strong disavowal of any religious characteristics to Confucianism. Confucian thought, often expressed in the language of "personal cultivation" (*shūshin*), cut across a wide range of groups and scholarly traditions in pre-Meiji Japan, including, for example, Ishida Baigan's *Sekimon shingaku*. The identity and social function of those traditions as either religion or learning, with its ethical emphasis, continued to be debated through the Meiji period.[39] Even as the Meiroku Society called for conforming popular practices and beliefs to the project of constructing a nation-state, the simultaneous disavowal of the contestable—that is, religious—character of state authority illustrated the difficulty of distinguishing between religion and moral learning, and, by extension, between the contestable and the uncontestable.

Tsuda first muddied the waters by placing the founders of Buddhism, Christianity, and Confucianism in the same frame when he credited them with expounding "the great foundation of human morality [*jindō*]" that is "solid and unchanging as heaven and earth."[40] Sakatani Shiroshi (1822–1891), the oldest member of the Meiroku Society and a Confucian scholar of considerable repute, followed with the most developed discussion of morality, religion, and government thus far, in a two-part essay entitled "Questions concerning the Political Indoctrination" ("Seikyō no gi"). Sakatani clearly intended to distinguish the term *seikyō* from *hōkyō*, or religion, yet, he relates both to faith: "Nations are founded upon men, and the only reason that a nation exists is to pursue the good. Moreover, establishing this good relies solely on deep faith. Only political [*seikyō*] and religious [*kyōhō*] teaching will provide immovable and deep faith."[41] Faith, or inner commitment, was required to establish the good, and both forms of teaching (religious and nonreligious) could instill this faith. Sakatani argued that it was a mistake to confuse, as the Europeans and Americans appeared to do, "religion" with the teaching that was required for governance (*seikyō*). They "consider it best to separate governance [*matsurigoto*] from teachings [*oshie*], leaving those who govern unrelated to teachings."[42] Even as they shielded themselves from the potential harm of "religion," these governments still understood the principles of good and evil, and, in effect, were ethical as a result. Thus arguing that Western norms did not exclude moral principles from the realm of government, Sakatani called for an explicit commitment to principles that were cemented by faith but nonetheless remained distinct from "religion." The need to shape proper belief again stood in tension with the need to disavow the religious.

Nishimura Shigeki (1828–1902) pleaded more explicitly for the role of ethics in government. Although separating scholarship from governance might be a welcome development, Nishimura deeply regretted "personal cultivation [*shūshin*] and government [*seiji*] diverging into two different paths." He set about demonstrating that the two were not separate by pursuing a rationalist line of argument, beginning with the claim that only humans are endowed with a rational instinct—"heaven's reason" (*tenri*). He claimed that ethics is a matter of reason and thus shares its rational base with the government of a country: "Since what they hold to be good and bad are identical, they are completely alike."[43] As a rationally founded domain of normativity, ethics remained within the purview of government, while "religion," founded on irrationality, belonged to an entirely separate and superficial domain of human concern. Nishimura consistently situated ethics (either as *rinri*, *dōtoku*, or *shūshin*) in contrast to "religion" in his subsequent writings. The fact that Confucianism (Jyukyō), once counted as one of three teachings (*sankyō*: Buddhism, Shinto, and Confucianism), was rarely identified as a "religion" in Japan following the Meiji period stems in large measure from this discursive strategy and its broad application in education.[44]

Fukuzawa Yukichi, in his influential *Encouragement of Learning* from 1874, suggested that a new form of government, one focused on the interior lives of its subjects, came into existence following the Meiji Restoration: "Governments of old robbed the people of power; the current government robs them of their hearts. Governments of old violated the people outwardly; the current government controls them internally."[45] Nishi Amane echoed Fukuzawa in a more affirmative form when he identified "faith" as the indispensable foundation for government, morality, and progress: "Faith [*shin*] . . . is the source for all virtue and the origin of all conduct. It is the foundation for managing oneself and ruling others. The safety and health of our bodies as well as the peace and prosperity of our country begins by establishing great faith [*daishin*]."[46] Seeking to intervene in the interior lives of the populace, however, raised the question of how "faith" related to the imperial myths, international law, religion, or morality. The principles of faith had to be "established," but how would the state establish something understood to be mutable and unstable? Nishi conceptually resolved the tension between the demand for stability and the admission of instability with temporal displacement: faith would move closer and closer to stable knowledge as human civilization progressed. Still, a clear and confident definition of religion and its boundary in relation to government, education, and morality did not emerge from the Meiroku Society's debates. Instead, a muddled compromise between two seemingly irreconcilable postulates remained. On the one hand, the state should not risk its authority by involving itself in the inherently volatile realm of belief. On the other hand, the state must regulate outward forms of "religion" and instill proper morals in its subjects for Japan to achieve civilization and enlightenment. Inextricably caught up in these two commitments were the formulations of imperial sovereignty and the status of Christianity, especially as it pertained to relations with the treaty powers. The resulting dilemma may be rendered thus: the state was best served by disassociating itself from religion, but it could not risk placing religion "outside" its power, in a position capable of radical critique. The solution to this Gordian knot in the Meiroku Society debates—freedom of private, individual belief versus the regulation of communal institutions and ritual practice—emerged in the form of a "subjectified" construct of religion embraced by Buddhist critics of the Ministry of Doctrine.

Administering an Absolute Yet Mediated Doctrine

While the *Meiroku Journal* provided a forum for debating the theoretical challenges that accompanied the introduction of a general conception of religion to early-Meiji Japan, the Ministry of Doctrine was the institutional site where the boundary between religion and political authority was worked out in practice during the 1870s. The creation of the Ministry of Doctrine in early 1872 had marked the Meiji government's retreat from explicitly promulgating an imperial doctrine that would "convert" the Japanese populace. Seeking to defuse theological debates within the Missionary Office concerning the afterlife and prevent the imperial ancestor from being confused with a "founder of a doctrine," the government sought to separate imperial rituals from the Great Promulgation Campaign by dismantling the Ministry of Divinities and creating two new entities, the Bureau of Rites and the Ministry of Doctrine—in effect maintaining the "unity of rite and rule" by distinguishing doctrine from ritual.[47] The ministry, therefore, reflected the political will to pursue a more mediated projection of imperial doctrine, one that did not place the emperor in direct opposition to other creeds. That mediation was immediately noticeable in the joint mobilization of Buddhism and Shinto under the new ministry; ostensibly, the doctrine propagated by the ministry was neither Shinto nor Buddhist but transcended their sectarian differences. For this reason, from the perspective of the Buddhist sects at least, the ministry promised a nonsectarian framework through which Shinto and Buddhist clerics alike could be mobilized to disseminate a doctrine that would secure the loyalty of the masses and prevent the spread of Christianity.

Still, as indicated by its project to disseminate a doctrine, the Ministry of Doctrine did not signify that the government had abandoned altogether the project of capturing the "people's hearts" (*jinshin*). Just as the Meiroku Society attempted to strictly separate religion from the imperial institution while also calling for interventions in the beliefs of the "ignorant" populace, the Ministry of Doctrine attempted to disavow any identification of religion with the imperial institution, while at the same time "teaching and directing" the populace. The institutional posture of the ministry, in other words, mirrored the religious discourse of the Meiroku Society—separate the imperial institution from the unstable realm of belief, but also effectively intervene in the beliefs and practices of the populace. For this reason, the ministry sustained, rather than defused, a political conversation sensitive to the destabilizing identification of the imperial institution with religion.

The mandate of the Ministry of Doctrine was to disseminate a national doctrine that "would serve as the ideal ideological apparatus: absolute, self-perpetuating, and common sensical."[48] From its inception, this "absolute" and all-encompassing doctrine was undercut by the premise of mediation. In other words, even as Shinto partisans ambitiously sought to resurrect and retain an explicit identification between Shinto and the imperial institution, there existed within the Meiji government an abiding concern that such an apparatus should be related only indirectly to the imperial institution. This concern was expressed in the semiprivate character of the doctrinal instructors and the academy system used to disseminate the putatively absolute national doctrine. From the outset, the conflicted pursuit of an absolute national doctrine and its mediated dissemination ensured the eventual demise of the Ministry of Doctrine. Buddhist critiques of the ministry, led by Shimaji Mokurai and the Shin sect, facilitated its demise by promoting a subjectified construct of religion and religious identity, a construct that emphasized the private (subjective) and loyal (subjected) nature of authentic religion.

The theoretical promise of the Ministry of Doctrine to mediate the boundary between the imperial institution and the realm of "religion" proved illusory in the face of the inherent contradictions that informed its creation. In the first place, the caretaker government created the ministry in the absence of the Iwakura Embassy, violating the agreement to maintain the institutional status quo while the embassy traveled abroad. As a result, the ministry, with its stated goal of preventing the spread of Christianity, stood in tension with the policy priorities that members of the Iwakura Embassy brought back from their travels. The Foreign Ministry, sensitive to the diplomatic climate, opposed the ministry's creation outright.[49] The removal of the public notice boards banning Christianity in early 1873, moreover, signaled that any overtly anti-Christian mandate of an official state ministry would be superseded by diplomatic considerations. Second, despite the stated goal of separating the imperial institution from religion, the Ministry of Doctrine provided an opportunity for Shinto partisans to develop Shinto into a religion (*shūmon*) with doctrines and institutions analogous to, and in competition with, Buddhism. The pursuit within the ministry of doctrinal formulations and institutional structures favorable to this vision of Shinto provoked Buddhist resistance, while the development of "churches" (*kyōkai*) began transforming prominent Shinto shrines (notably Ise and Izumo) into the headquarters of nationwide denominations.[50] Both the ongoing Buddhist-Shinto competition and the presence of a proselytizing form of Shinto within a state ministry undermined the goal of firmly separating the emperor and imperial rituals from the messy realm of "religious" competition. Third, the Ministry of Doctrine, with its mandate to "teach and direct" (*kyōdō* or *oshie michibiku*) the populace, overlapped and competed with the nascent public-education policy of the state.[51] The nominal and short-lived consolidation of the ministry into the Ministry of Education in

October 1872, for example, betrays how easily indoctrination collapsed into education at this time.[52] As separating the narrowly "religious" from education became an increasingly explicit priority for the government, the Ministry of Doctrine became a redundant and potentially embarrassing organ of the state. Fourth, narrowing the scope of *saisei itchi* by separating the rituals of the imperial house, now conducted within the palace by the emperor himself, from doctrine remained an unchanged priority.[53]

From its inception in early 1872, then, the Ministry of Doctrine carried within it unresolved tensions arising from the attempt to clarify the relations between the imperial institution, Shinto, Buddhism, Christianity, and "religion" in general. Ōhara Shigetomi (1833–1877), reporting the creation of the ministry to Iwakura Tomomi, who remained abroad at the time, expressed significant misgivings about its prospects:

> It would be fine if enough was done to prevent the spread of the evil doctrine, but there have only been fierce debates. The ministry has [already] been revised, Fukuba has been removed and Shishido appointed director [*daiho*] and Kuroda, a counselor [*sangi*] from Tokyo, has been appointed deputy director [*shōho*]. Fukuba argued for mixing Buddhism and Shinto, while the Council of the Left insisted on placing Shinto at the head of the ministry, and it is rumored the assembly got its way. In this manner, only arguments have been active and no action can be seen. As the years and months pass, the doctrine [i.e., Christianity] will enter even more and we will no longer be able to prevent its intrusion.[54]

As Ōhara observed, the relationship between Buddhist clerics and Shinto partisans proved particularly contentious. Fukuba Bisei, a prominent leader within the former Department of Divinities had attempted to create a degree of formal parity between Buddhism and Shinto within the new ministry. His replacement in 1872 by Kuroda Kiyotsuna (1830–1917) from Satsuma and Shishido Tamaki (1829–1901) from Chōshū allowed the pro-Shinto Satsuma clique to exert considerable influence over the ministry and privilege Shinto over Buddhism.[55] While the institutional advantage enjoyed by Shinto partisans over Buddhist sects under the Ministry of Doctrine was considerable, the mediating conceit of the ministry—"joint proselytizing" (*gōdō fukyō*) by Buddhist and Shinto clerics—provided the grounds for Buddhist critiques.

The formal administrative jurisdiction granted to the Ministry of Doctrine further illustrates how the government attempted to mediate its relationship to Shinto and Buddhism through the ministry. The minister of doctrine received administrative authority to open or close temples and shrines, as well as designate the rank of Buddhist and Shinto clerics; license new priests, monks, and nuns; publish texts concerning doctrinal matters (*kyōgi*); grant licenses to proselytize, study doctrine, and form congregations (*kōsha*); and adjudicate doctrinal disputes. The minister required prior authorization from the Council of State before revising or adding to ministry doctrine (*kyōsoku*), or revising the structure of the ministry itself; altering a sect (*kyōha*) or altering the name of a sect, temple, or shrine; closing or establishing a shrine or temple; granting court ranks to Shinto or Buddhist clerics; revising shrine and temple ranks; revising or adding to ministry regulations; and promoting, transferring, or demoting any member of the ministry appointed by the court.[56] In other words, the executive branch of the state—the Council of State—retained strict control over actions that could affect relations between the court, Buddhist sects, and Shinto shrines. Conferring court ranks on Buddhist and Shinto clerics and altering the status of a shrine or temple, for example, could unsettle the delicate distinction sought between imperial rituals and the doctrinal activities overseen by the ministry. As these administrative regulations made clear, the state remained directly concerned with the activities of Buddhist and Shinto clergy, but was devising increasingly indirect means of control.

The clearest expression of the liminal state of relations between the government and religion under the Ministry of Doctrine was its system of doctrinal instructors (*kyōdōshoku*).[57] Only clerics—Buddhist, Shinto, or otherwise—licensed by the Ministry of Doctrine as doctrinal instructors were allowed to preach and perform rituals, most significantly funeral rites.[58] In fact, the system proved more durable than the ministry itself; the ministry ceased to exist in 1877, while the final vestige of the doctrinal instructor system was not eliminated until 1884. The instructors provided a system whereby the state could effectively control who could publicly preach and conduct funerals while disavowing any direct involvement in sectarian ordinations (especially in the case of Buddhist clerics). The clearest indication of this double move came in the form of two successive ordinances issued by the Council of State on the same day in early 1872. The first, ordinance number 132, decreed the creation of doctrinal instructors and their fourteen ranks. The second, ordinance number 133, decreed that Buddhist clerics would thenceforth be free to eat meat, marry, grow hair, and wear civilian clothes when not performing rites of their office.[59] The oaths one took to become a Buddhist cleric, in other words, lost all public character and were transformed into private oaths, relevant only within the sect to which the cleric would belong; the state no longer enforced or prohibited such oaths of ordination. Richard Jaffe observes that "the various changes in the status of clergy" during this period worked to harden "the distinction between so-called private religious concerns and the public realm."[60] At the same time, the doctrinal instructor system retained a direct connection between state recognition and the public activities of Buddhist clerics.

Doctrinal instructors were organized into a hierarchy consisting of fourteen ranks.[61] Seven Buddhist sects were recognized (Tendai, Shingon, Jōdo, Zen, Shin, Nichiren, and Jishū) under the system, each with its own superintendent (*kanchō*); smaller Buddhist sects and subsects, such as the Hossō and Kegon sects, were initially required to place themselves under a superintendent of one of the seven recognized sects (this was amended in early 1874). For the Buddhist sects, the system provided a transitional framework that forced Tokugawa-era sect structures—especially the head temple/branch temple relationship (*honmatsu kankei*)—to recast themselves into religious corporations with modern administrative relations to the state. Under the superintendent system, the hierarchical authority of a Buddhist sect, formerly secured by state fiat, was secured through the creation of centralized corporations that were granted private jurisdiction over the administration of their sects.[62] A "private" domain of Buddhist sectarian autonomy took shape through the Meiji government's efforts to withdraw from any direct administration of Buddhist affairs while regulating the public function of Buddhist clergy.

Buddhists and Shinto clerics were not the only individuals appointed as doctrinal instructors, moreover. The Ministry of Doctrine decreed in early 1873 that regional authorities could nominate individuals other than clerics, and figures such as the Kabuki actor Ichikawa Danjūrō IX (1838–1903) and the Rakugo raconteur Sanyūtei Enchō (1838–1900) were made doctrinal instructors.[63] Prefectural officials were also registered as doctrinal instructors, further complicating the category of instructor. For purposes of this study, the focus will remain on Buddhist and Shinto doctrinal instructors whose activities and regulation created complications that were addressed through appeals to religion as a distinct category.

The fiscal status of Buddhist sects vis-à-vis the Meiji state is significant in relation to the doctrinal instructor system. When the Meiji government revised the tax structure in 1871 in order to reform its finances, temples and shrines were forced to surrender their landholdings (*shajiryō no jōchi*), which were formerly guaranteed by Tokugawa and domain authorities. The Buddhist sects heavily reliant on landholdings—Tendai,

Shingon, Rinzai, and Jōdo—were most adversely affected, while sects that possessed significant parishioner-based financial resources in addition to private land—Shin, Nichiren, and Sōtō—were relatively unscathed by these reforms.[64] Although the government continued to pay stipends to the sects at levels pegged to the amount of land seized, the stipends were to be phased out over a ten-year period. The willingness of the Shin sect to actively lobby the Meiji government for the autonomous administration of its affairs, ahead of the other Buddhist sects, stems to some extent from its ability to achieve financial independence more quickly than the others.

The relation of the doctrinal instructor system to Shinto, reflecting its unsettled institutional identity, proved more complicated. In the summer of 1872, all shrine priests were automatically appointed doctrinal instructors, but how to oversee those instructors became a contentious question. Initially the Ministry of Doctrine recognized two Shinto superintendents, one for an eastern district and another for a western district, with the head priests of the Ise and Izumo shrines, respectively, filling the positions. This arrangement was amended in January 1873 with the creation of a unified structure for Shinto under a single superintendent. However, the pretense of a singular structure was abandoned in 1876 when Shinto priests were divided up again, first into three sections, then into four, each with its own superintendent; Shinto doctrinal instructors were thenceforth allowed to freely choose which section they would affiliate with.[65] The rapid and confusing realignment of Shinto doctrinal instructors reveals that, unlike with the Buddhist sects, whose sectarian framework predated the Meiji period, the doctrinal instructor system was insufficient as a vehicle to create a centralized Shinto organization out of nothing. In fact, as the Pantheon Dispute of 1879–1881 would later indicate, the instructor system, by introducing the premise of private religionists operating under the aegis of the state, further alienated the Shinto priesthood from the state.

In 1874 there were 7,247 licensed doctrinal instructors, of whom 4,207 were registered as Shinto instructors. Among the Buddhists, the Shin sect registered the largest number of instructors, 728.[66] By 1880, the total number reached 103,000, with Buddhists numbering 81,000.[67] These numbers reflect a reversal of fortune between Shinto and Buddhism, a reversal rooted in, among other things, the fiscal realities of the doctrinal instructor system. The 1873 state budget allocated 50,000 yen for the Ministry of Doctrine, compared with 1.3 million yen for the Ministry of Education. Not only did the Ministry of Doctrine receive a mere one-twenty-sixth of what the Ministry of Education was allocated, but its budget was the smallest among all state ministries.[68] Reflecting this, doctrinal instructors, while officials of the state, were given no financial support from the state. As Tokoyo Nagatane recalled: "Doctrinal instructors were given no stipend. The intent was for them to rely upon the faith [*shinkō*] of the people for their support."[69] The need for financial self-sufficiency proved a challenge for Shinto doctrinal instructors who, unlike their Buddhist counterparts (especially Nichiren and Shin clerics), possessed little if any experience soliciting financial support directly from believers. This explains why so much effort of the Shinto partisans was directed toward having shrine priests and doctrinal instructors conduct funeral rites—even going so far as forbidding cremation, ostensibly to motivate more people to hold Shinto funerals.[70]

The attempt to transform shrine priests from liturgists into pastoral clergy, in order that they would have to "rely upon the faith of the people," proved particularly vexing, both for the priests themselves and for the government. The government had completed its formal survey of Shinto shrines in May 1871, with the total numbering 123,705. Of that total, 97 shrines were ranked as national (*kokuheisha*) and imperial shrines (*kanpeisha*). The remainder were designated either prefectural (*fusha, kensha*), county (*gōsha*), or village shrines (*sonsha*).[71] These ranks corresponded to the ranks of their affiliated priests. The state supported Shinto shrines and their priests, but that support continued to decline in both scope and amount as the government sought to limit its direct involvement in shrines at the local level. For example, even though the state initially promised to pay a salary to all shrine priests in 1872, priests at shrines ranked beneath the prefectural level were excluded the following year, and this was later extended to prefectural priests as well.[72] Yet because the government had formally declared Shinto shrines to come under the purview of the state and had ended all hereditary appointments of priests as unacceptably "private" arrangements, fund-raising activities undertaken by priests who were officially associated with the state as doctrinal instructors appeared problematic. In early 1874, for example, the Ministry of Doctrine issued a warning to Shinto superintendents, complaining that Shinto doctrinal instructors were raising funds from the populace by falsely claiming they were doing so in an official capacity. This "betrayed the purpose of proselytizing [*fukyō no taishi*] and results in no small harm to governance [*seiji*]."[73]

For both Shinto and Buddhist clerics, then, the doctrinal instructor system forced significant realignments of their institutional structures and practices. The ambivalent, official-yet-private status of the instructors reflected the structural duality of the Ministry of Doctrine itself. The end of the doctrinal instructor system in 1884 marked a decisive attempt to "settle" that ambivalence and institute a stable boundary between religion and political authority, and the contours of that settlement emerged first from Buddhist efforts to reform the Ministry of Doctrine and doctrinal instructor system.

When the seven Buddhist sects petitioned the government in May 1872 to create the Great Teaching Academy (Daikyōin), they sought to exploit the private character of the doctrinal instructor system. The resulting academy, however, merely amplified the tensions built into the Ministry of Doctrine. The Buddhist sects argued in their petition that to adequately discharge their duties as doctrinal instructors, Buddhist clerics had to be educated broadly not only in Shinto but also in "Buddhism, Confucianism, and the sciences of Western Learning." For that purpose, and to overcome the divisions among themselves, the seven sects proposed creating a Great Teaching Academy with small academies (*shōkyōin*) in all prefectures. The government granted permission to establish the academy in January 1873, emphasizing that it be self-financed. Like the doctrinal instructor system, the academy system took shape as something in between an official state institution and a private organization. This liminality was highlighted when the Great Teaching Academy was given authority over the doctrinal instructor system as a whole, adding another institutional layer of mediation to the state's relationship to doctrine.[74] From 1873 until its effective dissolution in 1875, the Great Teaching Academy formed the front line, where the boundaries between Buddhism and Shinto, education and proselytizing, and state and religion were questioned.

Contrary to Buddhist expectations, Shinto partisans, bolstered by the Satsuma faction and the Council of the Left, quickly assumed control of the academy system and set about transforming it into a vehicle for creating a centralized Shinto organization. Following several relocations, the Great Teaching Academy was ultimately established at Zōjōji, the Tokugawa family's ancestral temple in Tokyo. The inaugural ceremony there, conducted according to Shinto ritual with Buddhist superintendents participating, amply demonstrated the sectarian colors of the academy system.[75] All Buddhist elements were removed from the main hall of the temple and a Shinto altar was erected, enshrining the three creator *kami* and the imperial ancestor, Amaterasu Ōmikami. The academy's regulations required all doctrinal instructors (Buddhist or Shinto) visiting the academy to first bow to the *kami* enshrined at the altar.[76] In both form and content, the Great Teaching Academy aspired to be the center of something that could only be labeled Shinto.

Even though the Shinto partisans took control of the academy system, they confronted problems in financing it. The Buddhist sects, which had proposed creating the Great Teaching Academy in the first place, were capable of marshaling significant financial resources relative to the Shinto sects, leading Shintoists to fear Buddhist leverage. In one instance, Shinto doctrinal instructors attempted to raise funds by levying a local tax, but the Ministry of Doctrine quickly halted that experiment.[77] The semiprivate nature of the academy system thus exposed the Buddhists' financial strength relative to that of Shinto shrines and their priests, threatening Shinto ambitions when attempts to increase direct financial support from the state were hampered by the principle of private support. As a result, so-called new religions and their confraternities (*kōsha*), hitherto at the margins of official recognition, were invited to join the academy system, further muddying the sectarian waters.[78] "Shinto" doctrinal instructors came to consist of an "uneasy coalition" of Kokugaku ideologues from competing scholarly lineages, prominent sacerdotal lineages from the larger shrines and the Yoshida and Shirakawa houses, priests appointed by local administrators, and "religionists" from the new religions, sacred mountain cults, and pilgrimage associations seeking legal shelter and legitimation.[79] These heterogeneous elements coalesced around anti-Buddhist resentment, fear of Christianity, and a desire to elevate their status through ties to the imperial institution, but they struggled to provide Shinto with a clear doctrinal or institutional definition. The Great Teaching Academy and the doctrinal instructor system exacerbated the problem by encouraging the combination of ritual and pastoral elements within the coalition of Shinto partisans. Whatever Shinto was to become, it looked increasingly "religious" under the Great Teaching Academy.

With the creation of the academy, the Ministry of Doctrine designated all shrines and temples either middle (*chūkyōin*) or small academies (*shōkyōin*), effectively bringing them under the control of the Great Teaching Academy.[80] "This basic national hierarchy," Ketelaar observes, "provided the foundation stones upon which the national education system was eventually built: lower schools in each local area, middle schools established at the prefectural level, and universities in select national administrative areas."[81] This characterization of the academy system alerts us to another source of ambivalence built into the Ministry of Doctrine and its operation. Just as the doctrinal instructors were caught in a liminal role between officials of the state and private religionists, the academies were ambivalently positioned as schools-cum-shrines or temples. Hence, even though Ketelaar characterizes the doctrinal instructor system as "a thinly veiled attempt by the state to create . . . a de facto state priesthood," one could just as well argue that it was an attempt to create an education system. Miyachi Masato proposes a functional motive behind the creation of the doctrinal instructor and academy systems. Following the abolition of domains and the creation of prefectures in 1871, the Meiji government rushed to centralize its authority, which had formerly been shored up by the military support of loyalist domains. Uniform taxation and conscription were cornerstones of that centralization, but the government faced the challenge of explaining and legitimating those policies to a restive populace. The only ones capable of directly explaining the government's policy to the population at large, and over whom the government possessed regulatory control, were the Buddhist and Shinto clerics. They were therefore mobilized to educate the masses, explaining the necessity and desirability of the new state policies.[82] Schools would not come to fulfill the function of mediating state ideology until the late 1880s. The doctrinal instructors and academies thus straddled an ill-defined line between educating and proselytizing, an ambiguity clearly admitted in 1874 in a Ministry of Doctrine directive clarifying that academies were not to be mistaken for schools and that young children were still required to enroll in elementary schools.[83] Given the ambitious scope of the doctrine that the doctrinal instructors and academies were charged with teaching, however, one could hardly fault any who were confused.

The basic triadic structure of the Ministry of Doctrine, the doctrinal instructor system, and the academy system both informed and reflected the unsettled boundaries between religion and political authority, Buddhism and Shinto, educating and proselytizing. The actual doctrine that the Ministry of Doctrine formulated and then disseminated through the doctrinal instructor and academy systems brings the ambiguities into further relief. The Three Standards of Instruction (Sanjō no kyōsoku), formulated by Etō Shinpei in June 1872, formed the basis of all doctrinal instruction at shrines and temples (Fig. 3.1). They were: (1) revere the *kami* and love the nation; (2) clarify the principle of heaven and the way of humanity; and (3) serve the emperor and obey the will of the court. The Three Standards, in their generality, sought to sidestep the theologically contentious topic of a "hidden world," or the afterlife and salvation, topics that had plagued the earlier Missionary Office.[84]

In 1873, however, the Eleven Themes (Jūichi kendai) were appended to provide greater scope to the doctrine, and these reintroduced some con-

FIG. 3.1. Preaching the Three Standards of Instruction at a shrine. From Kanagaki Robun, *Sansoku oshie no chikamichi* (Nakanishi Genpachi, 1873), 1. Courtesy of the National Diet Library of Japan.

tentious content. Written in cryptic and truncated phrases, the Eleven Themes are far more doctrinally expansive:

1. The *kami* and power, the emperor and gratitude
2. The spirit of man is immortal
3. The heavenly deities and creation
4. The worlds of the visible and invisible
5. Love of nation
6. Divine rites
7. Pacification of the spirits (of the dead)
8. (The relation between) lord and subject
9. (The relation between) father and child
10. (The relation between) husband and wife
11. The Great Purification (Ceremony)

These themes, with their discussion of divine rites, the visible and invisible worlds, and the pacification of the spirits, clearly grew out of ambitions to use the Ministry of Doctrine to create a Shinto doctrine. To the Three Standards and the Eleven Themes, another set, the Seventeen Themes (Jūnana kendai), was added in late 1873:

1. Imperial nation, national polity
2. The Way does not change
3. Organizations must correspond with the times
4. Renewal of imperial rule
5. Man is distinct from the beasts
6. Study is necessary
7. (The) Doctrine is necessary
8. International relations
9. National law, civil law
10. Development of laws
11. Taxes and conscription
12. Wealthy nation, strong army
13. (Agricultural) production and manufacturing
14. Cultural enlightenment
15. Different forms of government
16. Employing the heart, employing the form
17. Rights and responsibilities

As Ketelaar convincingly points out, these themes were so vague as to permit a nearly infinite array of interpretations. The resulting "polyphony" accounted at once for the utility and the futility of the ministry's doctrinal project.[85]

Still, at its inception the doctrine was intended, as Sakamoto Koremaru describes it, to be "the absolute foundation upon which the state stood," a foundation that "transcended religion [*kyōhō*]."[86] Like the institutions charged with its dissemination, however, the doctrine was plagued by inherent tensions from the very beginning. The eleven themes, for example, clearly articulated a Shinto-based vision of an afterlife, in sharp contrast to Buddhist doctrine. Yet the attempt to formulate a coherent Shinto theology of the afterlife risked reviving the interminable doctrinal debates of the Department of Divinities and the Missionary Office.[87] The doctrine thus fueled not only Buddhist-Shinto tension, but also doctrinal disputes among Shinto partisans themselves. The Great Teaching Academy attempted to contain the potential for dispute among the doctrinal instructors by overseeing the publication of authorized commentaries on the Three Standards and twenty-eight themes.[88] The difficulty of such an attempt at constraint, however, was readily apparent in the repeated rebukes issued against doctrinal instructors. For example, the Ministry of Doctrine issued a directive to Buddhist and Shinto superintendents in late 1872, demanding that the doctrinal instructors avoid precisely those tensions and disputes built into the doctrine itself. Shrine priests were often so poor at preaching that some even appeared incapable of reading their own prepared notes; others preached on "the hidden world" (*yūmei*) and "unfounded strange theories" (*mukon no kaisetsu*), running counter to the "orthodoxy" (*seikyō*) of the doctrine. Moreover, some Shinto priests preached against Buddhism (*haibutsu*), again contradicting the principle of joint proselytizing. As for Buddhist clerics, some preached the Three Standards in public but in private continued to preach only their sectarian teachings (*shūi*), teachings that in some cases contradicted the Three Standards. Others still taught the long-standing doctrine that the *kami* were but manifestations of Buddhas (*hotoke no keshin*).[89] Both Shinto ambitions and Buddhist resistance undermined the "ideal ideological apparatus" from the very beginning.[90]

Much like the Meiroku intellectuals, the Ministry of Doctrine recognized the utility of situating what they taught, however discordant, in opposition to what they deemed popular superstition and ignorance. In early 1876 the ministry banned fortune-telling, prayer healing, and mediums, declaring that such practices and their practitioners (often itinerant figures) led the people astray.[91] As a clear by-product of the dominant discourse of "civilization and enlightenment," or *bunmei kaika*, doctrinal instructors were prompted to attack superstition while simultaneously stressing reverence of the *kami*. A popular handbook on *bunmei kaika* explained at length the need to "revere the *kami*" without resorting to superstitious beliefs—"there are no strange deeds [*kikai*] with the *kami*."[92] Examining the juxtaposition of a theocratic emperor and the ideals of civilization and enlightenment in the seventeen themes, Fujiwara Masanobu suggests that combining the two did not pose a problem for most Shinto doctrinal instructors.[93] Indeed, relating true doctrine (or religion) to the self-evident legitimacy of civilization and enlightenment was a strategy widely employed by sectarian advocates, whether Buddhist, Shinto, Christian, or any of the multiple new religions.[94] Doctrinal instructors operating in Shizuoka prefecture, for example, stressed in their sermons how state policies would increase wealth and comfort through enlightened rule and modern technology.[95] Although doctrinal instructors combined calls to worship the *kami* with admonitions to adopt civilized dress and conduct, the potentially theocratic character of the emperor still troubled many involved in the doctrinal project. The Shin Buddhist movement to break free from the strictures of the academy system and, ultimately, the Ministry of Doctrine itself, leveraged precisely this threat of a "religious" Shinto and a potentially theocratic imperial institution.

Critiquing Doctrine and Subjectifying Religion

Shimaji Mokurai, a Shin sect cleric with close ties to the Chōshū clique within the government, led his sect in withdrawing from the academy system, and in the process contributed to the discursive clarification of Buddhism's boundary in relation to the state. Although Buddhism came under considerable pressure following the Restoration, the Shin Buddhists (specifically the Nishi Honganji branch), thanks to their regional and ideological connections to influential members of the Meiji government and their own financial contributions to the state treasury, successfully sought autonomy for their sect in particular, and for Buddhism as a whole. From the initial "serve the emperor, protect the dharma" movement (*kinnō gohō undo*) in 1870 and 1871, Shimaji served as the point man for those efforts, and as a result he has been credited with advancing the first general definition of religion in Japan.[96] In carving out a discrete and autonomous sphere for Buddhism by embracing its character as a religion, Shimaji also establishing the basic terms in which the nonreligious character of Shinto came to be articulated.[97] Shimaji articulated with particular force and clarity the solution to the problem of securing the inner commitment of subjects while disavowing a "religious" imperial institution—a "subjectified" religion and a nonreligious Shinto.

Buddhist attempts to recover from disestablishment began in earnest in March 1870 when Shimaji proposed the government create a Temple Bureau (Jiinryō) dedicated to the administration and reform of Buddhist temples.[98] His petition granted that the Missionary Office was pursuing a doctrine completely discrete from Buddhism and Confucianism but nonetheless insisted that Buddhism could better prevent the feared spread of Christianity. A Temple Bureau was created in December of that year, but with the Department of Divinities and the Missionary Office still in operation, it did little to improve the administrative and ideological treatment of Buddhism. Seeking better results, Shimaji petitioned again in September 1871, this time for the creation of a ministry dedicated to the regulation of all doctrinal matters, Shinto and Buddhist included. That petition appealed to Buddhist expertise in countering Christianity and notably stressed the inseparable nature of political rule (*sei*) and doctrine (*kyō*).[99] Shimaji clearly sought to capitalize on anti-Christian attitudes as he stressed the desirability of Buddhist involvement in state-directed ideological programs.[100]

Like the Temple Bureau before it, the Ministry of Doctrine proved an immediate disappointment for Buddhist aspirations. Shimaji, who traveled to Europe on the heels of the Iwakura Embassy in 1872, actively petitioned the Meiji government on behalf of his sect even while abroad. In Europe he was greatly impressed by the notion that the human conscience was inviolable, and his writings increasingly espoused a strict separation between religion and the state on those grounds.[101] In a letter written during this time, he insisted that only faiths capable of resisting political authority were true religions.[102] Accordingly, Shimaji applied the new taxonomy of religion to Shinto and the majority of Buddhist sects, none of which could be considered proper religions since they had all accommodated themselves to political authority. Only the Shin sect had ever properly resisted political authority and could thus be deemed a religion proper.[103] This dramatic shift in Shimaji's understanding of religion and its relation to the political did not mark an antagonistic split with the Meiji government, however. In fact, Shimaji strengthened his ties to leading members of government during his time in Europe, especially Kido Takayoshi, Itō Hirobumi, and Aoki Shūzō, all from Chōshū. Shimaji's new critique of the Ministry of Doctrine converged significantly with concerns Kido and other members of the Iwakura Embassy had formed in regard to religion.[104] Kido, for example, met with Shimaji eight times between October 1873 and March 1874, just as Shimaji was pressing for the fundamental reform of the Ministry of Doctrine. Shimaji's increasingly vehement call for the separation of religion from political power must be placed in relation to the backing he received from key members of the Meiji government.[105] Put another way, Shimaji embraced a discourse of religion as a category discreet from and privileged in relation to the state, with the implicit support of Kido and Itō within the government.

The first of Shimaji's new critiques demanding a clear boundary between religion and political authority came in December 1872 when he attacked the Three Standards of Instruction. His critique applied the confident taxonomy that differentiated a properly religious Buddhism from a problematically religious Shinto. His detailed critique of the standards began with the blanket claim that mirrored Nishi Amane's maxim in the *Meiroku Journal*: "Politics and religion are different and should never be confused. Politics belongs to human deeds [*jinji*] and controls only outward shapes [*katachi*]." Religion, or doctrine (*kyō*), on the other hand, "is the work of the divine [*shin*] and controls the heart." The Three Standards violated this basic truth, since the very first standard—revere the *kami* and love the country—blatantly mixed religion and politics. Shimaji warned that if the myriad *kami* in the land were to be revered by government decree, even European children would mock the Japanese.[106] Distinguishing superstition and mythology from rational religion, Shimaji insisted that defining the *kami* as deities would only discredit the state and, by implication, the imperial institution itself. Instead, the *kami* should be clarified to be ancestors worthy of veneration but not worship. Ritual respect conveyed to the imperial ancestors should never be construed as religion.

The second standard of instruction—clarify the principles of heaven and the ways of humanity—conveyed only the abstract essence of religion without any concrete doctrinal or institutional expression of that reality. Shimaji insisted religions must possess a sect, an institutional reality that can embody a sentiment. Without a well-established tradition of doctrine, leadership, and institutions, the "principles of heaven and the ways of humanity" would not "enter the people." And unless it enters the people, Shimaji asked rhetorically, what good can religion accomplish? The critique was clear: only Buddhism possessed the attributes needed to successfully implement this standard, but the Ministry of Doctrine stood in the way by privileging Shinto, which in contrast possessed none of the necessary attributes. Shimaji amplified this point in his critique of the third standard of instruction—revere the emperor and obey the court—when he claimed that the reverence owed to the emperor constituted the *kokutai*, or national polity, and was not a religion (*oshie*). While the Ministry of Doctrine's efforts arose from the "fear that the *kokutai* will be altered," those efforts were not only ineffectual as religion (*oshie*) but also threatened to realize that fear of an undermined *kokutai*.[107] Trying to endow Shinto with the institutional and doctrinal framework that properly belonged to religions such as Buddhism exposed the *kokutai* to potential harm.

Shimaji's critique of the Three Standards of Instruction strategically drew on the concern voiced by Etō Shinpei and the Council of the Left in late 1871, when they feared the emperor would be mistaken for a religious authority. Shimaji's petition addressed lingering concerns within the government over the persistent ambiguity surrounding the boundary between the imperial institution and religion. Kinoshita Masahiro (1824–1897), a bureaucrat serving the Council of State, expressed precisely this concern in relation to the Ministry of Doctrine: "However, the divine rites [*shinji*] were originally meant to answer the ancestors, but if this is what is preached [*sekkyō*], the rites of the imperial nation [*kōkoku no tenrei*] will stoop to become another religion [*shūshi*], and it will come to be that those who do not believe will be able to turn their backs on it [*somuku*]."[108] Shimaji deliberately hit a nerve by emphasizing how the ministry and its doctrine placed the imperial institution within the realm of belief (and thus potential disbelief). Taxonomically separating Shinto from religion proper, in order to carve out a sphere of legitimate utility for Buddhism qua religion, was an approach attractive to the government.

In the face of Shinto attempts to leverage a direct connection to the imperial institution, Buddhists could resist only by removing shrine rites from direct competition with Buddhist beliefs and practices. The *Kyōgi shinbun*, published between September 1872 and April 1875 and considered one of the first religious newspapers in Japan, provides a window into the discursive strategies adopted by Buddhists under the doctrinal instructor system.[109] The harmonious collaboration of Shinto and Buddhism under the Ministry of Doctrine had to be affirmed in principle, even if reality was different. Yet the possibility of critique could be created by insisting on the distinctly religious character of Buddhism relative to Shinto. The *Kyōgi shinbun*'s editorial policy affirmed the Three Standards of Instruction and thus constrained doctrinal discussions within the orthodoxy of the standards.[110] Although the paper carried a large number of Buddhist letters, few ventured an outright critique of the Ministry of Doctrine except to argue for the nonreligious character of Shinto. Buddhists wielded a double-edged sword, however, for denying the religious character of Shinto risked strengthening the claim that both the Three Standards and the demand that Buddhists conform to them were religiously neutral. Staking a claim for Buddhism's discrete character and mission as a religion nonetheless provided the best means to differentiate it from Shinto and to secure for Buddhism a unique role. Like Shimaji, many who wrote to the newspaper questioned the wisdom of turning Shinto into a religion: "If Shinto is taken to be a religion [*shūkyō*], will it not be called a mere polytheism [*shūjinkyō*], or worse, a syncretic religion [*zasshinkyō*]? If we allow the ritual veneration of the emperor's ancestors to be a religion, we would render the sacred spirits of all our emperors the same as the hidden and indeterminate gods of the various religions, gods who are believed by those who believe and are mocked by those who do not believe."[111] The proposition that Shinto was something less than or fundamentally distinct from religion found support across a relatively wide ideological spectrum. Key members of the oligarchic government as well as its critics, including Fukuzawa Yukichi,

Kume Kunitake, Inoue Kowashi, Motoda Nagazane, Sasaki Takayuki, and Mutsu Munemitsu (1844–1897), all expressed the view that Shinto did not belong in the classification of religion.[112] The concern to shield the imperial institution and the national polity combined with the increasing currency of religion as a category to create widespread assent among the political and intellectual elite that Shinto, however defined, would best be left outside of religion.

The central thrust of Shimaji's argument for Buddhist autonomy concerned the discrete social and political function of religion. Even as he pressed the case for distinguishing religion from political authority, Shimaji refused, therefore, to render religion superfluous or optional. Soon after the Ministry of Doctrine and the academy system was created, the prefectural government in Kyoto criticized the central government for relying too much on religion. The concern, specifically, was that under the Ministry of Doctrine the basic regulation of religion (appointment of clergy, creation of new shrines and temples, and so on) would be left in the hands of the religionists themselves, and local authorities would have little means to regulate them. The authorities in Kyoto, confronting a high concentration of prominent temples and shrines, wondered whether the Ministry of Doctrine could competently regulate from Tokyo the local actions of clerics. In addition to concerns specific to its jurisdiction, the prefecture questioned the utility of employing religion to aid government. In Europe the "King of Italy," the Kyoto government noted, had just "destroyed the authority of the pope," and Bismarck "worked to prevent religionists [*shūto*] from participating in governance." Why should the Japanese state pursue policies to the opposite effect? An attempt to mobilize Buddhism to counter Christianity, the prefecture warned, would either provoke conflict among the various sects [*kakushū ai arasou*] or would confuse the people. "Why," it asked, "should the government rely on irrational and false religion [*shūmon*] to teach and guide the people to protect and maintain the state?"[113] A corollary to this blanket rejection of religion, Kyoto prefecture proposed to exclude Shinto from the category of religion. Shimaji could not ignore the prefectural government's assertions that religion both was useless to governance and required strict oversight. Shimaji's response, Ketelaar explains, attempted "to constitute religion as a social institution on par with and yet distinct from organizations such as the government or the military. Service to one's religion would thus be seen as a legitimate social 'occupation.'"[114] Not only that, he insisted "religion" could be an effective means to "teach and guide the people." "Religion," Shimaji observed, "of course cannot be said to be harmless, but its benefits are also great."[115] The critique leveled by the Kyoto prefecture and

Shimaji's haste to rebuff it indicates the strategic liabilities from tactically embracing the category of religion as something distinct from the state. It could be rendered superfluous, even harmful, in contrast to necessary and public concerns such as education.

While Shimaji waged battle on many fronts against the marginalization of Buddhism qua religion, it was his campaign from the autumn of 1873 until early 1875 to withdraw the Shin sect from the Great Teaching Academy that yielded the desired result—Buddhist independence from the constraints of a Shinto-dominated institution. His initial petition to withdraw the Shin sect from the academy system summed up Buddhist grievances since the creation of the Ministry of Doctrine. The Great Teaching Academy at Zōjōji temple enshrined four *kami* and had all the appearances of a Shinto shrine. Officials at the academy, whether Buddhist or Shinto priests, had to employ Shinto protocols and preach only Shinto sermons.[116] There was no doubt that the academy system functioned to erase anything distinctly Buddhist by placing a Shinto veneer over it. With all temples converted into small teaching academies (*shōkyōin*), Shimaji feared they would eventually cease to be Buddhist at all. His argument for dismantling the academy system did not rely on Buddhist grievances alone, however. Erasing the differences between Shinto and Buddhism through a centralized academy system threatened to confuse the populace further, especially concerning the proper character of Shinto. Returning to an earlier theme, Shimaji observed that shrine priests had hitherto only conducted rituals directed toward the ancestors (*soshū no saishi wo tsukasadoru*). They had not yet created a body of teaching (*kyō*), which was why authorities through the centuries had relied on Buddhism and Confucianism to educate the populace. The problem, then, stemmed from replacing Buddhism with Shinto, and also from attempting to transform Shinto into a religion it had never been: "It is readily seen that a Shinto religion [*shinkyō*] did not exist in the ancient past."[117]

Not only should Buddhism not be subsumed under a deviant form of Shinto, Shimaji continued, but the state would be better served by recognizing a plurality of religious doctrines (excluding, of course, Christianity). Such a plurality would not threaten the state, because each doctrine would contribute to the welfare of the common whole. Different occupations and stations existed throughout the land, and each contributed to the strength of the entire nation. Likewise, given discrete autonomy, religions would contribute to the stability of the nation-state through their individual teachings. If, however, the Ministry of Doctrine and the academy system continued to turn the Three Standards of Instruction into a single religious doctrine, if "the teachings of the various religions [*kakushū*] are made one," it would herald the end of religion.[118] Shimaji appealed to the policies adopted by the government itself to support this point, arguing that the edicts separating Buddhism from Shinto were in fact the correct means to ensure that religion and political authority were not improperly confused. The Ministry of Doctrine undercut those policies, however, with its directives that effectively transformed Buddhist temples into Shinto shrines, thus returning to the "mixing" that the edicts had sought to correct. Shimaji reconceived the disassociation of Buddhism from Shinto, which had been so traumatic for the Buddhist establishment, into a new basis for Buddhist recognition and empowerment.

Shimaji refrained from detailing the precise character of Shinto as it related to the state, but he did repeat an increasingly familiar chorus: treating Shinto as a religion threatened the foundation of the state. As we have seen, at the root of that refrain was a conversation concerning how best to mold the populace in the image of a nation-state. As a subscribing member of the Meiroku Society, Shimaji would have been well aware of the debates and tensions produced by the intersection of a precariously theocratic imperial institution and the project to enlighten an ignorant populace. Directing and shaping the hearts of the people, of central concern to governance, proved treacherous when belief intervened: "If, claiming the original history of the opening of our country provides the basis for the imperial family, [the government] attempts to force the people to believe it, this would involve the authority of the court in attempting to control the people's hearts; this may prove a source of harm to the imperial house in the future."[119] By involving the state in the unstable realm of belief, a religious Shinto opened up the possibility of easy and open transgression. The only way to render state directives uniformly authoritative was to ensure their neutrality in regard to belief:

> I ask that what the court decrees be the standard for all people to follow, with not one who transgresses the decrees. If this is not the case, the only means of rectification is to transgress the decrees. Thus has religion [*kyōhō*] been mixed with the court's rule [*chōsei*]. By what law shall one who does not believe be ruled? It requires no argument that rule and religion [*seikyō*] should not be mixed. I ask that the court turn from its policy of treating religion as a toy.[120]

Government decrees belonged to "teachings of governance" (*chikyō*), while contestable belief belonged to "religion" (*shūkyō*). Thus, any solution required clarifying distinctions:

> We ask that the court swiftly perceive the source of harm and clarify the difference between teachings of governance and religion. What of-

> ficials execute should be teachings of governance . . . and what it teaches should have nothing to do with the hidden world or the afterlife. It should communicate the will of the court, the duties of the time, and accord with school education [*gakkō buiku*]. It is essential that disciplined and educated people not turn their backs upon it [*chikyō*].[121]

Calling for a strict distinction between religion and government decrees (or perhaps ideology), Shimaji turned his petition into a call for secular governance. The secular comes into focus only in its contrast to the religious.

The most successful critique leveled against the Ministry of Doctrine boiled down to two points: religion marked a discrete sphere of human life that the state cannot effectively regulate, and by granting autonomy to organized religions (i.e., Buddhism), the state could indirectly and more successfully guide the populace. Shimaji plainly made this point when he called religion the basis for "'a hundred governments" (*hyakusei no konpon*) because it could reach where the government could not—the hearts of the people. Shinto, primarily conceived as a body of standardized shrine rites that venerated politically significant ancestors, did not constitute a religion and should not be confused with one. By defining Buddhism as a private faith willing to serve the nation, if only given the autonomy to do so, Shimaji effectively subjectified religion as a category of administrative recognition by the state. That is to say, he rendered religion subjective (discrete and private) while also subjected to the nation-state. The idea of "subjectification" draws our attention to the way in which the claim for an authentic and self-determining religious identity that stands apart from state power actually presumes that power and responds to its demands. All subject positions are subjected to discourses and authorities that precede them. In the context of early-Meiji Japan, the subjectivity of the religious, to paraphrase Foucault, articulated itself on the already-begun political project of the Meiji state.[122] This was not, to be sure, a clear endorsement of religious freedom or even toleration, but rather a differentiation of roles played by religion and the state. Buddhism qua religion, in Shimaji's arguments, derived its legitimation from its contribution to governance. As a result, this articulation of the role and position of religion accorded with the discursive demands placed on Buddhism by the Meiji government and reflected modern modes of state sovereignty.

Scholars have repeatedly stressed the role Shimaji played in defining the boundary between religion and the state in the early-Meiji Japan. Most focus on Shimaji's use of a Shin sect doctrine called *shinzoku nitai*, or the division between absolute and relative truth; Buddhist dharma belongs to absolute truth, while political authority belongs to relative truth.

Shigaraki Takamaro, for example, argues that the doctrine of *shinzoku nitai* was developed in the early-modern period as a means to justify Shin sect acquiescence to Tokugawa rule.[123] The distinction Shimaji makes between religion and political authority, then, appears to be a natural extension of *shinzoku nitai*. Fujii Takeshi observes, though, that Shimaji employed the binary schema to remove Shinto from the picture. The basic early-modern distinction between the claims of Buddhist teaching and the claims of political authority is maintained, but Shinto is placed outside of that opposition, enabling the Shin sect to accommodate state rituals as nonreligious.[124] At the root of this analysis rests a narrative of Shin sect decline; at its inception, the Shin sect defied political authority, the narrative goes, but under the Tokugawa shogunate it acquiesced and forfeited the antisecularism characteristic of Buddhism.[125] As Ketelaar is quick to point out, such an analysis tends to idealize the origins of Shin sect Buddhism and reenacts a simplistic narrative of decline and decadence.[126] Significant continuities clearly exist between Tokugawa-era discourses concerning the relationship of Buddhism and political authority, and any claim of a radical, modern rupture would be facile.

At the same time, however, I want to stress the significantly modern features, or what Fukushima Kanryū calls the "active" (*sekkyokuteki*) character, of Shimaji's discourse.[127] First, the boundary he posits no longer separates political authority from Buddhism but rather political authority from religion, as a discrete and generic domain of private belief. Second, he justifies that boundary in relation to the effective operation of the imperial institution and national polity (*kokutai*). Religion must be rendered private and discrete precisely because the foundation of state authority must not be rendered an object of belief. These two features add up to a form of liberal logic similar to Vattel's legal theory. Defining state sovereignty (especially the effective exercise of that sovereignty) went hand in hand with defining "religion" as individual, private belief. The "subjectification," and hence reification, of religion occurs through and against modern forms of centralized state sovereignty.

Appeals to concepts derived from European precedents—the inviolability of private conscience, the discrete character of religion, and the separation of political authority from religion—provided a compelling argument for placing Shinto outside the realm of religion.[128] Indeed Shimaji, and Meiji Buddhists in general, relied on "'modern' discursive strategies of political and social efficacy" to secure their relevance and survival.[129] It is important, therefore, to pay attention to how the modern discourse of liberty and its relationship to foundations of political authority—in this case, the imperial institution—engendered complex complicities. Fujiwara

Masanobu suggests Shimaji succeeded in producing only a false religious liberty by insisting Shinto was not religious.[130] Whatever restrictions qualified the "liberty" that Shimaji pursued on behalf of Buddhism, we should not ignore the degree to which Shimaji's discourse mirrored the purportedly "enlightened" discourse of the Meiroku Society—freedom remained subservient to the demands of effective governance.

Shimaji's drive to withdraw the Shin sect from the academy system spanned three years and produced more than thirteen petitions and proposals (*kenpaku, kengensho*), two enquiries (*ukagaisho*), and thirty-four essays (*ronbun*).[131] The actual process through which the Shin sect achieved independence from the academy system naturally involved more than Shimaji's individual efforts. The six other Buddhist sects resisted Shin sect efforts and sought to maintain the academy system, compelling the Shin sect to frame the matter in terms of its own sectarian autonomy rather than a pan-Buddhist movement. The Shinto-leaning leadership of the Great Teaching Academy also sought to prevent the Buddhist sect from departing, but the premise of the academy's voluntary creation prevented an overt rejection of Shin sect requests.[132] The result was a slow but inevitable progression toward secession, which finally came about in May 1875.[133] The notice, issued by the Ministry of Doctrine, declared an end to joint Shinto and Buddhist proselytizing (*gappei fukyō*), and granted the superintendent of each sect the authority to open that sect's own academies (*kyōin*). The Council of State lifted the ban on cremations in the same month, further signaling the end of the anti-Buddhist policies adopted under the Great Teaching Academy.[134]

Reporting on the Shinshū departure from the Great Teaching Academy, the *Yomiuri shinbun* observed that this apparent victory came as the result of the sect's possessing many scholarly clerics capable of winning arguments.[135] The weight of words alone did not force the reluctant hands of the Ministry of Doctrine and Great Teaching Academy, however. Clearly, Shimaji and the Shin sect succeeded in synchronizing their interests with concerns present within the Meiji government itself. A hint of that concern can be seen in a letter Kido Takayoshi sent to Itō Hirobumi in early 1873. In it, Kido explained that he managed to convince Shishido Tamaki, then in charge of the Ministry of Doctrine, that there was no other choice for the government than to grant the freedom of belief.[136] Confirmed Shinto partisans from Satsuma were the only obstacle within the government to abolishing the ministry and granting a degree of liberty to religious belief, but Kido reported that he was slowly bringing one of them, Kuroda Kiyotaka (1840–1900), around to his view. Kido concluded his letter by reassuring Ito that he was keeping their decision to abolish the Ministry of Doctrine hidden for the time being.[137] In a subsequent letter to Itō, Kido discussed the need to reform the government and clarify "the great law upon which the nation is built" (*kenkoku no taihō*). To that end, Kido recommended eliminating and consolidating unnecessary state ministries and institutions, chief among them the Ministry of Doctrine, and proposed moving the regulation of shrines and temples into the Home Ministry.[138] Shimaji's petition drive provided the theoretical basis for promoting these envisioned reforms within the government.

Characterizing the demise of the academy system and its vision of doctrinal unity, James Ketelaar makes the following point: "The Meiji government's attempt to define the Other failed to recognize the sheer radicality of the Other—be it called 'Buddhism,' 'religion,' or 'culture'—and was finally unable to accommodate characteristics of true difference produced by their own system of definition."[139] The contradictions inherent in subsuming "the radicality of the Other" through a national doctrine had been recognized from the inception of the Ministry of the Doctrine. The Meiji leadership was aware of the impossibility of erasing all difference through an unmediated national doctrine, and had been since at least late 1871. The success of Shimaji and the Shin sect in withdrawing from the academy system suggests their articulation of a "subjectified" form of religion provided the best solution to a dilemma confronting the government—how to accommodate difference while placing the imperial institution beyond the operation of that difference.

The end of joint Shinto-Buddhist proselytizing under the academy system in 1875 left unresolved much of the ambivalence built into the Ministry of Doctrine, however. An editorial carried in the May 17 issue of the *Yomiuri* newspaper characterized the new development as a mere half-step toward clarifying the state's relationship to religion. Faith (*shinkō*), the editorial declared, did not exist to provide wealth or to answer wishes; rather, it was a means to "correct peoples' actions and help them join human society [*ningen no nakama iri*]." For this reason, it would be worthless to force someone of the Nichiren sect, for example, to listen to the teachings of the Shin sect. This was why belief must be made free, and why the government had abandoned efforts to combine the various Shinto sects. While the editorial clearly approved of the step, the question of who should control the appointment of doctrinal instructors remained unsettled: the superintendents of each sect, or the state? So long as the doctrinal instructor system remained in place, clerics remained officials of the state. The editorial, eschewing any direct criticism of the government, merely concluded with the observation that since the times were moving away from monarchy toward an elected assembly (*minsen giin*), the government could start listening more to the voice of the people.[140]

While the press noted the lingering ambivalences, the end of "joint proselytizing" threw those directly involved in the Ministry of Doctrine–doctrinal instructor–Great Teaching Academy triad into disarray. By late 1874, rumors of the Shin sect's departure from the academy system elicited anxious letters from regional doctrinal instructors demanding that the Great Teaching Academy clarify the matter.[141] Shortly after the formal secession of the Shin sect from the Great Teaching Academy, rumors spread that the Ministry of Doctrine itself would soon be abolished.[142] Although the Ministry of Doctrine continued to exist for two more years after the end of joint proselytizing, it was clear to all involved that it would no longer provide a framework through which a unified national doctrine could be promulgated. The Shin sect's departure from the academy system established a crucial precedent for the new principle that each sect (Buddhist or otherwise) and affiliated doctrinal instructors would fulfill their obligations to the state by preaching their own particular doctrines. How these particular—and in principle, private—doctrines would relate to the continued requirement to affirm the Three Standards of Instruction posed an immediate problem, however, and indicated a still porous boundary between religion as private belief, and political authority.

The Ministry of Doctrine attempted to clarify matters in November 1875 when it decreed how the superintendents, freed from the academy system, were to regulate their respective doctrinal instructors. This so-called "notice of the freedom of belief" (*shinkyō jiyū no kutatsu*) sought to indicate where the administrative reach of the state ended and the private jurisdiction of the sects began. Doctrinal instructors were to teach and direct the people according to their respective doctrines (*kakuji no kyōgi*), and superintendents were to oversee that doctrine and be responsible for its propagation.[143] Thus, although the state continued to administer exams to doctrinal instructors, it did not do so to evaluate the competence of the instructors in their respective doctrines (*sono shūgaku*). Rather, the state remained interested only in the "administrative protection" (*gyōseijō no hogo*) of the doctrinal instructors. "If religionists [*kyōhōka*] are granted the freedom of belief [*shinkyō no jiyū*] and receive administrative protection, they must recognize the will of the court, pay attention so as not to become a hindrance [*bōgai*] to politics, and work to guide the people into good and thus assist governance."[144] Tracing Shimaji Mokurai's argument, the freedom granted to religion was premised on its ability to assist governance. Needless to say, the freedom "guaranteed" in this declaration was limited to Shinto doctrinal instructors and the Buddhist sects, and was conditioned on their continued adherence to the Three Standards of Instruction. Significantly, the declaration recast the standards as an "administrative matter" that did not constitute a doctrine. Moreover, the Eleven Themes, with their overt Shinto theology, were no longer employed, and greater emphasis was placed on the Seventeen Themes.[145]

Even as it freed Buddhist sects from the stricture of the academy system, this "guarantee" of free belief did little to clarify the terms on which Buddhism and Shinto would intersect and compete with each other. In January 1876 the Ministry of Doctrine issued a notice seeking to reign in abuses stemming from the recently granted liberty to convert between sects (*tenshū/kaishiki*). The notice observed that this had led to unseemly competition among sects for the business of conducting funeral rites, and decreed that henceforth anyone switching sects was to notify the original sect and local authorities of their conversion.[146] Doctrinal confusion also remained a problem for some. One confused soul sought clarification in the press:

> Last year, on December 15, I attended a sermon given by the Izumo church, where I was told that one's soul [*tamashii*] is given by the *kami* and returns to the *kami* upon death. That made sense to me, but recently I attended another sermon at a temple where I was told that although one's soul is indeed given by the *kami*, there are originally two souls: one returns to the *kami* and the other goes to the Buddha, so unless you are buried with proper rites, you will be in trouble. These two teachings don't accord with each other. Can someone clarify the matter?[147]

The competition between Buddhist clerics and Shinto doctrinal instructors for adherents and their funeral rites continued unabated, and was likely exacerbated by the new independence of Buddhism. Absent any doctrinal and ritual practices standardized by the Ministry of Doctrine, the continued operation of the doctrinal instructor system merely sowed confusion.

Amid the shifting relations of state, Shinto, and Buddhism, the status of Christianity in Japan, too, remained ambiguous.[148] Shimaji, even while embracing the principle that religion served the state best when given autonomy, had noticeably excluded Christianity from the frame of his discussion. Meanwhile, three years had passed since the notice boards banning Christianity had been removed, and the government had issued no formal pronouncement concerning the status of the foreign faith. Even in its "guarantee of the freedom of belief," mention of Christianity was conspicuously absent. This undetermined state of affairs did not go unnoticed, and letters submitted to *Yomiuri*, the leading newspaper in Tokyo and Yokohama, in the spring of 1876 provide some indication of how the reading public in the capital region viewed the matter.[149] In a March 20 letter from a "resident of Yokohama," the writer began by observing the visible presence of Christianity in that treaty port; many missionaries were openly active there, and they were attracting many who were interested in the faith. The prefectural offices even closed on Christmas. These signs suggested to the writer that the Christian faith would eventually spread beyond the confines of the treaty port, while in other prefectures those seeking to practice or spread the faith were either jailed or driven off. It remained unclear whether the faith would be allowed or banned. The writer concluded: "If it is a good teaching they should quickly permit it; if it is bad, they should quickly ban it."[150] Responses to this letter were overwhelming, and in April the editors printed a front-page tally of the opinions sent to the paper. Approximately a third of the letters argued that the government remained silent because belief cannot be forced or prohibited, another third stated it would be acceptable to believe in Christianity, and the final third argued that the Japanese should not believe in it.[151] While these numbers do not constitute a representative poll by any means, they point to an urban public keenly interested in the fate of Christianity in Japan and generally skeptical about the state's ability to control matters of belief.

The absence of any formal recognition or regulation of Christianity certainly posed challenges for Japanese Christians, especially when it came to funeral rites. Conducting funerals remained the formal prerogative of doctrinal instructors licensed by the Ministry of Doctrine, and "private burials" were strictly forbidden. When one Japanese convert to Orthodox Christianity passed away and her husband asked the Russian Orthodox missionary Nikolai (1836–1912) to conduct her funeral, the resulting complications attracted notice. According to the newspaper report of the affair, Nikolai and the husband approached the family's hereditary parish temple, Enrinji, to request written permission to conduct a Christian burial and the priest refused. Only after they appealed through numerous bureaucratic channels was a provisional burial service by Nikolai allowed. The report concluded by observing how "inconvenient" the whole matter was.[152]

Given the prevailing state of affairs, few were surprised when the government moved to eliminate the Ministry of Doctrine entirely in 1877. Ironically, perhaps, the Council of the Left, which had played a central role in the creation of the ministry, also played a part in its demise. In a formal proposal to eliminate the ministry, submitted to the government in March 1875, the council suggested the ministry had failed, like the Department of Divinities and Missionary Office before it, because national laws could neither instill nor erase the faith of the people. The authority of the court could not rob the people of their Buddhist loyalties, and law could not control the sentiments of faith. In the face of these impossibilities, the government should abolish the Ministry of Doctrine, again placing all rites under the jurisdiction of the Bureau of Rites. Shrine priests should be directed to conduct the rites of their respective shrines and be free to preach (*sekkyō wa katte shidai*). The various religious sects (*shūshi*) should be left to the free belief of the people (*jinmin jiyū no shinkō*), and be required to uphold only two of the Three Standards of Instruction: revere the *kami* and love the nation, and serve the emperor and obey the laws. The Home Ministry would supervise both Buddhist and Shinto clerics.[153] Save for its affirmation of the two standards, the content of the proposal was strikingly similar to Kido's recommendations to Itō and suggests the Council of the Left was echoing the prevailing concerns within the government. Inundated by petitions echoing Shimaji's arguments, including a lengthy one by Ōuchi Seiran (1845–1918), the council had been signaling a gradual shift in its attitude toward religious liberty.[154] Compounded by the fact that the Council of the Left was significantly reorganized in February 1874, rendering it a more passive advisory organ to the executive core of the government, there is little reason to doubt that the proposal reflected the views of Kido and Itō.[155] More important, the proposal was a frank admission that the concerns that informed the creation of the Ministry of Doctrine remained unaddressed. By eliminating the Ministry of Doctrine and leaving Buddhist sects and shrine priests to the "faith of the people," the council called for inscribing a more explicit boundary between doctrine and state authority, a "separation of rule and doctrine" (*seikyō bunri*) that would complement the "separation of rite and doctrine" (*saikyō bunri*) that occurred three years earlier.

The Council of State formally closed the Ministry of Doctrine in January 1877 and transferred the regulation of temples and shrines to the newly created Shrine and Temple Bureau (Shaji kyoku) of the Home Ministry. This section would handle all bureaucratic regulation of Buddhist temples and Shinto shrines for the next twenty-three years, until it was split into the Shrine Bureau (Jinja kyoku) and Religion Bureau (Shūkyō kyoku) in 1900. Even though the end of the Ministry of Doctrine granted considerable autonomy to the Buddhist sects, the continued operation of the doctrinal instructor system until 1884 ensured that the state remained entangled in the regulation of clerical status. Only Buddhist clerics licensed as doctrinal instructors could be appointed abbots of temples (*jūshoku*); even formally ordained Buddhist priests or nuns had to be appointed as doctrinal instructors.[156] Shrine priests who were doctrinal instructors faced similar constraints; if they were to do more than conduct the rites of their shrines (proselytize, conduct funerals, and so on), they had to be licensed as doctrinal instructors. By requiring license from the state, the doctrinal instructor system provided the primary means by which Shinto doctrinal instructors could connect their proselytizing activities to the state, and it also created the appearance of a functional equivalence between Buddhist clerics and Shinto doctrinal instructors. With the government moving to separate doctrine from government by embracing the concept of religion as a sphere outside the direct purview of the state, the ungainly composition of Shinto, with shrine priests and "religionists" yoked together as doctrinal instructors, remained to be resolved. The need to distinguish between the religious and ritual activities of Shinto doctrinal instructors informed the ultimate discontinuation of the system, as we will see in Chapter 4.

Conclusion

The conceptual vocabulary of religion began to organize the policy debates of the Meiji government in the early 1870s. This was, in part, a result of the Iwakura Embassy's experiences abroad and the factional shifts within the government that left members of the embassy in positions of influence. The grammar of religion, what counted as religion, how it related to the state, the imperial institution, and the existing sectarian landscape of Japan remained ill-defined, however. The public discourse of the Meiroku Society helped disseminate the premise that religion existed as a discreet object of regulation. As a result, what had in 1871 been only a nascent conception of doctrine as a sphere to be separated from imperial rites assumed a more definite designation. Private, mutable belief came to be associated with religion, and while it could be valorized in contrast to superstition, if confused with the imperial institution, religious belief could threaten the integrity of the national project. Adopting religion as an organizing category, as the Meiroku Society's debates revealed, called for carefully distinguishing contingent religious belief from necessary claims to state sovereignty and national integration.

The Ministry of Doctrine, with its semiprivate doctrinal instructors and Great Teaching Academy, designated the front lines on which the administrative and regulatory implications of the grammar of religion were first contested. Specifically, Shimaji Mokurai's criticism of the ministry and its elevation of Shinto ambitions thrust claims about religion and its proper relationship to the state to fore. Celebrating the ability of religion to reach and shape the interior lives of the populace, Shimaji embraced the identification of Shin Buddhism as a proper religion. The utility of religion relied on the autonomy of its institutional expression, and thus the Shin sect called for the freedom to withdraw from the Great Teaching Academy and teach its own particular doctrines. This demand and its conceptual grounding conformed to the views of Kido Takayoshi and Itō Hirobumi within the government and received a positive hearing. In dismantling the Ministry of Doctrine and freeing the Buddhist sects and Shinto doctrinal instructors from the strictures of the Great Teaching Academy, the Meiji government also embraced the grammar of religion. From this point on, religion would be primarily administered as a privileged private belief and a regulated public practice. Following 1875, Buddhist sects served as archetypes for how the avowedly religious would be formally recognized and regulated by the state.

Applying this archetypal "separation of doctrine from rule" (*seikyō bunri*) beyond Buddhist sects proved a challenge that would not be resolved until the early 1880s. In the first place, Shimaji's celebration of religion as an autonomous sphere excluded Christianity and failed to resolve the question of whether the foundational posture of the state toward religion would be toleration or freedom. Well into the 1890s, Buddhist sectarians continued to aspire to a form of toleration that recognized Buddhism as the national religion of Japan. The diplomatic calculus of treaty revision continued to call for the full liberalization of Christianity and compelled the government to answer how Buddhism and Christianity would relate to the state and to each other as "religions," not as incommensurable rivals. Second, the separation of doctrine from rule in 1875 was accompanied by a broad consensus that Shinto was best placed in a conceptual and regulatory space distinct from religion. Yet the doctrinal instructor system had encouraged the growth of Shinto into an untidy amalgamation of shrine priests, clerics representing new religions, confraternities, and so on. Beyond the doctrinal and institutional confusion within Shinto, the combination of ritual and pastoral dimensions to the Shinto doctrinal instructors proved embarrassing to the government. Shrine priests conducted rites at their shrines that were synchronized with imperial rites, yet those very same priests might proselytize on behalf of a particular sect and even conduct funerary rites; the ill-defined role of Shinto clerics frustrated the separation of both rite from doctrine and doctrine from rule.

In sum, the category of religion began to structure policy debates in the first half of the 1870s. Frustrated by those debates and the entanglements they made visible, in the 1880s the government actively began to pursue what it called a "religious settlement."

CHAPTER 4

Seeking a "Religious Settlement," 1877–1884

> Many problems have already resulted from directly involving the government in religion. However, the benefits [of that involvement] are not yet apparent.
>
> —Yamagata Aritomo, 1884

> The foundation has been laid to prevent any religion from relating to national governance in the future.
>
> —Kitagaki Kunimichi, 1884

The closure of the Ministry of Doctrine in 1877 signaled the end of the Great Promulgation Campaign—or at least its premise of subjugating Buddhist sects within a Shinto-derived doctrine. Instead, Buddhist sects began to operate more as private, autonomous entities, administered by their respective superintendents. They did so in accordance with the discourse of subjectified religion put forward to great effect by Shimaji Mokurai, who argued for religion as an intensely subjective belief that serves the common good best when freed from state intervention—a position that suited the pragmatic priorities of the oligarchic leadership under Kido Takayoshi. How this construct of subjectified religion was to be translated into regulatory practice and applied beyond Buddhist sects to an as-yet amorphous Shinto practice and even to Christianity remained to be seen.

The outbreak of the Satsuma Rebellion a month after the Ministry of Doctrine was closed distracted the Meiji government from the matter of religion until the early 1880s, when the controversy known as the Pantheon Dispute (Saijin ronsō) and the Freedom and People's Rights Movement returned people's attention to the theocratic character of the imperial institution. Promising to produce a constitution and a representative assembly to deflect the *minken* movement, Itō Hirobumi and other key architects of the modern state engaged anew the matter of religion, apprehending it as the "greatest problem" confronting the state. The ease with which the imperial institution was criticized as theocratic, the intrasectarian disputes within the Shinto establishment, and the open sectarian tensions between Buddhists and Christians all compelled the government to pursue what it called a "religious settlement" by the mid-1880s.

The Japanese term *shobun*, translated here as settlement, carries with it the connotation of disposal, and it becomes clear that Itō Hirobumi, Inoue Kaoru, Yamagata Aritomo (1838–1922), and other key oligarchs set out to dispose of religion as a politically threatening category in Meiji Japan by applying the subjectified grammar of religion uniformly to all religions, thereby erecting a wall between private, sectarian concerns and the public domain of state authority. The pursuit of this settlement produced a number of corollary actions. First of all, the Home Ministry forced on Shinto its modern contours, administratively bifurcating it into Shinto shrines and their priests, who were to be state ritualists, and Shinto sects and their clerics, seen as private religionists. This division of Shinto, and the substantial diminishment in state support for shrines that accompanied it, placed the majority of shrines and their priests outside the scope of government attention and marked what Fridell and others have identified as Shinto's low point.[1] Second, by announcing the intent to regulate all religions uniformly, the settlement also exposed significant anxieties among Buddhist sectarians, who imagined Christianity would spread unchecked if Buddhism were not granted special recognition. Third, the settlement encouraged ideological formulations concerning the imperial institution, whether by the government or civilian ideologues, to explicitly disavow sectarian identification, setting the stage for the Imperial Rescript on Education and the increasing significance of state control over education.

In effect, the religious settlement pursued by the Meiji government in the mid-1880s attempted to place sectarian organizations outside the realm of politics by firmly associating them with private, individual belief and administering them indirectly, thus preventing them from "relating to national governance in the future."[2] Separating sectarian organizations from the political realm addressed not only diplomatic considerations but also the fear that sectarian conflicts, be it they intrasectarian disputes among Shinto clerics or potentially violent clashes between Buddhist adherents and Christian missionaries, would undermine the state. The settlement was by no means thorough or fully realized, to be sure, but it established the parameters by which the avowedly religious, as well as those who would be designated religious, could negotiate and challenge their participation in the constitutional politics inaugurated by the Imperial Diet in the 1890s.

Disputing a Pantheon, Adjudicating Shinto

The end of the Ministry of Doctrine in 1877 left in its wake the framework for increasingly autonomous Buddhist sects. The ministry's demise followed from a logic most forcibly put forward by Shimaji Mokurai and the Shin sect: religion, to be effective in supporting the nation-state, must be rendered discrete from the state. As Buddhist sects increasingly embraced this functional definition of religion, whether and how it would be applied to Shinto remained an open question. Arriving at an answer unavoidably revolved around the relationship of Shinto both to the construct of religion and to the state. While clarifying those relationships exposed schisms within the Shinto community, most among the intellectual and political elite preferred a Shinto neutered of religious pretensions.

Few outside observers believed Shinto was in fact, or should ever be, a religion. Writing in 1875, Fukuzawa Yukichi observed: "Of late, one hears Shinto mentioned, but borrowing a small amount of the monarchy's [*ōshitsu*] glory at the time of the Restoration, it mustered a very small movement. Only a temporary state of affairs allowed this to happen, and by my view, it [Shinto] is not a determined religion [*shūshi*]."[3] However, the "very small movement" of Shinto that Fukuzawa belittled did not disappear along with the Great Teaching Academy and the Ministry of Doctrine. In spite of those clear setbacks, Shinto partisans did not abandon efforts to determine a doctrinal and institutional framework for Shinto. Largely as a result of their continued efforts, the years between 1877 and 1882 proved pivotal for establishing the institutional and discursive posture of Shinto prior to the creation of the Imperial Diet. Under the Department of Divinities, then the Ministry of Doctrine, shrines, their priests, confraternities associated with prominent shrines (*kō*), Kokugaku ideologues, and even new religions redefined and realigned themselves under the vague rubric of Shinto. When those state institutions ceased to provide a focal point for the ill-fitting components of Shinto, tensions about definitions and orthodoxy and, ultimately, control over the Shinto enterprise erupted into public debate, principally in the form of an internecine conflict between factions aligned with the Grand Shrines of Ise and the Izumo Grand Shrine. That conflict took the form of the so-called Pantheon Dispute, a public dispute among competing Shinto factions that brought the question of religious definition directly to bear on Shinto. The state-mediated resolution of the dispute in early 1881 forced the Shinto establishment to address the question of whether or not it wanted to be recognized and treated as a religion.

When the secession of the Shin sect from the Great Teaching Academy appeared imminent in 1875, Soejima Taneomi (1828–1905), Tokoyo Nagatane, and others moved to create a new centralized institution to regulate Shinto doctrinal instructors.[4] In March they created the Bureau of Shinto Affairs (Shintō jimukyoku), which combined functions analogous to those of the head temple of a Buddhist sect and an institution administering doctrinal instructors.[5] Among Buddhist sects, the headquarters, or head temple, was often clearly defined, as in the case of the Honganji temples in Kyoto. Shinto, however, lacked a centralized sectarian hierarchy, except for the shrine ranks conferred by the imperial court and the credentialing roles once played by the Yoshida and Shirakawa houses. Designating a single shrine to be the headquarters of Shinto thus proved predictably contentious. At its creation, the Bureau of Shinto Affairs declared the Grand Shrines of Ise to be the "root of Shinto" (*shintō no konpon*) and appointed the head priest of Ise the superintendent for Shinto.[6] Placing Ise at the pinnacle of Shinto reflected the post-Restoration policy of reorganizing shrines into a centralized hierarchy with the imperial house at its apex, except that the bureau no longer possessed a direct institutional connection to the imperial house. Still, because it enshrined the imperial progenitrix Ise promised the best means to secure the identification of Shinto with the imperial state.

Even as it attempted to provide a unified framework for Shinto and thus to secure its institutional status, the Bureau of Shinto Affairs harbored significant divisions, owing to the heterogeneous composition of Shinto's clerics and their bifurcated regulatory treatment. First, although the bureau sought to provide an institutional representation of a unified Shinto, in reality the interests represented with the bureau operated at cross-purposes. Reforms introduced at the Grand Shrines of Ise soon after the Restoration removed the Watarai family from its hereditary positions of authority and attempted to shift popular focus from the outer Toyouke shrine to the inner shrine dedicated to the imperial progenitrix. These reforms allowed Tanaka Yoritsune (1836–1897) from Satsuma to organize the early-modern devotional confraternities into a sectarian organization, the Jingū-kyō. The Izumo Grand Shrine, which remained under the hereditary control of the Senge family, also organized its confraternities, into the Ōyashiro-kyō. Competition between these two dominant shrines within the bureau split the loyalties of Shinto doctrinal instructors. In addition to this rivalry, so-called new religions, ranging from shrine-based churches to those with charismatic founders, such as Kurozumi-kyō, were nominally aligned with the bureau but were by no means doctrinally or organizationally compliant.[7] Second, the Bureau of Shinto Affairs appeared caught between presenting Shinto as a sectarian religion on par with Buddhism and as a nonreligious entity that transcended the category of religion altogether. The presence of new religions and their churches (*kyōkai*) further complicated matters; the use of the ideogram *kyō* associated these elements with doctrine and the voluntary nature of the belief they preached. The bureau, in short, struggled to balance the advantages of autonomy attached to the category of religion (private belief) with the security and prestige promised by direct affiliation with the state.

These fault lines built into the Bureau of Shinto Affairs and its attempts to define Shinto are readily apparent in the bureau's efforts to secure state support for its activities. For example, it requested "special protection" (*tokushu hogo*) from the state so that Shinto could establish itself as a self-sustaining creed capable of competing with Buddhism and, by implication, Christianity. When Ōtori Sessō (1814–1904) petitioned Iwakura Tomomi on behalf of the bureau, he explained that Shinto was struggling, not because it lacked purity or goodness as a religion (*kyōhō*), but because a framework conducive to its development had not been created.[8] Calling the existing framework the "feeble efforts of a few individuals," he pleaded for the special protection of the government. Ōtori's proposed framework underscored the easy slippage between Shinto as a religion and Shinto as state rites. First, Ōtori proposed the bureau's superintendent of Shinto should appoint and promote priests at the elite imperial and national shrines, which were at that time monopolized by the state and kept out of the bureau's hands. The bifurcated character of Shinto clerics under the doctrinal instructor system informed Ōtori's request. For administrative purposes, shrine priests (*shinkan*) who served in imperial and national shrines and conducted the "rites of the state" were officials appointed by the state. Doctrinal instructors, on the other hand, were private "religionists" regulated by their respective superintendents. Many shrine priests, however, also served as doctrinal instructors, leaving them straddling the administrative distinction between state ritualists and private religionists. The Ministry of Doctrine treated shrine priests as officials of the state (*kanri*), while doctrinal instructors were treated according to the principle of separating rule and religion (*seikyō nizu*). When Buddhist sects were granted basic independence, doctrinal instructors were rendered private (*jinmin ni zokushimetaru*), creating a problem for shrine priests who were also doctrinal instructors. Priests attached to official shrines received financial support from the government for the conduct of rituals, but their activities as doctrinal instructors remained unfunded, apart from private sources of support.[9] Beyond the financial limitations, the administrative distinction between shrine priests and doctrinal instructors also undercut the Bureau of Shinto Affairs' ability to centralize control over a unified Shinto. With his petition, Ōtori sought to resolve this bifurcation by placing both shrine priests and doctrinal instructors under the administrative authority of the bureau. He insisted shrine priests and instructors, who shared the same essential character (*seishitsu*), should be no different from Buddhist clerics who were also doctrinal instructors. In other words, as Buddhist sects controlled the appointment and promotion of their own clerics among their temples, the bureau should be allowed to the do the same for all shrine priests.

Even as Ōtori and the bureau pressed for a level of administrative authority and autonomy analogous to that of Buddhist sects, they simultaneously sought to restore the privileged relationship of Shinto with the imperial institution. Ōtori's petition argued that the court should appoint the Shinto superintendent, in order to affirm the principle of imperial control over Shinto (*shugo tōkatsu no kiso*). Many petitions submitted by Shinto partisans repeated this plea to connect the imperial court to the Bureau of Shinto Affairs, specifically requesting that a member of the imperial family be made superintendent of Shinto (*shintō sōsai*). The head of Shinto, one petition insisted, should aid the emperor's personal ritual observances (*shinsai*) and govern all of Shinto.[10] Recognizing the government's attempts to separate governance, religion, and imperial rites, Ōtori observed that the government was adopting such principles only because they accorded with and benefited the national polities (*kokutai*) and religions of Europe and America. When applied to Japan's imperial polity and religions, he warned, those principles not only failed to provide any benefit to the throne but also threatened to harm the security of the nation. Ōtori further lamented that Shinto—the *religion* of the imperial nation—had come under sustained criticism and ridicule in the press due to the popularity of foreign ideas. In the face of such adversity, Ōtori feared Shinto might fragment into factions competing for converts unless the principle of "imperial control" was reaffirmed.[11] Ōtori's petition betrays no sense of contradiction in categorizing Shinto as a religion while fearing its descent into sectarian competition.

Ōtori's petition, and many others like it, gave voice to a clear sense of betrayal even while pleading for support from the government. The ambitious goal of creating a national doctrine and promulgating it through a government organ had been abandoned. In its efforts to administratively distinguish state rites (conducted by shrine priests) and doctrinal proselytizing (conducted by doctrinal instructors), the government had placed Shinto in a liminal position—as neither a full-fledged private religion nor a state creed. The solution proposed in Ōtori's petition, however, indicates the Bureau of Shinto Affairs wanted it both ways. The petition sought to consolidate control over a unified Shinto in the hands of the bureau, just as Buddhist sects were given basic autonomy over their internal affairs. At the same time, the petition called for a reinforced connection between the bureau and the imperial institution, effectively placing Shinto above Buddhism and all other "religions." Tanaka Yoritsune, Senge Takatomi, and others within the Bureau of Shinto Affairs conceived of Shinto in terms that transcended and contested the emerging construct of religion as private, individual belief discrete from political authority, even as they employed it to expand the definition and institutional scope of Shinto.[12] Constructing Shinto as a suprareligious entity in this way resisted the state's attempt to separate rites from doctrine. As a result, the discursive and institutional reach of Shinto imagined by the bureau far outstripped what the state officials envisioned. By maintaining the administrative distinction between shrine priests as officials of the state and doctrinal instructors as private religionists, and thus suggesting a potentially permanent divide between priests as public ritualists and doctrinal instructors as sectarian proselytizers, the government threatened the bureau's ambition to establish Shinto as the "Great Teaching" (*taikyō*) of the imperial nation.

The absence of significant financial support from the state had hampered Shinto ambitions ever since the Ministry of Doctrine was created in 1872. The need to secure financial support had not eased since the creation of the Bureau of Shinto Affairs, and the salaries and the number of priests at even the elite imperial and national shrines were reduced in late 1877. Tokoyo Nagatane complained that so long as shrine priests relied on a small state-subsidized salary for their ritual duties at a shrine, they could rarely devote any energy to proselytizing.[13] Raising money directly from the people was unattractive in principle because it undercut Shinto's unique position in relation to the imperial institution, and so, Ōtori explained, Shinto clerics should not stoop to solicit money from the people. Hence, Ōtori petitioned the government to issue a bond to finance Shinto proselytizing. The goal of the bureau and its doctrinal instructors, he wrote, was to "bring all people of the imperial nation [*kōkoku jinmin*] into the realm of our teaching [*waga kyōiki*]."[14] Absent significant government support, the only means to pursue that goal was to incorporate new religions and confraternities, along with their networks of adherents, into the Bureau of Shinto Affairs, and to rely on newly created "pastoral" elements in Shinto, such as funeral rites. The government flatly denied the request for a bond, and thus as Ōtori and the bureau sought to place Shinto above and beyond the petty realm of sectarian competition, the need to secure financial support led them to rely on precisely those elements most easily identified as "religious." Doing so, moreover, also meant that the Bureau of Shinto Affairs and its activities would only appear more problematic in the eyes of the government.

Under the Great Teaching Academy, Shinto partisans confronted the challenge of competing with Buddhist sects in raising funds. The Buddhists, especially the Shin sect, possessed the advantage of well-organized parish organizations capable of raising funds. To offset the Buddhist advantage, Shintoists recruited and co-opted folk and new religions, organizing them into *kōsha*, or confraternities.[15] Under the Ministry of Doctrine, forty-three confraternities were permitted to function as *kyōkai*, or churches.[16] These included shrine-based confraternities (such as Keishin-kō of the Izumo shrine, which became the Ōyashiro-kyō), mountain-based confraternities (such as Fuji-kō), and confraternities with charismatic founders (for example, Kurozumi-kō).[17] Beyond these confraternities, many of which grew out of Tokugawa-era practices and organizations, so-called new religions, for instance Konkō-kyō and Tenri-kyō, with their charismatic founders, also came to support such Shinto-controlled institutions as the Great Teaching Academy and the Bureau of Shinto Affairs. For many new religions, identifying themselves with Shinto and supporting the academy system and, later, the Bureau of Shinto Affairs, provided an opportunity to secure official recognition and a measure of public legitimacy. The state had issued a series of edicts criminalizing many popular spiritual practices, including prayer healing, divination, and mediums, making it difficult for many new groups to gain legal sanction to practice and proselytize.[18] The best solution for many was to identify as Shinto and thereby gain a connection to the state.[19] The struggles of these individual creeds to gain recognition mark a significant chapter in the history of "religion" in modern Japan.[20] Here, we note how elements later designated "sect Shinto" (*kyōha shintō*), in distinction to "shrine Shinto" (*jinja shintō*), were initially incorporated into Shinto under the Bureau of Shinto Affairs in the interest of financial self-sufficiency. The fact that Shinto doctrinal instructors included both shrine priests and clerics from potentially heterodox new religions and their churches makes the definition of Shinto during this period particularly ambiguous.

If the placement of churches and new religions under the umbrella of Shinto further obfuscated its definition and relation to the construct of religion, Shinto funerals further complicated matters. Shrine priests, who resented the requirement for Buddhist funeral rites, first advocated Shinto funerals during the Tokugawa period.[21] In 1868, the Meiji government permitted Shinto funerals, but only for shrine priests; this permission was extended to their entire households the following year.[22] Shinto funerals were not permitted extensively until the Ministry of Doctrine was created in 1872; in June of that year, shrine priests were granted permission to conduct funerals for any who requested such rites. Reflected in the fact that cremation was banned the following year, Shinto funerals were clearly intended to compete with Buddhist funeral rites. Initially, only shrine priests and Buddhist clerics were permitted to conduct funerals—the newly created doctrinal instructors were not permitted to do so until 1874.[23] When the Ministry of Doctrine decreed in July 1874 that the populace was free to choose between Shinto and the various Buddhist sects for funeral rites, a free market of sorts for funeral services emerged.[24] Shrine priests varied in their attitudes toward conducting funeral rites, however. Some resisted violating the traditional taboo against defilement, while others found the funeral rites to be an effective means of attracting believers and raising much-needed funds.[25] By the late 1870s, many of the shrine priests who were also doctrinal instructors operating under the Bureau of Shinto Affairs had come to depend on funeral rites as a source of income, and in some areas entire villages adopted the new rites in lieu of Buddhist rites.[26]

In sum, even though the Bureau of Shinto Affairs sought to position Shinto as a Great Teaching that transcended the category of religion, the need to secure financial support led it to behave like a religion in the eyes of many. The bureau oversaw the development of pastoral, as opposed to ritual, elements of Shinto, such as churches and funeral rites; the ritual practices of shrines such as Ise were increasingly connected to the pastoral activities of "churches," chief among them funeral rites. It was precisely this amalgamated form of Shinto that the head priest of the Grand Shrine of Ise, Tanaka Yoritsune, proudly promoted when he petitioned Iwakura Tomomi for "special attention" in June 1880. "The peoples' hearts are like water," he wrote—they would flow in any direction unless controlled with dikes and dams. Religion (*kyōhō*), Tanaka proposed, provided the most effective dikes and dams, and the state "should not lack religion for even one day." Shinto doctrinal instructors were developing churches throughout Japan and successfully winning the hearts of the people: "Truly, if we labor as today without ceasing, in a few years the state will not lack for support." The key to that support rested with the inseparable connection between revering the *kami* (*keishin*) and the *kokutai*; "One who understands the national polity will surely come to revere the *kami*, and if one comes to revere the *kami*, one will reach the domain of security [*anshin*]."[27] Tanaka's optimistic vision of a Shinto expanding through proselytizing belied the significant conflict that plagued the Bureau of Shinto Affairs.[28] The Pantheon Dispute that grew out of that conflict prompted the Meiji state to finally attempt a clear determination of how or whether Shinto would be treated as a religion.

The roots of the Pantheon Dispute of 1879–1880 can be traced back to theological disputes concerning the status of the afterlife, or hidden world (*kakureyo*), that plagued the Missionary Office and Department of Divinities after the Restoration.[29] More specifically, the dispute was triggered by Senge Takatomi (1845–1918), the head priest of the Grand Shrine of Izumo and leader of the Ōyashiro-kyō, when he requested that the tutelary *kami* of his shrine, Ōkuninushi-no-kami, be enshrined within the Bureau of Shinto Affairs. In effect, he asked that the bureau sanction the deity of his shrine and the teachings of his church as part of orthodox Shinto. The doctrine of the Izumo church, formulated by Senge, situated Amaterasu, the imperial progenitrix, as the ruler of the seen world, and recognized Ōkuninushi, enshrined in Izumo, to be the ruler of the hidden world—that is, the afterlife. The emperor ruled the seen world according to the mandate bestowed on him by Amaterasu, while Ōkuninushi ruled all who died and entered the unseen realm, mirroring in the afterlife the emperor's sovereignty.[30] In short, Izumo, with its doctrine of a hidden world ruled by Ōkuninushi-no-kami, provided a focus of Shinto veneration that distracted from—or at least diluted the singular importance of—Ise, where Amaterasu was enshrined. With the Bureau of Shinto Affairs dominated by Tanaka Yoritsune and others affiliated with the Grand Shrines of Ise, any effort to qualify its supremacy was inevitably rejected.[31] After his request that Ōkuninushi be enshrined within the new shrine constructed by the bureau was rejected in 1875, Senge continued to press his case in increasingly public forums.[32] The dispute reached its zenith in the spring and summer of 1880, and essays advocating both the Ise and Izumo positions were printed in the Shinto paper, *Kaichi shinbun*.[33] The dispute was public enough to attract the attention of the wider press; the pro-government *Tokyo Nichinichi shinbun*, for example, carried an editorial by Fukuchi Ōchi (1841–1906) on the issue, decrying the dispute for treating Shinto as though it were a religion. The state, Fukuchi observed, had never declared Shinto to be a religion (*shūkyō*) and had always employed it as a doctrine for governance (*chikyō*). Because religion concerned the afterlife and the bureau's dispute revolved around this, he declared the government should not dignify it by intervening.[34] Whether the government intervened or not, the dispute was principally understood to be an undignified religious controversy best confined to the private space of sectarian affairs.

The dispute quickly reached a stalemate, with the Ise faction controlling the leadership of the bureau and the Izumo faction attracting the sympathies of doctrinal instructors and shrine priests disaffected by the ascendance of Ise. By October, both factions were begging the government to intervene. Tokoyo Nagatane, Ochiai Naoaki (1827–1894), and other Shinto clerics petitioned Iwakura Tomomi on behalf of the Ise faction. Chiefly concerned that the dispute introduced the element of private, sectarian interests to Shinto, they denounced Senge's arguments as groundless and private (*shisetsu*), lacking any basis in the official and public orthodoxy of Shinto. His drive to include the *kami* of Izumo—carried out, they wrote, for purely selfish reasons—threatened to undermine Shinto, which was confronting "an age of free belief" (*shinkyō jiyū no meisei*). Were the debate allowed to continue, the petitioners feared that it "may come to affect the *kokutai*, or may provide an excuse for contemporary proponents of people's rights [*minkenronja*]" to press for a representative form of government. Notably, they anticipated the government would hesitate to intervene directly in the dispute: "We understand the reasons why the government has not directed which *kami* the doctrinal instructors should serve." Still, to put an end to private, sectarian interests, an "official determination of the truth or falsehood" of Senge's claims had to be made.[35] Pointing, as precedent, to political authorities' adjudications of Buddhist sectarian disputes, the petitioners pressed the government to clarify why it would refuse to act: "If, because the times are different, [the government] cannot rule on the foregoing matter, we request a clear indication of the reasons why."[36] Whether it determined the winner of the Pantheon Dispute or refused to adjudicate the dispute, the government was confronted with a demand for clarification.

The Izumo faction also petitioned Iwakura in October, making the case for including Ōkuninushi in the Shinto pantheon. Honjō Munetake (1846–1893), a former daimyo and chief priest of the Kono shrine, and Furukawa Miyuki (1810–1883), chief priest of Ōmiwa shrine, explained to Iwakura that the Ise faction had privatized the Bureau of Shinto Affairs, sacrificing the interests of Shinto as a whole for the parochial interests of Ise alone. From their perspective, the bureau was run by individuals out of touch with those most invested in successfully propagating Shinto, especially doctrinal instructors and regional shrines priests serving in lower-ranking shrines. What the Ise faction declared to be the public and orthodox shape of Shinto was an arbitrary creation, and the true contours of Shinto remained to be established. To avoid a private and arbitrary determination of Shinto, the petitioners argued, only the state could provide an official framework to resolve the dispute. That framework, moreover, should allow for the majority of shrine priests and doctrinal instructors to determine the shape of Shinto. They specifically requested that the home minister direct the Shrine and Temple Bureau to resolve the following issues by convening a Shinto convention (*shintō daikaigi*): the treatment of the Bureau of Shinto Affairs as a branch of Ise, the inclusion of Ōkuninushi in the pantheon, and the appointment of new, non-Ise-affiliated staff to the bureau.[37]

Between the public nature of the dispute and the repeated petitions, the government was effectively forced to intervene in the Pantheon Dispute. It fell to Sakurai Yoshikata (1844–1898), head of the Home Ministry Shrine and Temple Bureau, to design the intervention. Noting that the conflict between the two factions grew more intense by the day, Sakurai warned his superiors that the situation could even threaten the state if left unchecked. The Izumo faction was attracting radical followers and the Bureau of Shinto Affairs, controlled by the Ise faction, had declared a fiscal crisis. Thus even though the dispute appeared to concern only matters of doctrine, Shinto priests were not focusing on their ritual duties but, by involving themselves in this dispute, were instead "coming to affect the affairs of state." Concerned about politically mobilized Shinto priests, Sakurai recommended that the government intervene before the dispute could cause any direct harm to the state. He concluded that the authority to adjudicate doctrinal disputes, formerly invested in the minister of doctrine, had passed to the home minister in 1877, thus providing a legal basis for issuing a decree adjudicating the dispute. Matsukata Masayoshi, the home minister, agreed with Sakurai's assessment, emphasizing that "this matter relates to Shinto rites [*jingi*] and echoes through the foundations of the state." He ordered Sakurai to circulate his recommendations to all government ministers, asking the Council of State to approve a course of action.[38]

The means of settling the Pantheon Dispute that Sakurai proposed scrupulously avoided a direct edict from the state, much less from the emperor. Instead, he proposed ordering the Bureau of Shinto Affairs to hold a convention to establish internal regulations, regulations that would in turn provide the means for settling the doctrinal dispute. This was to become the Home Ministry's standard means of intervening in intrasectarian disputes, especially among Buddhist sects. Still, the semipublic, semiprivate character of shrine priests-cum–doctrinal instructors made balancing the private and public aspects of the convention a difficult proposition. Sakurai attempted to achieve that balance by recommending the appointment of a superintendent prior to the convention:

1. If the convention were to be convened first, it would be a private conference, and what is determined in private [*watakushi*] cannot be made law and applied to all doctrinal instructors. Therefore, the government should appoint a superintendent first; the convention can then be convened according to his proper authority.
2. The superintendent shall declare, under his authority, that the agenda will be determined by a majority.
3. Both factions will submit agendas for the convention, and the agenda will be put to a vote first.
4. The superintendent will be appointed according to the founding principles [*sōken taii*] of the Bureau of Shinto Affairs. This means the head priest of Ise will be appointed superintendent.[39]

If these measures were followed, Sakurai concluded, the Pantheon Dispute and the reform of the bureau would both be settled by majority votes at the convention and the government would not have to involve itself in any more details, although "some degree of government direction will be necessary" to resolve the matter, he acknowledged.[40]

The Council of State approved Sakurai's recommendations, and Matsukata announced a Shinto convention would be convened on January 25, 1881, to determine the appointment of a superintendent, the organization of the Bureau of Shinto Affairs, and the pantheon.[41] The declaration announced the government's willingness to intervene, but the premise of mediation also made clear that the doctrinal dispute would be treated essentially as a sectarian concern to be settled among Shinto doctrinal instructors. This posed a problem for the Shinto doctrinal instructors on two levels: if the dispute were settled by vote, it would create a precedent for treating Shinto as an autonomous (and even democratic) sect with little, if any, official relation to the state; not only that, the Izumo faction appeared likely to win any vote, threatening the primacy of Ise.[42] Partially to protect its position and partially to preserve a direct connection to the imperial institution, the Ise faction pushed to request an imperial edict that would settle the pantheon dispute *before* the convention.[43] A majority of doctrinal instructors came to support this initiative, largely because the doctrinal dispute itself proved more of a liability than any potential outcome of the dispute.[44] Rather than setting the precedent of a privately—that is, religiously—determined Shinto, an imperial edict would affirm the official and suprareligious character of Shinto. Senge Takatomi, as head priest of the Izumo shrine and leader of Ōyashiro-kyō, resisted the proposal to seek an imperial edict before the convention; his faction appeared to possess the upper hand and he could ill afford to reject an imperial edict if it ruled against Izumo. In the end even he could not resist the prevailing concern to preserve the appearance of a suprareligious Shinto. On January 29, 1881, representatives of the Bureau of Shinto Affairs formally requested an imperial edict adjudicating the Pantheon Dispute. This was forwarded from the Home Ministry to the Council of State; by refusing to resolve the matter by a vote, the Bureau of Shinto Affairs compelled the government to intervene directly in a doctrinal dispute concerning which *kami* the bureau should enshrine and worship.[45]

The Shinto convention began on January 31, only after its participants were satisfied that the government would issue an edict to settle the pantheon. One hundred eighteen Shinto doctrinal instructors attended the convention, which focused on the organizational bylaws that would govern the Bureau of Shinto Affairs. Of particular interest was an answer that Sakurai, representing the Home Ministry at the convention, gave to a question concerning the government's view of Shinto. Asked if the organizational bylaws proposed by the Home Ministry included all forms of Shinto activity, both ritual and proselytizing, Sakurai answered in the affirmative.[46] This suggests that, as of February 1881, the Home Ministry did not consider Shinto priests and doctrinal instructors to be separable; whether Shinto was to be religious or not, it was understood to include both the rites conducted at shrines and the proselytizing activities undertaken by the "churches." At this time, at least, the Shinto clerics and the government appear to have been in agreement regarding the scope, if not the character, of Shinto.

With the Shinto convention concluded, the government issued an official adjudication on February 23, 1881. The short decree, issued in the name of Sanjō Sanetomi, head of the Council of State, carefully avoided declaring an explicit winner to the dispute. It merely enumerated three points: (1) the *kami* enshrined *within* the imperial palace (the three imperial Deity Halls) could be worshiped from afar (*yōhai*); (2) Prince Takahito (1812–1886) was appointed superintendent of Shinto (*shintō sōsai*); and (3) Iwashita Masahira (1827–1900), a *genrōin* senate member from Satsuma, was appointed vice superintendent.[47] As Tokoyo Nagatane observed in 1884, although the decree did not explicitly favor either faction, because the Kashikodokoro Deity Hall within the imperial palace mirrored both the Ise shrine and the shrine within the Bureau of Shinto Affairs (that is, they all excluded Ōkuninushi), the Ise faction won the dispute by default.[48] At the same time, the ruling did not resoundingly affirm imperial jurisdiction over Shinto, as many had hoped it would, and few Shinto partisans were pleased.[49] Tellingly, Senge Takatomi and Tanaka Yoritsune, the primary antagonists in the Pantheon Dispute, soon afterward jointly petitioned the government to create a state department dedicated to Shinto alone (*daikyōkan*). Recognizing that the Bureau of Shinto Affairs had potentially lowered Shinto to the level of a religion, the two called for a state institution that would firmly place the Great Teaching above religion and in direct relation to the emperor.[50] The government had been reluctant to intervene in the Pantheon Dispute in the first place, and it was even less interested in overtly promoting Shinto in the wake of the dispute. In fact, following the Pantheon Dispute, the Home Ministry began to discuss a dramatic shift in how the state would regulate and relate to Shinto. That policy discussion and its outcome in early 1882 must also be understood in light of the rise of the Freedom and People's Rights Movement and the Crisis of 1881.

Directing the People's Hearts and Bisecting Shinto

By the late 1870s, the Freedom and People's Rights Movement had developed into a clear opposition movement critical of the oligarchic government, and policy debates within the government increasingly revolved around responses to the opposition movement. Educational policy proved one prominent focus for those debates. While the government had achieved some success in shaping elementary education, its control over middle and higher education remained less secure, with numerous private academies exercising considerable influence over political conversations. It was in this context that Motoda Nagazane, Confucian tutor to the emperor, authored an imperial statement on education (*kyōgaku seishi*) in July 1879 at the behest of Emperor Meiji.[51] The statement, internally presented by the emperor to Home Minister Itō Hirobumi and Education Minister Terashima Munenori, called for adopting an overtly Confucian doctrine as the cornerstone of school curricula, thereby instilling loyalty in the populace and defusing any potential for republican agitation. In the background of this statement stood attempts by the *jiho* (attendant advisers to the emperor), Motoda chief among them, to involve the emperor more directly in government affairs (the so-called *tennō shinsei undō*)—which meant allowing the *jiho* to participate in policy formation.[52] For Motoda and his colleagues, placing a doctrinal component at the center of education went hand in hand with placing the emperor at the executive center of national government.

The Choshū- and Satsuma-based oligarchy, which virtually monopolized the government and of which Motoda and the *jiho* were critical, was reluctant to allow the *jiho* to participate in the government. Motoda and the *jiho*, best labeled conservative, were critical of not only the progressive Freedom and People's Rights Movement but also the pragmatic modernism of the oligarchic leadership, represented by Itō. Itō was naturally reluctant to introduce an explicitly doctrinal component into the school curriculum. When Itō Hirobumi learned in September that Motoda, not the emperor, had been the author of the *kyōgaku seishi*, he quickly moved to rebut it. Drafted by Inoue Kowashi at Itō's behest, the rebuttal acknowledged the need to address the Freedom and People's Rights Movement and promoted an education policy robust enough to rein in popular agitation, yet restrained enough to appear enlightened and progressive.[53] Inoue blamed the rapid changes wrought by the Restoration for unsettling popular customs and discontenting the masses. The remedy to popular agitation lay in education, he asserted, for "the cause of these ills rests mainly in the failure of education [*kyōiku*]."[54] Only a firmly established education policy would rectify the situation, and Inoue suggested that such a policy, though not specifically defined, could be expected after a few more years of "civilizing" (*bunmei no ka*). He did, however, identify two pitfalls to be avoided in developing such a national education policy. First, students involved in higher education (*kōtō seito*) should not be enticed into political debate (*seidan*); they should study history, literature, and customs—the elements of the national structure. Elements of Kokugaku nativism, once cast out with the demise of the Ministry of Doctrine, were rehabilitated as fields of empirical scholarship, not theological speculation, and included in the frame of education.[55] Second, the government should avoid the mistake of "establishing a single national doctrine [*kokkyō*]," since this did not belong to a realm the state could successfully regulate. The government would have to wait for enlightened leaders capable of weighing all teachings, past and present, to establish such a doctrine.[56] Inoue's first pitfall clearly referred to the political instability that accompanied the push for popular representation, a push informed in large measure by the translation and circulation of European and American political theory in the burgeoning press.[57] The second, however, was aimed squarely at the conservative elements within the government and firmly rejected any move to establish a "national doctrine." In the eyes of Itō and Inoue, a formally adopted national doctrine was not an effective means to address the Freedom and People's Rights Movement. Rather, the memorial suggested that any attempt on the part of the government to implement such a doctrine would involve it in necessary failure and undercut its efforts to co-opt elements of the Freedom and People's Rights Movement.

Motoda countered Itō's rebuttal to the throne with a detailed commentary, the *Kyōikugi-fugi*, devoting a disproportionate amount of space to Inoue and Itō's rejection of a national doctrine. Motoda blamed the absence of Confucian education for the confusion and discontent evident among the masses. Although he agreed with the home minister that a suitable education policy was needed, he insisted texts for teaching ethics and customs should come from the Confucian classics, not from Western texts. As for formally establishing a national doctrine, Motoda insisted that it remained the emperor's prerogative to determine a doctrine for the nation. Such a doctrine need not be created anew, moreover; all that was called for was the respectful inheritance of the teachings handed down by the imperial ancestors (*sokun*), specifically, the moral values of benevolence (*jin*), righteousness (*gi*), loyalty (*chū*), and filial piety (*kō*). Whether the people (*jinmin*) believed in such a doctrine or not, though, would depend solely on whether they *believed* themselves to be subjects of the emperors. In short, whether a national doctrine "stood" or not depended on how deeply the people believed.[58] Motoda conceded that the state could not control the belief or disbelief of the people—"Buddhism has long since entered [this country], and Christianity is no longer prohibited." Clarifying and implementing a national doctrine (*kokkyō*) would have to rely on the absolute conviction and honest action (*kakushin tokkō*) of the emperor and his ministers. In the end, then, Motoda's confident call for a national doctrine returned to an anxious acknowledgment of the limits to state power when it came to matters of belief. Even as Motoda sought to distinguish Confucian precepts from religion (*shūkyō*), he still articulated his "national doctrine" in terms functionally analogous to religion in Europe.

The oligarchic core of the government not only rejected Motoda's push for a national doctrine but also abolished the position of *jiho* in October 1879. Motoda continued to lobby for an explicitly Confucian ideology in school curriculums in the years that followed, culminating in the 1890 Imperial Rescript on Education. That rescript, discussed in Chapter 5, explicitly situated its moral precepts and thus imperial authority in the realm of public duty, outside of private religious belief. But an intervening decade was required before the imperial institution could be confidently situated in relation to religion, and the early 1880s saw a considerable amount of debate concerning the desirability of a religious emperor. Itō Hirobumi's reluctance to involve the state in the business of national doctrines was understandable in light of how the theocratic nature of the imperial institution continued to be an object of easy critique.

In fact, in the wake of the Pantheon Dispute a debate concerning the religious nature of the emperor was waged on the pages of several prominent newspapers. At issue was where the Freedom and People's Rights Movement would locate sovereignty as it produced various draft constitutions.[59] The *Tokyo Nichinichi shinbun*, known for its pro-government editorial stance, initiated the debate with a March 26, 1881, editorial, likely by Fukuchi Ōchi, warning that any denial of the sacred (*shinsei*) and divine (*shinshu*) nature of the imperial office would ultimately lead to the abolition of the imperial institution itself, clearly a position too radical to be countenanced.[60] The editorial did not promote a specifically Shinto-based doctrine, but rather attempted to preempt public discussion of popular sovereignty by appealing to the transcendent origins of imperial sovereignty. Newspapers aligned with the Freedom and People's Rights Movement responded by questioning the wisdom of declaring the imperial office divine and sacred, suggesting that such a move would be far more destabilizing. An April 2 editorial in *Chōya shinbun*, for example, observed that if one were to ask why the emperor is divine and why his office is sacred, one could answer only tautologically: "It is divine because it is divine and sacred because it is sacred."[61] In short, the editorial concluded that insisting on a sacred emperor merely perpetuated primitive notions of authority that did not accord with constitutional monarchies.[62] The *Tokyo-Yohokama Mainichi shinbun*, affiliated with the Ōmeisha political association, echoed this line of argument five days later when its editors observed that appeals to a divine right to rule had not saved Charles I from regicide in seventeenth-century England, noting, "Because it was a wild and irrational theory, who would believe it?"[63] The debate continued through the month of April, but the central argument put forward by the *minken* papers foregrounded the threat that any insistence on a theocratic emperor posed to the institution itself. Proponents of the Freedom and People's Rights Movement considered any demand to view the emperor as divine and sacred to be a hallmark of autocratic regimes, and that such regimes inevitably incited the people to revolt. The best way to secure the loyalty and affection of the people, they warned, was to place the emperor within an enlightened constitutional framework.

Press censorship silenced such "progressive" arguments. When the *Tokyo Nichinichi shinbun* challenged its opponents to explain how they were not slighting the *kokutai* by insisting the emperor was not sacred, they could reply only that the limited scope for free expression prevented an open discussion of the issue. The institution of a lèse-majesté ordinance in January 1882 would further limit the scope of such discussion. Still, the Freedom and People's Rights Movement at its zenith reinforced the perception within and outside the government that the imperial institution had to be formally separated from religion. When the *Tokyo-Yokohama Mainichi shinbun* revisited the issue of the emperor and religion in December 1881, it warned that any monarchy relying on the force of religion to support itself would inevitably fail when human wisdom progressed and religion was exposed to be false.[64]

The decisive shift in the government's response to the Freedom and People's Rights Movement came with the Crisis of 1881. Internal division over the desirability and form of a constitutional government came to a head in March, when Ōkuma Shigenobu secretly recommended adopting a British form of constitutional monarchy. His call for the swift adoption of popular sovereignty destabilized the government, which was already struggling in its attempt to recover from Ōkubo Toshimichi's assassination in 1878. Three forces competed within the government at this time to shape the fundamental direction of the state: those seeking a more "progressive" constitutional order (Ōkuma Shigenobu), those seeking to further consolidate state authority (Itō Hirobumi), and conservatives within the court seeking to realize the ideals of direct imperial rule (Motoda Nagazane). As it tried to settle this internal struggle, the government was further rocked by the fallout from the questionable sale of government assets in Hokkaidō. Kuroda Kiyotaka, the head of the Hokkaido Colonization Commission (Hokkaidō kaitakushi), had arranged to sell government assets worth 14 million yen to a compatriot from Satsuma for merely 387,000 yen, payable over thirty years with no interest.[65] The public outrage over this sale, fanned by the press, caught the government off guard.

The Crisis of 1881 was forcibly brought to an end on the evening of October 11, when the three ministers of state (*daijin*) and seven out of the nine state councilors (*sangi*) met in the presence of the emperor. At this meeting it was decided that Ōkuma would be dismissed from his position as state councilor, the sale of government assets in Hokkaidō would be canceled, and an imperial rescript announcing the opening of a national assembly in 1890 would be issued.[66] The immediate result of the October 11 meeting was the emergence of Itō Hirobumi as the undisputed leader within the government. As his close adviser, Inoue Kowashi also cemented his position as a significant voice within the government. It was Inoue who proposed using an imperial rescript to effectively silence the Freedom and People's Rights Movement and its demand for a national assembly. By promising such an assembly while monopolizing the prerogative to craft the constitution, Inoue argued, the government could grant its critics a hollow victory.[67] At the same time, he proposed that the government develop the means to direct the people's hearts.

Inoue Kowashi's November 7 policy proposal "to instruct and direct the people's hearts" (*jinshin kyōdō ikenan*) explicitly identified a way to regain a sense of control over a populace agitated by the Freedom and People's Rights Movement. Inoue observed that the rescript promising a national assembly had bought the government some time, time in which mechanisms for guiding popular attitudes could be put in place. If the government failed, he warned, "the majority of people would fall into the hands [of extremists] and . . . there were be no means to correct the situation." At the heart of Inoue's proposal stood the firm belief that the populace could never be controlled by force. The way lay "not in covering the people's mouths, but in directing their hearts."[68] To that end, Inoue proposed five policies: (1) establish government-controlled newspapers at both the national and regional levels; (2) mobilize conservative *shizoku* (former samurai) to support the state at the regional level; (3) create regional middle and technical schools, to keep youth away from the capital (and its political associations); (4) encourage Confucianism (Kangaku) in the schools; and (5) promote German studies.[69] This policy paper was significant on many levels, especially in its overt call to replace French and English language training with German studies, but it is particularly noteworthy that as Inoue sought indirect means of influencing the populace, he made no references to religion, to Shinto, or to the imperial institution. His goal lay in discovering less overt and more effective means to "direct the peoples' hearts."

Given Inoue Kowashi's close ties to the Home Ministry, it is more than likely that he was aware of the policy discussions taking place within the ministry through 1881 concerning Shinto. As mentioned, the resolution of the Pantheon Dispute in early 1881 did not end deliberations over the administrative status of Shinto. The perceived vulnerability created by a religious Shinto had to be dealt with, especially in light of the government's efforts to shore up state authority in response to the Freedom and People's Rights Movement. Buddhist sects, fearful of any resurgence of Shinto ambitions, also maintained pressure on the government. The Shin sect, which had first promoted a religious Buddhism, in contrast to a nonreligious Shinto, petitioned Home Minister Matsukata in March, arguing that so long as the doctrinal instructor system continued to place Shinto and Buddhist priests in the same administrative category,

Shinto would be regarded a religion. Instead, doctrinal instructors should be abolished and Shinto must be clearly placed beyond the realm of religious competition so that "those who believe any religion cannot object [to Shinto], and all can revere and venerate it."[70] If Buddhism was to be officially recognized as a national religion, as many Buddhist clerics hoped it would be, Shinto had to be removed as a rival candidate.

Sakurai Yoshitaka, still the head of the Shrine and Temple Bureau, recommended the government consider the Shin sect's petition, given its "convincing argument."[71] Indeed, the Home Ministry appears to have advocated a more explicit separation of Shinto from religion, and Matsukata wrote to Sanjō Sanetomi in July that, "unless doctrine is separated from scholarship [as in Kokugaku], ritual, rule, and religion will remain mixed, resulting in administrative problems." By October the Home Ministry had drafted a proposed outline for reforming the regulation of Shinto and the "various religions" (*shokyō*). Its central purpose was to firmly separate aspects of Shinto closely associated with the state and imperial institution from the domain of religion. The first article in the proposal thus declared: "Rites [*shinsai*] shall be conducted by the state [*kokka*] while religion [*kyōhō*] shall be believed in by individuals and their households [*shinka*]."[72] To achieve this distinction, the proposal called for placing all regulation of shrine rites in the hands of the Bureau of Rites, a part of the imperial palace, and trimming the Shrine and Temple Bureau within the Home Ministry to just the Temple Bureau.

The government upheaval leading up to October 11 sidelined the Home Ministry's proposal, and new developments did not emerge until Yamada Akiyoshi (1844–1892) assumed the post of home minister on October 21. Inheriting his predecessor's concerns, Yamada informed Sanjō that it was no longer prudent to handle Buddhist and Shinto "religionists" (*shūkyōsha*) in the same fashion administratively—that is, as doctrinal instructors. Clearly referring to the Pantheon Dispute, Yamada explained that handling them the same way "has resulted in treating the *kami* enshrined by the court as objects of religious belief [*shūkyō honzon*] and has led to religious conflict." He recommended fully disassociating shrine priests (*shinkan*) from doctrinal instructors, and allowing only the latter to conduct funeral rites. Doing so would make it clear that only doctrinal instructors concerned themselves with soteriological issues of the soul's repose in the afterlife and were, therefore, "plain religionists" (*tanjun no shūkyōsha*). Doctrinal instructors who, under the Ministry of Doctrine, once served as semiofficial propagators of a national doctrine would be unambiguously designated private religionists in order to place Shinto shrines and their priests outside the administrative domain of religion.

Yamada concluded by observing that such a solution would "accord with the currents of the time" (*jisei ni tekishi*).[73]

These proposals having been approved by the Council of State, the Home Ministry issued the following ordinance on January 24, 1882: "Shinto priests [*shinkan*] will no longer serve jointly as doctrinal instructors and will not involve themselves in funeral rites." The ordinance, the culmination of the foregoing policy discussions, attempted to explicitly disassociate shrine priests as public liturgists (*kōmu wo shoben suru kan*) from doctrinal instructors as religionists (*shūkyōsha*). That distinction, however, was simultaneously qualified by a caveat that accompanied the order: "Shrine priests serving at prefectural shrines and below may continue as before for the time being."[74] This qualification came as the result of opposition by the Bureau of Shinto Affairs and its sympathizers within the government. It was, above all, an acknowledgment of the crucial financial role funeral rites played in post-Restoration Shinto.[75] The caveat notwithstanding, the order crystallized the divide between the state's approach to Shinto and the aspirations of the Shinto establishment represented by the Bureau of Shinto Affairs. By declaring the Grand Shrines of Ise, along with the elite imperial and national shrines, strictly nonreligious and regulating the doctrinal and pastoral efforts of the bureau as private religion, the state introduced a regulative divide between shrines and "sects" (*kyōha*).[76] The bureau, even as it rejected the premise that Shinto was a religion, consistently included both the liturgical (shrines) and the doctrinal/pastoral (churches) within its scope of Shinto. Unwilling to treat the overtly conversionary form of Shinto, with its funeral rites and competing church organizations, as a nonreligious extension of state authority, the government moved to bisect Shinto.

The legacy of this separation order is complex, in large measure because the Shinto establishment's approach to the question of religion was ambivalent to begin with (as it continues to be). Shinto partisans never constituted a united force during the Meiji period, and attitudes toward Shinto funeral rites were mixed from the outset.[77] Regulating shrine Shinto as a nonreligious and ritual extension of the imperial institution did provide channels of support for state shrines. The 1882 order, however, formally placed the so-called "civic shrines" (*minsha*) outside the scope of state support. Naturally, "it was a matter of great frustration for the priests of civic shrines that they and their shrines received no support from the national government."[78] This frustration provided the basis for the "victim narrative" noticeable in many postwar histories of modern Shinto: the Meiji government robbed Shinto of the ability to serve as a vibrant and developing focus of popular spirituality when it artificially cut off the centers of veneration (chiefly, Ise) from the pastoral activities of the various churches (*kyōkai*) and confraternities (*kōsha*). At the same time, as shrine priests continued to press for increased state support by appealing to the logic of the 1882 separation order, the utility of being placed above and beyond the category of religion could not be denied. One result of the order was that some Shinto partisans lobbied to extend the scope of nonreligious Shinto by separating all shrine priests from doctrinal instructors.[79]

Not all elements of Shinto possessed the option to formalize a direct relationship to the state, however, and in the wake of the order the already divided array of Shinto churches, confraternities, and new religions broke free from the Bureau of Shinto Affairs. On May 15, the Home Ministry acknowledged the independence of six Shinto "churches": the Jingū church, the Izumo Ōyashiro church, the Fuyō church, the Jikkō church, the Honkyō Taisei church, and the Shinshū church.[80] Where the role of shrine priests and doctrinal instructors overlapped, the recognition of independent Shinto sects forced difficult choices. Senge Takatomi, for example, had ceded his position as head priest at Izumo to his son and assumed the role of superintendent for Izumo Ōyashiro church in March. The legal separation of shrines from their confraternities and churches hampered the scope of activities available to many, but it also opened the way for new religions to gain recognition as sects of Shinto, including Konkōkyō and Tenrikyō. These operated as "subjectified" religions, much like the Buddhist sects, and gained a measure of autonomy previously unavailable to them.[81]

Placed in the context of the Crisis of 1881 and its aftermath, it becomes apparent that the government separated state shrines and their priests from the realm of "religion" in January 1882 largely as a defensive measure, not as a means to actively employ shrines as a prominent ideological device. The fact that a theocratic emperor and the Pantheon Dispute proved easy targets for a press critical of the government, combined with the formal commitment to draft a constitution, was enough to remind the oligarchic leadership of the potential pitfalls arising from employing Shinto as a legitimating device. Although they may have seen in Shinto "a tool useful in the legitimation of the political regime," they were far more interested in safeguarding the continued and increasing utility of the imperial institution itself.[82] The ordinance of 1882 reinscribed the imperative to secure the emperor from religion. Inoue Kowashi's proposed methods of controlling the people's hearts tellingly make no mention of Shinto or shrines. Shinto shrines, designated a nonreligious extension of the Japanese state, did come to serve as a significant forum for nationalizing rituals. How they would do so was by no means evident in 1882, however, and it took the emergence of a robust parliamentary system and two costly imperial wars for shrines and their priests to significantly rectify their reduced stature, a point we will return to in the next chapter.

In sum, Shinto, as it was imagined and pursued under the Bureau of Shinto Affairs, posed a problem for the government as it confronted the need to develop more effective means of directing the "people's hearts" and prepared for a constitutional order. By resisting a subjectified position for Shinto as a "private religion," the Bureau of Shinto Affairs frustrated efforts to place the imperial institution outside the realm of religious competition. The Pantheon Dispute and its aftermath coincided with a significant political crisis and resulted in the administrative separation of shrine Shinto from sect Shinto. That separation, moreover, is best understood as a defensive maneuver made by the state as it began the process of creating a constitutional form of government, which would expand the space of political participation beyond the confines of the oligarchy. The separation was less than complete, however, with priests at shrines at the prefectural level and below still allowed to conduct funeral rites. And even if the 1882 order managed to distinguish government shrines from Shinto sects, the continued operation of the doctrinal instructor system maintained some connection between the state and "religionists." To this mix must be added the continued ambiguity surrounding the status of Christianity—private funerals remained illegal, thus maintaining a de jure if not de facto ban against Christianity. As the government, led by Itō Hirobumi, moved toward drafting a constitution, the status of Christianity within Japan and its relation to renegotiating the unequal treaties surfaced again as a leading concern. The contours of how Buddhism and Shinto would relate to the state were sketched by early 1882, but the regulatory contours of Christianity remained undefined, and it would take a "religious settlement" to define them.

Rumors of Conversion

The Crisis of 1881 produced an imperial rescript promising a constitution and a national assembly by 1890. Visions of a British constitutional monarchy perished when Ōkuma Shigenobu was forced from the government, and they were replaced by a Prussian model, commensurate with Inoue Kowashi's proposed encouragement of German studies in Japan. The constitutional model of Prussia retained greater authority in the hands of the monarch and hence the state.[83] The government's position relative the Freedom and People's Rights Movement was already strengthened by the edict, which promised a constitution issued in the emperor's name, as a gift to the people; the government retained control over all aspects of drafting the constitution. At the center of that endeavor stood Itō Hirobumi, who traveled to Germany and Austria in the spring of 1882 to study constitutional law. Although the German influence on the Meiji constitution is a well-rehearsed point in modern Japanese history, the manner in which it addressed the problem of religion requires closer attention.[84]

While in Germany and Austria, Itō sought out the advice of Rudolf von Gneist (1816–1895), a professor at the University of Berlin, and Lorenz von Stein (1815–1890) of the University of Vienna. Among other significant topics, both men addressed the matter of how the constitution should deal with religion.[85] Gneist had already recommended to Aoki Shūzō, during his stay in Germany, that Japan adopt Buddhism as its national faith, and he repeated the advice to Itō.[86] Stein, by contrast, reportedly advised Itō against formally adopting a national creed but did emphasize the need to retain state control over religion.[87] Moreover, Stein's opposition to a state creed does not appear to have been a principled one, as he later recommended the adoption of Shinto as a national creed to Maruyama Sakura (1840–1899) and Kaeda Nobuyoshi (1832–1908) in 1887.[88] Gneist and Stein held in common the firm conviction that any legal system had to be an organic outgrowth of a given polity's history; for that reason, both men impressed on Itō the need to formulate a constitution compatible with the historical peculiarities of the Japanese polity. In Gneist's case, this meant adopting Buddhism as a state creed; for Stein, this meant, at a minimum, retaining a significant symbolic role for Shinto.

Itō received a very different message from the politicians and aristocrats he met during his stay in Europe. In a letter to Matsukata Masayoshi, then finance minister, Itō observed that German elites, particularly the aristocrats he came into contact with, would never accept Japan as a civilized nation unless Christianity was given a prominent place there. He referred specifically to a conversation with Prince Charles Anthony of Hohenzollern-Sigmaringen (1811–1885), former prime minister of Prussia. Though praising the impressive progress Japan had made since the Restoration, the prince noted that there remained one "obstacle" to further progress and asked Itō what his government intended to do about the matter. Itō wrote that he understood the prince to mean that if Christianity were not officially tolerated, "true civilization would be difficult to achieve." Itō deflected the question, suggesting that so long as the matter followed the direction of the people's hearts, it should not be terribly difficult to resolve. He observed in his letter to Matsukata that among the members of the upper classes of Europe, eight or nine out of ten were fervently religious, believing religion to be the best means to rule their country's subjects. Even though scientists (*rigakusha*) were calling religion into question, he wrote, they could do nothing about the fact that society currently "lives in the atmosphere of religion."[89] The subject of religion was raised again in a subsequent conversation with the kaiser's brother-in-law, Karl Alexander August Johann, Grand Duke of Saxony (1818–1901). With Itō as Japan's proxy, an aristocratic Christian Europe was interrogating a non-Christian Japan.

"Nothing other than the difference of race and religion," Itō concluded, explained how the yardstick of civilization was applied to countries. Why was it that Bulgaria, Serbia, Montenegro, and Romania—nations "no different than wild monkeys in the mountains"—are deemed civilized and independent nations (*bunmei dokuritsu no ikkoku*)? The answer: "The so-called civilization and morality of Europe applies only among Christians; there is no honest desire to grant them to heathens [*ikyō no hito*]."[90] The lesson, as far as Itō was concerned, was unmistakable; only by adopting Christianity in a prominent way could Japan hope to win the sympathetic recognition of Europe, the Christian West. Without that sympathy, Japan could not expect the ideals of international law and justice to be applied, and its quest to revise the unequal treaties would most likely fail.

The cultural politics of Christianity on the diplomatic stage, largely dormant since the conclusion of the Urakami Incident in 1873, emerged once again and confronted Itō with a dilemma in drafting the constitution: either adopt a state creed rooted in Japanese history, such as Buddhism, and pursue a policy of tolerance, or avoid a state creed altogether and formally pursue religious neutrality.[91] If he were to heed Gneist's advice and establish Buddhism as the state religion, he would constitutionally confirm Japan's status as a non-Christian and heathen nation. If, on the other hand, he adopted religious neutrality as a constitutional principle, the imperial institution and its mythic foundation would attract easy criticism and potential rejection. This dilemma had already been confronted in embryonic form during the early 1870s in the Meiroku Society's debates, but Itō's constitutional research brought it out of the realm of hypothetical debate and into the realm of political decision. While Itō did not announce his intended solution to the dilemma while he was abroad, his earlier rejection of an overt national doctrine suggests he was never interested in establishing either Buddhism or Shinto as the official religion of the Empire of Japan.

Ironically, Itō was forced to deal with a rumor that he favored a far more radical solution to the question of how the Meiji state would relate to religion. After his return from Germany in August 1883, Itō was dogged by the rumor that he had converted to Christianity while abroad and was planning to convert the emperor, if not all of Japan. A prominent basis for this rumor was furnished by the *New York Herald*, which carried a short report entitled "Japanese Converts":

> One of the most prominent men in Japan is Mr. Ito Hirobumi. He has just recently returned from a long stay in Germany, where he saw much of Bismarck and Emperor William. Mr. Ito was much impressed with the character of these men, both of whom, he says, advised him to accept Christianity for his own welfare and happiness, as well as for the good of his country. Since his return, he has formally addressed the Mikado on the subject; and such has been the influence of his report, that the chief officers of the Cabinet are becoming interested in the study of Christianity.[92]

The report, the source of which is unknown, was carried by a Japanese press happy to attack the most prominent oligarch. The *Marumaru chinbun* satirized Itō's rumored conversion in its May 31, 1884 issue with a cartoon employing obscure visual puns. Perceiving the potential for political damage from this rumor and the satire it produced, Itō demanded the censure of *Marumaru chinbun*. He denied ever "entering that religion myself" in his complaint to the police censor.[93] While Itō never adopted the Christian faith, evidence suggests he returned from Europe determined to formally permit its free exercise in Japan; his efforts to do so may account for the persistence of the rumors. In fact, it was clear to many observers in 1884 that the government was preparing to alter significantly its regulatory treatment of religion and Christianity.

Rumors of Christian conversions circulated within the government as well. In February 1884, Mutsu Munemitsu reportedly advanced the argument that the "sympathy" (*shinpasê*) of the "Western nations" would need to be won in order for Japan to recover full sovereignty and achieve parity. Converting the nation to Christianity, Mutsu was rumored to have argued, would provide the best means of winning that sympathy.[94] The call to convert to Christianity on a national scale, however expedient, alarmed many within the government. Ozaki Saburō (1842–1881), secretary to the Privy Council, met with Higashikuze Michitomi and Miura Yasushi (1829–1910), both members of the council, on April 30 to discuss the rumor that the government would soon officially establish Christianity as the national religion (*kokkyō*). That influential members of the government appeared to be promoting the plan added a measure of veracity to the rumor. Even if adopting Christianity would aid the cause of treaty revision, Ozaki and his colleagues feared that the government would first have to kill tens of thousands sectarians in order to implement such a plan.

Although the plan to convert the nation was attributed to statements made by Mutsu Munemitsu, it was believed that Itō Hirobumi stood behind them. When Ozaki confronted Itō about the rumors on May 16, Itō denied outright any connections between Mutsu's statements and his own position on the matter; instead, Itō accused Ozaki of spreading the rumor. Ozaki pointed out that the government was funding Mutsu's planned travels to Europe, implying that Itō was rewarding him for serving as a spokesman. Itō reportedly responded emphatically:

> Mutsu's own argument is in no way the government's position. Aside from the personal veneration [*shinsai*] of its ancestors, our imperial family has no religion [*shūshi*]. It is not even clear whether this veneration could be called a religion; in any case, it is completely different from what the foreign nations call religion. The only policy that we can adopt is for the imperial family to maintain its several-thousand-years-old customs [*kanshū*] and not interfere at all in the religion of the people.[95]

This answer reaffirmed the principles set forth in the 1882 separation order and apparently satisfied Ozaki. It is clear from other statements that Itō comprehended the need to fundamentally disassociate the imperial institution from sectarian identifications. He explained the difficulty confronting the state in a letter sent to Yamagata Aritomo in July: "However, in order to maintain the scope of opening the country, we can no longer criminalize and prosecute those within the nation who become ardent followers of various religions." As a result, the imperial institution must not be affiliated with either Buddhism or Christianity, he maintained.[96] Itō's position as he set about drafting the constitution is strikingly similar to the postwar constitutional treatment of the imperial household and its ritual observances, wherein the emperor participates in the personal and private veneration of his ancestors. Whatever treatment of Christianity Itō had in mind presumed the conceit of a religiously neutral imperial institution.

While any plan to convert en masse to Christianity was disavowed within the government, the unsettled status of Christianity did cast a cloud over attempts to revise the unequal treaties. Inoue Kaoru, then foreign minister, believed that the diplomatic representations made by the government were repeatedly undermined by domestic politics. He submitted a policy paper to the cabinet in July 1884, demanding that diplomatic concerns be reflected in domestic policies, most particularly policies concerning religion. Renegotiating the unequal treaties, Inoue stressed, was the "most urgent diplomatic concern for our nation," and the unsettled regulatory treatment of Christianity impeded those negotiations. Like Mutsu, Inoue emphasized the importance of securing the trust of the treaty powers, insisting that in order to do so the government must determine a diplomatic policy that is implemented across the entire government.[97] Above all else, Inoue feared that apparent divisions within the government would prevent him from securing the trust of the treaty powers.

In referring to divisions within the government, Inoue was pointing specifically to divisions over the treatment of religion and Christianity. He noted that among the various political associations forming at the regional level, some had organized around religious or moral causes and were actively attacking Christianity. The Kiyūkai (Apprehension Society) and the Myōdō kyōkai (Society for Illuminating the Way), for example, were both founded in the early 1880s, counted more than ten thousand members, and were continuing to grow. Both societies sought to defend against pernicious foreign currents of thought, especially Christianity, and, Inoue suggested, advocated *jōi*, or the expulsion of all foreign influence. The foreign minister reminded the cabinet that the government had maintained an open-country policy as the cornerstone of its diplomacy since the Restoration, and said that any contradiction of that policy would undermine its credibility abroad. The Kiyūkai and Myōdō kyōkai counted regional and court officials among their membership, creating the appearance that the government was not necessarily committed to diplomatically declared state policies. As proof of his concerns, Inoue reported that members of the Kiyūkai had already publicly confronted Christian missionaries, actively hindering their proselytizing efforts. Incidents of violence had been reported in the Kyoto area and it appeared it would be only a matter of time before deaths would result. Inoue warned that "when foreigners see those serving in significant positions and important offices calling for and praising such actions, they would not be without reason to believe our government to be aiding and directing such groups." Simply put, he wrote, "If ever a missionary were to be harmed or even killed, the goal of negotiating treaty revisions would be lost and the hope of recovering legal jurisdiction severed."[98]

Diplomatic expedience and domestic agitation thus converged at the status of Christianity in Japan. Invoking the Urakami Incident, Inoue reminded his colleagues that "relations among Christians are a very important [diplomatic] matter, and if we were to mistake our treatment once, the resulting difficulties would be unpredictable." He noted that the pretext of aiding persecuted Catholic missionaries had allowed the French to steadily increase their hold over Vietnam, culminating in what would become the Sino-French War in the summer of 1884. Besides, Inoue asked, how could the tide of Christianity be stemmed in the first place? The Western nations were Christian nations; the people of those nations were Christian, and thus the foreigners who instructed Japanese students in Japanese universities were also Christians. The institutions and laws that the government was in the process of adapting were first developed in Christian nations. "Therefore, to now take only the civilization and reject Christianity alone is impossible."[99] The status of Christianity in Japan had already resulted in diplomatic complications, but those complications had remained manageable so far, thanks largely to diplomatic promises of future liberalization. If the government were to put off establishing a clear national policy regarding Christianity, Inoue cautioned, greater and far less manageable complications might result.[100] The promises of liberalization made to the treaty powers and the silent toleration (*mokkyo*) of Christianity had produced a status quo in which the state's legal treatment of Christianity no longer corresponded to the facts on the ground; missionaries were winning more converts by the day, and the government was taking no action to prevent the spread of Christianity. Without a formal declaration legalizing the practice of Christianity, conservative elements within the government would continue to use organizations outside of the government's control, such as the Kiyūkai, to resist the inevitable spread of Christianity. Fearing his proposal might be equated with Mutsu's radical call for mass conversion, Inoue did not forget to include the following caveat: "However, I do not believe in Christianity and do not advocate on its behalf."[101]

Instead of advocating special treatment for Christianity, Inoue called for defining the state's regulatory relation to religion in uniform terms. Reviewing the treatment of Buddhism and Shinto, Inoue wrote: "Until now in our country, the government has created offices [to regulate] religious organizations [*shūkyō no soshiki*] and has intervened in appointing and promoting their clergy, even bestowing special privileges and treating them as though they were a state religion [*kokkyō*]." Given this precedent, if the government allowed the free practice of Christianity while maintaining its direct regulation of Buddhism and Shinto (the doctrinal instructor system), Buddhist and Shinto clerics might well complain that Christians were enjoying greater freedom. Moreover, if the regulative treatment of Buddhism, Shinto, and Christianity were not uniform, rumors that

Christianity would be made the national religion might again arise. Inoue thus recommended that the cabinet create a single regulatory framework within which the state would permit the free exercise of religion without privileging one creed over any other. He appealed to examples provided by Britain and other nations, where the selection of one religion over others for preferential treatment resulted in political difficulties (*seijijō no konnan*). If Japan was to avoid the same political (not to mention diplomatic) difficulties, "there [would be] no better path than for the government to bestow the same liberties to all religions from the beginning."[102]

In practical terms, this meant lifting the ban on private burials (that is, permitting Christian burials) and devising uniform regulations for religion (*shūmon no toriatsukai*). Requesting the speedy adoption of a clear and uniform policy on this matter, Inoue concluded his proposal with a specific agenda for the cabinet to consider:

1. The government, enacting the principles of imperial rescripts since the Restoration, will adopt the policy of open progress [*kaishin no shugi*] in determining its diplomatic strategies [*gaikō seiryaku*].
2. The government will determine its diplomatic strategies with the understanding that Christianity will not be prohibited.
3. Once the government determines its diplomatic strategies, all officials are to recognize them and not act in a manner that would betray those strategies.
4. The method of handling religion in general [*shūkyō ippan*] will be determined.[103]

Inoue translated the basic lesson Itō had learned in Europe into a policy proposal: If Japan could regain full sovereignty only by becoming the first Asian country to adopt Western civilization, then the only prudent choice was to permit the free exercise of the Christian faith. Unlike Mutsu's unrealistic call for mass conversion to Christianity, however, Inoue proposed the pragmatic solution of casting the state as religiously neutral, neither pro-Christian nor anti-Christian. To this point, the government had organized religious regulations in a piecemeal fashion, as it first disestablished Buddhism then began disentangling the imperial institution from the liabilities of the Great Promulgation Campaign. As a result, the Home Ministry's Shrine and Temple Bureau regulated Shinto shrines, Shinto sects, and Buddhist sects, each according to different administrative categories and precedents. In contrast, the creation of a generic Religion Bureau promised the potential of transposing those multiple regulatory efforts into a uniform administrative approach to religion in general, making it easier to incorporate Christianity without appearing to endorse it or subjugate it to other religions. The foreign minister's call to regulate religion in uniform terms clearly articulated the grammar of religion employed by the architects of the modern Japanese state. Creating uniformity, and its corollary, neutrality, in the state's regulation of religions would not come easily, however.

Settling the "Greatest Problem"

Clearly, the foreign minister's policy paper did not emerge from a vacuum. Itō Hirobumi and other leaders within the government shared the belief that a general religious settlement (*shūkyō shobun*) was required to address both diplomatic and domestic concerns. Any settlement, it was understood, would entail the legalization of Christianity and the abolition of the doctrinal instructor system, the final vestige of the project to promulgate a national doctrine. By 1884 the system functioned merely to confer a small measure of state recognition on Buddhist and Shinto clerics. Nonetheless, the government confronted a surge in sectarian conflict and internal dissent through the summer of 1884, as it prepared to abolish the system in the name of a religious settlement. As Buddhist, Shinto, and conservative voices sought to dissuade the government from legalizing Christianity, the specter of Christian conversion and the accompanying social fragmentation was raised anew.

Inoue Kaoru did not exaggerate when he cited incidents of religious conflict. During the early 1880s many believed in the inevitable ascendance of Protestant Christianity in Japan. The press widely reported on a national convention of Christian converts in 1881, along with the opinion that Japan would be fully Christianized within twenty years.[104] In April 1884, press reports counting more than 62,000 Christians in Japan contributed to the impression of a rapidly growing movement.[105] Combined with rumors of government support for Christianity (if not outright conversion to it), groups opposing the spread of Christianity grew increasingly agitated through the early 1880s. The press during this time is full of reports of Christian speeches violently disrupted by opposition groups, often led by Buddhist clerics, and local police being called on to protect the Christian speakers from physical harm. In one such incident, more than 300 Buddhist clerics and adherents disrupted a Christian evangelical meeting in Kyoto.[106] Rumors that the government was planning a "great change in how it handles religion," including the possibility that the government would itself actively promote Christianity, circulated during the summer months of 1884, adding to the perception of heightened sectarian tensions.[107] At the same time, all sides appeared to agree on one point: they assumed that once legalized, Christianity would inevitably overwhelm Buddhism and Shinto and emerge as the dominant religion in Japan. The specter of Christian conversion remained easy to invoke.

Organizations opposing Christianity that Inoue identified expanded rapidly against this backdrop, fueling the "religious friction." The Kiyūkai, for example, was founded in 1884 in Nagasaki, where the Urakami Incident occurred, and developed into a national organization pursing three declared goals for its members: to revere the will of the court and discharge one's duty as a national citizen (*kokumin*); to recover morality (*dōtoku*) and work to secure and strengthen the nation; and to prevent the spread of the evil doctrine.[108] The Myōdō kyōkai caused the greatest headache for the Meiji government because its leadership included government officials who were critical of the "civilization and enlightenment" promoted by the oligarchs. Founded in Tokyo in January 1884, the Myōdō kyōkai was a predominantly Buddhist organization, in which Imperial Army general Torio Koyata (1847–1905) served as chairman and court chamberlain Yamaoka Tesshū (1836–1888) served as vice chairman.[109] With government officials such as these working to prevent the spread of Christianity in Japan, the treaty powers may well have believed the government approved of such activities. Itō Hirobumi wrote to Matsukata in July, warning him that "Torio's teaching and agitation is enough to significantly misdirect Buddhists."[110] The concern that Buddhist sectarians might "generate sentiments of aversion toward Christianity" prompted the vice minister of the Home Ministry, Hijikata Hisamoto (1833–1918) to personally denounce the Myōdō kyōkai in front of assembled Zen leaders in March 1884.[111] The governor of Kyoto, Kitagaki Kunimichi (1835–1916), also pressed Buddhist superintendents in July, instructing them to avoid violent conflict with Christians. He admonished them to keep the larger political picture in mind, especially since diplomacy would only increase in importance as the government moved closer to treaty revision.[112] The governor reminded them, as loyal subjects whose sectarian interests were to be subjected to the nation-state's interests, to direct their clerics and adherents to refrain from violent confrontations.

Addressing the role of government officials within the society was a more delicate matter. In a letter to Yamagata, Itō reported that he had discussed the public agitation over religious debates with Tani Tateki (1837–1911), another conservative critic of the oligarchs within the government. Itō impressed upon Tani the impossibility of criminalizing the religious identifications of the people (*kokumin*) and asked him to convince Torio to resign from the Myōdō kyōkai.[113] Finally, Itō, Yamagata Aritomo, and Inoue Kaoru meet with Torio in person on August 1; although we do not know what was said in the meeting, it was reported that Torio and other government officials, with the exception of Yamaoka, resigned from the Myōdō kyōkai.[114] This apparent concession did not silence Torio as a conservative critic of the government for long, however; he went on to found another organization, the Nihon kokkyō daidōsha (Society of the Great Way of the Great Japanese National Teaching), and a political party, the Hoshu chūseitō (Conservative Impartial Party), both in 1888.[115] Resistance to the liberalization of Christianity died hard because it also served the purpose of criticizing the autocratic character of the oligarchic government. The political conservatism of Torio, Tani Tateki, and others like them played an important role in promoting the interests of Shinto shrines in the Imperial Diet during the 1890s, a point we will return to in Chapter 5.

These conservative critics within government were learning to employ the grammar of religion to press their arguments. Motoda Nagazane, still serving as an adviser to the emperor, for example, circulated two essays in July and August 1884, as the government moved closer to issuing a formal policy on religion.[116] The first, entitled "Concerning National Doctrine" ("Kokkyōron"), summarized the situation confronting the government: "If with one statement we reject religion, then it will lead to bloodshed in our relations with other countries, and there is no way to fathom what strife would follow. If with another statement we accept religion, then disorder will occur within our land and violence will increase." The only option, Motoda affirmed, was to assume the posture of "neither rejecting nor accepting" any specific religion and to allow the people to believe in any religion they pleased. For liberty of belief to be both feasible and harmless, however, the fundamental basis of the state had to be determined and communicated to the people; if "the people do not know where to place their faith," how will stable governance take place? The government, therefore, must establish a national doctrine (*kokkyō*).[117] Though the content of Motoda's national doctrine differed little from what he advocated in 1879, he had grown more explicit in attempting to place that doctrine above and beyond religion (and hence belief).

That attempt is more evident in his August essay on religion, written when it was evident that doctrinal instructors would be abolished and Christianity legalized. In that essay Motoda acknowledged that the trend (*ikioi*) of the day prevented the government from resisting the free practice not only of Buddhism but also of Christianity, neither of which would threaten the state so long as "the court stands outside of religion." The liberalization of religion, in other words, required "placing the true appearance of the court outside of religion." The best means of doing that, naturally, involved "clarifying the national doctrine, which includes no discussion of the afterlife." Observing that most who become religiously fervent do so as adults, Motoda proposed that the state inculcate the national doctrine in the young (between ages three and fifteen).[118] While Motoda did not discernibly influence the Home Ministry's policy deliberations, his concern to link the liberalization of religion to a confident separation of the imperial institution from the realm of religious belief mimicked the language employed by Itō and others at the center of the government. His mastery of this political grammar of religion helps explain Motoda's central role in drafting the Imperial Rescript on Education in 1890 under Yamagata Aritomo's cabinet.

Shinto clerics, both shrine priests and doctrinal instructors, feared the prospect of a legalized Christianity as much as Buddhists did, and numerous petitions were submitted in the summer of 1884, most seeking the resurrection of a state department dedicated to the separate regulation of all Shinto shrines. Notable among them was one submitted by eighty-one Shinto doctrinal instructors. Responding to rumors concerning government plans to legalize Christianity and abolish doctrinal instructors, the petition challenged the presumed rationale for such a move by attacking the logic of legalizing Christianity in order to appease the treaty powers and thus secure the revision of the unequal treaties. Whatever diplomatic benefit such a policy would provide, the petition argued that Christianity, as a monotheism that prohibited the worship of other gods, would lead to republicanism and sectarian division within Japan. "The hearts of the people will thus fracture," the Shinto petitioners wrote, leading the nation to become a mere "confederation" (*gasshūkoku*). As if this warning were not dire enough, the petition concluded with a thinly veiled threat that "men of noble purpose" (*shishi*) might oppose Christianity by force.[119]

Representatives of the Bureau of Shinto Affairs, including Ōtori Sessō, took a less confrontational approach in their petition. Accepting the legalization of Christianity and the end of doctrinal instructors as inevitable, the bureau insisted that these policies be implemented only after the unparalleled (*sekai muhi*) national polity was secured by resurrecting the Department of Divinities. Court rites, while they were being conducted, remained in the hands of the Bureau of Rites, and though shrines were administered by the state, they fell under the jurisdiction of the Home Ministry; an administrative divide stood between the imperial court and the shrines. The petition acknowledged the state's prerogative to alter its organization to accommodate the "needs of the day," but also demanded that the Department of Divinities be resurrected as of old, because it alone related to the foundation of the national polity. The government must "eradicate the source of evil teachings and impudent arguments before the treaties are revised and the national assembly is convened."[120] Presumably, resurrecting the Department of Divinities, and thus placing shrines firmly within the administration of the court and above all forms of religious competition, would silence all "impudent arguments." Shrine priests and their allies pursued this movement to revive a state ministry dedicated to Shinto (the so-called *jingikan saikō undō*) beyond 1884, but, as examined in the following chapter, it was the representative function of the Imperial Diet, which they feared most, that gave the priesthood the greatest amount of political leverage.

If special treatment of any religion was being promoted within the government at this time, it was on behalf of Buddhism, not Shinto. Inoue Kowashi yet again stood at the center of the policy deliberations concerning a religious settlement. Called upon by Home Minister Yamagata Aritomo to draft an opinion on abolishing the doctrinal instructor system, Inoue submitted proposals on March 17 and 18. In these he was quick to denounce the failings of earlier policies adopted by the government, warning that "the matter has been mistaken once, it should not now be mistaken again." In order to avoid further mistakes, Inoue revisited the choice between religious toleration and religious freedom and advocated the former. The crucial difference between the two policies, according to Inoue, rested in the government's ability to harness the power of religion as a tool for governance: "It would be exceptional if religion did not exist in the world. When it is practiced, however, a government must borrow some religious power and render it a tool for governance. There are many examples wherein a government failed to rule well and, opposing the force of religion, incited the people's hearts, bringing about internal unrest and inviting external enemies."[121] Reprising his earlier concern to direct the people's hearts, Inoue worried that opposing the passions of the people—by either forcibly endorsing or radically disestablishing a dominant religion—would lead to greater harm. Referring in a separate policy paper to the friction arising from the spread of Christianity, Inoue warned against underestimating the sway of Buddhism among the people. The state should not weigh the relative merits of one religion against another but should instead recognize which religion holds sway over the majority of the population. Buddhism clearly remained the religion of the majority in Japan.[122] In addition, the state must discriminate between religions based *within* national borders and those based abroad. To illustrate, Inoue appealed to contemporary European concerns directed toward the Catholic Church, with its supranational organization (the ultramontane authority of the pope). Inoue thus sought to strike a balance in how the state would relate to religion: an overt accommodation of Christianity at the expense of Buddhism would exacerbate already present friction, while continuing to reject Christianity would complicate diplomatic relations. Inoue summarized his position with three options or recommendations: even if religious freedom is legally granted, a distinction should be made between recognized and unrecognized religions; if religion is to be made a tool of governance, a religion that commands the adherence of the majority should be employed; if religion is to be harmonized with political policy, one with foreign institutional ties (such as Christianity) should be avoided and instead a religion well accustomed to the nation should be used.[123] All three options pointed to a unique role for Buddhism that differentiated it from other religions.

In calling for a special role for Buddhism, Inoue did not deviate significantly from the principles that informed the separation of Buddhism from the Great Teaching Academy in 1875. He recommended recognizing Buddhist sect organizations (*bukkyō no danketsu kyōkaitai*) as autonomous bodies governed by head temples. At the same time, he said, a system of state-recognized ordination ought to be implemented, with imperial ranks conferred on prominent clerics and exemptions from conscription granted to ordained clerics. With these changes, Inoue suggested, Buddhism could be "co-opted" (*rōraku*), and further conflict between Buddhists and Christians could be prevented. At the same time, potential diplomatic protests over the preferential treatment of Buddhism over Christianity could be deflected by legally tolerating Christianity while restricting privileges (court ranks, formal ordination, exemption from conscription, and so on) to religious "organizations" formally recognized by the state. Limiting recognized organizations to those with more than 300,000 believers would effectively exclude Christianity from formal recognition for the time being, even as it was allowed free exercise.[124] In this way, Inoue sought to balance popular sentiments in favor of Buddhism with the diplomatic expedience of liberalizing Christianity. That balance had little to do with a doctrinal preference for one religion over another and more to do with pragmatic calculations of demographic representation. A four-part editorial on religion in the *Jiji shinpō*, a paper that touted its political impartiality, echoed Inoue's concern when it observed that "what does not obey the will of the government is a populace fervent in religion."[125] Any sudden move on the part of the government to spread Christianity, the editorial warned, would likely provoke violent responses because many remained fervently religious.[126]

Few were surprised when the Home Ministry announced a significant shift in its regulation of religion on August 11, 1884. The Council of State's ordinance number nineteen abolished the doctrinal instructor system and placed all control over the ordination and promotion of Buddhist and Shinto clerics in the hands of their respective superintendents. It completed the creation of self-regulating religious organizations initiated in 1875 with the secession of the Shin sect Buddhists from the Great Teaching Academy. The order contained two noteworthy caveats. First, religious sects were not to splinter or enter into disputes with one another. Second, regulations established by superintendents to govern their sects required the Home Minister's approval before they could take effect.[127] These caveats, along with the fact that no mention was made of Christianity and its legalization, betray the delicacy of the balance between the competing demands of addressing diplomatic requirements and diffusing sectarian friction at home.

The rationale behind the August 11 order was clearly expressed in the explanatory opinion that the Home Ministry had submitted to the cabinet in July. Signed by Yamagata Aritomo, that document begins with a blunt assessment of how the government had hitherto related to religion: "Many problems have already resulted from directly involving the government in religion [*shūkyō*]. However, the benefits (of that involvement) are not yet apparent." Given that history, it continued, the primary objective of the new policy was to regulate and manage religious sects in an indirect manner, preventing them from destabilizing governance and complicating diplomatic relations. By granting the superintendents the authority to draw up regulations for their sects while retaining the home minister's prerogative to authorize those regulations, the Home Ministry suggested it could achieve the ideal mode of religious regulation: "Even if the power of the government does not touch their bodies directly, it can easily shape the regulations of the religious organization. Thus, the government can control them by freeing them externally while controlling them internally." This ideal mode of indirect control could prevent "internal and external religious conflict," and it "accords well with the current of the day, causes no internal harm and aids diplomacy."[128] The policy, moreover, relied on a clearly articulated construct of religion: "In the first place, religion concerns the souls of the people." Since there existed no immanent means of intervening in this concern, and with seven-tenths of the population still ardently religious, the government would risk unrest if it meddled directly in their beliefs. "Religion is a category in which the government should not be deeply involved."[129]

At the same time that the Home Ministry explained the rationale for withdrawing the state from any direct relations with religion, however, it acknowledged how the history of close relations that bound the court to Buddhism and Shinto complicated matters. Buddhist and Shintoist clerics were likely to feel slighted as a result of the new regulations, and just as likely to agitate. To solve this problem, the ministry proposed granting the superintendents of each Buddhist and Shinto sect imperial appointments (*chokunin*), using the "honor" to control the individual superintendent; if the individual could be thus controlled, the sect beneath the superintendent would also be controlled.[130] To this extent, the final order produced by the ministry echoed Inoue Kowashi's proposals.[131] Still, Yamagata rejected Inoue's proposal to grant Buddhism a prominent position as a religion specifically recognized by the state.[132] So far as possible, Yamagata attempted to place distance between the government and religion to achieve a mode of indirect control. The continued prerogative of the home minister to sanction sect regulations was to be the bare minimum of direct control maintained over what remained, in the eyes of the Yamagata and others within the government, a volatile realm of competing beliefs.

As a corollary, the government assiduously evaded an announcement on the legal recognition of Christianity, largely to avoid further social unrest over the matter. Instead, private funerals (that is, non-Buddhist, non-Shinto) were quietly legalized by October 1884, removing the final legal barrier to the free exercise of the Christian faith. The fact that the government did not issue an explicit declaration of liberalization reminds us that perceived limits to state authority underlay the "religious settlement" sought in 1884. That is to say, the acknowledged inability to directly quell religious passions—be they Buddhist, Shinto, or otherwise—motivated Yamagata and the Home Ministry to create a system of indirect control, a system premised on the discrete character of religion. By placing religion in a private realm administered by superintendents, the government attempted to put distance between the religious demands of clerics and their adherents and the political and diplomatic priorities of the state. As Kyoto governor Kitagaki explained to Shinto clerics after the August 11 order was issued, "With the announcement of ordinance number 19, the foundation has been laid to prevent any religion [*shūkyō*] from relating to national governance in the future."[133] The undercurrent of containment was clear; by instituting an administrative divide between private religion and public governance, the state sought to prevent its policies from being held hostage by "religious" interests.

In the aggregate, the goal and effect of the separation order in August 1884 was the creation of a realm of autonomous religious organizations that were in competition with one another outside the direct concern of the state. The prestige of the state was unlikely to be affected by the sudden success or rapid decline of a particular religious group, Buddhist, Shinto, or Christian. Above all else, the Meiji government sought to avoid favoring any specific religion in order to defuse the religious friction that flared in 1884, and to separate the state, in the eyes of the treaty powers, from both Shinto and Buddhism. Needless to say, that neutrality was premised on placing the imperial institution "outside of religion." The August 11 order marked the decisive expression of that premise, and subsequent utilizations of the imperial institution, especially the Imperial Constitution and Rescript on Education, would expand on it.

Conclusion

The press responded immediately to the end of the doctrinal instructor system, with many papers running lengthy editorials. The pro-government *Meiji nippō*, for example, ran a four-part editorial in which it noted that the "government has already painfully seen through the harm unique to religion [*shūkyō koyū no heigai*]," and that the policy of "noninterference" was the only way to deal with the unavoidable fragmentation and competition among religions.[134] The August 11 ordinance, the editorial concluded, marked a clear break with the *saisei itchi* policies initially pursued by the Meiji government, and the full legalization of Christianity was expected to follow soon after.[135] The editorial rehearsed the narrative of how religion emerged as a political concern in the first place, and how the regulative creation of religion as a sphere of private belief marked an attempt to address that concern. The unavoidable fragmentation and competition that religion came to represent stood in stark contrast to the vision of a unified nation administered by the uncontested authority of the state. The government attempted to position itself "above the fray," beyond the private beliefs that fragmented the populace, by refusing to "interfere" in religious competition. Absent a construct of religion, the government could not have adopted a policy of "noninterference," especially given the unmistakably mythic foundation of imperial authority. Following the separation order of 1882 and the abolishment of the doctrinal instructor system in 1884, however, the government signaled its determination to replace its multiple relationships to Shinto sects, Buddhism, and

Christianity with a uniform relation to "religion" as a discrete or sui generis category.

To be clear, declarations of policy and administrative practices did not render the Meiji state and the imperial institution religiously neutral or benign. To the contrary, by rendering religion a private and discrete realm, the government sidestepped the political and diplomatic complications entangled in the "matter of religion" and opened a space for a public orthodoxy that superseded sectarian interests. Yamagata justified the granting of autonomy to religious superintendents in terms of its effectiveness as a mode of governance; defining and regulating religion as a discrete and private domain allowed the state to effectively get around or elide differences within a diverse population (such as the religious friction evident in 1884), while setting the groundwork for molding that diverse population in the image of a centralized nation-state. At the same time, a "sacralized" conception of authority—specifically, imperial authority—unquestionably continued to develop through the Meiji period. For example, on August 7, just as the Home Ministry was preparing to issue its August 11 ordinance, 292 newly titled aristocrats (*jushakusha*) took an oath before the Three Deity Halls within the imperial palace.[136] The government continued to use the ritual veneration of the imperial ancestors, including the sun goddess Amaterasu, as a visual, ritual, and doctrinal means to discipline loyal subjects. Nonetheless, those new aristocrats took an oath *within* the imperial palace, sequestered from public view, and disassociated from the realm of private religious belief. The architects of the Meiji state, such as Itō Hirobumi, were well aware not only of the potential utility of a sacralized imperial institution, but also of the potential liabilities presented by having a blatantly "theocratic" basis for political authority. The grammar of religion provided them a means to articulate and police a division between private, contingent identifications and the public identifications necessary for national subjects.

The diplomatic negotiation of belief clearly informed the emergence of this grammar of religion in Meiji state policy, and Helen Hardacre makes the following point in a related vein: "That the oligarchs were prepared to guarantee religious freedom in any form was due more to the pressure exerted from abroad than to their convictions about fundamental human rights."[137] When one combines the conversations informing the 1882 order and the 1884 settlement, however, the picture grows more complicated. Politics and diplomacy together shaped the government's discovery of religion as an object of policy. Just as diplomatic calculations aimed toward treaty revision shaped the government's approach to religion, internecine conflict among Shinto clerics, culminating in the

Pantheon Dispute, also illustrated the political expedience of placing such disputes beyond the administrative jurisdiction of the state and into the domain of private belief and sectarian affairs. Continued sectarian competition within Shinto and between Shinto and Buddhism provided ample incentive to adopt what might loosely be termed a liberal approach to religion. Beyond that, the government's desire to control and direct the people's hearts in an indirect fashion also informed the end of direct government intervention in the realm of religion. The Meiji oligarchs may never have believed in "fundamental human rights," but they believed in pragmatically pursuing effective governance, a belief evidenced in their approach to religion.

This much, then, is clear: as of 1884 the core of the Meiji government—Itō Hirobumi, Inoue Kaoru, Inoue Kowashi, Yamagata Aritomo, Matsukata Masayoshi, and the others—were opposed to adopting a formal national doctrine and using Shinto shrines in a systematic way to project imperial authority. The so-called shrine reform case (*jinja kaisei no ken*) of 1885–86 amply reflects the ongoing priorities animating policy discussions during this crucial phase of preparing for constitutional government. The Home Ministry, under Yamagata, was not completely satisfied with the religious settlement obtained by the August 11 ordinance; while sects (both Buddhist and Shinto) were placed under the private administration of superintendents, Shinto shrines remained formally linked to the state. Together with the Finance Ministry, which was interested in reducing state expenditures to the shrines, in July 1885 the Home Ministry proposed revising how Shinto shrines were ranked and funded. Under the proposed plan, state support for the Grand Shrines of Ise was to be increased, while the ranks of all other imperial and national shrines were to be revised and their maintenance support cut off. Instead, the state would offer "preservation funds" (*hozonkin*) for ten years, during which time the shrines were supposed to accumulate their own endowments. After ten years, the shrines would rely entirely on the income from their endowments and private donations. The notable exception to this dramatic reduction in government support was Yasukuni shrine, whose entire budget was to be drawn directly from the ministry budgets of the Imperial Army and Imperial Navy. This plan faced stiff opposition from Shinto partisans within the government, who feared it would give the appearance that the state was intent on destroying Shinto (*haishin no mokuteki*).[138] The opposition was successful only in delaying the implementation of the shrine reform plan, however, and the order was issued in November 1886, signed by Yamagata Aritomo as home minister and Matsukata Masayoshi as finance minister.[139] The policy unmistakably privileged Ise and treated it as a ritual extension of the state, while it simultaneously intimated that the majority of shrines might ultimately be privately funded, and hence religious. Though the government could not but support the shrine dedicated to the imperial ancestor, all other shrines were deemed more of a financial and ideological liability than an asset. In short, along with any attempt to fully utilize the imperial institution we can find a corresponding attempt to minimize its potential for exposing the fundamental fissures and divisions within Japanese society throughout the archipelago; constructing religion as a discrete realm of private belief marked such a minimizing move.

The separation order of 1882, the abolishment of the doctrinal instructor system in 1884, and the shrine reform of 1886 together comprised the religious settlement by which the architects of the Meiji state attempted to dispose of all liabilities associated with the pursuit of *saisei itchi* and the Great Promulgation Campaign. The settlement marked the bottom of the trough Fridell describes in the state support for Shinto shrines; shrine priests were cut off from sectarian expansion and shrines were starved of state funds and official recognition.[140] While dissenting voices persisted within the Meiji government, this approach—to minimize the religious footprint of the imperial institution—guided government policy with little alteration into the "Meiji Settlement" of the 1890s that followed the promulgation of the Imperial Constitution.[141] The representative politics of the Imperial Diet provided a forum in which the parameters of this religious settlement were subsequently challenged and adjusted.

CHAPTER 5

The Religious Constitution of Meiji Japan, 1888–1900

In our nation . . . religion possesses little power and none can serve as an axis for the nation. Buddhism once prospered and connected the hearts of people high and low, but today it is in decline. Shinto passes on the teachings of the ancestors, but lacks the power to attract the people's hearts as a religion. Only the imperial institution [*kōshitsu*] can serve as the axis of our nation.

—Itō Hirobumi, 1888

The 1889 Imperial Constitution explicitly rejected religion as a component of Japan's national definition. Both Shinto and Buddhism were deemed insufficient to unite the nation around its constitutional state. As a corollary, the constitution adopted the principle of religious freedom instead of toleration (whereby minority religions were tolerated alongside a majority religion established by the state). This deliberate articulation of imperial sovereignty in opposition to religion grew out of the religious settlement of the 1880s and implied a secular, religiously neutral state. Yet at the end of the first decade of constitutional rule, the Home Ministry created the Shrine Bureau and nominally placed it above the Religion Bureau. This administrative move in 1900 marks for many scholars the end of the "trough" in state support for shrines and the beginning of "State Shinto."[1]

How did a constitution that explicitly rejected a state religion and adopted the principle of religious freedom facilitate this apparent resurgence in state support for shrine Shinto? In his pioneering essay "The Establishment of Shrine Shinto in Meiji Japan," Wilbur Fridell ascribes the late-Meiji resurgence of shrine Shinto to the creation of a "theoretical and administrative base" for state support.[2] He does not, however, explain how that theoretical and administrative base was produced. The architects of the constitution, including Itō Hirobumi, did not mendaciously advocate a secular state while plotting to dramatically increase the state's support for the shrines; most of the oligarchic leadership saw the shrines and their priests as fiscal and political liabilities. Nor were shrines unambiguously assumed to have been nonreligious when the constitution was promulgated. In fact, shrine priests and their allies feared that the Imperial Diet, inaugurated by the constitution, would treat the majority of shrines and their priests as religious, further eviscerating them both ideologically and fiscally.

It was the decade-long negotiation of the political disposition of religion in the Imperial Diet that produced the theoretical and administrative basis for placing shrines outside the regulatory space of religion and closer to the state. For contemporaries, the promulgation of the constitution on February 11, 1889, marked a threshold separating the early-Meiji period from the late Meiji—a period of uncertainty and experimentation that was followed by a period of stability and institutional settlements.[3] The Imperial Constitution, in short, ushered in a decade during which the operative parameters of constitutional government were negotiated, the unequal treaties were revised, and Japan emerged a victorious imperial power in East Asia. Negotiating how constitutional government would operate through the 1890s necessarily entailed negotiating the boundary of religion, or, more specifically, the manner in which the avowedly "religious" would participate in the political sphere, namely the Imperial Diet.

This chapter surveys how the Imperial Diet furnished the dominant stage for negotiating the statutory and administrative boundaries of religion. The freedom of belief, conditionally guaranteed in Article 28 of the constitution, formalized an interpretive distinction between the religious and the secular, or what Inoue Kowashi referred to as the "domain that governs all people." In theory, what fell outside that domain, such as religion, was unrestrained by virtue of its exclusion from public and political recognition. For the state, the utility of the religious settlement depended on dismissing the political relevance of sectarian distinctions by regulating religions in a uniform fashion. The constitution thus offered the avowedly religious the promise of freedom in proportion to their irrelevance to and undifferentiated treatment by the state. Recognizing this theoretical exchange, shrine priests sought to escape the category of religion, and to avoid political irrelevance, by demanding a revived Department of Divinities, while Buddhist sects demanded a formal distinction between established and tolerated religions. Both mobilized to gain access to the Imperial Diet.

The 1890s thus confronted the potential for sectarian politics. The attempts by shrine priests and Buddhist sects to press their cases through the Imperial Diet generated considerable public commentary, most of which expressed concern that sectarian interests would fragment the nation. In this context, it was the representative function of the Imperial Diet, the premise that it represented the national will (*yoron*), that proved crucial to the manner in which the regulatory grammar of religion took form. The political parties in the Diet, for example, employed the shrine priests' cause as a means to discredit the oligarchic government, employing the demotic conceit of the Imperial Diet to place shrines outside of religion and in the "domain that governs all people." Buddhist sects, in contrast, were criticized for attempting to press a majoritarian claim for special recognition. Buddhism qua religion could be not but be private, and the Imperial Diet worked to enforce the nonsectarian definition of the nation-state. In both cases, the Diet provided the primary stage on which the political disposition of religion under the constitution was negotiated and enforced.

The theoretical and administrative base that Fridell identifies thus emerged from a decade's worth of laws and ordinances debated and enacted by and in response to the Imperial Diet. From forestry custodianship regulations to the Ancient Shrine and Temple Preservation Law, the minutiae of statutes and bureaucratic administration proved as important in shaping the discursive contours of religion in Meiji Japan as intellectual discourse outside the formal policies of the state. These codes and administrative practices were untidy and often mutually compromising, and the failure of the highly anticipated Religion Bill in 1900 demonstrates that the government was never able to define and regulate religion entirely on its own terms. At the same time, the repeated disavowals of authority by Home Ministry bureaucrats, claiming that the state did not determine what was and what was not religious through its statutes and regulatory practices, appear disingenuous at best. The history of parliamentary politics during that formative decade suggests that the Imperial Diet played a significant role in interpreting the constitutional application of the religious settlement.

Constituting the Religious Settlement

The Imperial Constitution, framed under the direction of Itō Hirobumi and Inoue Kowashi, simultaneously sacralized and secularized the imperial institution. Sacralization, to borrow Kino Kazue's useful formulation, refers to "the process of incorporating the emperor system, a symbol of irrational authority derived from historical tradition, into the state apparatus." Secularization worked to "maintain the legitimacy of politics by seeking the universal validity of law" in designing the state apparatus, "while accommodating social pluralism and cognitive relativism."[4] The religious settlement, worked out in the mid-1880s, set the stage for this critical double move, dividing a competitive realm of religious plurality from a circumscribed realm of imperial rites.

Itō's famous declaration to the Privy Council (Sūmitsuin) in June 1888 explicitly links the language of religion to the project to secure the transcendent authority of the imperial institution while accommodating "social pluralism and cognitive relativism." In Japan, he asserted, "religion possesses little power and none can serve as an axis for the nation." Accordingly, Itō rejected the constitutional precedents of Europe, precedents that commonly combined a state religion with religious toleration.[5] In rejecting a state religion, Itō not only sought to avoid the diplomatic complications feared and experienced since the Urakami affair, but he also wished to place the imperial institution above the fray of sectarian competition *within* Japan. Explicitly identifying the Japanese state as Shinto or Buddhist would not only have accentuated the divide between a "heathen" Japan and the "Christian West" but also inflamed sectarian divisions rooted in "social plurality and cognitive relativism."[6] To Itō, the ambiguous term *kokkyō*, employed since the early 1870s to denote a state-authorized doctrine, evoked coercion and conversion. The abject failure of both had given birth to the imperative to place the imperial institution beyond the realm of conversionary competition in the first place. According to Itō's own commentary on the constitution, following the "direction taken since the Restoration," he did not adopt a state religion because "to compel belief with a national religion" would only hinder the progress of the nation.[7]

The Imperial Constitution thus adopted the principle of religious freedom over toleration. Article 28 declared: "Japanese subjects possess the freedom of belief to the extent that it does not disrupt peace and order, and does not contradict one's duties as a subject."[8] Recognizing belief, but not practice, the article codified the subjectified construct of religion, placing the self-articulation of belief beneath and after the public and political demands of the state. The freedom of religious belief followed an interpretive division between private belief and public duty that preceded it; thus Itō could confidently assert that the "freedom of reverencing a teaching [*hōkyō*] internally receives absolutely no restraint."[9] According to this logic, restraint precedes the articulation of belief and is contained in the presumption of boundaries that separate the religious from the secular, the contingent from the necessary, the private from the public. Thus, in practice, Article 28 generated a constitutional imperative to continually interpret and police the boundary separating the two realms of freedom and constraint, a boundary entirely dependent on how "religion" was to be defined through the administrative practices of the state. Put another way, the treatment of religion within the Imperial Constitution did not codify a distinction already widely agreed upon in existing administrative practice and institutional arrangements so much as it formalized the political significance of religion as the repository of purportedly unconstrained private belief.

The Privy Council confronted this interpretive imperative when it met to discuss Article 28. Sasaki Takayuki and Torio Koyata, both noted critics of Christianity and frequently opposed to Itō's pragmatism, questioned the limit to the freedom of belief by raising the possibility that state officials might refuse to attend palace rites conducted by the emperor, on the grounds of religious belief. Itō Miyoji, speaking for the drafting committee, emphasized the conditional nature of the right to belief and indicated that the rules governing state officials sufficiently clarified official duties. (He hastened to add, moreover, that existing regulations did not require officials to attend imperial rites.) Unsatisfied, Torio cautioned that the full consequences of openly tolerating all religions without distinction needed to be carefully weighed. "It does not particularly affect the national polity [*kokutai*] nor does it infringe upon [questions of] duty if civilians [*jinmin*] do not participate in court rites," he conceded, while insisting matters would be different for state officials. Itō Hirobumi, chair of the council, refused to debate anew the wisdom of the religious settlement and ended the discussion by dismissing Torio's concerns. Torio was asking, Itō observed, "what the state's policy toward religion would be in the future." Declaring that "this question belongs to the attitude of politicians of each era and cannot be answered now," Itō bequeathed the interpretive requirement to subsequent political debate.[10]

The Privy Council's deliberation of Article 28 helps frame three points relevant to the contours of the "religion problem" (*shūkyō mondai*) as it came to be debated during the first decade of constitutional government. First, the constitution was widely interpreted to openly legalize Christianity by replacing silent toleration with an explicit guarantee of free belief, an interpretation shared and welcomed by many in the press.[11] At the same time, Christianity remained outside the regulatory reach of the Home Ministry, specifically the superintendent system in place since the mid-1880s. How to place Christianity, Protestant, Catholic, and Orthodox alike, within the framework of the religious settlement proved a recurring regulatory concern through the 1890s. The concern to bring Christianity under the administrative recognition of the state also exacerbated

Shinto and Buddhist fears of marginalization and defeat at the hands of a better-supported foreign rival. For shrine priests and Buddhist sectarians, the constitutional guarantee of free belief formalized a regulatory domain of religion in which, in theory, the state recognized no meaningful distinctions between specific religions qua religion. Shrine priests and their allies considered it imperative to lift all shrines out of that regulatory domain, while Buddhist sectarians pressed for the state to recognize meaningful historical and demographic distinctions between Buddhism and Christianity.

Second, the Privy Council, including Torio Koyata, accepted the proposition that state rites were confined to those conducted in person by the emperor within the palace, and concerned the official realm alone. Many within the government feared the introduction of elective politics could compromise the boundaries of that official realm; the unpredictable composition of the elected lower house of the Imperial Diet, and its attitudes toward imperial rites, in particular, generated considerable anxiety. Inoue Kowashi resisted requiring newly elected members of the House of Representatives to swear oaths of office before the Three Deity Halls within the palace, for fear that it would invite protests on the grounds of religious conviction.[12] *Saisei itchi*, the unquestioned principle of uniting rite and rule in the person of the emperor, had been carefully circumscribed as a defense against the unpredictable partisanship that the legislative organ was anticipated to produce. Critics of the limited scope given to *saisei itchi* also feared the approach of constitutional government, though for different reasons. Rather than serving as a bulwark against the unpredictable partisanship of an elected lower house, shrine priests and their allies within the government believed the Imperial Diet would further diminish the fiscal and institutional standing of the shrines. In both cases, the approach of constitutional government was met with significant apprehension.

Finally, and more broadly, Article 28 and its subjectified contract of religious freedom framed the terms under which the avowedly religious would negotiate their political participation in public life under the constitution. That negotiation was complicated by the fact that private belief was unregulated in direct proportion to its public irrelevance; the guarantee of freedom came at the potential cost of rendering religion completely marginal or hidden from public recognition. The struggles of Japanese Christians to accommodate themselves to the ideological demands of the state under these conditions are relatively well known, but the extent to which Buddhist sectarians struggled to reconcile their embracing of religion as a category with its potential for marginalization has been easier to overlook. Religious commentators in the 1890s, especially Buddhist clerics, were painfully aware of the potential for exclusion from the secular realm inherent in the subjectified contract of religious identification, and they were thus quick to assert an essential connection between religion and the public good generally, as well as a unique historical connection between Buddhism and the Japanese nation specifically.[13] By the same token, the Meiji state, for all its anticlerical inclinations, recognized that organized sects and professional clerics provided the surest means to "measure," and hence retain some control over, internal belief. Belief could never be strictly individual or unrelated to practice, and no nation-state could remain completely disinterested in the internal lives of its subjects. Hence, both the state and the "religious" converged to negotiate over how much public space and political recognition religion could claim.

The axiom that religion was inherently sectarian and competitive nonetheless shaped fundamentally how the political position of religion was negotiated under the Imperial Constitution. In a speech given to the Center for the Study of Imperial Classics (Kōtenkōkyūjo) in February 1889, Inoue Kowashi explained that the study of the classical texts and ceremonies of the imperial institution was "necessary to state governance, and . . . for the education of the nation"; it was not necessary, however, "for religion [*shūkyō*] . . . to furnish material for a political party's argument." He impressed upon his audience of shrine priests the proposition that transforming the imperial classics into sources for "religious argument" or using them "as religious signboards with which to attack Buddhism or Christianity" would be sacrilegious (*mottainai*).[14] Religious sects, like their political counterparts, were inherently partisan, reflecting fragmented and fragmenting interests.[15] It was imperative on the eve of constitutional government, therefore, that no single political party or religious sect could lay claim to the classics of the nation, because "the study of the rites and ceremonies of the nation belongs to a domain [*kūiki*] that governs all people."[16] The 1882 order to separate shrine priests from sectarian clerics had exempted priests serving at prefectural-level shrines or below. That exemption had allowed the majority of the Shinto priesthood to simultaneously serve as shrine priests and sectarian clerics.[17] With so many low-ranking priests affiliated with Shinto sects, the possibility that they would fall out of the "domain that governs all people" appeared all too real.

The ceremonies surrounding the promulgation of the Imperial Constitution confirmed for many the suspicion that the new political order would continue to marginalize Shinto. February 11, 1889, did begin with the emperor ritually announcing the event to his divine ancestors before the Three Deity Halls within the palace grounds. The date for the ceremonies was chosen to coincide with the *kigensetsu* holiday that commemorated the mythic ascension to the throne of the first emperor, Jinmu, and the founding of the imperial state in 660 BCE. In spite of those concessions to the principle of united rite and rule, however, the visual focus of the day lay squarely on the modern throne room (*seiden*) of the palace, where the emperor personally handed down the constitution as representatives of the treaty powers looked on.[18] The visual emphasis placed on the "secular" ceremony, in contrast to the rites hidden from view underscored the limited weight invested in Shinto rituals and amplified the frustrations of Shinto partisans.[19]

The level of frustration caused by the state's treatment of Shinto shrines was sensationally illustrated by the assassination of Minister of Education Mori Arinori on the morning of the promulgation. Rumors had been published to the effect that Mori, while visiting the Grand Shrines of Ise as a cabinet minister, had lifted the blinds concealing the inner sanctum of the shrine, using his walking stick.[20] As a prominent representative of the government's Westernizing policies, Mori's rumored act of desecration circulated in the press with considerable credence.[21] Anti-Western nationalists celebrated his assassin, Nishino Buntarō (1865–1889), as a martyr who had defended the dignity of the *kokutai*.[22] When some in the press characterized the violent attack as sectarian violence rooted in religious animosity, Kuga Katsunan (1857–1907), the journalistic voice of the conservative nationalism of the 1890s, vehemently rejected that view. Any defense of the dignity of Ise, and of shrines in general, he insisted, stood beyond petty sectarian concerns.[23] It was precisely this tendency to associate shrines with sectarian competition that most agitated shrine priests and their allies. The political grammar of religion as it was taking shape at this time rendered illegitimate political acts, including violence, in the name of religion. For Kuga, shrines therefore could not be religious, because political action in the name of the imperial dignity represented by shrines had to remain legitimate.

Provoked by these frustrations, a group of officials sympathetic to the Shinto cause and fearful of unbridled representative politics mounted a concerted campaign through the summer and fall of 1890 to reestablish a state department that would be dedicated to the supervision of all shrines, prior to the commencement of constitutional government.[24] Including Sasaki Takayuki, Motoda Nagazane, and Yamada Akiyoshi, this group challenged directly the circumscribed character of imperial rites in order to securely place shrines outside religion by more explicitly linking them to the imperial institution. They demanded a revived Department of Divinities that would reconnect palace rites with the administration of imperial and national shrines, while at the same time restoring permanent fiscal support for those select shrines.[25] Although attitudes within the government toward the shrines were far from uniform and the most influential oligarchs were either hostile or indifferent, Sasaki's memorial to establish an Institute of Divinities (Jingiin) secured support from Privy Council members, members of the Genrōin senate, and even the head of the Home Ministry Shrine and Temple Bureau.[26] Reaching beyond the imperial and national shrines to also include "large and small shrines," Sasaki asked explicitly to reverse the 1872 separation of rite from doctrine. "There is nothing more important and pressing," he declared, "than the maintenance of the national order and the unification of the hearts of the people as the first steps toward constitutional politics."[27] Whereas Itō had dismissed using either Buddhism or Shinto as a potential axis for national unification, Sasaki countered that Shinto shrines were vital to the maintenance of stability in the face of parliamentary politics.

In reality, the opposite was closer to his concern: the maintenance of Shinto shrines depended on quickly reversing government policy before the Imperial Diet could finish the job of eviscerating them, begun in the 1880s. The shrine reform of 1886, which formed a cornerstone of the religious settlement, had abandoned perpetual state support for shrines in favor of a preservation fund that was to be distributed to imperial and national shrines over a period of fifteen years; fiscal independence was to follow. The preservation fund was as unpopular as it was ungenerous; the majority of shrines and their priests were excluded form its provisions, and Sasaki chaffed at the premise that even imperial and national shrines should be fiscally independent of the state and vulnerable to the shifting tides of popular support.

The government revisited its treatment of shrines in anticipation of the commencement of constitutional rule, but for reasons distinct from Sasaki's movement. Article 67 of the constitution granted the government the prerogative to place certain budget items beyond the ratifying authority of the Diet.[28] The cabinet, led by Yamagata Aritomo, reviewed which expenditures could be classified as either the prerogative of imperial sovereignty or legal obligations incurred by the state, a process that included the shrine preservation fund. Funds set aside for the repair of shrines damaged by natural disasters, for example, had been pooled within the Ministry of Finance, but new accounting rules introduced by the constitution prohibited undifferentiated budget lines. Unless those funds were moved to a budgetary line secured under Article 67, the government would lose the ability to supply repair funds without parliamentary approval. In response to this new requirement, the Home Ministry proposed folding the disaster funds into the preservation fund by amending the division of those funds and extending the number of years they would be provided to shrines. In effect, the ministry suggested doubling the duration of the preservation fund to thirty years while effectively reducing the annual contribution to shrine endowments by 15 percent.[29] On the eve of constitutional rule, the Yamagata cabinet thus confronted two proposals affecting Shinto shrines. The Cabinet Legislation Bureau, then headed by Inoue Kowashi, affirmed the Home Ministry's proposed revisions to the shrine preservation fund as reasonable but rehearsed a cardinal tenet of the religious settlement in its formal opinion: "Ceremonies [*reiten*] should belong entirely to the royal house and should not be mixed with state affairs."[30] At the same time, Inoue's bureau appeared to endorse a key element of Sasaki's memorial—reviving direct fiscal support of imperial and national shrines—but with a significant difference. While Sasaki insisted that fiscal support of shrines fell under the sovereign prerogative of the emperor (*taiken*) according to Article 67, and hence was beyond the purview of the Imperial Diet, the Legislation Bureau proposed reviving fiscal support for shrines by passing legislation in the Imperial Diet.[31] Shrines were to be supported as a voluntary legal obligation of the state adopted by the Imperial Diet, not as an inherent expression of imperial sovereignty that transcended parliamentary procedure. With this recommendation, Inoue and the Cabinet Legislation Bureau rejected outright the central preoccupation of those seeking to resurrect a shrine department: ensuring the status and funding of shrines were never placed at the mercy of parliamentary politics.

In its attempt to square the two contradictory recommendations presented by the Legislation Bureau, the cabinet expanded the scope of its discussion to include Buddhist temples. The ministers accepted the Home Ministry plan to double the duration of the shrine preservation fund, but criticized the fund for excluding not only the majority of shrines but Buddhist temples as well. Perhaps influenced by Buddhist petitions pleading fiscal distress, the cabinet considered undoing some elements of the 1871 *jōchirei* by which the majority of land held by temples and shrines had been confiscated by the state. Doing so would expand the central premise of the shrine preservation fund, which was to provide for the eventual fiscal independence of all shrines and temples. The cabinet proposed returning to shrines and temples forestland (*sanrin*) held by the state, in the interest of securing their fiscal independence.[32] Though the proposal was blocked by the Agriculture and Commerce Ministry's refusal to relinquish its management of state-owned forestlands, the cabinet's discussion indicated the state viewed shrines and temples as administrative equivalents and set the stage for subsequent parliamentary debates concerning property rights and cultural preservation in which shrines and temples were treated as equivalent entities.[33]

As the first session of the Imperial Diet approached, then, not only did the oligarchic core of the government appear unwilling to alter the parameters of the religious settlement, but it also signaled a willingness to bureaucratically yoke shrines and temples together in order to render them fiscally independent. The leaders, including Yamagata and Itō, had not forgotten the lessons accumulated in the religious settlement of the 1880s and they were in no mood to overreach, either fiscally or ideologically, on the eve of parliamentary governance.[34] Any achievable consensus within the government would not have moved very far beyond the parameters set by the religious settlement. Convinced time was running out, proponents in a flurry of last-minute memorials sought at least a nominal change to the supervision of shrines "prior to the implementation of the constitution," but when the Imperial Diet convened for the first time on November 29, 1890, any chance of leaving the disposition of shrines and their priests outside the theater of parliamentary politics was lost.[35] Only the Home Ministry's proposal to extend the duration of the shrine preservation fund until 1917 was issued as an ordinance, two days prior to the first session of the Imperial Diet.[36]

The Imperial Constitution formalized the Meiji state's commitment to religious neutrality in order to insulate the imperial institution from "social pluralism and cognitive relativism." The theoretical implications of that commitment were clearly anticipated by stakeholders as the convocation of the first Imperial Diet approached. The freedom of belief threatened Buddhist sects and shrine priests alike with the potential of being rendered politically irrelevant, while Christian voices welcomed the formal legalization of Christianity. Shrine priests and their allies were quick to contest those theoretical implications by demanding the state unequivocally place shrines above and beyond the regulatory grammar of religion. The government, for its part, refused to reconsider the premise of religious neutrality built into the constitution and further signaled a willingness to treat shrines and temples as bureaucratic equivalents.

The Parliamentary Politics of Escaping Religion

The convocation of the first Imperial Diet in the fall of 1890 inaugurated a forum in which state policies would be debated in the open. Even though the Diet's ability to directly dictate state policy was limited by the sovereign prerogatives reserved by the cabinet in the name of the emperor, the legacy of the Freedom and People's Rights Movement ensured that no one could easily dismiss the principle that the elected House of Representatives and the appointed House of Peers represented the public will of the realm. In practical terms, the Diet brought to an end the memorial system (*kenpaku seido*), which since the early-Restoration period had meant the government received large numbers of petitions from disgruntled constituents; in the absence of a representative assembly, inconvenient memorials could be ignored with little consequence.[37] With both houses allowed to adopt memorials to the throne (*jōsō*) and recommendations to the government (*kengi*), the legislative body could now compel the oligarchy to debate policy in the open and on the record.[38] Memorials or recommendations formally adopted by the Imperial Diet could force the government to openly commit to a position on highly controversial issues, even if it did so by maintaining silence. Faced with political parties adamantly opposed to the *hanbatsu* oligarchy, an active press sympathetic to the parties, and a foreign diplomatic corps alert to the policy choices of the Japanese state, the government had every reason to fear that shrine priests and their allies, not to mention Buddhist sectarians, would attempt to access the Diet to press their grievances.

Indeed, the National Shinto Priest Conference was quick to turn to the Diet. Its frustration with the failure to move the government from within, prior to the commencement of constitutional government, was compounded by the rapid loss of its supporters from positions of influence within the government during the early 1890s.[39] These priests and their allies feared that, absent a clear institutional expression of the premise that all shrines, regardless of rank, stood outside the administrative category of religion, the anticipated religion ordinance or law would leave the majority of shrines and their priests in the same regulatory space as Buddhist temples and clerics, not to mention Christian churches and their clergy.[40] To prevent this from happening, the conference circulated a petition to members of both houses during the first Imperial Diet. Though limited in direct leverage, the possibility of the elected and appointed representatives of the empire adopting a memorial to the throne held out the promise of addressing the grievances of the shrine priests, not out of sectarian self-interest but as a matter of public or national interest, or what the petition called "national feelings" (*kokkateki kansō*).[41]

Many Buddhist sects and clerics were no less keen to access the Imperial Diet.[42] Unlike the shrine priests, however, their concern was not to place Buddhism outside of religion but to formalize distinctions between religions in the eyes of the state. As early as June 1889, Buddhist clerics representing central Japan and the Kansai regions gathered in Tokyo to protest their exclusion from the Diet through the House of Representatives Election Law. More generally, Buddhists focused their attention on the two issues foregrounded by the "Conflict between Education and Religion," a public debate that raged between 1892 and 1893. The first concerned the perceived advantages Christians enjoyed in accessing the public sphere, especially education and political office. The second concerned the view that Article 28 of the constitution appeared to indiscriminately recognize religions in Japan.[43]

Though framed as a debate concerning the relationship between religion and education in general, the Conflict between Education and Religion assailed Christianity's apparently privileged access to education. In addition to its well-known attacks on Christianity's theological compatibility with the *kokutai*, the debate drew attention to regulations, or the lack thereof, constraining the public presence of religion, especially in the realm of education. The two incidents that precipitated the public debate not coincidentally involved Christian faculty accused of committing lèse-majesté in their capacity as educators.[44] Though Christianity was denounced for its purportedly seditious nature, these incidents were also used to foreground the advantages that Christians were perceived to enjoy in using education as a proselytizing tool.

Buddhists and nationalist critics had long complained that Christians and their foreign missionary supporters employed schools as a means to wield a disproportionate influence on the future leaders of Japan. Kuga Katsunan ran a series of editorials in September 1893 criticizing the advantages enjoyed by Christian missionary organizations, capable of raising funds abroad and receiving diplomatic support in Japan to build churches, schools, and hospitals.[45] These perceived advantages made even the relatively small number of Christian schools appear dangerous.[46] For critics such as Kuga, Christianity remained a potent symbol and means of foreign encroachment, and its unrestrained access to education was only part of the problem. As the example of Yuasa Jirō (1850–1932) indicated, prominent Protestant Christians, with their tradition of lay leadership and lack of direct state regulation, were able to participate openly in government by standing for office at the local and national levels.[47] By formally legalizing the practice of Christianity without placing it under the regulative constraints of the Home Ministry, the Imperial Constitution appeared to grant Christians unacceptable access to the public sphere.[48]

The fact that Christianity escaped constraints placed on other religions fed the expectation that the government would produce a "religion ordinance" (*shūkyō jōrei*) to address that deficiency. Yet, because the regulatory constraint of Christianity under the constitution had to take the form of uniformly regulating the domain of religion, any ordinance would have affected Buddhist and Shinto organizations and clerics alike.[49] Therefore, even as they denounced Christian advantages, Buddhist commentators resisted what they considered the marginalization of Buddhism in the public domains of education and politics.[50]

The secular press generally argued that the constitution and Article 28 had inaugurated a secular politics by codifying the lessons of the religious settlement; hence, the public role of the religions had to be brought in line with the constitution.[51] In a series of editorials, the *Yomiuri* granted the possibility that religion might play a constructive societal function, but predicted a "religious war" as a result of the formal legalization of Christianity. Therefore, separating religion from the state and insulating the constitutional order from sectarian competition were declared to be vital to social and political stability. At the same time, the editorial had to concede that the distinction between what was religious and what was not remained ambiguous. Securing the stable operation of the constitutional order required resolving that ambiguity, presumably by defining the regulatory boundaries of religion.[52]

As a response to its potential marginalization and a bulwark against any general regulation of religion, a segment of the Buddhist establishment prominently sought official recognition for Buddhism (*kōninkyō*). The Nichiren cleric Furuya Nisshin (n.d.) and Tendai leader Murata Mokujun (1835–1905) pressed their case with Yamagata Aritomo in November 1889 by warning that "the people of shallow learning may use the freedom of belief as an excuse to overstep the bounds of propriety to the extent that peace and stability will be harmed." Official recognition, though essentially symbolic, promised to draw the "bounds of propriety" that the unrestrained exercise of free belief might violate. Specifically, they proposed criteria by which the state would "recognize" religions: those possessing a history of more than 100 years in Japan and counting more than 100,000 adherents, or those possessing 200 years of history in Japan and counting fewer than 100,000 adherents. Any religions relying on foreign sponsorship and subservient to foreign organizations would be automatically excluded from consideration. Any recognition conferred by the state in this manner would not imply fiscal support for Buddhism, but the activists considered it an important safeguard against the further marginalization of Buddhism in the public sphere. For them, the anticipated religion ordinance offered a welcome opportunity to interpret the limits of free belief and differentiate the treatment of religions based on historical particularity and numerical representation.[53]

As shrine priests and Buddhist clerics organized to try to openly influence state policy, the government moved quickly to curtail their ability to directly influence the Imperial Diet through elections. Targeting the political activity of clerics, however, raised anew the interpretive requirement to distinguish between the religious and nonreligious. When the Privy Council first deliberated the House of Representatives Election Law in 1888, for example, Mori Arinori questioned the wisdom of listing shrine priests and Buddhist clerics (*shinkan sōryo*) together in the article designating those disqualified from standing for election. Itō Hirobumi defended the wording and disingenuously denied that the law made any determination of what was or was not religious. In addition to preventing clerics from running for office, the Home Ministry directed Shinto and Buddhist superintendents to prevent their clerics from endorsing or campaigning on behalf of any political parties.[54] Such partisan activity, the ministry warned, not only threatened to divide adherents (*shinto*), but also risked undermining the state itself by leading believers astray (presumably by introducing a religious component to partisan affairs). The Home Ministry also warned shrine priests (*shinkan shinshoku*) formally unaffiliated with Shinto sects and their superintendents not to involve themselves in elections.[55]

Ironically, the ambiguous status of the majority of shrine priests as both officials of the state and private religionists facilitated their political organization. The Shrine Priest Service Regulations issued in July 1891 for priests serving at shrines at the prefectural shrines and below, for example, affirmed the status of the priests as officials subject to the direct oversight of the state. By allowing the shrine priests themselves to draft specific regulations at the local level, however, the service regulations provided the impetus for the organization of local associations across the country, which in turn facilitated the formation of a national shrine-priests movement.[56] Their truncated status as officials of the state allowed shrine priests to evade direct state control and lobby the Imperial Diet through the 1890s, while their vestigial claim to official status enabled them to claim they were pursuing public, not sectarian, interests.

The prospect of the shrine priesthood's forming a permanent political movement and employing the Imperial Diet as a means to press its grievances frightened many within the government. Aoki Shūzō, who spearheaded treaty revision negotiations as foreign minister between 1889 and 1892, warned Home Minister Inoue Kaoru that a memorial to the throne demanding a revived Department of Divinities would prove fatal to the negotiations. Should the Diet appear poised to adopt such a memorial, he wrote, "We must employ an imperial edict to stop it." Adopting a memorial sure to scuttle the attempt to revise the unequal treaties was, in Aoki's view, effectively "treasonous" (*bōkokuron*).[57] Although the supraconstitutional authority of the emperor was not preemptively invoked, the fear that the shrine priests would present a memorial to the throne through the Imperial Diet compelled Kunishige Masafumi, head of the Home Ministry Shrine and Temple Bureau, to admonish shrine priests to desist from their efforts to lobby the Diet in the fall of 1890.[58]

The government was not alone in condemning the introduction of sectarian politics to the Imperial Diet. Politically active clerics were widely criticized in the secular press, where the apparent pursuit of sectarian self-interest was frequently denounced as antithetical to the principles of parliamentary government.[59] The *Yomiuri* ran a series of editorials in the summer of 1889 castigating Buddhist clerics who demanded the right to stand for office, arguing that clerics elected to the Diet would inevitably seek to legislate in favor of one religion and would provoke sectarian conflict that would only discredit the representative function of the Imperial Diet. The paper had to concede, nonetheless, that nothing stood in the way of clerics organizing their votes or from laicizing in order to stand for office, thus circumventing any attempt to divide electoral politics and religious activism.[60]

The desire of some clerics to participate in the political process appeared to violate the subjectified contract of religion, a point felt acutely by those who had most actively embraced the category of religion in the 1870s. The *Reichikai zasshi*, a journal first published in 1885 by a group of clerics belonging to the Honganji faction of the Shin sect and under the influence of Shimaji Mokurai, expressed discomfort with politically active Buddhist clerics.[61] Concerning five laicized clerics who represented Hiroshima, Gifu, Hyōgo, and Shimane prefectures in the House of Representatives, the journal's editors cautioned that any appearance that they were promoting a "religious agenda" would only discredit them and the Buddhist community as a whole.[62] Having embraced religion, Buddhist voices were hard-pressed to find avenues to escape the constraints built into the category.

Shrine priests, in contrast, though also criticized for their overt political lobbying, were better poised to use the Imperial Diet as a means to escape the category of religion all together. The National Shinto Priest Conference found fervent advocates in both houses of the Diet, chief among them Ōtsu Jun'ichirō (1857–1932) and Hayakawa Ryūsuke (1853–1933) in the House of Representatives, and Maruyama Sakura and Iwashita Masahira in the House of Peers.[63] Ōtsu was by far the most effective advocate for the shrine priests' cause, and his political biography illustrates how representative politics, born of the Freedom and People's Rights Movement, connected to reinvigorated articulations of *kokutai* and *saisei itchi*. Born to a Mito-domain retainer the year Perry sailed into Edo Bay, Ōtsu saw his father and elder brother fight for the loyalist cause. Following the Restoration, he participated in local political associations demanding representative government, eventually joining Ōkuma Shigenobu's moderately conservative Constitutional Reform Party (Rikken kaishintō). Ōtsu served two terms in the prefectural assembly before winning election to the House of Representatives in the first general election.[64] A former samurai from Mito, steeped in the intellectual tradition of Aizawa Seishisai's Mito Learning, Ōtsu became the leading advocate of the *kokutai* and the principle of *saisei itchi* in the Imperial Diet.

Critical to understanding the political support shrine priests garnered in the Imperial Diet is the fact that Ōtsu and others promoted the ideals of the *kokutai* and the unity of rite and rule as a means to criticize the oligarchic government. Demanding a revived Department of Divinities was an effective cudgel with which to challenge the legitimacy of a government that attempted to remain "transcendent" in relation to the Imperial Diet.[65] In addition to instrumentalist support, the shrine priests' cause had undeniably idealistic supporters; Ōtsu himself was clearly a true believer. As a result, Diet members who sponsored the call to revive a Department of Divinities cut across a relatively broad partisan spectrum, including veterans of the Freedom and People's Rights Movement, such as Ōtsu, and members of parties more closely aligned with the government.[66]

Ōtsu and his fellow sponsors drafted memorials to the throne (*jōsōan*) requesting the revival of the Department of Divinities and submitted them to the House of Representatives during each of the first three Diet sessions between 1890 and 1892. These sessions were frequently cut short, however, by the intractable conflict between the parties and the government over the budget, and the draft memorials never reached the floor for debate.[67] The repeated dissolutions of the Diet resulted in frequent general elections, which, in turn, created opportunities for electoral activism on the part of shrine priests.[68] The political utility of the shrine priests' cause was increased when the political parties attempted to leverage foreign policy to undermine the legitimacy of the government.[69] A draft memorial to the throne finally made it onto the agenda of the lower house during the fourth Diet session in late 1892, for example, just as the final negotiations for a revised treaty with the British government were under way.[70] Most parties, even those nominally aligned with the government, adopted a hard-line posture (the so-called *taigai kōha*) in the fierce debate over treaty revision and chose to express their disapproval of the government's position by supporting the revival of the Department of Divinities. Public outrage had already scuttled negotiations in 1887, when the government was denounced for granting concessions, including negotiated tariff rates and the appointment of foreign judges to the judiciary, in the interest of hastening treaty revision.[71] As a new round of negotiations commenced under the second Itō cabinet in 1892, the oligarchic government's willingness to officially elevate the administrative status of shrines became a litmus test for its perceived strength or weakness in relation to the treaty powers.[72] The government was incapable of openly rejecting appeals to the cardinal virtues of safeguarding the *kokutai* and promoting *saisei itchi*, making the shrine priests' cause a very effective weapon to wield in the name of representing the public will and national self-respect. A draft memorial submitted to the House of Representatives in December 1893 carried the supporting signatures of more than 120 out of 300 members, a level of support clearly tied to the intensifying treaty negotiations then being conducted by Foreign Minister Mutsu Munemitsu.[73] The moment of political opportunity was lost, however, when a vote of no confidence was taken against the scandal-ridden speaker of the House of Representatives, Hoshi Tōru (1850–1901).

The contest between the parties and the government over the issue of treaty revision thus promoted electoral cooperation between clerics and party politicians. For shrine priests and Buddhist clerics alike, treaty reform promised mixed residence and the uninhibited influx of foreign Christians, whose missions had ample funds to purchase real estate and establish churches, schools, and hospitals. Material advantage alone appeared destined to obliterate shrines and temples alike, in the absence of active support from the state. For party politicians, Buddhist clerics provided the promise of organized votes and shrine priests delivered the grounds to criticize the oligarchic government. Parties adopting a hard line on treaty negotiations in the general election that followed the dissolution of the fifth Diet in March 1894, for example, appealed to shrine priests and Buddhist clerics by emphasizing the likelihood that mixed residence would inevitably lead to the spread of "foreign religion."[74] The Itō government responded to the electoral activism by clerics with a Home Ministry directive explicitly prohibiting clerics from "directly or indirectly participating in political debate, joining political parties, and involving themselves in the competition of elections."[75] This and more overt forms of government suppression cost five of the original six sponsors of the lower house draft memorial, including Ōtsu, their seats.[76]

The success of treaty revision and a surge of patriotism that accompanied the Sino-Japanese War in the second half of 1894 altered the political dynamics of the Imperial Diet considerably and a new modus vivendi replaced the near paralysis of the early Diet sessions.[77] The revised Commerce and Navigation Treaty with Great Britain, exchanged in July 1894, set the clock for the commencement of mixed residence five years later. This prompted a wide-ranging review of laws and regulatory practices by the government and refocused attention on an anticipated religion ordinance or law. At the same time, the Sino-Japanese War temporarily neutralized the budget as the primary topic of contention in the Imperial Diet and allowed debate on a range of issues, including the revival of the Department of Divinities.

Convened in December 1894, in the midst of the Sino-Japanese War, the eighth Imperial Diet thus proved remarkably productive in debating bills and motions related to the disposition of shrines, temples, and religion more generally.[78] A forestry bill containing provisions for the return of state-owned forestlands to shrines and temples reintroduced questions concerning their fiscal independence and administrative equivalence. A bill to revise the superintendent system provoked debate concerning the autonomy of religious sects and extracted an explicit promise of a religion bill from the government, while a draft memorial to revive the Department of Divinities was put to a vote for the first time.

The government's forestry bill, with its provision to return confiscated land to shrines and temples, reinforced the conception of religion as a private matter involving private property. The constitutional affirmation of the integrity of religious belief as a private concern gave the confiscation of shrine and temple property at the beginning of the Meiji era the appearance of flagrantly violating property rights and threatening the self-sufficiency of shrines and temples. Proponents of the bill framed the debate as a matter of property rights and demanded that confiscated land beyond the precincts of shrines and temples that remained in the state's hands be returned. As in the Yamagata cabinet's deliberations in 1890, the fault line of the deliberations lay between the desire to preserve historical shrines and temples and the desire to conserve forestry resources. The forestry bill faced stiff opposition in the Diet, however, where concerns to safeguard state assets, as well as lingering skepticism about the ability of clerics to manage the land, blocked the forestry bill and subsequent attempts to return confiscated property outright.[79] The forestry law that was finally promulgated five years later in the spring of 1899 provided a framework called Shrine and Temple Forest Custodianship Regulations, whereby shrines and temples could take custody of, but not repossess, confiscated forestlands.[80] Crucial to our interests here, these regulations created an administrative precedent for treating shrines and temples as equivalent entities in the eyes of the state.

The eighth Diet also debated a draft bill submitted to the House of Representatives by Hatoyama Kazuo (1856–1911) from Ōkuma Shigenobu's Constitutional Reform Party.[81] The bill aimed to redress the perceived failure of the 1884 superintendent system to prevent disputes within Buddhist sects. Intrasectarian disputes concerning the appointment of superintendents, the designation of head and branch temples, and attempts by some temples to break off into new sects or branches had been widely reported in the press, and these reinforced the perception that religious entities were not only prone to disputation and schism, but often for petty reasons.[82] The Sōtō sect of Buddhism provided the most notorious example of schism, and the dispute had proven so intractable that the Home Minister had assumed provisional administrative control of the sect.[83] The vague statutory basis for the government's response to the Sōtō dispute came under criticism in the Diet as an unwarranted intervention into what should have been the autonomous sphere of religious life.[84] The superintendent system, intended to facilitate the self-governance of religious sects and indirect supervision by the state, had ironically resulted in direct state intervention. The bill Hatoyama and his colleagues submitted would have amended the 1884 Home Ministry ordinance to make a law that safeguarded "as much as is possible" the self-governance of sects by strengthening the authority of superintendents over the affairs of their sects.[85] The debate on the floor of the House of Representatives did not question the premise that the state was ill-served by being drawn into sectarian disputes. The language of Hatoyama's bill only addressed Shinto and Buddhist sects, however, and contained no generic language applicable to Christianity. When the Home Ministry, fearful of losing control over the drafting of a religion bill, promised a bill regulating religion in general, Hatoyama's bill was quickly voted down.[86]

These debates made it clear that the Imperial Diet was perilously close to affirming the understanding of "religion" as a sphere of autonomous, private competition wherein the state had little incentive to differentiate its regulatory treatment of specific religions. The explicit promise of a general religion bill compelled the shrine priests and their parliamentary allies to redouble their efforts to place as much of shrine Shinto outside the reach of that legislation and its equalizing logic as possible. A draft memorial to the throne calling for a Department of Divinities finally reached the floor of the House of Representatives against this backdrop. Sponsored by Ōtsu Jun'ichirō, Hayakawa Ryūsuke, and three others, the draft's signed supporters had dwindled to thirty-one members of the lower house, nearly a quarter of the number of supporters during the fifth Diet. The shrinking support reflected the diminished partisan utility of the shrine priests' cause following treaty revision.[87]

Because this was the first draft memorial seeking a Department of Divinities to be debated on the floor of the Imperial Diet, the manner in which its authors framed their demand deserves some scrutiny. As indicated earlier, the oligarchic government took the position that the principle of *saisei itchi*, unifying rite and rule, was institutionally satisfied so long as the emperor conducted rites within the imperial palace and all shrines followed a standardized calendar of rites. A separate department of state dedicated to administering all shrines and their priests and to conducting its own rites, as was envisioned in the immediate aftermath of the Restoration, threatened to compete with the emperor's personal and well-circumscribed role as chief ritualist of the state. Tellingly, the draft memorial did not challenge directly the government's limited vision for *saisei itchi*. The Department of Divinities was necessary, it argued, not for the emperor to conduct rites, but as a site in which his *subjects* could express veneration; hence it would not intrude on the existing institutional arrangement of palace rites.[88] This was a significant concession that reflected the diminished ambitions of the Shinto cause; by abandoning the premise that a revived department would establish a direct link between the emperor's rites within the palace and all shrines across the realm, a relatively minor bureaucratic adjustment would suffice to separate the supervision of shrines from that of Buddhist temples and other sects. The shrine priests and their advocates abandoned the grand project of uniting rite and rule and instead sought a modest bureaucratic adjustment to escape the administrative logic of religion. The draft memorial debated by the eighth Diet thus explicitly disassociated the Kashikodokoro within the palace from any shrine department that would be created, and instead focused its demands on removing the supervision of the Grand Shrines of Ise and all other shrines from a small bureau within the Home Ministry.[89]

When Ōtsu rose to present the draft memorial and field questions, he accordingly disavowed any interest in reviving the eighth-century Department of Divinities. He refused, nonetheless, to abandon the principle that all shrines conducted rites of the state (*kokka no sōshi*).[90] Because it left the imperial institution largely untouched, this diminished vision for a Department of Divinities did secure a measure of support from within the palace as well. Debate in the House of Representatives accordingly revolved less around the desirability of placing shrines outside of religion and more around the constitutional authority of the Imperial Diet.[91] Distinguishing the new department from the imperial institution appeared to undercut the need to move it outside of the Home Ministry, and even if the department were to be created within the Imperial Household, the Diet did not appear to possess the authority to dictate the organization of the Imperial Household. Motions to send the draft to committee or to extend debate were defeated by narrow margins in the face of these concerns, and a final secret ballot defeated the draft memorial by ten votes.[92]

Ōtsu and his supporters returned to the ninth Imperial Diet with a draft recommendation (*kengian*) to the government. The recommendation, addressing the cabinet instead of the throne, neutralized the constitutional concerns, and the draft secured more than twice the number of supporters (eighty-two).[93] The sponsors again proclaimed the public and nonsectarian character of the recommendation; Kitahara Nobutsuna (1849–1901) of the Constitutional Reform Party rhetorically challenged anyone in the Imperial Diet to oppose the need to maintain the "dignity of the *kokutai*" (*kokutai no songen*). Komuro Shigehiro (1858–1908), a former journalist and veteran of the Freedom and People's Rights Movement, however, countered that the recommendation was nothing but an expression of sectarian self-interest. The shrine priests assumed, he observed, that if a state department dedicated to shrines were revived, they would "receive a salary"; in short, the draft recommendation was, "crass, incoherent, sloppy, and negligent." Ōtsu retorted that the principle of *saisei itchi* had never been formally denied by the state and that to "treat the Department of Divinities in the same manner as the filthy religion of foreign countries is to shame Japan's *kokutai*."[94] While the petty self-interest of shrine priests was easily denounced, few were willing to directly oppose appeals to the national polity and the premise that imperial rites were part of the state.

The vote in the House of Representatives was taken not by closed ballot but by a standing vote, and it passed by a clear majority. The more conservative House of Peers passed a similar recommendation without debate.[95] This success in early 1896, coming nearly six years after the first Imperial Diet convened, marked a significant threshold for the political position of Shinto shrines and their priests. The passage, in both houses of the Imperial Diet, of recommendations calling for a special department dedicated to the administration of Shinto shrines served to validate the public and nonsectarian claims of the shrine priests, and vindicated their investment in the representative function of the Diet.

This apparent victory in lifting shrines beyond the category of religion was undercut, however, by the very same Imperial Diet in the name of preserving the art and history of the nation. As an outgrowth of the debate to return forestlands to shrines and temples, during the eighth Diet the House of Representatives had passed a recommendation to the government calling for the conservation of ancient shrines and temples in the name of art.[96] Even those opposed to elevating the status of shrines were eager to support the cultural and artistic value of shrines and temples. Komuro Shigehiro, who loudly criticized the revival of a Department of Divinities, declared from the floor of the lower house that the "first thing to insist upon is the preservation of art."[97] Clearly willing to support shrines and temples in the name of national heritage, the Itō cabinet submitted a bill that was promulgated as the Ancient Shrine and Temple Preservation Law (Koshaji hozonhō) on June 10, 1897. The law permitted shrines and temples to request preservation funds from the Home Minister, and a preservation committee would weigh their historical significance, provenance, or artistic merit to determine whether preservation was merited. A structure or object with particular historical or artistic merit could be designated a special protected building or a national treasure, turning what had been the treasure of a particular shrine or temple into something designated as valuable to the entire nation. Shrines and temples that received the preservation funds and that possessed items designated as national treasures were obligated to submit them to museums for display, in exchange for compensation.[98]

In practice, the law introduced a system through which a select group of shrines and temples could be singled out for direct state aid by creating a distinction between the religious function of the buildings and items and their value as repositories of national heritage.[99] For those seeking to revive permanent state support for imperial and national shrines, such as Senge Takatomi, onetime chief priest of the Grand Shrine of

Izumo, leader of the Taisha-kyō sect, and then member of the House of Peers, the law appeared to be a favorable first step toward their goal. The transposition of the private religious possessions of shrines and temples into the public cultural heritage of the nation-state had its limits, however. The law included the caveat that treasures employed for rites and services (*saiten hōyō*) would be exempted from the requirement to lend them to museums for exhibition; those private religious instruments could never fully become public symbols denuded of their particular functional significance.[100] Thus, if shrines were to seek exemptions from the provisions of the preservation law, they would have to do so in the name of ritual practices that were religious in nature. The shrines and temples recognized by the Ancient Shrine and Temple Preservation Committee in effect joined the ranks of the imperial and national shrines and received state aid, with one crucial distinction. Under the Shrine Preservation Fund, shrines were expected eventually to achieve self-sufficiency; the Ancient Shrine and Temple Preservation Law, in contrast, placed the artistic and cultural merit of select shrines beyond the struggle for self-sufficiency.[101]

For this reason, the press was critical of the preservation law as it applied to Buddhist temples. *Taiyō*, the general interest journal with the largest circulation of the day, observed critically that, under the provisions of the law, "temples no longer stand on faith but under the state's preservation of art," and as a result, a temple ceased to be a "religious building" and became an "exposition hall."[102] Also, the law created yet another regulatory space in which temples and shrines were recognized as functional equivalents by placing both within the common framework of art preservation. Rejecting the regulatory category of religion in favor of art secured state funds, but at the cost of muddying the distinction between shrines and temples and undercutting the premise that shrines belonged to an entirely different regulatory sphere from temples and even religion more generally.

This point was not lost on parliamentary supporters of the shrine priests' movement. In a letter to Prime Minister Matsukata, Maruyama Sakura, Negishi Takeka (1839–1902), a *kokugakusha* appointed to the House of Peers, and Hayakawa Ryūsuke denounced the state's inconsistent treatment of shrines since the Restoration and singled out the Ancient Shrine and Temple Preservation Law as a particular point of protest: "Worst of all, what does it mean to treat shrines as individual objects in the name of preservation?"[103] Pressed to resolve the intolerable confusion created by the overlapping regulative grammars—of art preservation, religious freedom, sectarian autonomy, and a suprareligious *kokutai*—the

Matsukata cabinet sent a patently unsatisfying response to the House of Representatives in the spring of 1897: "The matter of creating a government office dedicated to Shinto rites [*jingi*] is of grave importance and cannot be implemented casually. Therefore, it is currently being studied by the government."[104] Bureaucratic inertia, generated by regulatory practices accumulated since the Restoration, became as much an obstacle as the reluctance of the leadership.

In light of the cabinet's manifest reluctance to adopt the demotic voice of the Imperial Diet, the formation of the first party cabinet with Ōkuma Shigenobu as prime minister and Itagaki Taisuke (1837–1919) as home minister in June 1898 generated considerable anticipation among shrine priests and their advocates.[105] Ōkuma and Itagaki, both prominent opponents of the domain-clique (*hanbatsu*) mode of government, assumed positions with the constitutional authority to amend the bureaucratic structure of the state as leaders of political parties that had expressed support for reviving a Department of Divinities.[106] In fact, the Ōkuma cabinet planned to extensively revise state departments, with the avowed goal of reducing the oligarchic hold over the government. The cabinet drafted an edict creating a Shrine Bureau (Jinja kyoku) as part of that process.[107] A leaked draft was welcomed by the more conservative press, but the Ōkuma cabinet was too short-lived to implement it.[108] Support for the shrine priests' cause remained closely associated with the political parties' attempt to undermine the oligarchy's hold on the government.

The National Shrine Priests Association (Zenkoku shinshokukai), the first truly national Shinto priest association, formed in November 1898, just as the Ōkuma-Itagaki government collapsed. With mixed residence commencing the following summer, the association declared blocking any potential legislation that would regulate shrines as religious institutions as its foremost objective.[109] Spurred by the new association, both houses of the thirteenth Imperial Diet adopted recommendations in early 1899 calling for the separate regulation of shrines and religion. In the House of Peers, Kii Toshihide (1870–1940), himself from a family of shrine priests, reiterated that with mixed residence fast approaching no one expected "something as grand as a Department of Divinities [Jingikan]"; all that was being asked was that the government "take the shrine section within the Shrine and Temple Bureau and create a separate Shrine Bureau or Shrine Department" inside the Home Ministry.[110]

Insisting that these newly adopted recommendations legitimated their demands as reflecting public opinion, the National Shrine Priests Association pressed the cabinet ministers to respond.[111] In a petition to Prime

Minister Yamagata, for example, regional priests declared confidently that "adopting public opinion [*yoron*] is the purpose of constitutional government."[112] The government could not overtly question the legitimacy of public opinion validated by the Imperial Diet, and the priests felt they received favorable responses from cabinet ministers, including Home Minister Saigō Tsugumichi (1843–1902), even as they chaffed at the evident lack of movement on the part of the government: "Not one member of the government has voiced opposition, yet the matter is not being acted upon today."[113]

Unable to ignore the recommendations adopted by the Imperial Diet, the cabinet under Yamagata Aritomo considered its options. Saigō Tsugumichi presented the Home Ministry's view: "Not only is no need recognized for creating a special office [for shrines] in view of the current system's administrative scope, there is considerable overlap in the regulatory work that deals with shrines and temples. It is therefore impossible to separate them into different offices." The Ancient Shrine and Temple Preservation Law and the Shrine and Temple Forest Custodianship Regulations placed shrines and temples within a common bureaucratic framework, and the Home Ministry claimed that creating a separate office for shrines was impossible in view of its regulatory mandates. In effect, the piecemeal accumulation of legislation meant to secure the fiscal health of shrines and temples stood in the way of a clean administrative break between shrines and their religious counterparts. In addition to its own bureaucratic logic, the Home Ministry also rejected the theoretical premise that the state could employ ordinances and regulatory practices to establish any distinction between religion and shrines: "The distinction between shrines and religion relies entirely on the original character of shrines."[114] This disingenuous disclaimer suggests Home Ministry bureaucrats were reluctant to admit the arbitrary and hence continually contestable character of that distinction.

Despite the Home Ministry's manifest reluctance to overtly define the boundary separating shrines from religion, the Civil Code required a clear demarcation. The thirty-third article of the code, passed in 1896, stipulated that "corporations or foundations that promote the public interest through rites, religion, charity, learning, or the arts, and do not operate for profit, may incorporate as juridical persons [*hōjin*] with the authorization of competent authorities." Admitting the potential implications of this dry formulation, the law promulgating the code in 1898 included a caveat: "The stipulations concerning juridical persons within the Civil Code will not, for the time being, apply to shrines, temples, fanes [*shiu*] and Buddha halls [*butsudō*]."[115] This exemption purchased some time for the government to clarify how these disparate entities would be allowed to incorporate as legal entities.[116] The Home Ministry was thus legally compelled to draft legislation that would clarify the distinction between shrines and temples, Shinto and religion, and hence safeguard the reverence due to shrines without radically altering bureaucratic practices. The Home Ministry conveyed to the House of Representatives its decision to prioritize legislation over the executive creation of an administrative department dedicated to shrines:

> The decision whether or not to establish a special office for shrines concerns primarily the nature and scope of executive administration [*gyōsei jimu*]. The nature and scope of executive administration is primarily determined by statute, and the government hopes to enact special legislation concerned with shrines and thus prevent any loss of reverence for shrines. Therefore, the decision whether or not to establish a special office for shrines will await the determination of the nature and scope of executive administration through the enactment of such legislation.[117]

The emphasis on legislation here is significant, for it credits the Imperial Diet with the authority to legislate the interpretive divide between religion and shrines. It was also a consistent application of the government's refusal to elevate shrines through sovereign prerogatives exercised in the name of the emperor. This, and a nearly identical response sent to the House of Peers, came very near the end of the thirteenth Diet in early 1899 and was interpreted as yet another oligarchic rejection of the Imperial Diet's demotic will.[118] It was, all the same, a clear promise that the government would legislatively place shrines outside of the regulatory grammar of religion. The enthusiastic increase in support for the Grand Shrines of Ise granted by the Imperial Diet in 1898 also underscored the success with which prominent segments of the Shinto community were supported as public entities.[119] All the shrine priests and their allies had to do was ensure that the Home Ministry excluded all shrines from the religion bill it would draft and submit to the Imperial Diet.

Legislating Religion in Meiji Japan

By early 1899, advocates for Shinto shrines had successfully employed the Imperial Diet to set shrines apart, at least in principle, from the regulatory and administrative domain of religion. What remained was the promised legislation to uniformly define the state's regulatory relationship to religion, and with it the separate regulation of shrines. For

Buddhist sectarians, incapable of extracting themselves from the discursive and regulatory space of religion, the prospect of legislation that did not differentiate among the state's relationships with various religions was disquieting. The final years of the nineteenth century thus witnessed a critical clash between Buddhist sects and the government over legislation debated in the Imperial Diet. The debates that accompanied the submission and ultimate defeat of the Religion Bill during the fourteenth Diet defined the political limits of religion under the Imperial Constitution. Buddhist sects were unable to escape the constraints imposed by a normative grammar of religion defined and policed through regulatory practice.

The impending commencement of mixed residence in July 1899 provided the immediate backdrop to the political focus on the regulatory disposition of religion. The elimination of extraterritoriality and the end to most legal constraints on travel, residence, and property ownership by foreign residents generated a sense of foreboding and exposed an ambivalence in Japan as it wavered between its growing confidence as an emerging imperial power in Asia and its abiding sense of vulnerability in relation to a more powerful West.[120] In 1898, the journal *Taiyō* laid out the anticipated effects of mixed residence on education in a detailed diagram (Fig. 5.1).[121] Direct effects included the growth of schools established by foreigners (assumedly Christian missionaries), an increase in foreign children entering "our schools," and an increase of "mixed race" students in the schools. Indirect influences on the realm of thought included shifting morals, changes in principles, religious conflict, heightened xenophobia, and an increase in material knowledge. Language and writing would be influenced by the need to use foreign terms, and customs would be affected by changing lifestyles, etiquette, and mores. Livelihoods would be affected by increased competition with foreign capital as well as the need to improve knowledge and skills.

The effects, as enumerated by one of the most popular magazines of the Meiji era, indicate the threat of foreign encroachment still carried the shadow of Christian conversion. Accordingly, the approach of mixed residence, and an assumed influx of foreign missionaries and mission funds, reignited public interest in the regulation of Christianity. Rehearsing the script of the Conflict between Education and Religion debate from earlier in the decade, the apparent overrepresentation of Christian institutions in the educational sphere attracted the greatest amount of concern.[122] Home Ministry bureaucrats were no less concerned. In anticipation of mixed residence, the Home Ministry informed the Foreign Ministry that British and American Christian denominations were

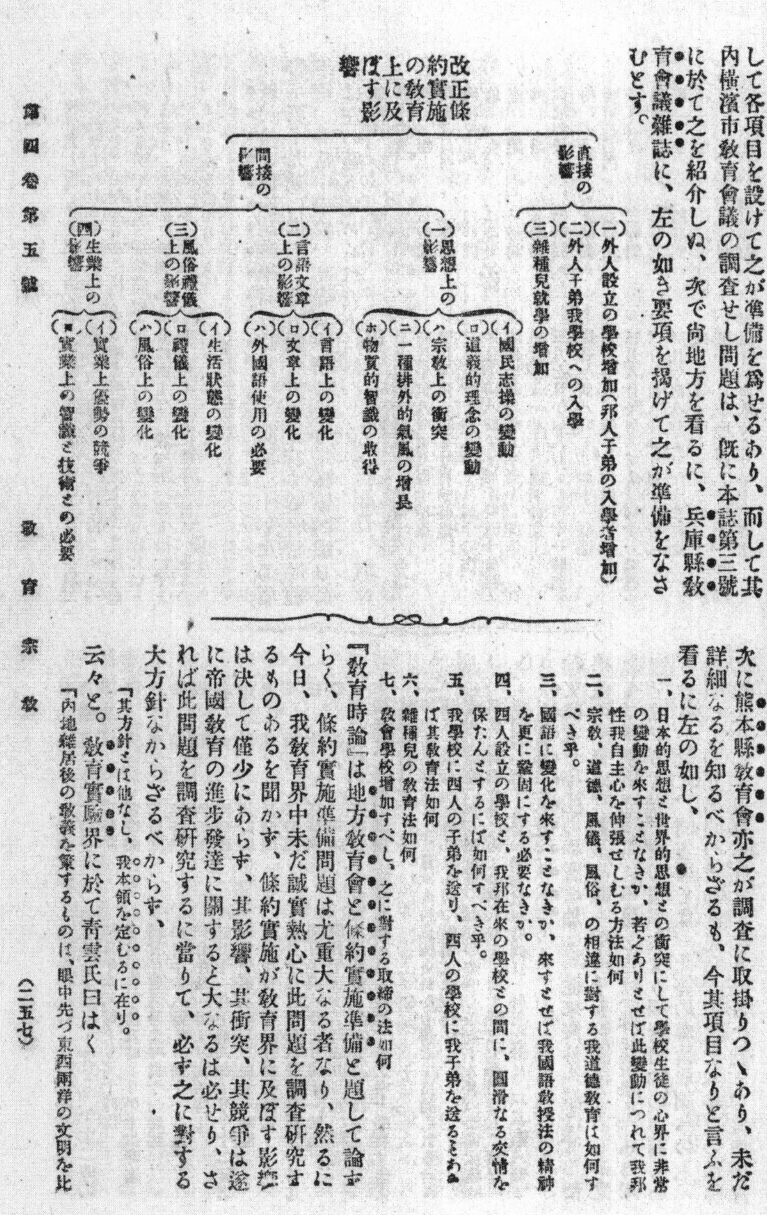

して各項目を設けて之が準備を爲せるあり、而して其內橫濱市教育會議の調査せし問題は、既に本誌第三號に於て之を紹介しぬ、次で尚地方を看るに、兵庫縣教育會議雜誌に、左の如き要項を掲げて之が準備をなさむとす。

改正條約實施の教育上に及ぼす影響

- 直接の影響
  - （一）外人設立の學校增加（邦人子弟の入學者增加）
  - （二）外人子弟我學校への入學
  - （三）雜種兒就學の增加
- 間接の影響
  - （一）思想上の影響
    - （イ）國民志操の變動
    - （ロ）道義的理念の變動
    - （ハ）宗教上の衝突
    - （ニ）一種排外的氣風の增長
    - （ホ）物質的智識の收得
  - （二）言語文章上の影響
    - （イ）言語上の變化
    - （ロ）文章上の變化
    - （ハ）外國語使用の必要
  - （三）風俗禮儀上の影響
    - （イ）生活狀態の變化
    - （ロ）禮儀上の變化
    - （ハ）風俗上の變化
  - （四）生業上の影響
    - （イ）實業上優勢の競爭
    - （ロ）實業上の智識と技術との必要

次に熊本縣教育會亦之が調査に取掛りつゝあり、未だ詳細なるを知るべからざるも、今其項目なりと言ふを看るに左の如し、

一、日本的思想と世界的思想との衝突にして學校生徒の心界に非常の變動を來すことなきか、若之ありとせば此變動につれて我邦性我自主心を伸張せしむる方法如何
二、宗教、道德、風儀、風俗、の相違に對する我道德教育は如何すべき乎。
三、國語に變化を來すことなきか、來すとせば我國語教授法の精神を更に鞏固にする必要なきか。
四、西人設立の學校と、我邦在來の學校との間に、圓滑なる交情を保たんとするには如何すべき乎。
五、我學校に西人の子弟を送り、西人の學校に我子弟を送るとあらば其教育法如何
六、雜種兒の教育法如何
七、教會學校增加すべし、之に對する取締の法如何

『教育時論』は地方教育會と條約實施準備と題して論ずらく、條約實施準備問題は尤重大なる者なり、然るに今日、我教育界中未だ誠實熱心に此問題を調査研究するものあるを聞かず、條約實施が教育界に及ぼす影響は決して僅少にあらず、其影響、其衝突、其競爭は遂に帝國教育の進歩發達に關すると大なるは必せり、されば此問題を調査研究するに當りて、必ず之に對する大方針なからざるべからず、

「其方針とは他なし、我本領を定むるに在り。」

云々と。教育實驗界に於て靑雲氏曰はく

「內地雜居後の教義を策するものは、眼中先づ東西兩洋の文明を比

第四卷第五號　教育宗教　（二五七）

FIG. 5.1. “The Effects of Treaty Revision on Education.” From “Naichi zakkyo to chihō kyōiku kaigi,” *Taiyō* 4, no. 5 (1898): 257.

planning a large missionary push involving 300 male and 500 female missionaries who would arrive in Japan by 1902 and would seek to gain 8 million converts, at an estimated expense of 4.5 million yen. The memo warned that these foreign missions were intent on "capturing the people's hearts" (*jinshin wo shūran*).[123] One commentator in the press summarized the issue confronting the state in two questions: should Christianity be treated on equal terms with Buddhism and Shinto, and should Christian schools be allowed to teach religion in accredited curricula?[124] For most people the answer was simple—Christianity had to be placed under constraints applicable to all religions.[125]

The approach of mixed residence, fueled by a general anxiety, reinforced the political salience of the religious settlement. The state could not specifically target Christianity, but it could contain the most onerous effects of increased missionary activity by producing a general religion law that regulated all religions equally. Buddhist sects for their part approached the prospect of new legislation affecting their relationship to the state and to Christianity by waging a two-front war. On the one hand, they frequently attacked Christianity as incompatible with the *kokutai* and called for restricting Christians' access to educational and correctional institutions, while on the other hand, they lobbied for an expanded public role for Buddhism.[126] The long-standing *kōninkyō* movement thus increased in intensity in the final two years of the nineteenth century, with Buddhist clerics organizing "mixed residence preparation committees" across Japan.[127] Spearheaded by Ishikawa Shuntai (1842–1931), the modernizing reformer of the Ōtani branch of the Shin sect, these committees submitted more than 300 petitions and 200,000 signatures to the Imperial Diet by the time the government submitted its Religion Bill in December 1899.[128] The scale and intensity of the movement to secure state recognition for Buddhism naturally attracted considerable commentary, which in turn articulated anew the increasingly normative grammar of religion.

Critics of the Buddhist movement, both from within the Buddhist establishment and from the secular press, consistently reinforced the conception that a religion, to be authentically religious, had to accept unfettered competition, free from state support. For Buddhist reformers like Nakanishi Ushirō and Inoue Enryo, the movement appeared a "cowardly" retreat from the "daily competition to survive." Mixed residence to them seemed to be an opportunity worth embracing in order to shed the decadent and retrograde features of Buddhism and better compete with Christianity.[129] The Shingon journal *Dentō* invoked Herbert Spencer and exhorted Buddhist clerics and sects to prepare themselves for "natural selection" (*shizen tōta*).[130] The secular press likened the *kōninkyō* movement to the voice of "a jealous woman," and denounced associations such as the National Alliance (Kokumin dōmeikai), the Buddhist Youth Alliance (Bukkyō seinenkai), and the Recognized Religion Establishment Alliance (Kōninkyō kisei dōmeikai) for operating in the "style of political parties" (*seitōsharyū*).[131] Perhaps nothing summarized the criticism and ridicule directed toward Buddhism better than a political cartoon published in the September 10, 1899, issue of the *Jiji shinpō* newspaper (Fig. 5.2). A line of clerics representing Buddhist sects is depicted force feeding Saigō Tsugumichi, the home minister, with ladles of their own miso (*temae miso*), a metaphor for self-centered convenience, while a weeping Buddha looks down from the middle of a sun setting on the horizon.[132] The press policed the normative schema in which religion properly belonged to a sphere of conversionary competition; any religion seeking to avoid competition was clearly not properly religious.[133] Competition was considered salutary and essential to producing "civilized religion," by eliminating epistemically flawed and socially malignant forms of religion through a process akin to natural selection. The very fact that a vocal segment of the Buddhist community wanted to avoid competition only confirmed in the eyes of many its decadence and backwardness.[134]

FIG. 5.2. "Buddhist Dharma in the Latter Age." From "Masse no buppō," *Jiji shinpō*, September 10, 1899, 3.

In addition to its transparent desire to avoid unfettered competition in the wake of mixed residence, the *kōninkyō* movement was criticized for its appeal to Buddhism's status as the faith of the national majority. Buddhist critics attacked the very premise that Buddhism should stake a majoritarian claim on the nation-state, since doing so would "produce within a single nation those who look upon others as enemies."[135] The rejection of toleration as a constitutional principle invalidated any association of sectarian identity with national identity, and this accounts for a fundamental distinction between the shrine priests' movement and the Buddhist movement. By rejecting the category of religion, the shrine priests and their allies could employ the Imperial Diet to represent their cause as a national cause. The Buddhists' embrace of religion in the 1870s as a means to secure greater autonomy, in contrast, invalidated in principle any attempt to represent Buddhism qua religion as national. The Ancient Shrine and Temple Preservation Law afforded special recognition to Buddhism as a source of art, or cultural heritage, not as religion. To speak or be addressed as a religion precluded certain political articulations. Appeals to be a religious majority—and its corollary, a religious minority—were both foreclosed by the normative grammar of religion in place by the late 1890s.

For its part, the government's path to drafting the Religion Bill, though guided by the clear goal of bringing Christianity under the supervision of the Home Ministry, was not a simple one. To prepare for mixed residence, the government pursued legal and administrative adjustments covering a broad range of matters as they applied to foreign nationals, including the regulation of Christianity.[136] In late 1897 the Revised Treaty Preparation Committee compiled a list of statutes and ordinances that required adoption or revision, and ministries were ordered to submit draft bills to the cabinet by the following April. In this communication the Foreign Ministry reminded the Home Ministry that, under current administrative arrangements, "no religions apart from Shinto and Buddhism were recognized as religion," and that "it is absolutely necessary to take measures to recognize Christianity and other foreign faiths (*gaikyō*) as religion."[137]

Admitting it could not draft a comprehensive legislative solution to religious regulation prior to mixed residence, the Home Ministry opted in the summer of 1898 to issue a provisional ministerial ordinance to bring Christianity under state supervision. The cabinet-level deliberations of this ordinance indicate an abiding concern to shield the state from engaging in the doctrinal particulars of religions. As Saigō Tsugumichi summarized it, the crux of the ordinance was to "treat it [Christianity] as a religion." That seemingly simple task was complicated by the fact that the state's supervision of "religion" had evolved in relation to the doctrinal and institutional particulars of Shinto and Buddhist sects. Integrating Christianity into the regulatory framework while maintaining the "balance" (*kenkō*) between the three raised difficult questions, questions that the Home Ministry repeatedly stated could be resolved only by future legislation that it promised would deal with "religion in general" (*shūkyō ippan*).[138]

As the draft ordinance passed through the Legal Codes Research Committee (Hōten chōsakai) and returned to the cabinet for deliberation, the ordinance's implicit regulation of doctrinal content provided a point of contention.[139] Article 1 of the draft ordinance required all religious proselytizers to submit information to local governors, including the essentials of their doctrine and ritual (*kyōshi oyobi gishiki no taiyō*). To critics like Aoki Shuzō, then foreign minister, this requirement implied that the state would judge doctrinal content and ritual practice.[140] The ordinance returned to the cabinet with an appended amendment that removed all requirements to submit doctrinal and ritual information, warning that it would otherwise "enter the realm of the intangible and contradict the spirit of the Constitution." The Yamagata cabinet accepted Aoki's objections and the ordinance was limited to regulating tangible facilities, while the regulation of intangible entities, such as sects, was left to existing regulations concerning associations (*kessha*) and to future legislation.[141] The home minister was denied the authority to unilaterally rescind the recognition of religious entities, Shinto and Buddhist clerics and organizations were to be regulated according to prior ordinances, and the ordinance was to expire with the passage of a comprehensive religion bill.[142] The difficult work of legislating regulatory equality among Buddhism, Christianity, and Shinto sects was left for the Religion Bill.

While Christian clerics and churches were provisionally brought under the supervision of the Home Ministry, the government also moved to curtail further Christian encroachment into the domain of education.[143] The state readily apprehended the significance of education as a means to tame social plurality and cognitive relativism. As a consequence, education provided a crucial site for debating the public footprint of religion after the Conflict between Education and Religion. State control over higher education, in particular, progressed through the 1890s, producing a pyramid structure with the imperial universities at the pinnacle. The dominance of the state in this process cemented the meritocratic legitimacy of state-directed education and compelled private schools to accommodate themselves to the directives of the Ministry of Education.[144] Private schools, especially, depended on the ability of their students to qualify for advancement into the higher schools and imperial universities as well as for the privilege of exemption from conscription. The Private School Ordinance (Shigakkōrei) issued in 1899 participated in this larger process of consolidating state control over the educational system, while also addressing the place of religion within state-sanctioned education.[145]

The ordinance transparently aimed to counter the anticipated influx of foreign missionaries intent on expanding Christian education. The initial draft of the ordinance allowed only those who had resided in Japan for five years or more and who were fluent in the Japanese language to establish private schools.[146] It also prohibited religious education and rituals in accredited schools. The Legal Codes Research Committee, sensitive to diplomatic implications, recommended these controversial provisions be amended or removed.[147] In its final form, the Private School Ordinance weakened the provisions meant to restrict foreign access to education in Japan.[148] Rather than abandoning the language excluding religion from accredited curricula, however, the Ministry of Education issued a separate directive that proscribed religious education and rituals in private schools accredited by the state.[149] As a suggestive side note, the decision to forbid religious education through a ministry directive rather than a more formal ordinance was reportedly made to avoid issuing it with the emperor's signature.[150] Through such details the imperial institution was meticulously kept aloof from the matter of religion.

Christian schools greeted the directive with dismay.[151] Representatives of six leading Christian schools (including Dōshisha, Meiji, Rikkyō, and Aoyama) immediately met in Tokyo and condemned the directive for violating parents' rights to educate their children in the Christian faith and for violating the spirit of the Imperial Constitution.[152] In challenging the constitutionality of the directive, Christian commentary appealed to the divide between the secular public sphere and the religious private sphere. Editors of the theologically liberal journal *Rikugō zasshi*, for example, accepted the premise that publicly financed schools should not teach religion but argued that removing religion from private schools made little sense unless all religion was considered harmful (*yūgai*). The problem, in their view, was that "religion" remained narrowly associated with Christianity in the eyes of xenophobic nationalists who considered religious education to be "no different from having our soil invaded, the hearts of the people tempted, and the appearance of national independence harmed."[153]

In practice, the effect of the directive on Christian schools varied, and in many cases it was temporary. In discursive terms, however, the directive enacted the divide between contingent and necessary identifications by subordinating religious identifications to secular education.[154] Responding to protests that the directive violated the freedom of religious belief, for example, government officials underscored the necessity of protecting education from the conversionary character of religion. Okada Ryōhei (1864–1934), a consultant (*sanyo*) within the Ministry of Education, claimed the directive was intended to prevent religious proselytizing in the classroom but nothing stood in the way of students voluntarily conducting rites or studying a religion outside of the classroom.[155] He disingenuously suggested that, if anything, the directive would protect Christians by prohibiting teachers from denigrating Christianity in the classroom.[156] Kabayama Norisuke (1837–1922), the minister of education, expressed regret that Christian schools suffered as result of the directive but suggested the ordinance provided enough freedom to retain the "spirit" of religious education if not the form. Kabayama appealed to the norms of the religious settlement, assuring the public that the directive was nothing new and reflected long-established principles.[157]

Though some in the press took a jaundiced view of the government's intentions, few contested the premise that religion had no place in the "education of the nation" (*kokumin kyōiku*).[158] Kuga Katsunan wrote that missionaries and Japanese Christians could not complain, since all religions were equally removed from the schools.[159] Reprising the lessons learned during the Iwakura Embassy, he reminded his readers that Europe had shown the way by removing Roman Catholicism from public education and by diluting the sectarian foundations of ethics.[160] Such characterizations of European precedents did not go unchallenged, however. Kamata Eikichi, the president of the private Keiō University, countered that the Ministry of Education's directive betrayed a misunderstanding of European "secularization." Education and religion were separated only to protect minorities within the borders of the European states, as in the case of Catholics in the United Kingdom. No European state, he observed, rejected outright the role of religion in education.[161] A functional corollary to the majoritarian claim of the Buddhist *kōninkyō* movement, few commentators were interested in validating Christians as a religious minority. Between these competing visions of secularization, Meiji discourse consistently rejected Kamata's vision, one that granted special recognition to religious majorities or minorities. The religious were to be equally removed from education, regardless of their numerical, historical, or doctrinal particulars.

For this reason, Buddhists, while critical of the overrepresentation of Christianity in private education, felt equally threatened by the Ministry of Education's directive. In fact, even voices within the Buddhist community critical of the *kōninkyō* movement reversed their position when it came to education. *Dentō*, for example, employed the metaphor of a family to suggest that education and religion were like a pair of parents to a nation; any attempt to define the nation by excluding religion would be a profound mistake.[162] The editors struggled to reconcile their rejection of the *kōninkyō* movement with their call for a special role for Buddhism in the schools. Because the state admitted an interest in restraining foreign access to the educational system with the Private School Ordinance, the journal proposed, a commensurate interest in restraining the access of foreign religion to the schools was justified. Limiting the legal privileges of foreign religions should be no different than distinguishing between national citizens and foreign nationals. Hence, the editors concluded, although Buddhists had no legitimate grounds to seek a special recognized status, the state had legitimate grounds to grant Buddhist clerics special access to classrooms in the name of national interest.[163] The stakes appeared so high that, "whatever happens with the *kōninkyō* [movement], whatever happens with the Religion Bill, if the foundation of education is solidified with Buddhism, that would be best for the nation [*kokka*], the best for Buddhism, and also the best for society."[164]

The ordinances issued by the Home Ministry and the Ministry of Education in the successive summers of 1898 and 1899 not only satisfied the need to bring Christianity under some form of state supervision prior to the commencement of mixed residence but also indicated the government was not likely to deviate from its stated goal of regulating all religions as equivalent. This required a legislative framework that clarified the legal status of shrines, temples, and churches, as well as their respective clerics and sectarian organizations. The administrative habits of the Shrine and Temple Bureau, formed in the decade following the promulgation of the Imperial Constitution, reflect the difficulties confronting the effort to produce a single legislative framework for religion. Although it was initially divided simply into shrine (Shinto) and temple (Buddhist) sections, combining the supervision of Shinto sects and their clerics with the supervision of Shinto shrines and their priests grew more objectionable as efforts to place shrines firmly outside the realm of religion gained traction in the Imperial Diet. As a result, in 1893 the bureau adopted a three-part approach, with a shrine section, a temple section (for Buddhist sects and their clerics), and a *kyōmu* (doctrinal affairs) section that supervised Shinto sects.[165] This three-part division of the bureau into shrines, temples, and religion grew out of the piecemeal ordinances and regulations issued since the Restoration, and provided a flexible means of addressing the particularities of Buddhist sects, shrines, and Shinto sects. Some officials recognized the advantages of this arrangement, and the Home Ministry contemplated drafting three separate bills addressing shrines, temples, and religion.[166] The government's refusal to differentiate the treatment of Buddhism and Christianity, however, doomed the three-way organization of the Shrine and Temple Bureau, and in April 1899 the home minister submitted to the cabinet a plan to establish a separate Shrine Bureau and a reorganized Religion Bureau. The Home Ministry reiterated that the "difference between shrines and religion is not decided by policy or departments," but conceded that creating a Shrine Bureau would both satisfy the recommendations passed by the Imperial Diet and pave the way for adding Christianity to the administrative workload of the current bureau. To justify the creation of a permanent bureau dedicated to shrines, the Home Ministry also recommended the cabinet abolish the Imperial and National Shrine Preservation Fund.[167] Even though both proposals were blocked by the Finance Ministry's refusal to fund any new programs, they announced that the Home Ministry intended to satisfy the demands of the Imperial Diet and the legislative requirement of the Religion Bill by splitting the Shrine and Temple Bureau into a Shrine Bureau and a Religion Bureau.[168]

With the groundwork laid over the course of the decade, the press followed the Yamagata cabinet's introduction of the Religion Bill in the House of Peers in early December 1899 with intense interest.[169] The *Yomiuri* declared it one of the most important pieces of legislation before the fourteenth session of the Imperial Diet. Validating that characterization, few members of the Diet were absent when the bill was presented and the gallery was reportedly full, with many Buddhist clerics and foreign missionaries present.[170] Further underscoring the significance of the bill, instead of the home minister, Yamagata Aritomo personally presented the bill to the upper house. In his address, Yamagata declared the intent behind the bill in the now-familiar language of the religious settlement:

> Because the freedom of belief is guaranteed by the constitution, regardless of differences among religions, the state of course cannot step into the content of faith and interfere but must endeavor to maintain that freedom. However, activity that manifests externally, such as the establishment of temples and churches, the gathering of adherents, or the regulations of sects, must be supervised by the state so as not to threaten

security and order nor contradict the duties of subjects; this is not only the duty of the state but also its responsibility.[171]

Consisting of five chapters and forty-six articles, the sprawling bill legally defined churches (*kyōkai*), temples (*tera*), denominations (*kyōha*), and sects (*shūha*), as well as clerics (*kyōshi*). The bill allowed churches to incorporate as associations (*shadan*) or foundations (*zaidan*) and temples to incorporate as foundations, while denominations or sects could not incorporate. Churches and temples were required to submit bylaws to competent authorities for authorization, and any disputes touching on those bylaws would be adjudicated by a Religion Committee (Shūkyō iinkai). Anyone who had their civil rights stripped or suspended could not be ordained a cleric, and clerics were forbidden from making political statements or participating in political activities.[172] To substantiate its claim to balance the "supervision" (*torishimari*) of religion with its "protection" (*hogo*), Yamagata's government also submitted a Revised Conscription Ordinance that exempted from military service all clerics with at least a middle-school education.[173] The Religion Bill and its ancillary Conscription Ordinance attempted to frame religion in relation to the public good, a broader utility, to satisfy the language of the Civil Code, which juxtaposed religious corporations with charitable organizations.

The press devoted a considerable amount of space in its usual coverage of the Diet session to the so-called "Religion Bill problem," and the editorial reception of the bill was generally positive.[174] Particularly welcomed were the provision of the bill that denied clerics the right to express political opinions, and its clear rejection of the Buddhist demand for official recognition.[175] Hara Takashi (1858–1921), then president of the *Osaka Mainichi* newspaper, wrote that the bill treated "the three religions" equally and was not very far from what he would have drafted himself.[176] *Taiyō* praised the bill for rendering sects voluntary organizations and for weakening the clerics' hereditary control of temples by forcing them to incorporate as foundations with trustees.[177] Criticisms, when made, typically took the form of suggested amendments that placed religion more completely in a private sphere.[178] The *Yorozu chōhō* criticized the redundancies and potential contradictions created by the bill's attempt to retain terminology specific to Buddhism alongside generic terminology applicable to all religions.[179] The *Jiji shinpō* complained that the bill did not grant complete autonomy to religious organizations and believed the Religion Committee would only mire the state in sectarian disputes, as the precedent of the Sōtō sect suggested.[180]

The response from Shinto quarters to the bill was muted. Both houses of the Diet had passed recommendations and the Home Ministry had already signaled its intent to create a separate Shrine Bureau. The absence of any language touching on shrines in the Religion Bill only confirmed the growing sense of immunity. Representatives of the Shinto sects, including Taisha-kyō, Ontake-kyō, Kurozumi-kyō, Jikkō-kyō, Shinshū-kyō, Shūse-kyō, Shinri-kyō, Fusō-kyō, Misogi-kyō, Taisei-kyō, and Shinto Honkyoku, conferred in late December. They decided to forgo submitting a formal petition seeking amendments to the bill because in their judgment it affected Buddhism to a greater extent, and it seemed unlikely to pass.[181]

Protestant Christian responses to the Religion Bill were measured, in contrast to their resistance to the Private School Ordinance and the Ministry of Education Directive, in part because the bill erased regulatory distinctions between Buddhism and Christianity.[182] Kozaki Hiromichi (1856–1938), the Congregationalist leader, welcomed the bill, believing it would help bring an end to the friction between Buddhism and Christianity. Nonetheless, he and other Protestant leaders were critical of Article 37, which prohibited political speech by clerics.[183] When representatives of the Protestant churches met in Tokyo, they also expressed concern that the bill granted the state a role in determining the qualification of clerics and that the Religion Committee effectively prevented religious organizations from seeking redress in the civil courts. Nonetheless, these representatives believed select amendments would render the bill acceptable and circulated their concerns to members of both houses of the Imperial Diet in early January.[184] Protestant missionaries were also generally pleased with the Religion Bill; in a letter to a colleague, H. M. Landis, a Presbyterian missionary, described the bill as "very liberal & free from annoying particulars as compared with regulations in Germany."[185] There was no appreciable response from Roman Catholic quarters, perhaps because Catholics had been reassured by the successful reception of a Vatican envoy at the imperial palace in 1885, and the fact that sect-level organizations were largely left outside the purview of the bill.[186] Any restriction of Vatican involvement in diocesan appointments was left out of the provisions of the bill, which precisely characterized what most irritated the Buddhist establishment.

Buddhist organizations had vigorously sought formal recognition from the government in anticipation of the Religion Bill, and their responses to the bill were predictably negative.[187] Buddhist sects had even collectively published a "Buddhism Bill" (the Bukkyō hōan) in hopes of influencing the Home Ministry's legislation. Comprising eight chapters and forty-six articles, their bill attempted to safeguard the organizational integrity of the sects by granting them the right to incorporate.[188] The bill aimed to limit the potential of intrasectarian schisms by creating a conference of superintendents representing existing sects and granting it considerable authority over the recognition of new sects and branch sects. Buddhist superintendents were also to receive ranks and titles via imperial ordinances, granting the sects a measure of official recognition that differentiated them from Christian denominations.[189]

The Buddhism Bill anticipated the chief Buddhist criticisms leveled against the Religion Bill. First, the government's bill ignored a millennium of Buddhist history in Japan in favor of an ahistorical and hence artificial equivalence with Christianity.[190] Second, sects were not allowed to incorporate as public corporations. The editors of *Dentō* complained the bill granted religions only the prerogatives of private corporations while subjecting them to the oversight of public corporations. The absence of any public recognition of sects and the curtailment of political speech amounted to placing "clergy outside of society."[191] Third, the bill weakened head- and branch-temple relations. Rendering the hierarchical relations between head and branch temples a matter of private contract was perceived as an existential threat to the Buddhist sects.[192] The majority of sects, with the notable exception of the Nishi-Honganji branch of the Shin sect, which maintained close ties to Yamagata's Chōshū clique, united to oppose the bill and sought to either block it or radically amend it to recognize Buddhist sects as public corporations (*kōhōjin*).[193] Superintendents conferred, clerics and adherents were mobilized, and organizations like the Recognized Religion Establishment Alliance, under Okamoto Ryūnosuke (1851–1912), lobbied the House of Peers, submitting an additional 162 petitions with more than 30,000 signatures.[194]

Particularly vexing to these Buddhist sectarians, as articulated in a pamphlet published by the Great Japan Buddhist Alliance (Dai nihon bukkyōto dōmeikai), was the government's refusal to formally validate a form of religious nationalism. The pamphlet declared that "religion is a significant element in the unity of a nation [*kokka minshin*], and along with race and language possesses an important relationship to the independence and growth of a nation," and challenged head on Itō Hirobumi's constitutional premise. Any law affecting how the state relates to religion must, therefore, pay particular attention to "the faith of the greatest majority." Appealing to the laws of Western nations that distinguished the treatment of religious organizations based on their relative size, the Buddhist Alliance argued that any legislative treatment of religion should avoid altering the "faith condition" of the nation.[195] For this reason, the alliance insisted that its demand that Buddhist sects be recognized as public corporations (the pamphlet invoked the German example of *Oeffentlich aufgenommene Religions-gesellschaft*) did not arise from a self-serving desire for fiscal support or special protection. Rather, because "religion is an element unifying the national spirit and must be treated with great caution," the Buddhists' demand reflected only a "small aspiration to prevent a change to religious attitudes within the Japanese empire." Invoking the weight of a national majority, the pamphlet concluded by directly addressing government officials and cautioning them that legislating matters so close to the sentiments of the people must not occur in secret. Like the shrine priests did before them, these Buddhist clerics appealed to the Imperial Diet as a forum to translate their sectarian concerns into a discourse of the national public.[196]

The fault lines within the Buddhist community and the criticism by the secular press that greeted the Buddhist movement to block the passage of the Religion Bill remained consistent with that of the *kōninkyō* movement.[197] Press commentary reprised earlier critiques of the public and political pursuit of sectarian self-interest. The principle that the freedom of religious belief formalized the distinction between "faith" (*shinkō*) and the external organizations of religion was repeatedly cited to dismiss Buddhist complaints; the bill, in the words of one editorial, had no bearing on "matters of faith."[198] The *Asahi* newspaper declared that no single religion could be privileged in its relationship to the state without exacerbating sectarian conflict; the state, as evidenced by the failure of the Tokugawa policy of prohibiting Christianity, could never completely control religion.[199] The more populist *Yorozu chōhō* complained that Buddhist opposition to the religion bill evoked the "bitter historical precedent" of the monks of Mount Hiei marching on the imperial palace during the medieval period. If the use of divine authority to press for worldly concerns was inappropriate then, the attempt to manipulate the levers of parliamentary power to secure sectarian interests appeared no less problematic at the turn of a new century.

Again, the very majoritarian logic that the Buddhists attempted to employ to their advantage generated the greatest censure, because it justified the sectarian form of politics that the secular press had repeatedly denounced as antithetical to national unity and the proper function of constitutional government. Reports that some sects were directing their adherents how to vote contributed to the sense that a form of sectarian politics was emerging in opposition to the Religion Bill. The Ōtani branch of the Shin sect, in particular, reportedly pressured members of the House of Representatives whose constituencies in the northeast contained large concentrations of adherents.[200] The prevalence of Buddhist funerary rites, some feared, meant the majority of Diet members were vulnerable to influence through their ties to parish temples and sects. Even a meeting of Buddhist representatives near Ryōgoku Bridge in late December appeared to be a threatening "show of force" intended to intimidate Diet members. As reports of Buddhists' use of money and votes to pressure Diet members circulated in the press, some within the Buddhist fold again feared that such activity would only further undermine the public standing of Buddhism.[201] The Shingon sect's *Mitsugon kyōhō* decried the proposition that numbers alone justified the demand for special status. Pointing out that Buddhist congregations (*kyōkai*) numbered more than 1,370, with more than 1.5 million adherents, the journal wondered whether numbers were the only measure of Buddhist strength and vitality. Habit and custom, it suggested, were not the same as "faith."[202]

Critical of Buddhist attempts to influence the Imperial Diet, the press paid close attention to the political parties' response to the Religion Bill.[203] Diet members sympathetic to Buddhist concerns organized a Religion Study Group (Shūkyō kenkyūkai) to study legislative approaches to regulating religion, and even politicians outside of the Diet attempted to organize in opposition to the bill.[204] The tangible result of these alliances came in the form of the Constitutional Government Party's Buddhism Club (Bukkyō kurabu), which pressed for a lower house resolution calling for a postponement of any vote on the Religion Bill.[205] No resolution was introduced, much less passed, and these Buddhist attempts to lobby the Imperial Diet faded quickly in a way that suggests a contrast with the shrine priests' movement. The *Yorozu chōhō* reported that Ishikawa Shuntai's dogged pursuit of the right of Buddhist sects to incorporate as public corporations had resulted in turning the political parties against them, with many expressing regret for having supported them in the first place.[206] Even Tani Tateki, a former general and noted critic of the oligarchic government, found vulgar and unbecoming the Buddhists' attempts to differentiate themselves from other religions.[207] The political grammar of religion clearly handicapped the ability of Buddhist sects to openly lobby the Imperial Diet.

The Religion Bill itself had been sent to a fifteen-member special committee after extensive questions from the floor of the House of Peers indicated it would not pass unamended.[208] From December 1899 through the following January, all interested eyes were thus focused on the special committee charged with deliberating the Religion Bill, and it was here that Home Ministry bureaucrats provided detailed explanations for the key provisions of the proposed legislation. Shiba Junrokurō (1861–1931), head of the Shrine and Temple Bureau, explained, "The desire was to establish regulations for religion in general [*ippan no shūkyō*]."[209] The difficulty of synchronizing the statutory treatment of Buddhism, sectarian Shinto, Christianity, and any other conceivably recognizable forms of religion was reflected in the terminology employed by the lengthy bill. Despite criticisms, the bill did attempt to communicate a measure of deference toward Buddhism by incorporating elements of the Buddhism Bill. Temples were designated by a distinct term (*tera* 寺) and were subject to more specialized regulations than the generic category of "church" (*kyōkai* 教会), which applied to both Christian and Shinto sects. Nonetheless, as foundations, temples were treated identically to churches, and most articles of the bill addressed "temples or churches," creating a basic equivalence between the two even as it retained the plural nomenclature.[210] The Home Ministry stressed to the committee that "this bill can be applied equally to any religion," and stated unequivocally that any legal distinction between established and tolerated religions, though common in Europe, was not being applied in Japan.[211] Because the superintendent system could not be applied to Christianity, where the supervising authority of sects and denominations, especially in the case of the Catholic, Anglican, and Orthodox Churches, resided abroad, the draft bill focused on individual churches and their clergy who resided in Japan. As a result, Buddhist and Shinto sects, which had developed organizations within the superintendent framework, were forced to adapt to the regulatory needs of Christianity. This apparent deference to the regulatory requirements of Christianity proved most contentious.

The question of uniformity and equality also applied to the privileges religions were to receive from the state. Buddhist temples, for example, had been granted a special tax-exempt status as a result of property confiscated in 1871.[212] The bill took this privilege and expanded it into a general tax exemption for all property put to religious use by temples or churches.[213] The cost of the tax exemption to the national budget, estimated at 300,000 yen, was criticized by those who questioned whether religion needed to be "protected" by the state at all. Tani Tateki found little reason to oppose the bill, except for the fear that a tax exemption would sap the state budget.[214] With no apparent sense of irony, the Home Ministry justified the tax exemption in terms of a functional symmetry between schools and religious organizations; the state had an interest in extending a measure of protection to schools for educational considerations, and to religion for moral considerations.[215]

Members of the committee charged to consider the Revised Conscription Ordinance also questioned the wisdom of exempting clerics from conscription. The revised ordinance had been submitted to the Imperial Diet in tandem with the Religion Bill, and the Imperial Army Ministry justified the exemption as a means of "protecting religion" (*shūkyō no hogo*), since "it is not sensible to forcibly conscript into military service those whose work is to instill morals [and compel them] to kill people." Members of the committee, referencing the history of Buddhist participation in armed conflict, questioned outright the premise that Buddhist clerics were pacifists by conviction.[216] Press commentary was no less favorable, with some claiming the exemption was a blatant attempt to appease Buddhists and silence their opposition to the Religion Bill.[217] Despite a personal push by the home minister, the Revised Conscription Ordinance was voted down in committee, and some in the House of Peers came to oppose the Religion Bill because of the privileges it conferred on religion. Exemptions from taxes and conscription appeared an unnecessary form of state intervention in what was supposed to be a realm of free competition; Miyoshi Taizō (1845–1908), a lay Christian member of the House of Peers, declared in committee that "there is no need for the state to provide any protection to religion."[218]

By the end of January 1900, the strength of criticisms levied against the Religion Bill convinced the special committee that it required substantial revisions.[219] A five-member amending committee—consisting of Soga Sukenori (1844–1935), Tsuzuki Keiroku (1861–1923), Hozumi Yatsuka (1860–1912), Matsuoka Yasutake (1846–1923), and Kikkawa Chōkichi (1860–1915)—was appointed to craft a bill with a better chance of success.[220] This amending committee quickly split into two factions, however; one sympathetic to the Home Ministry's basic approach and the other fundamentally opposed. Suggestively, Hozumi, a leading proponent of "national morality" (*kokumin dōtoku*) and a strident advocate of the emperor's sovereign prerogatives, supported the uniform regulation of religions.[221] Tsuzuki Keiroku, a career diplomat recently appointed to the House of Peers, questioned the very premise of the bill to treat "the three religions" as equivalent, saying, "What is good for one will create problems for the other." The deadlock resulted in two separate amended bills produced outside the formal framework of the committee.[222] Because it most resembled the original bill submitted by the government, the special committee chose to take up the amended bill drafted by Matsuoka, Hozumi, and Kikkawa.[223] Amendments included removing provisions specific to temples, further eliminating differences between temples and churches. At the same time, the amended bill attempted to address a central point of criticism by adding language that required sect bylaws to define relations between head and branch temples. To address concerns that tax-exempt property could increase without limit, the language was amended to read "taxes may be exempted," thus granting a measure of discretion to the home minister.[224] After some additional amendments, the Matsuoka bill was adopted by the committee and referred back to the House of Peers.

As the Religion Bill floundered in committee, the Yamagata government was frustrated by the lack of direct leverage to contain the organized opposition led by Buddhist sects. Not all Buddhist sects opposed the bill; the Nishi-Honganji branch of the Shin sect, in stark contrast to the Ōtani branch, had published its support of the bill and instructed its branch temples and adherents to refrain from participating in opposition movements.[225] Nonetheless, the broad Buddhist opposition to the Religion Bill proved troublesome enough that Yamagata ordered his home minister to restrict all Buddhist assemblies opposing the bill.[226] The prime minister also attempted to entice compliance by signaling that the government would accept amendments, short of granting public recognition to Buddhist sects. In a secret meeting with Ōtani Kōei (1852–1923), the head of the Ōtani branch of the Shin set, the home minister's private secretary reportedly conveyed a message that the government was willing to grant aristocratic titles to high-ranking Buddhist clerics in exchange for their support.[227] At the same time, the head of the Home Ministry Shrine and Temple Bureau summoned Ishikawa Shuntai to upbraid him for leading the opposition to the bill.[228] Failing with both the carrot and the stick, the government turned to the legislative body itself; Matsukata Masayoshi, the finance minister, approached Konoe Atsumaro (1863–1904), the speaker of the House of Peers, in an attempt to smooth the passage of the bill.[229] On February 14, Yamagata expressed frustration with the parliamentary process in a letter to Matsukata: "Since I cannot directly press them, I have been repeatedly urging them through indirect means."[230] Although many assumed the more conservative House of Peers was essentially in Yamagata's hands, factional dynamics proved complex and difficult to control.[231]

In the end, what Yamagata's Religion Bill failed to overcome was less the Buddhist opposition than the constitutional premise of a religiously neutral state. The Religion Bill returned to floor of the House of Peers for a vote on February 17, 1900. The gallery was once again full of onlookers, many dressed in the formal garb of Buddhist clerics, and Ozaki Saburō, then a member of the upper house, noted wryly in his diary that fifty to sixty unfamiliar faces were seated in the House of Peers that day, apparently induced to attend by the Yamagata government in its effort to pass the bill at all costs.[232] The debate that greeted the amended bill amounted to a dramatic showdown between the opposing sides of the special committee, with the chairman of the committee, Kuroda Nagashige (1867–1939), commencing the debate with the announcement that he would oppose the bill.[233]

When Matsuoka Yasutake and Shiba Junrokurō, head of the Shrine and Temple Bureau, stood to field questions on behalf of the amended bill, members of the amending committee proved the most vocal critics. Soga denounced the bill as the most arcane submitted so far to the Imperial Diet and argued that it made little sense to pass something so poorly understood, only to regret it later.[234] Tsuzuki pointed to the ambiguous legal character of the rules governing sects and the ill-defined authority of the Religion Committee; he asserted that the bill would merely make it easier for sects to splinter and would destabilize the religious sphere. His summary, that the bill "appears fair but in reality is small for adults and large for children," struck the crux of the matter. By altering the regulatory framework to accommodate Christianity, the state was in effect abandoning its neutrality and forcing Buddhist and Shinto sects to alter their shape and mode of operation. Hozumi Yatsuka defended the bill for addressing the pressing need to secure religious freedom by moving the regulation of religions out of the executive discretion of the home minister and into statutory definition. Matsuoka insisted the bill would introduce no discernable change to the social order, and argued it maintained the principle of separating state and religion established under the Imperial Constitution. Under the provisions of the bill, Shinto sects, Buddhism, and Christianity were "each treated fairly, given fair supervision and fair protection."[235]

The Religion Bill was defeated 121 to 100, and the Revised Conscription Ordinance, already voted down in committee, was also defeated in the House of Peers.[236] The relatively tight vote suggests that while Buddhist assertions of historical and numerical distinctions swayed some members of the conservative upper house, sympathy for the Buddhist cause alone did not affect the vote.[237] If anything, the length and density of the bill reflected the difficulty of applying a uniform regulatory scheme to the plural and idiosyncratic traditions and organizations of religion in Japan, and it was the premise that the state could legislatively equalize the status of divergent religions that generated the greatest resistance. Regardless, the letter of thanks sent by the representatives of thirty-two Buddhist sects to the House of Peers only underscored how the failure of the Religion Bill marked a humiliating defeat for the Yamagata government and a surprising rebuke from the typically compliant House of Peers.

Reflecting the immediate damage to the government, Senge Takatomi, a member of the upper house and also serving as the governor of Tokyo, submitted his resignation for opposing the bill, and the lower house demanded Yamagata's resignation.[238] At the same time, Itō Miyoji, who had a position on the Privy Council, reassured Yamagata in a letter that even Bismarck had struggled to pass similar legislation in Germany, and insisted the House of Peers was not swayed by the "stubborn and ignorant" Buddhist clerics who sought to confuse state and religion. It was, in his opinion, the upper house's unbalanced focus on legal details that prevented the bill from passing. The crucial lesson, therefore, was to pursue a "decisive punishment" (*danzen taru shobun*) against the Buddhist movements that violated the separation of religion and state.[239]

Hence, while some observers believed the defeat of the Religion Bill demonstrated the political force of Buddhist adherents across the country, their success was widely assumed to be temporary.[240] Buddhist sects achieved no positive victory as a result of their extensive lobbying; neither house of the Imperial Diet adopted recommendations in support of recognizing Buddhism as a majority faith or in support of turning Buddhist sects into public corporations. If anything, the sects remained vigilant in anticipation of another religion bill.[241] Moreover, the Yamagata government did not wait to punish Buddhist sects. Instead of preparing another bill for the next session of the Imperial Diet, the government quietly secured the statutory means to achieve its prime objective of rendering religion politically impotent.

The Home Ministry had from the outset intended to employ its police powers to constrain the intangible dimensions of religion, such as doctrinal content and ritual practice, dimensions that had been explicitly left out of the Home Ministry ordinance issued in 1898. For this reason, the Religion Bill was expected to function in tandem with the Peace Police Bill (Chian keisatsu hōan), which was also submitted to the fourteenth Imperial Diet. The police bill addressed the rise of urban labor disputes and did not explicitly mention religion, but following the defeat of the Religion Bill, a stipulation prohibiting "monks, priests, and other religious instructors" from joining political associations was added to the bill.[242] The Buddhist movement opposing the Religion Bill had amply demonstrated, however, that the boundary between political and religious associations was murky at best, a point admitted by the Home Ministry author of the Peace Police Bill: "If as a result of mixed residence the foreign religion expands within our country, religious conflicts will occur.

Therefore, associations of a religious purpose will likely expand as well. In that eventuality, the need to regulate those associations in the same manner as political associations will arise." As a result of these concerns, Article 3 of the police bill, which stipulated that any public associations and assemblies may be required to notify authorities prior to meeting, was given an expanded interpretation to include religious associations.[243]

After the Imperial Diet passed the Peace Police Bill into law, Home Minister Saigō Tsugumichi issued a ministerial instruction (*kunrei*) on March 12, 1900, making clear that the law applied to any public preaching or sectarian political movements:

> Assemblies and associations related to religion have recently formed with the purpose of shaping religious regulations [*shūkyō seido*], as in the case of associations insisting on making Buddhism an officially recognized religion. Since these express opinions concerning the institutions of the state, they must be viewed as political assemblies and associations. Therefore, according to Articles 1 and 2 of the Peace Police Law . . . they are to be strictly regulated. As the recently promulgated Peace Police Law prohibits monks, priests, and other religious instructors from joining political associations, this provision is to be applied.[244]

The Imperial Diet also expanded the language banning religious clerics from seeking political office in the Revised House of Representatives Election Law, which was passed in February 1900.[245] Strikingly, while the need to constrain Christianity remained a concern, the political activity of Buddhist sects and their clerics provided the primary motivation to place religion outside the public realm of politics.

The Home Ministry quickly complemented these legislative adjustments with two ministerial directives (*shōrei*) in August 1900 that put in place procedures for religious organizations to incorporate and thus minimally equalized the bureaucratic treatment of Shinto, Buddhism, and Christianity. These directives did not, however, confer benefits such as general tax exemptions and exemptions from conscription. To incorporate, churches or temples had to submit information, including their sources of funding, to local authorities, who then forwarded the information to the Home Ministry for authorization. This allowed the Home Ministry to regulate where Christian churches could be built in order to avoid generating friction with local temples and shrines, though in reality the anticipated clash between Buddhists and Christians as a result of mixed residence never materialized to the extent anticipated.[246]

While the Religion Bill dominated the press coverage of the fourteenth Imperial Diet, the movement to create a separate administrative organ for Shinto shrines quietly progressed in the background.[247] On February 15, as the conclusion of the Diet session loomed, the government submitted a supplemental budget request of 7,994 yen for the creation of a Shrine Bureau (Jinja kyoku) and both houses of the Imperial Diet passed the supplemental bill without delay.[248] The Home Ministry pointed out to the cabinet that creating a Shrine Bureau would accord with the Imperial Diet's recommendations and "remove the concern that the public [*sejin*] will confuse shrines for religion."[249] Imperial Ordinance number 163, issued on April 27, created a Shrine Bureau within the Home Ministry, and the Shrine and Temple Bureau was renamed the Religion Bureau (Shūkyō kyoku).[250]

The new Shrine Bureau was nominally listed as the first department within the Home Ministry and the first administrative responsibility of the home minister.[251] Despite this symbolic gesture, most contemporaries recognized the new bureau as a minimal accommodation of Shinto aspirations.[252] Ōtsu Jun'ichirō, the stalwart champion of a revived Department of Divinities, characterized the Shrine Bureau as a small section taken out of the smallest bureau in the Home Ministry, but he also recognized that it was the natural and only option available after a decade of parliamentary compromise.[253] That decade of compromise produced a triangular relationship between shrine priests, Diet members, and Home Ministry bureaucrats, a relationship cemented with the formation of the Shrine Bureau. The new bureau, moreover, arguably increased pressures on shrines and their priests by intensifying the demand that shrines and Shinto-as-religion be thoroughly separated. For example, Jingū-kyō, which had been a Shinto sect organized in response to the religious settlement of 1882, dissolved itself in 1899 and reincorporated as the nonsectarian Jingū hōsankai to ensure that the devotional organization affiliated with the Grand Shrines of Ise escaped being regulated as a sectarian organization.[254] Even after the creation of the Shrine Bureau, in the editorial view of *Taiyō*, not only were religious elements still present at shrines but those elements were the most worldly and vulgar elements of religion, which encouraged worshippers to seek wealth, health, and success. The segment of the priesthood that relied on those elements appeared particularly regressive, leading some to call for them to be exposed to natural selection (*tōta*).[255] The apparent victory, in short, also opened shrines and their priests to greater scrutiny and supervision. In accepting the premise that both shrines and the priests stood outside of religion, shrine Shinto secured a powerful bureaucratic position linking a national organization of shrine priests, Imperial Diet members, and a bureaucratic department dedicated to shrines. This rendered the priesthood increasingly dependent on the state and justified nearly unlimited bureaucratic interference, a point amply demonstrated in the traumatic experience of forced shrine mergers that accompanied the restoration of permanent fiscal support between 1906 and 1912.[256]

Conclusion

Remarking on the defeat of the Religion Bill, Hirata Tōsuke, a close aide to Yamagata Aritomo, suggested that if it "informed the nation, which is so deficient in religious thought, of the relationship between the state and religion, and if it gave monks [*sōryo*] devoted to proselytizing the opportunity to study religion, then the submission of the religion bill was not a complete waste."[257] Indeed, for most Japanese living at the end of the nineteenth century, the term *shūkyō* remained unfamiliar and alien to their daily lives, and the public discourse created by the Imperial Diet provided an important vehicle for explaining the significance of religion as a category of political recognition.[258] The decade of debates that culminated in the Religion Bill cumulatively institutionalized the assumption that separating a realm of public obligation from religious commitments was both possible and desirable. This provided the grammar of religion by which the avowedly religious would participate in the political sphere; to speak in the name of religion was to speak for private, sectarian identifications that could make no claim on the state, which itself remained neutral in relation to the inherently competitive realm of belief.

This overriding concern to render the state and imperial institution immune to social pluralism and cognitive relativism carried through the Imperial Diet's deliberations. The government and the Imperial Diet rejected Buddhist claims to majoritarian status. The oligarchy, the political parties, and even the secular press were unwilling to champion a messy epistemic and social plurality reflected in sectarian difference. Defining the nation and speaking in its name through the Imperial Diet was easier in monolithic and uncontestable formulations. When the Ancient Shrine and Temple Preservation extended state support and validation for shrines and temples, for example, it did so in the name of art and national heritage, not religion. Bringing Christianity under the supervision of the Home Ministry provided an opportunity to further clarify the distinction between the public character of education and the private character of religion. The Religion Bill, even in defeat, affirmed the rejection of sectarian politics.

Constitutional government in Meiji Japan, in short, negatively organized itself in reference to the category of religion, and this provided the "theoretical and administrative basis" for reviving state support for Shinto shrines. Hence, although the last of the five separations, the separation of the Shrine and Religion Bureaus in early 1900, marked the beginning of expanding state support for shrines through the first half of the twentieth century, it was within a more general grammar of religion that the treatment of shrines as nonreligious made sense.[259] Linking themselves to the cardinal principles of a *kokutai* with a sacerdotal emperor who united rites with the prerogative to govern, the shrine priests and their allies successfully argued that shrines, regardless of rank, should never be confused with the private and contestable category of religion. The oligarchic government was never animated by a coherent ideological concern to elevate Shinto shrines, especially the priesthood. Rather, concerns to prevent sectarian organizations from participating in parliamentary politics, facilitating treaty revision, and preparing for mixed residence reinforced the lessons of the religious settlement. In insisting on the essentially secular character of the state, the government created an opportunity for the Imperial Diet to demand the elevation of shrines.

At the same time, the recurring sensitivity of the Imperial Diet, the bureaucracy, and the oligarchic leadership to the fundamentally arbitrary and contestable boundary between religion and nonreligion reminds us that settlements are always incomplete and under negotiation. The 1890s nonetheless institutionalized a basic grammar of religion in Japan that would direct state policy through the first half of the twentieth century. From the rejection of a state religion to the separation of education and religion, the Meiji state assumed an avowedly secular form, relying on the ability to articulate in regulatory terms a distinction between the contingent and the necessary to police a realm of public duties distinct from the realm of contingent beliefs. Precisely because it was "protected" as a privileged realm of private belief, religion provided the means to posit public and national values not subject to competition, critique, or conversionary choice. Religion, in effect, freed categories such as the *kokutai* and *saisei itchi* from the politics of conversion and provided the foundation for the production of increasingly narrow ideological orthodoxies during the first half of the twentieth century. The sacralization of the nation-state relied on a secularization that placed a multiplicity of sectarian positions outside the realm of political representation; in the eyes of the modern Japanese state there would be no religious minorities or majorities—only Japanese subjects. It was the Imperial Diet that brought into focus the conceptual and political stakes involved in the definition and regulation of religion.

Conclusion
Assembling Religion in Meiji Japan

On the twenty-fifth of January 1912, five months before the emperor's death brought the Meiji era to a close, Buddhist, Shinto, and Christian clerics assembled at the Peer's Club (Kazoku kaikan) in Hibiya at the invitation of the undersecretary of the Home Ministry, Tokonami Takejirō (1866–1935). The assembly of seventy-one clerics representing the three religions—dubbed the Assembly of Three Religions (Sankyō kaidō)—in what used to be the Rokumeikan marked one culmination of the political construction of religion as an object of discursive and regulative attention in Meiji Japan. The meeting, ostensibly voluntary, was given a strong official flavor by the attendance of Hara Takashi, the home minister, as well as the justice minister, the communications minister, the naval minister, and bureaucratic representatives from most other government ministries.[1] The expressed purpose of the assembly was to counter the perceived rise in social instability, most famously illustrated by the Great Treason Incident of 1910, with religion. No longer itself the "greatest problem," religion now promised the state a means to address a new crisis of conversion.

Rapid urbanization and industrialization ushered in a period of civil unrest, beginning with the Hibiya Riots immediately following the Russo-Japanese War and leading up to the nationwide Rice Riots of 1918.[2] Much like their early-Meiji predecessors who saw Christianity as a threat, officials such as Undersecretary Tokonami viewed the potential spread of socialism, anarchism, and even liberalism as direct threats to political stability and national cohesion. The fact that Kōtoku Shūsui (1871–1911), the anarchist face of the Great Treason Incident, wrote a book entitled

Wiping Out Christianity while in prison prior to his execution only confirmed the impression that the new ideas threatening the *kokutai* were materialist in orientation and aggressively irreligious.[3] In this context, religion appeared as a resource to mobilize in opposition to new political heresies. Indeed, the clerics who assembled in early 1912 quickly adopted a joint resolution in response to this validation of their public function: "We will demonstrate our respective doctrines, and endeavor to support the imperial fortune and improve national morality. We desire that the authorities will respect and value religion, harmonize politics, religion, and education, and employ them to extend the nation's fortune."[4] Religion, which had once designated a realm of unstable competition among a plurality of identities, loyalties, and practices, had come to provide the conceptual and regulative means by which to contain and mobilize that plurality in the service of a centralized nation-state.

Even though formal legislative equality between the religions had been rejected in 1900 with the failure of the Religion Bill, the Assembly of Three Religions asserted the functional equivalence of sectarian Shinto, Buddhism, and Christianity in their private and voluntary service to the nation-state, a posture that the government consistently reinforced and encouraged through the first half of the twentieth century.[5] Following the Rice Riots of 1918, for example, Hara, by this time prime minister of the first democratic cabinet, and Tokonami, now the home minister, again invited representatives of the three religions to the prime minister's residence on May 24, 1919. After distributing a pamphlet entitled, *Democratic Thought in Japan*, Tokonami addressed the gathering of ninety-one clerics, representing thirteen Shinto sects, fifty-eight Buddhist head and branch sects, and seven Christian denominations. He stressed the limits to the government's ability to control the thoughts and attitudes of the populace and appealed to the clerics to communicate "national concepts" (*kokka kannen*) in their sermons.[6] He repeated, in essence, the subjectified contract for religious freedom: effective, voluntary service to the state in exchange for validated faith.

While these assemblies publicly affirmed the subjectified contract that structured the relationship between private religious belief and the state, the use of a generic definition of religion to uniformly affirm its public utility was still challenged by some in the name of theological difference. Members of the Ōtani branch of the Shin sect, which had so fiercely opposed the first Religion Bill and its legal equalization of Buddhism and Christianity, for example, remained critical of the state's undifferentiated treatment of religions. On the very morning that the Home

Minister addressed representatives of the three religions in 1919, more than seventy clerics and parishioners from Tokyo gathered at the Asakusa Honganji temple and adopted the following resolution:

> The gathering of the three religions of Shinto, Buddhism, and Christianity by Home Minister Tokonami repeats the previous Assembly of Three Religions. It is clear that religions that differ in their fundamental beliefs cannot be employed to achieve the goal of fostering the growth of the people's abilities [*minryoku baiyō*]. Not only that, it risks increasing the confused state of the national spirit [*kokumin seishin no konran*] and may harm the relationship between the state and religion. For this reason, we the priests and parishioners of the branch temples of the Shin sect Ōtani branch in Tokyo express our opposition.[7]

Although such assertions of sectarian particularity continued to challenge the political grammar of religion, both the state and the academy organized themselves around a construct of religion that subordinated theological difference to functional equivalence.[8] Functional equivalence implied interchangeability and helped render competition among the religions nonthreatening to the state. Thus, among the educated elite, the more common reaction to the assembly was to welcome it, so long as, in the words of the religious philosopher Hatano Seiichi (1877–1950), it did not alter the principle of "free competition and natural selection" among the various religions.[9] The assembly, in short, announced that such competition no longer appeared as a creditable threat in the eyes of the state.

As in other contexts, the academic discipline of religious studies played a significant role in shaping the modern grammar of religion in Japan. By introducing a comparative framework that presumed a common essence to diverse theological and ritual systems, religious studies worked to neutralize competition among religions. In effect, the academic authority of the discipline facilitated the Assembly of Three Religions by removing the primary excuse for marginalizing religion—conversionary competition.[10] Anesaki Masaharu (1873–1949), for example, considered the father of religious studies in Japan, demanded a more positive role for religion and worked closely with Home Ministry bureaucrats and religious leaders to organize the assembly.[11] At the same time, it is important to recognize that a functionally generic category of religion grew out of political imperatives and institutional adjustments that preceded the epistemic constructions of religious studies. The political function of *shūkyōgaku*, in other words, grew out of a broader political construction of religion that began with the Restoration.

As the government and religious studies scholars found a positive role to be played by religion and repeatedly assembled the religions, their attempts to "use religion" (*shūkyō riyō*) were criticized for violating the constitutional separation of religion and state and for undermining the secular premise of the nation-state, especially the separation of religion and education.[12] Nonetheless, the assemblies announced the state's consistent effort to apply the "one gaze, equal benevolence" (*isshi dōjin*) formula to religions to neutralize competition among them and employ them for public benefit.[13] Concluding his study of the modern reformation of Buddhism in Meiji Japan, James Ketelaar makes the following observation: "Within the Meiji era discourse on religion in Japan, the recognition of religion in general and Buddhism in particular as the source of a significant and powerful political critique was occasionally drawn upon but seldom sustained or recognized as viable."[14] When we see that the category of religion itself took form as a discursive technology to elide theological and ritual differences within the Japanese nation-state, it becomes much clearer why religion rarely provided a basis for political critique. To the extent that the modern grammar of religion valorized internal belief, as the conditional constitutional guarantee of religious belief did, it also rendered that belief marginal and potentially irrelevant to public politics. The only legitimate avenue to public politics available to the avowedly religious was through subjecting themselves to the secular demands of the state. In ceasing to be the greatest problem, religion had been tamed.

State Shinto, Again

The ambivalence built into the category of religion sheds light on a paradox at the center of current discussions of State Shinto. Few deny that state support for Shinto shrines expanded through the first half of the twentieth century, and that by the 1930s an increasingly narrow ideological orthodoxy emphasized the importance of shrine rites. At the same time, the majority of the shrine priesthood emerged from this period of increased state support with a deep sense of resentment and victimization.[15] How can State Shinto have been such a coercive force while those most intimately involved in it experienced only a sense of defeat? The inability to square these two points often results in either denying or downplaying the extent of one or the other.

We saw in Chapter 5 how the shrine priesthood successfully used the Imperial Diet to validate its concerns as nonreligious and nonsectarian, and hence as public concerns of national interest. As a consequence, the expansion of state support—which did not come smoothly, quickly, or evenly, we should note—relied on the discursive and institutional distinction between the public and the private and sectarian character of religion.[16] The conceit that shrines merited state support because they were "sites for the performance of state rites" justified considerable pressure to remove religious elements from low-level shrines at the margins, where "'religious' practices such as preaching, funerals, prayers, and the selling of charms" continued for economic reasons. Sakamoto Koremaru, the leading historian of modern shrine Shinto, summarizes how this generated a profound experience of victimization:

> With the possible exception of priests at "state shrines" (the so-called *kankokuheisha*), the prospects for the priests at shrines of prefectural and lower rank—who made up the vast majority of the 15,000 or so in the priestly population—were grim indeed. People had venerated at shrines and ensured their survival because they believed; priests were there to strengthen and deepen that belief. But the policy of the Meiji government was to declare shrines "nonreligious," and to suppress wherever possible their religious dimension.[17]

The need to remove "religious elements" from shrines, and the symbiotic relationship between shrine priests and Home Ministry bureaucrats resulted in policies such as the notorious shrine mergers, when between 1905 and 1929 a minimum of 83,000 *minsha* (civic shrines) were eliminated.[18] Those who criticized the merger program did so, tellingly, by affirming the religious character of Shinto shrines.[19] The subjectified grammar of religion had tamed sectarian difference, but it also valorized private belief and the organizational autonomy of sectarian organizations. It remained difficult, however, for shrine priests, especially at the lower levels and far removed from the elite circles of Tokyo, to embrace the validation of internal belief and resist the bureaucratic logic of the Home Ministry and its officials.[20]

As religious studies contributed another layer of authority to the grammar of religion, it also had the potential to threaten shrine Shinto by treating it as a primitive practice that was less evolved than a full-fledged religion. As early as Kume Kunitake's 1891 essay, which argued that Shinto was a vestigial form of Heaven worship, shrine priests and their advocates had been sensitive to this possibility.[21] Katō Genchi (1873–1965), writing from within the discipline of religious studies, consistently affirmed the essentially religious character of Shinto in order to prevent shrines from being denigrated as mere commemorative sites.[22] Writing soon after the Shrine Bureau was created, Miyaji Izuo (1847–1918), a former doctrinal instructor and palace official, tackled the taxonomic problem of whether shrines were religious or not. He identified seven elements that all religions share, and argued that shrines possessed all in some form. This did not mean, he was quick to emphasize, that shrines fell completely into the realm of religion. Unlike mere religions, which focused principally on the spiritual concerns of individuals, shrines principally directed attention to the nation.[23] Religion as competition between contingent identities remained anathema, but religion as a means to affirm interior belief remained attractive to many Shinto thinkers. As shrine priests and their advocates attempted to build on the gains of the late nineteenth century and increase the public significance of shrines and their priests, they chafed against the constraints imposed by the grammar of religion. This desire to simultaneously benefit from the category of religion while remaining above it runs through modern Shinto discourse into the postwar period.

The grammatical function of religion allows us, at the same time, to see how the coercive character of State Shinto and the marginalization of a subjectively dedicated priesthood could go hand in hand. As Shimazono Susumu has recently argued, State Shinto expanded principally through mechanisms that assumed a secular character and hence functioned as uniform demands on Japanese subjects. Holidays, school curricula, and civic rituals involving the war dead, for example, all relied on their distinction from religion to augment their coercive potential.[24] Built on the religious settlement and the parliamentary treatment of religion, it was difficult to resist these mechanisms in the name of religion, though few attempted to do so in the first place. In fact, the ideological significance of Shinto shrines increased through developments largely unrelated to the preceding debates concerning the boundaries of religion. The expanded scale of mobilization and the high casualty rates of the Russo-Japanese War of 1904–5, for example, significantly increased the civic function of the Yasukuni shrine, and the ritual commemoration of the war dead came to form one core of state Shinto through the first half of the twentieth century.[25] Focused as it was on wars of imperial expansion, few contemporaries associated the commemorative function of Yasukuni with the arcane theological debates of the early Meiji Department of Divinities and Missionary Office. Indeed, as a "special shrine" (*tokubetsusha*) whose budget was part of the Imperial Army and Imperial Navy's ministerial budgets, Yasukuni stood aloof from much of the controversy surrounding the religious character of Shinto shrines and their priests. The ritual commemoration of those who died for the nation, recognized to be common among modern nation-states, created a powerful means to instill a civic orthodoxy that transcended sectarian difference.[26] The separation of Shinto shrines from Shinto sects in 1882 and the creation of the Shrine Bureau did augment Yasukuni's function as a suprareligious commemorative device, but they certainly did not equal the effect of modern warfare, and mass death and its commemoration, in spreading an orthodoxy of state Shinto.

Religious Freedom Reconsidered

The boundary of religion in modern Japan remains ambiguous, and once the category of religion is historicized, the always already-contestable nature of religion as a category becomes largely self-evident.[27] The state continued its attempts to pass a uniform statute regulating all religions: religion bills were submitted to the Imperial Diet in 1927 and 1929, and both were defeated. The Religious Organization Law (Shūkyō dantai hō) was finally passed in 1939 and went into effect the following year. The timing and content of the law clearly signaled a desire to mobilize sect- and denomination-level organizations to support the war effort in China.[28] The repeated failures of the religion bills and the recurring debate over the religious character of Shinto shrines were at the forefront of the ongoing negotiation of religion in prewar Japan.[29] Religion retained its ambivalent character, designating a potentially volatile realm of conversionary competition that could rupture the sutured-together nation-state, while also providing a means to tame that potential and mobilize it in service of national goals. By the end of the Meiji period, however, religion ceased to be the country's greatest problem, in part because the premise that a boundary between the religious and the secular should govern the political and social order of the nation-state had been institutionalized.

The secularization of political institutions and discursive arrangements achieved through the construction of religion as a category laid the groundwork for the more coercive characteristics of the modern Japanese state. Minobe Tatsukichi (1877–1948), a scholar of constitutional law whose "emperor organ theory"—that the emperor served as an organ of the state—famously maximized the democratic potential of the Imperial Constitution during the interwar period, interpreted shrine Shinto to be a religion. In a detailed legal opinion published in 1930, Minobe argued that the inescapably religious character of the shrines and the state's support for them implied a policy of religious toleration, not freedom. The Imperial Constitution promised all individuals the right to believe or disbelieve the state religion, but it did not guarantee state neutrality toward all religions. Admitting that shrine Shinto is a state religion, he suggested, did not mean belief could be coerced; to the contrary, it would make coercion more difficult.[30] Minobe's argument exposed the liberal potential of tolerance and the illiberal character of secularism. By creating the administrative and conceptual conditions for declaring shrines irreligious, the Meiji-era construction of religion generated a coercive potential that had been hitherto absent. When combined with the successful nationalization of the masses through public education and foreign wars in the early twentieth century, the grammar of religion provided a key component to the exercise of state authority.

The general assumption that the "Meiji Constitution, in effect, established State Shinto as a state religion" has been repeatedly challenged in the scholarly literature, but it remains a durable view, in part because the political attention given to the boundary between religion and the state has not been emphasized enough.[31] In his introduction to an online database of Meiji-era laws, Delmar Brown suggests that "Japan's rulers during [the eighth century and the Meiji period] really did think and believe in the divine power of the Great Goddess Amaterasu . . . [and continued] to think and believe that state support for Imperial Shinto would add sanctity and strength to Japan, its emperors and the reforms."[32] Whatever merit there may be to this characterization, it should be clear that the state found as many liabilities in "Imperial Shinto" as assets during the formative decades of the middle Meiji. To the extent that Shinto achieved ideological prominence in the twentieth century, it relied on the religious settlement that gave birth to it.

We observe in early-Meiji Japan how the very idea of religion, instead of being a premodern remnant that resisted secularization, emerged as a corollary to modernization and secular authority. Japan, in short, offers no exception to Talal Asad's claim that the secular and the religious are interdependent.[33] Moreover, the secular in this context no longer designates a category free of sacred elements but instead operates as a means to obscure the contingent foundation of authority. Foundational principles and authorities are, by definition, circular in derivation.[34] The "greatest problem" thus directs our attention to how the contingent character of imperial authority was recognized in early-Meiji Japan and how the political establishment attempted to secure the sacred by secularizing it (that is, by defining imperial authority in opposition to contingent belief).

This analytical framework proposes two basic revisions to how we understand the Meiji government's relationship to religion. First, we see how the Restoration, conducted in the name of the imperial institution, produced as many problems as solutions for the political elite. The imperial institution, rather than simply providing a fail-proof means of legitimating political authority and uniting the populace, also produced the potential for sectarian fragmentation, particularly by generating an unprecedented sectarian divide between Buddhism and what fitfully came to be called Shinto. The political conversation concerning the disposition of religion must be read as a defensive effort to contain the liabilities produced by the political use of the imperial institution. Second, the Meiji state's approach to religion, religious toleration, and Christianity cannot be understood in terms of mere acquiescence to diplomatic pressures. Undeniably, the informal cultural politics that accompanied the unequal-treaty regime compelled the oligarchic leadership to render the state's configuration as compatible as possible with the so-called West. It should be clear, however, that the political and intellectual establishment in Meiji Japan quickly transposed diplomatic pressure concerning the status of Christianity in Japan into a shared conversation concerning how centralizing nation-states should regulate religion. Policies calculated to win the "sympathy" of the treaty powers, in other words, were also informed by pragmatic calculations for effectively neutralizing disruptive differences *within* the political space of the modern Japanese nation-state. The freedom of religious belief and the conceit of a secular political order were constitutive of the modern Japanese nation-state and imperial institution, not ill-fitting concessions to foreign constituencies. Put another way, as alien as *shūkyō* remains in Japanese self-articulations today, the modern Japanese nation-state could not have been imagined without it.

The resurgence in state support for Shinto shrines and the affirmation of the public function of religion through the Assembly of Three Religions has been seen as a departure from the government's negative treatment of religion through the middle Meiji. It should be clear, however, that the ideological function of shrines and the mobilization of religion in the twentieth century did not repudiate so much as rely on the religious settlement of the late nineteenth century. "Religion," to summarize, constituted the "greatest problem" in early-Meiji Japan because it provided a conceptual marker for a fragmented polity and the crosscurrents of global power relations. Its gradual reification in political discourse and regulatory practice as a discrete, private belief reflected and participated in the development of the modern nation-state in Japan. By approaching the category of religion in early-Meiji Japan in this manner, overly parochial readings of State Shinto and the emperor system as "native" developments give way to an understanding of how modern political and diplomatic demands and the definition of religion were interrelated, and how the very premise of a unified national public relied on the ability of religion to elide sectarian and theological difference.

Abbreviations

The following abbreviations are used when citing sources in the Notes and Bibliography.

DNGB	*Dai nihon gaikō bunsho*, ed. Gaimushō chōsabu. 73 vols. Tokyo: Nihon kokusai kyokai, 1936–63.
HZ	*Hōrei zensho*. Naikaku kanpōkyoku. 45 vols. Tokyo: Hara shobo, 1974–94.
JKGB	*Jōyaku kaisei kankei nihon gaikōbunsho*, ed. Gaimushō chōsabu and Nihon gakujutsu shinkōkai. 8 vols. Tokyo: Nihon gaiko bunsho ryofukai, 1941–53.
KNST: M	*Kindai nihon shisō taikei*, vol. 30: *Meiji shisōshū*, ed. Matsumoto Sannosuke. Tokyo: Chikuma shobo, 1976.
MBZ: BK	*Meiji bunka zenshū*, vol. 20: *Bunmei kaika-hen*, ed. Yoshino Sakuzō. Tokyo: Nihon hyōronsha, 1929.
MBZ: K	*Meiji bunka zenshū*, vol. 4: *Kensei-hen*, ed. Yoshino Sakuzō. Tokyo: Nihon hyōronsha, 1928.
MBZ: S	*Meiji bunka zenshū*, vol. 11: *Shūkyō-hen*, ed. Yoshino Sakuzō. Tokyo: Nihon hyōronsha, 1928.
MBZ: SH	*Meiji bunka zenshū*, vol. 21: *Shakai-hen*, ed. Yoshino Sakuzō. Tokyo: Nihon hyōronsha, 1930.
MBZ: Z	*Meiji bunka zenshū*, vol. 18: *Zasshihen*, ed. Yoshino Sakuzō. Tokyo: Nihon hyōronsha, 1928.
MZ	*Meiroku zasshi*, ed. Yamamuro Shinichi and Nakanome Tōru. 3 vols. Tokyo: Iwanami shoten, 1999–2009.

NKST: STK	*Nihon kindai shisō taikei*, vol. 5: *Shūkyō to kokka*, ed. Yasumaru Yoshio and Miyachi Masato. Tokyo: Iwanami shoten, 1988.
NKST: TK	*Nihon kindai shisō taikei*, vol. 2: *Tennō to kazoku*, ed. Katō Shūichi and Tōyama Shigeki. Tokyo: Iwanami shoten, 1988.
NST: HA	*Nihon shisō taikei*, vol. 50: *Hirata Atsutane, Ban Nobutomo, Ōkuni Takamasa*, ed. Tahara Tsuguo et al. Tokyo: Iwanami shoten, 1973.
NST: MG	*Nihon shisō taikei*, vol. 53: *Mitogaku*, ed. Imai Usaburō, Seya Yoshihiko, and Bitō Masahide. Tokyo: Iwanami shoten, 1973.
SKG	*Sūmitsuin kaigi gijiroku*. 96 vols. Tokyo: Tokyo daigaku shuppankai, 1984–85.
SMZ	*Shimaji Mokurai zenshū*, ed. Futaba Kenkō and Fukushima Kanryū. 5 vols. Kyoto: Honganji shuppan-kyokai, 1973–78.
TGKGS	*Teikoku gikai kizokuin giji sokkiroku*. 74 vols. Tokyo: Tokyo daigaku shuppankai, 1979–85.
TGKIS	*Teikoku gikai kizokuin iinkai sokkiroku Meiji-hen*. 28 vols. Tokyo: Tokyo daigaku shuppankai, 1985–88.
TGSGS	*Teikoku gikai shūgiin giji sokkiroku*. 86 vols. Tokyo: Tokyo daigaku shuppankai, 1979–85.
TGSIG	*Teikoku gikai shūgiin iinkai giroku Meiji-hen*. 72 vols. Tokyo: Tokyo daigaku shuppankai, 1985–89.

Notes

Introduction

1. Kamei Katsuichirō, "Giji shūkyō kokka."

2. Chamberlain, *Invention of a New Religion*, 6.

3. Quoted in Doak, "A Religious Perspective on the Yasukuni Controversy," 49, 50. Doak has argued more recently that the Meiji constitution and its conditional guarantee of religious freedom produced "not a unique Shinto theocracy, but a kind of modern secular state that put a primacy on political controls over religion"; see Doak, "A Naked Public Square?" 189.

4. Hardacre, *Shinto and the State*, 18.

5. See, for example, Bernstein, *Modern Passings*; Breen and Teeuwen, *Shinto in History*; Hardacre, *Religion and Society in Nineteenth-Century Japan*; Ketelaar, *Of Heretics and Martyrs in Meiji Japan*; Sawada, *Practical Pursuits*; Thal, *Rearranging the Landscape of the Gods*.

6. Inoue Kowashi, "Kyōdōshoku haishi ikenan," in *Inoue Kowashi den: Shiryō-hen*, 1: 389.

7. "Kyōdōshoku haishi narabini shinbutsu kakushūha mibun toriatsukai no ken," in *Kōbunroku* 2A-010-00 • 公03678100.

8. The secular can stand prior to or in distinction from secularism as an ideological project; see Asad, *Formations of the Secular*, 16.

9. I use the term Shinto here heuristically, well aware of its anachronism. Because no clear sectarian framework preceded the disassociation, it is more accurate to describe the separation of Buddhas and *kami*. The slow and contested definition of Shinto as a composite of shrines and ritualists forms an important component of the history of religion in modern Japan.

10. Veer, *Conversion to Modernities*, 7.

11. I have in mind particularly Sakamoto Koremaru's body of work, which is cited extensively throughout this book.

12. Holtom, *Modern Japan and Shinto Nationalism*.

13. Murakami, *Kokka shintō*, 225.

14. For representative expressions of this view, see Fujitani Toshio, "Kokka shintō no seiritsu," 289; Murakami Shigeyoshi, *Kokka shintō*, 225. For later formulations of

their views on State Shinto, see Fujitani Toshio, *Shintō shinkō to minshū, tennōsei*, 175–237; and Murakami Shigeyoshi, *Tennōsei kokka to shūkyō*, 71–162. Nitta Hitoshi notes that most scholars do not fundamentally depart from Murakami's basic schema; Nitta, "'Kokka shintō'-ron no keifu," *Kōgakkan ronsō* 32, nos. 1 and 2 (February and April 1999).

15. Sheldon Garon, for example, warns against "invoking the emperor system as an all-encompassing explanation of modern Japanese history before 1945," because it implies too much stability and consistency in state policies and authority; Garon, *Molding Japanese Minds*, 62.

16. Sakamoto Koremaru, *Kokka shintō keisei katei no kenkyū*, 9–11, 305–10.

17. Fridell, "The Establishment of Shrine Shinto in Meiji Japan," 145, 146, 161.

18. See, for example, Haga, *Meiji ishin to shūkyō*, 5–6; Yamaguchi, *Meiji kokka to shūkyō*, 12–19; Isomae, *Kindai nihon no shūkyō gensetsu to sono keifu*, 97–107.

19. See, for example, Veer and Lehmann, *Nation and Religion*; Yasumaru Yoshio, "Minshū shūkyō to 'kindai' to iu keiken."

20. Carl Becker provides an elegant and early articulation of this process in *Heavenly City of the Eighteenth-Century Philosophers*, 128–30.

21. Fitzgerald, *Ideology of Religious Studies*, 8. See also Asad, *Formations of the Secular*, 27–28.

22. Viswanathan, *Outside the Fold*, 12.

23. Ibid., 16.

24. Foucault, "Technologies of the Self," 18. See also Foucault, "Governmentality."

25. Itō Yahiko, *Meijin ishin to jinshin*. See also Katsurajima Nobuhiro's discussion of the discourse of "capturing the hearts of the people" (*jinshin shrūran*): Katsurajima, "Kindai tennōsei ideologii no shisō katei," 217–46.

26. Antoni, "Introduction," 8.

27. Quoted in Yamaguchi, *Meiji kokka to shūkyō*, 98.

28. See, for example, Aihara, "Yakugo 'shūkyō' no seiritsu"; Isomae, "Kindai ni okeru 'shūkyō' gainen no keisei katei," 161–96; Shimazono, "'Shūkyō' to 'Religion'"; Suzuki, *Meiji shūkyō shichō no kenkyū*, 13–17.

29. Hayashi, "Shūmon kara shūkyō he," 169–89.

30. As will be seen in subsequent chapters, the term *shintō* could be used in purely generic terms in early-Meiji Japan. Isomae, *Kindai nihon no shūkyō gensetsu to sono keifu*, 33–36.

31. See Sawada, *Practical Pursuits*.

32. Tanigawa, *Meiji zenki no kyōiku, kyōka, bukkyō*, 6–9.

33. Howland, *Translating the West*, 6.

1. The Crisis of Conversion in Restoration Japan

1. See, for example, Haga, "Shintō kokkyōsei no keisei"; Sakamoto Koremaru, "Kyōbushō setchi ni kansuru ichi kōsatsu"; Takagi Hiroshi, "Shintō kokkyōka seisaku hōkaikatei."

2. Bob Wakabayashi observes that *Shinron* had "a political and social impact probably unmatched by any other single work during the final decades of bakufu rule"; Wakabayashi, *Anti-Foreignism and Western Learning*, ix.

3. For a representative articulation of this vision, see Fujita Yūkoku, *Seimeiron*, in *NST: MG*, 10–14.

4. Matsumoto Takashi notes that while the phrase *saisei itchi* appears to have emerged in the eighteenth century from Yamazaki Ansai's school of Suika Shinto, it was Aizawa's *New Theses* that popularized the ideal; Matsumoto, "Kinsei ni okeru saisei itchi shisō no tenkai," 40–41.

5. Aizawa, *Shinron*, in *NST: MG*, 77, 94–95: 「妖教を用いて以てその民を誘ひ、民心皆一なれば、以て戦ふに足る。」.

6. For a vivid picture of the propaganda against Catholic missionaries produced in the early Tokugawa period, see Elison, *Deus Destroyed*.

7. Yasumaru, *Kamigami no meiji ishin*, 2–8; Koschmann, *Mito Ideology*, 76.

8. Aizawa, *Shinron*, 53, 144, 64–65, 104:「民の利を好み鬼を畏るるは、その情に免るる能わざるところ」,「民心を緝収」.

9. Ibid., 65.

10. Ketelaar, *Of Heretics and Martyrs*, 46–54.

11. For a discussion of the temple-registry system and the anti-Buddhist criticisms it generated, see Hur, *Death and Social Order in Tokugawa Japan*, 87–95.

12. Aizawa, *Shinron*, 66.

13. Ibid., 134: 「故に中国、常に一定の略ありて、以て夷狄を制御し」.

14. Ibid., 143; emphasis mine in the translation: 「神聖の夷俗を変ぜし所以の方を倒用し、反って以て中国を変ぜんと欲す」.

15. Ibid., 146: 「彼を変ぜざれば、すなはち彼に変ぜらる。」.

16. Katsurajima, "Kai shisō no kaitai to jitaninshiki no henyō," 242–44.

17. Yasumaru, "Kindai tenkanki ni okeru shūkyō to kokka," in *NKST: STK*, 493.

18. Yasumaru, *Kindai tennōzō no keisei*, 131.

19. John Breen, for example, has called into question the prevailing view of nativists serving within the early-Meiji government as xenophobes bent on suppressing Christianity and eliminating Buddhism; Breen, "Shintoists in Restoration Japan."

20. See Hoshino, "Bakumatsu ishinki ni okeru saisei itchi-kan," 93–117.

21. Kiri Paramore locates Aizawa within a broad current of anti-Christian discourse in mid- to late-Tokugawa Japan; Paramore, *Ideology and Christianity in Japan*, 103–30.

22. See, for example, Sakaguchi, "Bakumatsu ishinki no haiyaron"; Inoue Nobutaka, *Kyōha shintō no keisei*, 341–78.

23. *HZ*, 3: 6, no. 13.

24. For surveys of the factional competition within the Meiji government, see Breen, "The Imperial Oath of April 1868," 417–23, and Umegaki, *After the Restoration*, 111–23.

25. *HZ*, 3: 63, no. 153.

26. First revived as the Office of Divinities (Jingi jimuka) in February 1868, the office was quickly renamed the Bureau of Divinities (Jingi jimukyoku), before it was finally given its ancient title of Department of Divinities (Jingikan) in June. *HZ*, 3: 15–17, no. 36; 6: 316, no. 398.

27. Breen uses this formulation to question the characterization of *sasei itchi* as an anachronistic and xenophobic project within the early Meiji state; Breen, "The Imperial Oath of April 1868," 407–29.

28. Ketelaar, *Of Heretics and Martyrs in Meiji Japan*, 90.

29. Aston, *Nihongi*, 2: 180: "Then she commanded her August Grandchild, saying: 'This Reed-plain-1,500-autumns-fair-rice-ear Land is the region which my descendants shall be lords of. Do thou, my August Grandchild, proceed thither and govern it. Go! and may prosperity attend thy dynasty, and may it, like Heaven and Earth, endure for ever.'"

30. Breen, "The Imperial Oath of April 1868," 409–12.

31. It was, in fact, Sanjō who performed the most notable portions of the ceremony, reading both the oath to the deities and the accompanying imperial edict.

32. The courtiers were not the only ones marginalized by the ceremony. The five articles also marked the first significant step in replacing the semiautonomous prerogatives of the daimyo with the premise of a centralized state. For a discussion of the Charter Oath and the Restoration government's relations to daimyo domains, see Umegaki, *After the Restoration*, 52–59.

33. Breen, "The Imperial Oath of April 1868," 408.

34. *HZ*, 3: 137– 46, no. 331.

35. Published in the Council of State's gazette, the *Dajōkan nisshi*.

36. Kim, *Age of Visions and Arguments*, 272.

37. Ōkubo Toshimichi, "Osaka sento kenpakusho," in *NKST: TK*, 6–8: 「官武ノ別ヲ放棄」、「一天ノ主」.

38. *HZ*, 3: 223, no. 557; 224–25, nos. 852, 853. This designation made the Hikawa shrine a *chokusaisha*, a shrine to which imperial envoys are dispatched for the major rites, while twelve other notable shrines in the Tokyo area were also designated junior imperial shrines (*junchokusaisha*) at this time.

39. For an overview of the political use of the emperor at this time, see Fujitani, Takashi *Splendid Monarchy*, 51–66.

40. Of the many, the so-called six great imperial progresses (*junkō*) occurred between 1872 and 1885: the Chūgoku-Saigoku tour in 1872, the Tōhoku tour in 1876, Hokuriku-Tōkaidō tour in 1878, the Yamanashi-Mie-Kyoto tour in 1880, the Yamagata-Akita-Hokkaido tour in 1881, and the Yamaguchi-Hiroshima-Okayama tour in 1885. Pak Chinu examines the complex character of the popular veneration of the emperor that these progresses generated; Pak, "Tenno junkyō kara mita tennō sūhai to minshū," 321–55.

41. *HZ*, 3: 357, nos. 962, 963. For a comparison between the early-modern revival of the *niiname* rite and the post-Restoration version, see Sakamoto Koremaru, *Kinsei kindai shintō ronkō*, 103–22.

42. Takeda, *Ishinki tennō saishi no kenkyū*, 199–207. As a result of this abandonment of Buddhist funerary and memorial rituals for the imperial family, the *okurodo*, where the memorial tablets of the deceased emperors were kept within the palace and where Buddhist memorial rites took place, was dismantled. The memorial tablets were removed to Sennyūji temple, the parish temple of the imperial family, and imperial funeral and memorial rites were no longer conducted by Buddhist monks within the palace. When the Department of Divinities built its provisional shrine (*karishinden*) one year later in Tokyo, the ancestral spirits of the imperial family were enshrined as *kami*, along with the deities of heaven and earth and the eight guardian deities of the imperial house (*hasshin*).

43. I borrow the idea of "disassociation" of Buddhist and Shinto deities, as well as the characterization of "cultural revolution," from Allan G. Grapard's pioneering essay, "Japan's Ignored Cultural Revolution." For a classic discussion of the intertwined character of Shinto and Buddhism in premodern Japan, see Kuroda, "Shinto in the History of Japanese Religion."

44. Klaus Antoni provides a vivid example of this process in his study of Ōmiwa shrine; Antoni, "The 'Separation of Gods and Buddhas.'"

45. See, for example, the following orders spread between April and May 1868: *HZ*, 3: 69, no. 165; 77, no. 196; 97, no. 242; 108, no. 280; 133, no. 320; 203, no. 503.

46. Ketelaar traces the formation of anti-Buddhist attitudes among the ruling classes to the interplay of historicist, nativist, and economic concerns. Ketelaar, *Of Heretics and Martyrs*, 3–42.

47. See, for example, Hur's discussion of seventeenth-century reforms undertaken by the domains of Mito, Okayama, and Aizu, in Hur, *Death and Social Order in Tokugawa Japan*, 89–95.

48. Ketelaar, *Of Heretics and Martyrs in Meiji Japan*, 7.

49. Yasumaru, "Kindai tenkanki ni okeru shūkyō to kokka," in *NKST: STK*, 504; Breen and Teeuwen, *A New History of Shinto*, 108–11.

50. *HZ*, 3: 89–90, no. 226; 297, no. 752: 「破仏之御趣意ニハ決テ無之候」.

51. Murakami, Tsuji, and Washio, *Meiji ishin shinbutsu bunri shiryō*, 5: 1110–11.

52. The Ōhama uprising of 1872, led by Shin-shū priests and involving nearly 4,000 peasants, was sparked by rumors that government officials were adopting Christianity as the official creed. See Ketelaar, *Of Heretics and Martyrs in Meiji Japan*, 77–86; Tamamuro Taijō and Morioka Kiyomi, "Meiji ishin to bukkyō," in *Nihon bukkyō-shi*, vol. 3, ed. Tamamuro Taijō et al., 321–24.

53. *HZ*, 3: 203, no. 504: 「朝廷廃仏毀釈コレツトムナト」. The five head temples were East Honganji, West Honganji, Kyōseiji, Bukkōji, and Senjūji. The government repeated this appeal to the central temples of all Buddhist sects when it confiscated lands belonging to temples and shrines in the spring of 1871.

54. For the Nishihongan-ji sect's financial contributions and ties to the Chōshū faction, see Ketelaar, *Of Heretics and Martyrs in Meiji Japan*, 71–73.

55. *HZ*, 7: 93, no. 133.

56. Jaffe, "Meiji Religious Policy, Sōtō Zen, and the Clerical Marriage Problem."

57. One measure of their influence over policies relating to unifying rite and rule as well as disassociating Shinto and Buddhism is the length of their appointments. Kamei and Fukuba held executive positions within the Department of Divinities (in its various incarnations) from the spring of 1868 through the fall of 1871, while most other executives, especially those belonging to rival Kokugaku factions and hereditary Shinto houses, held only brief tenures. See Sakamoto Kenichi, *Meiji shintōshi no kenkyū*, 420–23, 436–56; Breen, "Ideologues, Bureaucrats and Priests," 231–38.

58. An account of Tsuwano retainers who served the loyalist cause and the Restoration government can be found in Inoue Mizue, *Ishin zengo tsuwanohanshi hōkō jiseki*.

59. For studies of Kokugaku as a philological and proto-nationalist project, see Burns, *Before the Nation*, and Sakai, *Voices of the Past*.

60. Quoted in Sakamoto Kenichi, "Meiji Ishin to Tsuwano Hongaku," 13, 17.

61. Yasumaru, "Kindai tenkanki ni okeru shūkyō to kokka," in *NKST: STK,* 502–3. John Breen characterizes the intent of Kamei and Fukuba to have been the demotion of Buddhism, not its elimination; Breen, "Shintoists in Restoration Japan."

62. Hur, *Death and Social Order in Tokugawa Japan*, 77–106.

63. Kawasaki, "Kaishū," 221–43. Controlling competition among temples for *danna* parishioners who sought to alter their affiliation based on marriage or relocation, proved difficult enough for the authorities, without even considering permitting free competition for parishioners; see Hur, *Death and Social Order in Tokugawa Japan*, 112–13, 125–27, 228–30.

64. For a detailed survey of early-modern attempts to transform Shinto into something institutionally equivalent to Buddhism, see Nishida, *Nihon shintōshi kenkyū*, 6: 13–102.

65. Bernstein, *Modern Passings*, 51–55; Hur, *Death and Social Order in Tokugawa Japan*, 321–22, 331–32.

66. *HZ*, 5: 1, no. 4:「億兆同心治教明」.

67. See Breen, "Heretics in Nagasaki," 10–16. In his survey of Tokugawa religious policy, Peter Nosco observes that by the end of the seventeenth century the Tokugawa authorities abandoned efforts to strictly police private belief and practice in favor of requiring external compliance with the rules of temple registration; Nosco, "Keeping the Faith."

68. *DNGB*, 2: 668.

69. Chapter 2 examines in greater detail the diplomatic negotiations surrounding the Meiji state's treatment of Christianity and religion.

70. Sawa was one of the seven loyalist courtiers famously exiled from Kyoto in 1863 for conspiring with the Chōshū domain.

71. Inoue Kaoru was reportedly most active in dealing with the Urakami Christians; Abe, "From Prohibition to Toleration," 122.

72. Kataoka, *Urakami yoban kuzure*, 102–6.

73. Shimizu Hirokazu, "Nagasaki saibansho no urakami kyōto shobunan," 75–79.

74. Kido, *Diary of Kido Takayoshi*, 9; Yamazaki Minako, *Iwakura shisetsudan ni okeru*, 56.

75. Satow, *A Diplomat in Japan*, 359–60.

76. Iechika, *Urakami kirishitan ryuhai jiken*, 16–19.

77. *HZ*, 3: 101–2, no. 256.

78.「皇国中一途ノ教法無之候テハ彼法ヲ圧倒イタシ候様ノ事難相成」.

79. Ōkuni, "Shinto kyōsei ni tsuki ikensho," in *NKST: STK*, 7:「日本本国之教法ヲ以テ異域ヲモ化導イタシ」.

80. Ueda, "Ōkuni Takamasa no shisōtaikei," 52–53.

81. A very good example of his exegetical strategy can be found in an essay that challenges the universal validity of the Law of Nations in light of the imperial myths. See Ōkuni, "Shin-shinkōhōron," in *NST: HA*, 494–96.

82. Katsurajima, *Bakumatsu minshū shisō*, 72.

83. Ōkuni, "Shinto kyōsei ni tsuki ikensho," 7: 「御一新之折柄、神道モ御一新御確定ニテ日本国中へ御布告ニ相成申度奉存候」.

84. Kido, *Diary of Kido Takayoshi*, 16–17. Murata Kakuzan provides a detailed analysis of the proposals circulated within the government at this time and notes that a majority favored converting the Christians through admonition; see "Meiji shonen no tai yasokyō seisaku kō," 245–49.

85. Nakamura Akira, "Kokugakusha ni okeru kyoka shiso," 121–54.

86. *HZ*, 4: 48, no. 98:「牧民之要領ハ政教並行ニ有之」.

87. *HZ*, 3: 126, no. 314; Kido, *Diary of Kido Takayoshi*, 27.

88. *HZ*, 3: 126:「懇切に教諭致し良民に立戻り候様厚く可取扱」.

89. For a detailed account of the debates regarding this initial exile plan within the government, see Iechika, *Urakami kirishitan*, 32–48.

90. Kataoka, *Nihon kirishitan junkyōshi*, 624–30.

91. *HZ*, 4: 385–86, no. 947; 400, no. 974. Kido, *Diary of Kido Takayoshi*, 56.

92. Fujii, "Senkyōshi no kenkyū," 3.

93. Tokoyo Nagatane, *Shinkyō soshiki monogatari*, in *NKST: STK*, 363.

94. Haga, *Meiji ishin to shūkyō*, 167–68; Nishida, *Nihon shintōshi no kenkyū*, 7: 447, 457. Officials at Tsuwano apparently employed a similar argument to press the Christian exiles to convert. See Haga, *Meiji ishin to shūkyō*, 187, n. 66.

95. Ono Nobuzane, *Shinkyō yōshi*, 469–70.

96. Katsurajima, *Shisōshi no jyūkyūseiki*, 143–45.

97. Fujii Sadafumi's research on the *senkyōshi* remains the most detailed account of these differences; see *Edo kokugaku tenseishi no kenkyū*, 42–64, and "Senkyōshi ni okeru kyōgi kakuritsu no mondai."

98. For an interpretation of the Hirata school's preoccupation with the hidden realm, see Harootunian, *Things Seen and Unseen*; for a social history of the Hirata school at the time of the Restoration, see Walthall, *Weak Body of a Useless Woman*.

99. *NKST: STK*, 364.

100. This was expressed, for example, in the doctrine that Ōkuninushi-no-kami ruled the hidden realm (the afterlife), while Amaterasu and her imperial progeny ruled the visible realm. Supported by those affiliated with the Izumo shrine, this view competed with those who sought to consolidate the pantheon and ritual order around Ise and Amaterasu. See Fujii Sadafumi, "Shiryō shōkai: 'Shinkon taishi,'" 58–59.

101. For a discussion of the divergent views on the Shinto pantheon during this period, see Hoshino, "Bakumatsu ishinki ni okeru saisei itchi-kan," 101.

102. Tokoyo blames Fukuba for slowing the construction of the Deity Hall by showing little interest in ritually venerating the eight tutelary deities; *NKST: STK*, 365–66.

103. Takeda, *Ishinki tennō saishi*, 217. This took place in February 1869.

104. Debate concerning the character of the afterlife was not new to Kokugaku, and Hirata Atsutane had courted controversy by emphasizing the sociopolitical significance of the afterlife. For an introduction to these earlier debates in English, see McNally, "The *Sandaikō* Debate."

105. *NKST: STK*, 371, 372:「其身一人ノ恥辱ニハアラズ、則官使ノ恥辱ナリ」.

106. *Kōgisho nisshi*, in *MBZ: K*, 52. The Kōgisho was a deliberative body created in late 1868. It was composed primarily of representatives selected by each daimyo domain. It was reorganized into the Shūgiin in July 1869. While it has been characterized

as a xenophobic and conservative body, its role in promoting the elimination of outcast status distinctions and the prohibition of seppuku, or ritual suicide, suggests the assembly was not entirely out of step with the reformist impulses of the state leadership; see Mimura, "Kōginin no sonzai keisei to kōgisho ni okeru 'giron,'" and Yamazaki Yūkō, "'Kōgi' chūshutsu kikō no keisei to hōkai."

107. *Kōgisho nisshi*, in *MBZ: K*, 84–85, 93, 97.

108. *NKST: STK*, 370.

109. The provisional system of registration was applied to eight jurisdictions that represented the political centers and treaty ports: Tokyo, Kyoto, Osaka, Hyogo, Kanagawa, Sado, and Nagasaki (*HZ*, 5: 248–54, no. 429). These were all areas with either treaty ports, planned treaty ports, or a foreign diplomatic presence. A permanent system was announced in September 1871 along with the intent to apply it nationally (*HZ*, 6: 270–72, no. 323), but it was effectively stillborn, owing to the civil registry law already issued in June (*HZ*, 6: 114–38, no. 170).

110. *HZ*, 6: 269, no. 321.

111. See Sakamoto Koremaru, *Kokka shintō keisei katei*, 172–90.

112. *HZ*, 6: 114–38, no. 170; 5: 254. Shrine parishioner registration was formally suspended in May 1873.

113. Takechi, "Meiji shonen no Nagasaki ni okeru taikyō senpu undō."

114. Quoted in Fujii Sadafumi, "Senkyōshi to Nagasaki kaikō," 25.

115. Ibid., 26.

116. Miyachi Masato, "Kokka shintō keisei katei no mondaiten," in *NKST: STK*, 574.

117. Fujii Sadafumi "Senkyōshi to Nagasaki kaikō," 28.

118. Sasaki Takayuki, *Hogohiroi*, 5: 197. Tokoyo blames Ono for not dispatching more missionaries because he feared they would not adhere to his doctrine; Tokoyo, *NKST: STK*, 378, 378.

119. Kataoka, "Nakano Takeaki no kōchi junshi," 154.

120. In many instances, the exiles were kept in extremely squalid conditions; Mitsumata, *Kanazawa, daishōji, toyama ni nagasareta urakami kirishitan*, 206–10.

121. These were Nagoya, Tsu, Kōriyama, Wakayama, Himeji, Tottori, Fukuyama, Matsue, Hiroshima, Okayama, Tsuwano, Yamaguchi, Tokushima, Takamatsu, Matsuyama, Kōchi, and Kagoshima.

122. The original reports can be found in the National Archives as under the titles *Oazukari ishūto koseki torishirabesho, Kirokuzairyō* 2A-035-01・記 00399100, and *Jūniken oazukari ishūjunshi gairyaku, Kirokuzairyō*, 2A-035-01・記 00399100. Reprinted versions of the reports are cited for convenience.

123. Kusumoto, *Jyūniken oazukari ishūto junshi gairyaku*, 16, 25, 33, 44, 50, 56, 60, 80, 93, 102, 126.

124. Ibid., 10, 11, 14.

125. For another example of strategies employed to convert the Urakami exiles, see Okuimiya Zōsai's lectures in Kataoka, "Nakano Takeaki no kōchi junshi," 151–83.

126. Kusumoto, *Jyūniken oazukari ishūto junshi gairyaku*, 65.

127. The *settoku taishi* is quoted in Junshin joshi tanki daigaku nagasaki chihō bunkashi kenkyūjo, *Yasokyō ni kansuru shorui*, 117–18: 「皇ノ大道ヲ以シ現

世所業ノ善悪ニヨリテ幽罰ノ有無又高天原黄泉等ノ説ヲ以テ死後霊魂ノ苦楽迄ノ懇々ト説諭シ」.

128. Ibid., 67, 68, 70. Exiled Christians who vowed to abandon their faith were ordered released in the spring of 1872, and those who remained unconverted were released a year later. Between 800 and 1,000 exiles swore to convert, leaving, by one estimate, 2,620 unconverted Christians in exile. Most who converted later returned to the Catholic Church. For a discussion of the timing and rationale for the release of the exiles, see Chapter 2.

129. Haga, *Meiji ishin to shūkyō*, 177.

130. *HZ*, 6: 276, no. 3261.

131. Haga, *Meiji ishin to shūkyō*, 178.

132. Yasumaru, "Kindai tenkanki ni okeru shūkyō to kokka," in *NKST: STK*, 511.

133. *HZ*, 6: 284, no. 353.

134. Sakamoto Koremaru, "Kyōbushō setchi," 105–12.

135. Shimaji, "Jinnryō setchi seigansho," in *SMZ*, 1: 1–4.

136. Miyachi, *Kindai tennōsei no seijishiteki kenkyū*, 114–15. Ironically, it was the persistent rumor that the imperial government was promoting Christianity that provoked Buddhist adherents the most.

137. The state assumed a "three council" structure comprised of the Council of the Center (Seiin), the Council of the Right (Uin) and the Council of the Left (Sain). The Central Council was the executive organ presided over by the prime minister (*dajōdaijin*); the Right Council housed the ministers and their deputies; and the Council of the Left performed deliberative functions. For an extensive discussion of the Council of the Left within the Meiji government, including its membership, see Matsuo, "Meiji shoki dajōkan seido to sain."

138. Quoted in Kitsunezuka, "Kyōbushō no setchi to Etō Shinpei," 149.

139. "Kyōbushō setchi ni tsuki sain kengi," in *NKST: STK*, 25.

140. Viswanathan, *Outside the Fold*, xvii.

141. Unlike the Kōgisho and Shūgiin assemblies it replaced, the Council of the Left was composed of individuals selected from within the government itself, and it proved an influential sounding board for the executive core of the government. Members represented a range of political backgrounds, including hard-line loyalists as well as former *bakufu* supporters. Prominent members included Ijichi Masaharu, Tani Tesunomi, Hosokawa Junjiro, Itami Shigetaka, Matsuoka Kikei, Nishioka Yumei, Takasaki Goroku, Nagai Naoyuki, Miyajima Seiichiro, Ikuta Kuwashi, and Ōtori Keisuke. See Matsuo, "Meiji shoki dajōkan seido to sain," 18, 28; Yamada and Ōsumi, *Kinsei jijō*, 11: 38–39.

142. For an account of the Mikawa uprising, see Ketelaar, *Of Heretics and Martyrs in Meiji Japan*, 77–86.

143. Miyachi, *Kindai tennōsei no seijishiteki kenkyū*, 147–48.

144. Sanjō was technically the head of the Ministry of Divinities for a month and a half during the summer of 1871.

145. *HZ*, 6: 347–48, no. 465; 7: 79, no. 87. The Three Deity Halls are the Kashikodokoro, enshrining Amaterasu; the Kōreiden, enshrining the imperial ancestors; and the Shinden, enshrining the deities of heaven and earth.

146. The Sain assembly, for example, included this in its reform recommendations; *NKST: STK*, 24.

147. *HZ*, 6: 186–87, no. 234.

148. *HZ*, 6: 187–200, no. 235.

149. For an explanation of the ranking system, see Hardacre, *Shinto and the State*, 84–86.

150. Annually distributing talismans from Ise (*taima*), for example, provided the primary interaction between Shinto priests and the local populace and also cemented the focus on the imperial institution; ibid., 86–87.

151. *HZ*, 7: 79, no. 82

152. Asad, *Genealogies of Religion*, 17.

153. Quoted in *NKST: STK*, 27.

154. Ketelaar, *Of Heretics and Martyrs in Meiji Japan*, 93.

2. Religion and Diplomacy in a Semicolonial World

1. Abe, "From Prohibition to Toleration"; Hardacre, *Shinto and the State*, 117.

2. See, for example, Isomae, "Kindai ni okeru 'shūkyō' gainen," 161–96; Yamaguchi, *Meiji kokka*, 29–46.

3. Viswanathan, *Outside the Fold*, 4.

4. Breen, "'Earnest Desires.'" Breen argues that the embassy's experience confirmed the anti-Christian views of many members and, ironically, worked to improve attitudes toward Buddhism.

5. The Roman Catholic Relief Act, granting Catholics the right to full political participation, was passed to avert an uprising in Ireland; McLeod, "Protestantism and British National Identity," 53–55. See also Webb, "The Limits of Religious Liberty"; and Viswanathan, *Outside the Fold*, 44–72.

6. Suzuki, *Meiji shūkyō shichō*, 14–17.

7. Tomes, *Americans in Japan*, 383 (Appendix, "Millard Fillmore, President of the United States of America, To His Imperial Majesty the Emperor of Japan"). The need to avow religious neutrality in the service of expansion was not unique to the United States. Britain, with its established Anglican Church, struggled more openly to balance its promise of secular impartiality with its proper endorsement of Christian faith. Queen Victoria's proclamation of 1858 following the Indian Mutiny attempts just such a balance: "Firmly relying ourselves on the truth of Christianity and acknowledging the solace of religion, we disclaim alike the right and the desire to impose our convictions on any of our subjects"; quoted in Cox, "Religion and Imperial Power," 348.

8. Fujii Sadafumi, *Kaikokuki kirisutokyō*, 6–7.

9. Quoted in ibid., 4.

10. Quoted in ibid., 15.

11. Ibid., 15–19.

12. Auslin, *Negotiating with Imperialism*, 9–10.

13. Fujii Sadafumi, *Kaikokuki kirisutokyō*, 8.

14. Harris, *Complete Journal of Townsend Harris*, 465–66.

15. In fact, Tokugawa officials attempted to remove even the article granting the right of religious freedom to American citizens; Harris refused to alter the language initially agreed upon; ibid., 512–13, 74–76.

16. Ibid., Appendix 9, 582–83.

17. For a list of articles pertaining to religious freedom in all treaties of amity and commerce, see Takagi Kazuo, *Meiji katorikku kyōkaishi,* 1: 183–85.

18. The Dutch had already convinced the *bakufu* to discontinue the practice of *fumie* (stepping on images of the virgin and child) in late 1857; Abe, "From Prohibition to Toleration," 112.

19. Auslin, *Negotiating with Imperialism*, 26–28.

20. Kenneth Anderson goes so far as to claim that "the unequal treaties were unequal precisely insofar as discriminatory exceptions were made to the purportedly rational and universal law for the purposes of sustaining colonial authority over a subject people"; Anderson, "The Foreign Relations of the Family State," 7.

21. For the commercial dimension of the treaties, see Beasley, "The Foreign Threat and the Opening of the Ports," 271–84.

22. Fujii Sadafumi, *Kaikokuki kirisutokyō*, 77–84.

23. The treaties signed in 1858 stipulated the opening of Kanagawa (Yokohama), Nagasaki, and Hakodate to foreign residents. Edo (later Tokyo) and Osaka were to be opened between 1859 and 1863.

24. Hoare, *Japan's Treaty Ports*, 36–37.

25. Marnas, *Nihon kirisutokyō fukkatsushi*, 198–200.

26. Lehmann, "Leon Roches," 284.

27. Quoted in Lehmann, "French Catholic Missionaries," 381, 382.

28. Inoue Katsuo, *Shirizu nihon kingendaishi*, vol. 1: *Bakumatsu-ishin*, 50–74. The Catholic missionaries in Yokohama, for example, insisted that de Bellecourt's order to cease preaching in Japanese was in fact merely a request; Marnas, *Nihon kirisutokyō fukkatsushi*, 198–99.

29. Marnas, *Nihon kirisutokyō fukkatsushi*, 239, 243–44; also Kataoka, *Nihon kirishitan junkyōshi*, 571.

30. Kataoka, *Nihon kirishitan junkyōshi*, 573–74.

31. Junshin joshi tanki daigaku nagasaki chihō bunkashi kenkyūjo, *Puchijan shikyō shokanshū*, 114.

32. The missionaries' insistence upon doctrinal and ritual orthodoxy, especially as preconditions for receiving the sacraments, must have also motivated the increased defiance; Marnas, *Nihon kirisutokyō fukkatsushi*, 265, 267–68.

33. The three prior *kuzure* occurred in 1790, 1839, and 1856.

34. Breen points out that the investigation in the 1790s coincided with the abolishment of the "*Shūmon Aratameyaku*, the Edo headquarters of the state's department for Christian investigation . . . in 1792. It would have been extremely awkward for the *Bakufu* to acknowledge that a Christian community had been thriving in secret for 150 years, now that the *Bakufu's* office concerned with Christians and Christianity had been abandoned"; Breen, "Heretics in Nagasaki," 16.

35. At least fifteen were arrested and tortured; eleven died in prison and others swore to convert to Buddhism. Of the four *mizukata* (elders who conducted baptisms),

only one survived to meet with the missionaries in 1865; Kataoka, *Nihon kirishitan junkyōshi*, 547–48, and Urakawa, *Kirishitan no fukkatsu*, 1: 270–79.

36. For a contemporary account of the arrests, see "Nagasaki omote kirishitan ikken," in *MBZ: Z*, 3–4.

37. Lehmann, "Leon Roches," 285–302.

38. The naval officer was referring to the 1858 naval expedition sent to punish Vietnam for killing several Catholic missionaries and force it to accept protectorate status. The 1862 Treaty of Saigon had ceded three southern provinces to the French, and by 1867 France had consolidated all of southern Vietnam into the colony of Cochin China, setting the stage for the Sino-French War of 1884; Gaikokugata, *Urakami sonmin ikyō ikken*.

39. Fujii Sadafumi, *Kaikokuki kirisutokyō*, 302, 303.

40. Ōta, "Senkyōshi no saitorai to kirisutokyō," 594–99.

41. Quoted in Marnas, *La "Religion de Jésus,"* 2: 19–20. This letter was followed by a formal demand sent to Petitjean on the twenty-eighth to cease violating the terms of the treaties; Fujii Sadafumi, *Kaikokuki kirisutokyō*, 321–22.

42. Lehmann, "French Catholic Missionaries," 382.

43. See, for example, the petition submitted by the villagers refusing to accept the funeral rites of the Buddhist parish temple; *NKST: STK*, 283.

44. The Nagasaki magistrate balked at the idea of releasing Christians who had not recanted and pressed Edo to release only those who had agreed to abandon the faith; Nakamura Hiromu, *Senkyō to juyō*, 202.

45. In a letter to Emperor Napoleon III dated September 14, 1867, Tokugawa Yoshinobu, the last shogun, suggested that the prohibition against Christianity had to remain in force as long as the majority of the population remained convinced that it was an evil teaching. The letter indicates the *bakufu* attempted to defuse the tension by intimating that Christianity might be legalized some point in the future; Abe, "From Prohibition to Toleration," 118.

46. Yūki Ryōgo et al., *Saigo no hakugai*, 216–19.

47. A government spy reported in January 1869 that men and women from as far as the Gotō Islands traveled to Urakami to study the "heretical scriptures" (*ishū kyōmon*); *DNGB*, 2: 668.

48. Quoted in Auslin, *Negotiating with Imperialism*, 148.

49. De Bary et al., *Sources of Japanese Tradition*, vol. 2: *1600 to 2000*, 672.

50. For a history of the *kōsatsu* and their function, see Suzue, *Kirisutokyō kaikin izen*.

51. *DNGB*, 1: 564, 640.

52. Letters of July 15, 1868, and October 5, 1868; quoted in Paolino, *Foundations of the American Empire*, 172.

53. The two revised notices read, respectively: "The *kirishitan* sect is strictly prohibited as before" and "Evil sects are strictly forbidden"; May 25, 1868, *DNGB*, 1: 644.

54. Satow, *Diplomat in Japan*, 368.

55. *DNGB*, 1: 695; Iechika, *Urakami kirishitan ryūhai jiken*, 32–48.

56. *DNGB*, 1: 835–36, 847.

57. Kataoka, *Nihon kirishitan junkyōshi*, 624–30.

58. "The Persecution of Christians," *New York Times*, October 18, 1868, 4.

59. In early 1869 Parkes revived the issue of Christianity in response to reports that formerly hidden Christians on the Gotō Islands northwest of Nagasaki were being tortured because of their faith. The treatment of the Gotō Christians was the subject of diplomatic conversations through the fall of 1869. *DNGB*, 2: 804; 3: 533–34, 666.

60. Kataoka, *Nihon kirishitan junkyōshi*, 633–34.

61. *DNGB*, 4: 542–43.

62. Ibid., 583, 560. Discrepancies exist between the Japanese and English minutes of the conference. The Japanese minutes include repeated disclaimers on the part of Sanjō and Iwakura that they do not wish to debate the correctness of Christianity (*shūshi no seija or ronji*), while the English minutes do not. Whether this was a function of the translation that occurred during the conference or an omission on the part of the U.S. diplomat who compiled the English minutes is not known.

63. Ibid., 584, 586, 593, 594, 598–99.

64. Ibid., 628–30.

65. Breen, "Beyond the Prohibition," 78.

66. Terashima, for example, silenced his counterparts by criticizing the illegal activities of the French missionaries who "have established a place of worship at Owakura, not within the limits of the foreign settlements, where they go at night and preach their faith"; *DNGB* 4: 597.

67. Ibid., 590. De Long's sharp criticism and threats are not included in the Japanese minutes of the conference.

68. Ibid., 602, 621–26.

69. Yamazaki Minako, *Iwakura shisetsudan ni okeru*, 22–23, 37, 53.

70. *DNGB*, 4: 115–18.

71. Sims, *Japanese Political History*, 25–27.

72. For the background of the embassy and its members, see Ōkubo Toshiaki, *Iwakura shisetsu*, 15–107.

73. Griffis, *Verbeck of Japan*, 259–62.

74. Yamazaki Minako, "Kume Kunitake to kirisutokyō," 159.

75. "Adamuzu shokan ni okeru Iwakura no tennōsei kenkai," in *NKST: STK*, 314.

76. Kume, "Shintō no hanashi," in *Kume Kunitake rekishi chosakushū*, 3: 320–22.

77. Ibid., 320–21.

78. "The Japanese Embassy," *New York Times*, January 20, 1872, p. 8.

79. For a detailed account of these arrests, see Kataoka, "Nihon kindai kokka keisei katei," 117–37.

80. Shunpokō tsuishōkai, *Itō Hirobumi-den*, 1: 643–44.

81. Sasaki Takayuki, *Hogohiroi*, 5: 264: 「宗旨ハ政府ノ権力相立候上ハ、妨害ナシナドノ識見ハ人民ニハ及ビ兼候」.

82. Ibid., 265, 266.

83. Ibid., 263–64.

84. Quoted in Yamazaki Minako, *Iwakura shisetsudan ni okeru*, 77.

85. Sasaki, *Hogohiroi*, 273.

86. Ibid., 293–94: 「人民ヲ維持スル道具ナレバ」,「此邊ヲ以テ考フルニ、合衆国ノ政治妙ナリト思フナリ」.

87. Hall, *Mori Arinori*, 151–61. See also Shunpokō tsuishōkai, *Itō Hirobumi den*, 1: 647.

88. Auslin, *Negotiating with Imperialism*, 181.

89. Mayo, "A Catechism of Western Diplomacy," 389–410.

90. Auslin, *Negotiating with Imperialism*, 183.

91. *JKGB*, 1: 90, 96–98.

92. Ibid., 114–115.

93. Ōkubo left Washington on March 20, and Itō left the following day; Takagi Kazuo, *Meiji katorikku kyōkaishi*, 2: 51–52.

94. Auslin, *Negotiating with Imperialism*, 185.

95. Shunpokō tsuishōkai, *Itō Hirobumi-den*, 1: 653–54.

96. Yamazaki Minako, *Iwakura shisetsudan ni okeru*, 117.

97. Article X: "The citizens and subjects of either country shall enjoy in the territories of each, the most perfect and entire security of conscience, without being annoyed or disturbed on account of their religious belief, or on account of their decorous worship in private houses or in other places appointed for the purpose, provided that due respect be paid to the laws and customs of the country"; Takagi Kazuo, *Meiji katorikku kyōkaishi*, 2: 72.

98. *JKGB*, 1: 224, 228–29.

99. Ruxton, "Britain," 66–67.

100. Breen, "'Earnest Desires.'"

101. Aoki, *Aoki Shūzō jiden*, 38–39.

102. Ibid., 41–43. As we will see in Chapter 4, the rumor that he advocated the adoption of Christianity as the official creed of Japan dogged Itō through the early 1880s.

103. *JKGB*, 1: 254–55, 262–63, 268.

104. Shunpokō tsuishōkai, *Itō Hirobumi den*, 1: 693.

105. Yasuoka Akio argues the embassy directly brought about the tacit toleration of Christianity in 1873, while Iechika Yoshiki places greater emphasis on the caretaker government's domestic concerns; Yasuoka, "Iwakura shisetsu to shūkyō mondai," 235–67; Iechika, *Urakami kirishitan ryūhai jiken*, 177–83. Also see Werf, "Deliberate Non-Communication," 57–70.

106. Iechika, *Urakami kirishitan ryūhai jiken*, 166, 177–83.

107. The number of converted villagers released in 1872 numbered between 800 and 1,000, leaving, by one estimate, 2,620 unconverted Christians in exile; Inoue Kaoru kō denki hensankai, *Segai Inoue kō den*, 1: 310–15.

108. John Breen argues that the decision to create the Ministry of Doctrine to more effectively counter Christianity betrays a long-standing expectation within the Meiji government that the prohibition could not be maintained indefinitely; Breen, "Beyond the Prohibition," 90.

109. Griffis, *Verbeck of Japan*, 264.

110. Suzue, *Kirisutokyō kaikin izen*, 110, 127.

111. "Religious Toleration in Japan," *New York Times*, June 4, 1873.

112. Suzue, *Kirisutokyō kaikin izen*, 5–8, 32, 99–103.

113. Two such cases are recorded in *NKST: STK*, 339–48.

114. This sense of the urgent—and possible—task of catching up with the treaty powers was famously conveyed by Bismarck himself during a toast he gave at a dinner held in honor of the embassy; see Wattenberg, "Germany," 76–77.

115. "Shōbenmushi Mori Arinori yasoshū ni tsuki ikensho," *Kōbunbetsuroku* 2A-001-00 • 別 00002100.

116. Mori Arinori, "Religious Freedom in Japan," in *MBZ: S*, 543–41 (printed in reverse order).

117. See Yoshino Sakuzō's introduction to the text in *MBZ: S*, 58–59.

118. For example, see Hall, *Mori Arinori*, 195–202.

119. Nakamura Keiu, "Taiseijin no jōsho ni gisu," in *MBZ: SH*, 225–28.

120. Mori, "Religious Freedom in Japan," 540.

121. Ibid., 542.

122. Ibid., 537, 536, 535.

123. Tanaka, *Riji kōtei*, 1: 7.

124. Ibid., 3: 21.

125. At this point, the dominant understanding of education among the Meiji leadership was primarily as a means to "enlighten" the populace and hence secure the material progress of a nation. Increased scientific and rational knowledge would, of its own accord, reduce the influence of religion and clergy. Using religion as an active means of indoctrination, at least, seems absent from Mori and Tanaka's discussions.

126. Smith, *German Nationalism and Religious Conflict*, 20.

127. Ross, "Kulturkampf," 174, 193.

128. Quoted in Yamazaki Minako, "Iwakura shisetsudan to shinkō jiyū mondai," 61–62.

129. Kume, *Iwakura Embassy*, 3: 324–25.

130. Ibid., 2: 28, 5: 156, 4: 63.

131. Ibid., 1: 367; 3: 41; 4: 24, 64, 291–92; 5: 135.

132. Ibid., 4: 292.

133. Kume credits a French scholar, a "Professor Block," with instructing members of the embassy that "so long as it is ensured that a country's government and its religion are as one, then it is certain that it will not split apart." Ibid., 5: 158.

134. Nishikawa Makoto, "Meiji shonen no Aoki Shūzō," 38.

135. Kume, *Iwakura Embassy*, 1: 367–68; 4: 62, 310.

136. Ibid., 1: 364–65.

137. "Christian Missions in Japan," *Times* (London), January 15, 1873.

138. "Christian Missions in Japan," *Times* (London), January 16, 1873.

139. "Christian Missions in the East," *Times* (London), January 29, 1873.

140. Ibid.

3. Civilizing Faith and Subjectified Religion

1. Kume, "Shintō no hanashi," 319–20. Isomae Junichi divides the establishment of *shūkyō* as a stable discursive category in Meiji Japan into four stages: when *shūkyō* began to serve as a translation of "religion"; when *shūkyō* represented Western civilization; when *shūkyō* came to be restricted as private and irrational; and

when religious studies secured the status of *shūkyō*, as an object of academic investigation; Isomae, *Kindai nihon no shūkyō gensetsu*, 31.

2. For a brief survey of the Korea issue, see Sims, *Japanese Political History*, 33–35.

3. Sakamoto Koremaru, *Kokka shintō keisei katei*, 200.

4. I employ the shorthand "Shinto partisans" to indicate the heterogeneous composition of those who promoted and gave shape to Shinto in its modern form during the latter half of the nineteenth century. Precisely because Shinto lacked a preexisting sectarian structure, Shinto partisans did not neatly correspond to the liturgical specialists serving at shrines. State officials sympathetic to Kokugaku nativists and ideologues, prominent shrine priests, and founders of new religions—sometimes a partisan like Senge Takatomi could pass through all of these roles—coalesced in unstable coalitions to promote the "Shinto" cause. Elected politicians joined the list in the 1890s.

5. As I elaborate below, I employ the term "subjectification" to draw attention to the way in which the claim for an authentic and self-determining religious identity that stands apart from state power actually presumes that power and responds to its demands.

6. The journal sold more than 3,000 copies per issue, a significant circulation for the time; Tozawa, *Meirokusha*, 197–229.

7. The ten founding members of the society were Mori Arinori, Nishimura Shigeki, Nishi Amane, Tsuda Mamichi, Katō Hiroyuki, Nakamura Masanao, Fukuzawa Yukichi, Sugi Kōji, Mitsukuri Shūhei, and Mitsukuri Rinshō.

8. Ōkubo, *Meirokusha*, 103.

9. A point made with particular force by Yasumaru Yoshio in *Ikki, kangoku, kosumologii*.

10. Michael Pye forcefully argues that eighteenth-century intellectuals like Tominaga Nakamoto subjected religion in the abstract to sustained rational critique; Pye, "East Asian Rationality in the Exploration of Religion."

11. Tsuda, "Kaika wo susumeru hōhō," in *MZ*, 1: 118–21.

12. Nishi, "Kyōmon-ron 1," in *MZ*, 1: 155–60.

13. Ibid., 156–57.

14. Ibid., 157, 159, 160.

15. Nishi, "Kyōmon-ron 2," in *MZ*, 1: 176–78.

16. Tsuda, "Tengu-setsu," in *MZ*, 2: 45–49; "Kaisetsu," in *MZ*, 2: 320–24; Sakatani, "Kosetsu no gi," in *MZ*, 2: 191–94.

17. Gerald Figal analyzes the way in which scientific authority and the "folk" operated in cofigured opposition; Figal, *Civilization and Monsters*, 77–104.

18. Nishi, "Kyōmon-ron 2," in *MZ*, 1: 181–82.

19. The Shugendō, whose livelihood depended on prayer healings, were abolished and forced to join to Tendai or Shingon sects in 1872. Mediums, diviners, and exorcists were banned in 1874; *HZ*, 7: 174–75, no. 273; 8: 1627, no. 2.

20. Nishi, "Kyōmon-ron 3," in *MZ*, 1: 209–10.

21. Ibid., 212.

22. Derrida, "Faith and Knowledge," 18.

23. Katō Hiroyuki, *Kokutai shinron*, 77–79.

24. Beginning in 1872, Katō had already translated Johann Kaspar Bluntschli's *Algemeines Staatsrecht*, published in Japan as *Kokuhō hanron*. In his introduction in the *Meiroku Journal* to Thompson's text, Katō drew his readers' attention to the fundamental similarity between the two jurists' opinions regarding the desirability of separating religion and state.

25. Katō, "Beikoku seikyō," in *MZ*, 1: 195.

26. Yamazaki Minako, "Iwakura shisetsudan to shinkyō jiyū mondai," 63–64.

27. Howland, *Translating the West*, 113.

28. The 1873 Echizen uprising, for example, involved about 3,000 peasants and was motivated in part by Buddhist fears that the imperial government was promoting Christianity under the guise of modernizing reforms, such as the three standards of instruction taught by doctrinal instructors under the Ministry of Doctrine's aegis. For a documentary record of the uprising, see *NKST: STK*, 135–51.

29. Nakanome, "Mori Arinori ni okeru 'bunmei' to shūkyō."

30. Ruddy, *International Law in the Enlightenment*, 33–57, 281–315.

31. Mori, "Shūkyō," in *MZ*, 1: 221–22.

32. Ibid., 224–26.

33. Ibid., 229.

34. Aoki Shūzō's 1873 constitution draft, for example, designated Buddhism as the national creed: 「日本国ニテ主トシテ信仰スベキ宗旨ハ釈迦教ナルベシ」; quoted in Nakajima, "Dai nihon teikoku kenpō dai nijūhachi-jō 'shinkō jiyū' kitei seiritsu," 6–7.

35. Dajōkan honyakukyoku, "Kyōkai ritsuryō."

36. In 1871 the Council of State declared that all shrines conducted rites of the state and removed hereditary priests from Ise and other prominent shrines; *HZ*, 6: 186–87, no. 234.

37. Nishi, "*Kyōmonron* 3," in *MZ*, 1: 210.

38. Tsuda, "Seiron," in *MZ*, 1: 320–21.

39. Sawada, *Practical Pursuits*, 89–117.

40. Tsuda, "Sansei-ron," in *MZ*, 2: 218.

41. Sakatani, "Seikyō no gi," in *MZ*, 2: 244: 「而シテ其善ヲ立テルハ唯信ノ厚キニアリ其信ヲ厚クセシメテ確然動カザルニ至ルハ唯政教教法ノニツニアル」.

42. Sakatani, "Seikyō no gi yo," in *MZ*, 2: 314–15.

43. Nishimura, "Shūshin jikoku hi-nito-ron," in *MZ*, 3: 81, 84–85.

44. Sawada, *Practical Pursuits*, 105–9.

45. Fukuzawa, "Gakumon no susume," 60.

46. Nishi, "*Kyōmonron* 7," in *MZ*, 1: 387.

47. Sakamoto Koremaru, *Meiji ishin to kokugakusha*, 162–64. For a chart of the shifts in government ministries charged with regulating Shinto, Buddhism, Christianity, and so on, see Umeda, *Kaitei zōho nihon shūkyō seido-shi*, 4: 21–22.

48. Ketelaar, *Of Heretics and Martyrs*, 105.

49. Sakamoto Koremaru, *Kokka shintō keisei katei*, 203–4.

50. The formation of Shinto churches and the related rise of "sectarian Shinto" will be discussed in Chapter 4.

51. Toyoda, *Shūkyō seidoshi*, 216.

52. *NKST: STK*, 449. See also Sakamoto Koremaru, "Nihongata seikyōkankei," 45.

53. Fujiwara, "Kyōdōshokusei to kyōinsei," 465.

54. Nihon shiseki kyōkai, *Iwakura Tomomi kankei monjo*, 5: 155.

55. Sakamoto Koremaru, "Meiji hachinen sain," 160–61. Satsuma had adopted the anti-Buddhist vision of the Mito school with particular zeal and purged Buddhism from the domain with particular vigor; by the early 1870s nearly 4,500 temples and halls had been eliminated; see Ketelaar, *Of Heretics and Martyrs*, 54–65.

56. *HZ*, 7: 448–50.

57. Toyoda, *Shūkyō seidoshi*, 201–2.

58. Rakugo performers, actors, and other public speakers were also mobilized as doctrinal instructors.

59. *NKST: STK*, 446.

60. Jaffe, "The Buddhist Cleric as Japanese Subject," 529.

61. For a list of individuals appointed to the top ranks, see "Kyōdōshoku Ichiran," in Inoue and Sakamoto, *Nihongata seikyō kankei*, 368–76.

62. Haga, *Meiji ishin to shūkyō*, 191–217; Hirano, *Meiji kenpō seitei*.

63. Sakurai, *Meiji shūkyōshi kenkyū*, 44; *NKST: STK*, 452.

64. Bunkacho, *Meiji ikō shūkyō seido*, 3; "Shūkyō kankei hōrei ichiran," in NKST: STK, 436; Umeda, *Kaitei zōho nihon shūkyō seido-shi*, 4: 32–35.

65. *NKST: STK*, 446, 447, 448, 452, 470. This freedom both reflected and exacerbated the competition within Shinto ranks.

66. Toyoda, *Shūkyō seidoshi*, 201.

67. Ketelaar, *Of Heretics and Martyrs*, 105.

68. Sakamoto Koremaru, *Kinsei kindai shintō*, 301.

69. Tokoyo, *Shinkyō soshiki monogatari*, in *NKST: STK*, 382.

70. *NKST: STK*, 448, 455, 467. The prohibition of cremation, initially decreed in 1873, was rescinded in 1875. The cremation debate is discussed in Bernstein, *Modern Passings*, 67–90.

71. Umeda, *Kaitei zōho nihon shūkyō seido-shi*, 4: 80.

72. *NKST: STK*, 444, 452, 456. See also Umeda, *Kaitei zōho nihon shūkyō seido-shi*, 4: 65–66.

73. *NKST: STK*, 436, 460.

74. Ibid., 447, 452, 453.

75. Tsuji, *Meiji bukkyōshi*, 233–34; see also Hardacre, *Shinto and the State*, 44.

76. *NKST: STK*, 457.

77. Toyoda, *Shūkyō seidoshi*, 206–13.

78. The status of the new religions and their role in shaping Shinto will be explored in Chapter 4.

79. Hardacre, "The Shinto Priesthood in Early Meiji Japan," 295–99.

80. Ibid., 202–6; *NKST: STK*, 451.

81. Ketelaar, *Of Heretics and Martyrs*, 99; see also Fujii Sadafumi, "Shimane-kenka," 15–16.

82. Miyachi, *Kindai tennōsei no seijishiteki kenkyū*, 115.

83. *NKST: STK*, 461.

84. "The Three Standards, in short, draw upon Nativist, Confucian, and utilitarian constructs to locate the precise social functions or 'occupation,' of the Emperor, the government, and the governed;" Ketelaar, *Of Heretics and Martyrs*, 110.

85. For the most part I have borrowed Ketelaar's translation of the themes, with a few alterations; ibid., 106, 107–21.

86. Sakamoto Koremaru, *Kokka shintō keisei*, 203.

87. Sakamoto Koremaru, "Nihongata seikyō kankei no keisei katei," 39–40. Tokushige Asakichi observes that Hirata-school attempts to insert into the doctrine specific references to the afterlife proved particularly contentious among the Shinto doctrinal instructors; Tokushige, *Ishin seiji shūkyōshi*, 662–64.

88. By 1873 there more than eighty-eight doctrinal commentaries accepted by the Great Teaching Academy; Kokugakuin daigaku nihon bunka kenkyūjo, *Shaji torishirabe ruisan*, 98–100.

89. *NKST: STK*, 451.

90. For a sense of how the doctrinal instructors and their activities were portrayed in the press of the day, see "Kaika sesō no ura omote," in *MBZ: BK*, 491, 504, 526.

91. *NKST: STK*, 452.

92. "Bunmei kaika," in *MBZ: BK*, 14–15.

93. Fujiwara, "Kyōbushō-gyōseika," 717–32.

94. Yamaguchi, *Meiji kokka*, 33–46.

95. Miyachi, *Kindai tennōsei no seijishiteki kenkyū*, 122–27.

96. Tokushige, *Ishin seiji shūkyōshi*, 198–287.

97. See, for example, Fujii Takeshi, "Nationalism and Japanese Buddhism," 114; Kleinen, "Nishi Hongan-ji and National Identity," 87–105; Fukushima, "Shintō kokkyō seisakuka no shinshū"; and Nitta Hitoshi, "Shinto as a 'Non-religion,'" 252–69.

98. Shimaji Mokurai, "Jiinryō setsuritsu seigansho," in *SMZ*, 1: 1–7.

99. "Kyōbushō kaisetsu seigansho," in *SMZ*, 1: 9.

100. Sakamoto Koremaru, *Meiji ishin to kokugakusha*, 144–51.

101. For a discussion of the formation Shimaji's ideas during this period, see Yoshida, *Nihon kindai bukkyōshi*, 94–103; Yasumaru, *Kamigami no meiji ishin*, 200–201.

102. *SMZ*, 5: 183:「宗旨ト云ハ . . . 抵抗力アル者ヲ云」.

103. It is not clear what specific precedents of Shin sect resistance to secular authority Shimaji has in mind, but it is likely that he is referring to the history of the *ikkō ikki* leagues and the late-medieval power of the Honganji temple. For a historical account of the *ikkō ikki*, see Tsang, *War and Faith*.

104. Breen, "'Earnest Desires,'" 151–65; see also, Yasumaru, *Kamigami no meiji ishin*, 201–5. Shimaji also submitted to the embassy his impressions of state-religion relations in Europe: "Ōshū seikyō kenbun," in *SMZ*, 1: 198–204.

105. Sakamoto Koremaru, "Meiji hachinen sain," 163; Miyachi, *Kindai tennōsei no seijishiteki kenkyū*, 132.

106. "Sanjō kyōsoku hihan kenpakusho," in *SMZ*, 1: 15, 18.

107. Ibid., 19–20.

108. Kinoshita, *Ishin kyūbaku hikaku-ron*, 205.

109. See *Kyōgi shinbun*; see also Fukushima, *Jinja mondai*, 393.

110. *Kyōgi shinbun*, 523–29.

111. "Shintō wo motte Shūkyō to Nasu wa Kōshitsu no Kakin taru koto," *Kyōgi shinbun*, no. 70 (August 1874).

112. Yamaguchi, *Meiji kokka*, 13.

113. "Kyōhō shūmon no gi ni tsuki kengen," in *Inoue Kaoru kankei monjo*, no. 703–2, pp. 150–51, 153, 155.

114. Ketelaar, *Of Heretics and Martyrs*, 102.

115. "Kyōtofu no kenpakusho wo yomu," in *SMZ*, 1: 207.

116. This refers to the stipulation that doctrinal instructors could preach only "doctrinal sermons" (*sekkyō*), and Buddhist instructors were forbidden from calling their talks "sermons of the dharma" (*hōdan, seppō*); "Shūkyō kankei hōrei ichiran," 451–52.

117. Shimaji Mokurai, "Daikyōin bunri kenpakusho," in *SMZ*, 1: 34–35.

118. Ibid., 36.

119. Ibid., 37:「若必ス開国元史皇家ノ所本タルヲ以テ、強テ之ヲ信ゼシメントスルハ、即是朝威ヲ挟ミテ人心ヲ制スル者ニテ、他日皇室ノ患ヲナス、恐クハ端ヲ此ニ発セン。」

120. Ibid., 39.

121. "Kyōbu kaisei ni tsuki kengen," in *SMZ*, 1: 54:「正身勉業文質ノ人タルニ背カザルヲ要トセシム可シ。」

122. Foucault, *The Order of Things*, 330.

123. Shigaraki, "Shinshū ni okeru shinzoku nitai-ron" and "Kindai Shinshū kyōgaku ni okeru shinzoku nitai-ron."

124. Fujii Takashi, "Shinzoku nitai-ron ni okeru shintō no henka."

125. See, for example, Futaba, "Shimaji Mokurai," in *SMZ*, 1: 542–78; Fukushima, "Shinto kokkyō seisakuka"; Mōri, "Meiji ishin to shinshū shisō"; Kashiwabara, "Kinsei shinshū"; Rogers and Rogers, "The Honganji"; Kuroda, *Kuroda Toshio chosakushū*, 4: 355–88; and Fujiwara, "Kokka shintō taisei to jōdo shinshū," 121–49.

126. Ketelaar, *Of Heretics and Martyrs*, 11–12.

127. Fukushima, *Jinja mondai*, 393.

128. Shintoists were divided over the desirability of Shinto's being declared "nonreligious." In fact, the Shin sect's attempt to withdraw from the academy system was met with a concerted effort on the part of Shinto doctrinal instructors to resurrect the Ministry of Rites (Jingikan) within the Meiji government; Toyoda, *Shūkyō seidoshi*, 235. The status of Shinto in relation to the emerging separation of political authority and religion will be discussed in the next chapter.

129. Ketelaar, *Of Heretics and Martyrs*, 135.

130. Fujiwara, "Kokka shintō taisei to jōdo shinshū," 139–42.

131. Yoshida, *Nihon kindai bukkyōshi*, 118.

132. For a Shinto partisan's account of the Shinshū secession movement, see *NKST: STK*, 390–92. The fact that the primary backers of the Ministry of Doctrine—Etō Shinpei and Gotō Shōjiro—left the government in October 1873 in response to the *Seikanron* (Punish Korea) debate also lent a degree of inevitability to the Shin sect's secession.

133. For a summary of the so-called academy secession movement, see: Yoshida, *Nihon kindai bukkyōshi*, 119–35; Tsuji, *Meiji bukkyōshi*, 294–350; Sakamoto Koremaru,

"Nihongata seikyō kankei," 50–71. Materials pertaining to the negotiations can be found in "Shinshū bunri shimatsu," in *SMZ*, 1: 502–41.

134. *NKST: STK*, 467.

135. "Zappō," *Yomiuri shinbun*, February 7, 1875.

136. Tokoyo Nagatane complains in his retrospective account that Shishido supported the Shin sect to such an extent that he might as well have been a Buddhist cleric; Tokoyo, *Shinkyō soshiki monogatari*, in *NKST: STK*, 391.

137. Nihon shiseki kyōkai, *Kido Takayoshi monjo*, 5: 122–23: 「尤此省ヲ廃シ候方向可然ト申愚案ハ一向未口外不致候」.

138. Ibid., 103–4.

139. Ketelaar, *Of Heretics and Martyrs*, 129.

140. "Hanashi," *Yomiuri shinbun*, May 17, 1875.

141. Kokugakuin daigaku nihon bunka kenkyūjo, *Shaji torishirabe ruisan*, 96.

142. *Yomiuri shinbun*, May 18, 1875.

143. *NKST: STK*, 468: 「夫教導職ハ各自ノ教義ヲ以テ教導スル者ニテ其管長ハ其部内ノ教義ヲ掌握シ布教上ノ責任ヲ担当スルモノトス」

144. Ibid.: 「教法家ハ信教ノ自由ヲ得テ行政上ノ保護ヲ受クル以上ハ能ク朝旨ノ所在ヲ認メ只政治ノ妨害トナラザルニ注意スルノミナラズ此人民ヲ善誘シ治化ヲ翼賛スルニ至ルベキ」.

145. Ibid.

146. "Kanpō," *Yomiuri shinbun*, January 20, 1876.

147. "Tegami," *Yomiuri shinbun*, April 22, 1876.

148. Umeda, *Kaitei zōho nihon shūkyō seido-shi*, 4: 130–31.

149. Founded by Koyasu Takashi, Motono Morimichi, and Shibata Masakichi in 1874, the *Yomiuri* newspaper increased its circulation rapidly thanks to its use of accessible prose. It boasted the top circulation in the Tokyo and Yokohama region until 1886.

150. "Tegami," *Yomiuri shinbun*, March 20, 1876.

151. *Yomiuri shinbun*, April 13, 1876.

152. Ibid., May 27, 1876.

153. "Kyōbushō wo shobun suru gi," *Sanjōke monjo*, no. 53–56.

154. Sakamoto Koremaru, *Kinsei kindai shintō ronkō*, 224–35.

155. Furuya Tetsuo, "Teikoku gikai no seiritsu," 11.

156. *NKST: STK*, 463, 471.

4. Seeking a "Religious Settlement"

1. Fridell, "The Establishment of Shrine Shinto in Meiji Japan."

2. Quoted in Yamaguchi, *Meiji kokka to shūkyō*, 98.

3. Fukuzawa, *Bunmeiron*, 224.

4. *NKST: STK*, 392.

5. Jinja shinpōsha, *Zōho kindai jinja shintōshi*, 80–81.

6. Quoted in Fujii Sadafumi, *Meiji kokugaku*, 19–20.

7. Inoue Nobutaka, *Kyōha shintō*, 25–30, 341, 350–55.

8. A Sōtō sect Buddhist cleric, Ōtori had been active in promoting anti-Christian efforts within the Restoration government. He laicized when appointed

to the Council of the Left in 1871 and went on to become the chief priest of the Kotohira shrine in Shiba, Tokyo, and later the superintendent of the Shinto sect Ontake-kyō.

9. *NKST: STK*, 394.

10. *Iwakura Tomomi kankei monjo*, no. 106-3.

11. "Shintō shinsaku no hōhō wo mōkete jissai shikō no tame seifu no tokushu hogo wo seigan suru kengen," in *Iwakura Tomomi kankei monjo*, no. 106-7.

12. Sasaki Kiyoshi, "Shintō hishūkyō," 89–96.

13. *NKST: STK*, 394.

14. *Iwakura Tomomi kankei monjo*, no. 106-7.

15. Yasumaru, "Kindai tenkanki ni okeru shūkyō to kokka," in *NKST: STK*, 531–36; Yamane, "Meiji-zenki shūkyō seisaku," 104–7; Hardacre, *Shinto and the State*, 46–48; Nishikawa Junji, "Meiji shonen ni okeru kyōkai kōsha."

16. Murakami Shigeyoshi, *Kokka shintō to minshū shūkyō*, 106.

17. Toyoda, *Shūkyō seidoshi*, 206–10.

18. *NKST: STK*, 452; Umeda, *Kaitei zōho nihon shūkyō seido-shi*, 4: 15–16.

19. Helen Hardacre observes: "Leaders of the new religions found religious meaning in state ideology, grafting it onto their individual soteriologies. Through participation in the Campaign, many of these leaders came to understand their own creeds as varieties of 'Shinto' and to preach this idea to their followers. They played an important role in creating a popular awareness of Shinto as an independent religion and in the process were able to legitimate themselves in the eyes of the state." Hardacre, "Creating State Shinto," 30.

20. See, for example, Katsurajima, "Kyōha shintō no seiritsu," and Ozawa, "Minshū shūkyō to kokka."

21. Nishida, *Nihon shintōshi kenkyū*, 6: 13–102.

22. *NKST: STK*, 427, 430. For a discussion of how Buddhists contested the ban on cremation, see Makihara, *Meiji sichinen no daironsō*, 81–117. See also Sakamoto Koremaru, *Kindai no jinja shintō*, 75–79.

23. *NKST: STK*, 448, 455, 460.

24. This order was reinforced in 1876 when the Ministry of Doctrine decreed that individuals were not to be prevented from switching sects and choosing a preferred form of funeral rites. Christian rites, however, were not an option at this point; ibid., 463, 468.

25. *NKST: STK*, 404.

26. Sasaki Kiyoshi, "Shintō hishūkyō," 103.

27. "Kyōgijō ni tsuki mikomisho," in *Iwakura Tomomi kankei monjo*, no. 106-8.

28. For the expansion of Shinto churches and the competition it engendered, see Nakajima, "Taikyō senpu undō to saijin ronsō," 45–57.

29. *NKST: STK*, 363–64.

30. Fujii Sadafumi, "Shimane-kenka ni okeru kyōdōshoku," 23.

31. Senge instructed adherents that the Izumo shrine was supreme so far as Shinto rituals were concerned; Senge, "Kyōshinto he no shiyusho," in *NKST: STK*, 57–62. See also Hara Takeshi, *"Izumo" to iu shisō*, 114–20.

32. Hara Takeshi, *"Izumo" to iu shisō*, 122–33.

33. *Kaichi shinbun*, no. 405–411.

34. *Tokyō Nichinichi shinbun*, February 3, 1880.

35. *Iwakura Tomomi kankei monjo*, no. 106-5: 「仰ぎ願くは尊福と對審教徒の真仮親しく公認の上御判決賜り度」.

36. Ibid.

37. "Shintō jimukyoku saijin no gi ni tsuki jōshin," in *Iwakura Tomomi kankei monjo* no. 106-9.

38. "Shintō kyōdōshokukan no ronsō hantei kyokō junjo," in *Sanjō-ke monjo*, no. 53-8:「此事教義上の係争に止まるに似たりと謂も各社神官皆社務に安せずして縷々奔走遂に官事に影響を来すに至る」.

39. Ibid.

40. Ibid.

41. Fujii Sadafumi, *Meiji kokugaku*, 520.

42. Hara Takeshi, *"Izumo" to iu shisō*, 122–33.

43. Fujii Sadafumi, *Meiji kokugaku*, 598–604.

44. Katsurajima, *Shisōshi no jūkyūseiki*, 244.

45. Fujii Sadafumi, *Meiji kokugaku*, 605–32.

46. Ibid., 634–702.

47. Ibid., 709–10.

48. *NKST: STK*, 402–3; see also Hara Takeshi, *"Izumo" to iu shisō*, 133.

49. Fujii Sadafumi, *Meiji kokugaku*, 710–12.

50. "Daikyōkan settchi kengen," in *NKST: STK*, 64: 「宗教と同視一列」.

51. *Seishi kyōgaku taishi*, in *Motoda Nagazane monjo, shorui no bu*, no. 110-2. For his role as tutor, see Motoda's memoir, *Kanreki no ki*, in Motoda, *Motoda Nagazane monjo*, vol. 1.

52. Hamaguchi, "Meiji-zenki no tennōsei"; Sims, *Japanese Political History*, 54.

53. Nakajima, "Meiji kokka to shūkyō," 34–35.

54. "Kyoikugi," in *KNST: M*, 266.

55. For a genealogy of an "empiricist" strain of Kokugaku, see Fujita Hiromasa, *Kindai kokugaku*.

56. "Kyoikugi," in *KNST: M*, 267.

57. This is best seen in the popularity of John Stuart Mill's works in translation; see Matsuzawa, "'Saigoku risshihen' to 'Jiyū no ri' no sekai."

58. "Kyōikugi fugi," in *KNST: M*, 268, 269:「則国教の立つと立たざるとは、我信ずるの厚きと厚からざるとに決するのみ」.

59. See Pittau, *Political Thought in Early Meiji Japan*, 99–130; Inada, *Meiji kenpō seiritsushi*, 2: 599–633.

60. *Tokyō Nichinichi shinbun*, March 26, 1881.

61. For a history of the *Chōya shinbun*, see Ukai, *Chōya shinbun no kenkyū*.

62. *Chōya shinbun*, April 2, 1881.

63. *Tokyō-Yokohama mainichi shinbun*, April 7, 1881. For the Ōmeisha's position in the Freedom and People's Rights Movement, see Kim, *Age of Visions and Arguments*, 163–73.

64. *Tokyo-Yokohama mainichi shinbun*, December 9, 1881.

65. Sims, *Japanese Political History*, 52–53; Itō Yahiko, *Meiji ishin to jinshin*, 128–31; Akita, *Foundations of Constitutional Government*, 31–57.

66. Sims, *Japanese Political History*, 55.

67. Itō, *Meiji ishin to jinshin*, 121–211.

68. Inoue Kowashi, "Jinshin kyōdō ikenan," in *Inoue Kowashi-den: Shiryō-hen*, ed. Inoue Kowashi denki hensan iinkai, 1: 248–49:「人口を塞ぐに在らずして人心を導くに在り」.

69. Ibid., 249–50.

70. Quoted in Sasaki Kiyoshi, "Shintō hishūkyō kara," 101.

71. Quoted in ibid.:「立論至当に付き、漸次御詮議可相成儀」.

72. Quoted in ibid., 107, 108; the opposition between *kokka* (国家) and *shinka* (身家) appears quite deliberate here and is difficult to render in translation. The state is opposed to private belief, but that private belief does not necessarily privilege individuals.

73. *NKST: STK*, 480–81.

74. Ibid., 480:「但府県社以下神官ハ当分従前之通」.

75. *NKST: STK*, 404.

76. In practice, shrines ranked at the prefectural level and below were caught in the split between doctrinal and pastoral functions, their priests being reliant on their role as doctrinal instructors to supplement their income. The perception that a majority of low-ranking shrines and their priests were inexorably sliding into the category of sectarian self-reliance fueled Shinto fears and lobbying efforts into the 1890s.

77. Tokoyo, reporting Shinto efforts to retain the right to conduct funerals, also observes that many were concerned about the ritual defilement that resulted from conducting those rites; *NKST: STK*, 404.

78. Hardacre, *Shinto and the State*, 85.

79. "Shinkan kyōdōshoku bunri ni tsuki ikensho," in *NKST: STK*, 66–68.

80. The Shinshū sect of Shinto (神習教) has no connection to the Shin sect of Buddhism (真宗); *NKST: STK*, 481.

81. For a survey of the emergence of "sect Shinto," see Inoue Nobutaka, *Kyōha shintō*.

82. Hardacre, *Shinto and the State*, 59.

83. Itō, *Meiji ishin to jinshin*, 141–45.

84. Pittau, *Political Thought in Early Meiji Japan*, 131–57.

85. For a detailed study of Itō's interaction with Stein and Gneist, including his lecture notes, see Shimizu Shin, *Meiji kenpō seiteishi*, vol. 1.

86. Pittau, *Political Thought in Early Meiji Japan*, 45; Yamaguchi, *Meiji kokka*, 59.

87. Hardacre, *Shinto and the State*, 118–19.

88. Yamaguchi suggests Stein may have been influenced by the Shintoist perspectives of Kaeda Nobuyoshi and Maruyama Sakura, both of whom were sent to research legal precedents for the Imperial Household Law; Yamaguchi, *Meiji kokka*, 59.

89. Shunpokō tsuishōkai, *Itō Hirobumi-den*, 2: 336:「現在の社会は宗教の空気の内に生息するを如何せん」.

90. Ibid., 337–38.

91. Yamaguchi, *Meiji kokka*, 63.

92. "Japanese Converts," *New York Herald*, March 2, 1884.

93. Quoted in Shimizu Isao, *Meiji manga uūransen*, 52–54.

94. Ozaki, *Ozaki Saburō nikki*, 1: 343:「即全国人民の宗旨を改むる」.

95. Ibid., 359.

96. Letter of July 28, 1884, reprinted in Shōyū kurabu, *Yamagata Aritomo kankei monjo*, 1: 114–15.

97. Inoue Kaoru, "Meiji jūnana-nen shichi-gatsu Inoue gaimukyō yori naikaku he no kengi," 359.

98. Ibid., 374, 376–77.

99. Ibid., 377–78.

100. Ibid.; "In fact, until this day our government has not adopted a consistent policy in regard to this creed, and what it decrees domestically and pronounces diplomatically have repeatedly been in contradiction."

101. Ibid., 390, 391–92.

102. Ibid., 392, 393.

103. Ibid., 394–95:「一般宗教の取扱方法を定むる事」.

104. *Yūbin hōchi shinbun*, July 14, 1881; *Tokyō Nichinichi shinbun*, December 5, 1881.

105. *Yomiuri shinbun*, April 5, 1884.

106. See, for example, *Tokyo Nichinichi shinbun*, July 9, 1883; *Yūbin hōchi shinbun*, June 9, 1884.

107. *Jiji shinpō*, July 29 and July 30, 1884.

108. *Meiji nippō*, February 3 and February 5, 1884.

109. Sawada, *Practical Pursuits*, 223–27.

110. Quoted in Yamaguchi, *Meiji kokka*, 93.

111. Quoted in Sawada, *Practical Pursuits*, 226.

112. *Jiji shinpō*, August 9, 1884:「大政全体ノ前後」; see also *Yūbin hōchi shinbun*, August 11, 1884.

113. Letter of July 28, 1884, in Shōyū kurabu, *Yamagata Aritomo kankei monjo*, 1: 114–55.

114. Yamaguchi, *Meiji kokka*, 94.

115. Sawada, *Practical Pursuits*, 230–35.

116. These essays do not seem to have been published but were likely circulated within the government, most likely through the Privy Council.

117. "Kokkyōron," in *Motoda Nagazane monjo*, no. 110-24.

118. "Shūkyōron," in *Motoda Nagazane monjo*, no. 110-23:「宗教の外に立」.

119. "Kokkyō wo sadamete jinshin no hōkō wo shimesu beshi," in *Sanjō-ke monjo*, no. 53-18:「驚嘆惜く能はざるの一説を聞く何ぞや曰く我大政府は不日耶蘇教を公許し教導職を廃せんとすと」.

120. "Jingikan saikō kengi," in *Inoue Kaoru kankei monjo*, no. 703-4.

121. "Kyōdōshoku haishi ikenan," in Inoue Kowashi denki hensan iinkai, *Inoue Kowashi-den, Shiryō-hen*, 1: 388, 390.

122. "Yamagata sangi shūkyō shobun iken," in ibid., 6: 162, 164.

123. "Kyōdōshoku haishi iken-an," in ibid., 1: 391–92.

124. Ibid., 392.

125. *Jiji shinpō*, July 27, 1884.

126. Ibid., July 31, 1884.

127. *NKST: STK*, 481–82.

128. “Kyōdōshoku haishi narabini shinbutsu kakushūha kanchō mibun toriasutakai no ken,” in *Kōbunroku*, 128:「政府ノ力直ニ彼徒ノ肉体ニ迫ル無シト雖、優ニ宗教組織ノ規定ヲ左右スルヲ得ベシ。然ラバ則チ、政府ガ彼徒ヲ支配スル道、外ニ縦テ内ニ操ルモノナリ。」

129. Ibid., 129:「抑宗教ハ民生ノ神魂ニ関ス。」

130. Ibid., 130.

131. Nitta, “Meiji kenpō seiteiki no seikyō kankei,” 186.

132. Sakamoto Koremaru, “Meiji zenki no seikyō kankei to Inoue Kowashi,” 187.

133. Quoted in Yamaguchi, *Meiji kokka*, 98.

134. *Meiji nippō*, August 12, 14, 15, and 16, 1884; quotes from August 12 and 14.

135. Ibid., August 16, 1884.

136. *NKST: STK*, 481.

137. Hardacre, *Shinto and the State*, 117.

138. Quoted in Nitta, “Meiji kenpō seiteiki no seikyō kankei,” 177.

139. *NKST: STK*, 481.

140. Fridell, “The Establishment of Shrine Shinto in Meiji Japan.”

141. Nakajima, “Dai nihon teikoku kenpō dai nijūhachi-jō ‘shinkō jiyu’ kitei seiritsu,” 30–31.

5. The Religious Constitution of Meiji Japan

1. For the representative view that State Shinto commenced with the birth of this bureaucratic arrangement, see Sakamoto Koremaru, *Kokka shintō keisei*, 305–11.

2. Fridell, “Establishment of Shrine Shinto,” 164–65.

3. As Carol Gluck describes it, the late-Meiji period “was less a time of upheaval than one of settlement, less of structural drama than functional adjustment, a time when change was absorbed and some sort of stability was wrested from the aftermath of crisis”; Gluck, *Japan’s Modern Myths*, 20.

4. Kino, *Inoue Kowashi kenkyū*, 368.

5. *SKG*, 1: 157. Great Britain, Germany, Portugal, France, Belgium, the Netherlands, Denmark, and Austria, for example, all possessed state churches, either Catholic or Protestant, while tolerating the freedom of belief. Karl F. H. Roesler (1834–1894) and Albert Mosse (1846–1925), two German advisers who collaborated with Itō in drafting the Imperial Constitution, never ruled out a state religion for Japan, whether Buddhist or Shinto; Yamaguchi, *Meiji kokka*, 143–55; Hardacre, *Shinto and the State*, 115–21.

6. It is interesting to note, however, that some within the government perceived a decline in the diplomatic sensitivity regarding the status of Christianity. As early as July 1891, for example, Inoue Kowashi gave a lecture arguing that the relationship between Christianity and international law, once so vital to European self-identification, was waning. See Inoue Kowashi, “Kokusaihō to yasokyō tono kankei,” in Inoue Kowashi denki hensan iinkai, *Inoue Kowashi den: Shiryō-hen*, 5: 734–38.

7. *SKG*, 1: 157.

8. Unlike other “rights” bestowed on Japanese subjects by the constitution, including the freedoms of speech, assembly, and association, the freedom of belief was

to be constrained not by legislation but by the inherent duties of imperial subjects. Nakajima Michio provides a rich a textual genealogy of Article 28 in a series of articles: Nakajima, "'Dai nihon teikoku kenpō' dai 28-jō 'shinkō jiyū' kitei seiritsu katei," "Dai nihon teikoku kenpō dai 28-jō 'shinkō jiyū' kitei seiritsu no zenshi," and "'Meiji kenpō taisei.'"

9. Itō Hirobumi, *Teikoku kenpō gikai*, 43.

10. Eighteen out of the twenty-two members of the council voted to adopt Article 28 without amendment; *SKG*, 1: 229–31.

11. A broad sample of press commentary on the constitution is reprinted in Meiji seijishi kenkyūkai, *Kenpō kaishaku shiryō*, 101–2, 107, 116, 127, 134, 139, 144.

12. Christians had been elected to prefectural assemblies in the 1880s, and it was assumed some would be elected to the Imperial Diet as well; see, for example, Gunma kenshi hensan iinkai, *Gunma kenshi tsūshi-hen*, 546. (Thanks to Emily Anderson for this source.) Though Inoue dismissed as ridiculous any potential protests on the grounds of religious conviction, he nonetheless believed such protests threatened to embarrass the government in the eyes of the treaty powers and to complicate its relationship with the Imperial Diet; "Giin sensei iken," in Inoue Kowashi denki hensan iinkai, *Inoue Kowashi-den Shiryō-hen*, 2: 250.

13. Namikawa Ryōjō, for example, pointed out the role religious figures played in aiding moral improvement in the West, citing the work of William Wilberforce and Henry Ward Beecher. He disclaimed any interest in asserting religious authority over political authority, but called on religionists (*shūkyōka*) to engage in the relevant debates of the day. Namikawa, "Shūkyōka wa seijika no nōzui wo shihai sezarubekarazu," *Dentō* no. 11 (November 1890): 18.

14. Inoue Kowashi, "Inoue Kowashi-kun enzetsu," *Kōtenkōkyūjo kōen* no. 1 (February 1889): 15–16.

15. Yamada Akiyoshi reinforced this message in July 1889 when he addressed a meeting of Shinto priests as head of the Center for the Study of Imperial Classics and attempted to calm them by flatly denying any religion ordinance was forthcoming. At the same time, he admonished the priests against participating in "religious movements" (*shūkyōteki no undō*). "Enzetsu," *Kōtenkōkyūjo kōen* 4, no. 34 (July 1889): 1–8.

16. Inoue Kowashi, "Inoue Kowashi-kun enzetsu," 17.

17. "Shinkan no undō," *Yomiuri shinbun*, August 12, 1890, 2; "Shinkan no fungi," *Yomiuri shinbun*, August 19, 1890, 2; "Shinkan kyodoshoku bunri hibunriron no gen'in," *Yomiuri shinbun*, August 21, 1890, 2.

18. Fujitani, Takashi, *Splendid Monarchy*, 77–79.

19. For a vivid image of the ceremony as it was presented to the public, see the Meiji-era woodblock print *Illustration of the Ceremony Promulgating the Constitution (Kenpō happushiki no zu)*, 1890 (Meiji 23), artist unknown, in the collection of the Museum of Fine Arts, Boston: www.mfa.org/collections/object/illustration-of-the-ceremony-promulgating-the-constitution-kenp-happushiki-no-zu-129892.

20. For a detailed account of Mori's visit to Ise and the rumors that circulated about it, see Nakanishi Masayuki, *Ise no miyabito*, 615–46.

21. "Ko Mori daijin sanchō no moyō," *Yomiuri shinbun*, February 24, 1889, 2.

22. Okada, *Shikyaku Nishino Buntarō*, 5–6.

23. "Shūkyō jō no onaku ni idetaru kana," *Nihon* no. 9 (February 20, 1889), reprinted in Kuga, *Kuga Katsunan zenshū*, 2: 13–14.

24. According to Maruyama Sakura's son, Maruyama Masahiko, advocates of a revived Department of Divinities felt the Imperial Constitution and the Rescript on Education merely "stated the passed-down teachings and institutions of the imperial ancestors" (祖宗の遺訓遺制を叙述せられた) and failed to provide any positive affirmation of Shinto shrines; see Itsumi Nakasaburō, "Jingi in kansuru tokubetsu kanga setchi no gi," in *Zenkoku shinshokukai kaihō* no. 6 (January 1900): 12.

25. Sasaki and Motoda, having served as tutors to the emperor, continued to wield some influence with the throne, even though they occupied marginal positions within the government, while Minister of Justice Yamada provided the primary conduit for the movement in its effort to influence the executive center of the government.

26. According to Sasaki Takayuki's own assessment, Yamagata Aritomo, then prime minister, continued to express an aversion toward Shinto (*jingi*), and Hijikata Hisamoto, the imperial household minister, was cool to the idea of resurrecting the Department of Divinities. Yanagihara Maemitsu, chairman of the Genrōin senate, and Yoshii Tomozane, undersecretary in the Imperial Household Ministry, on the other hand, expressed support. Home Minister Saigō Tsugumichi was so ignorant of anything related to shrines that he ordered subordinates to study the matter for him; Tsuda Shigemaro, *Meiji seijō to shin Takayuki*, 696. When a memorial submitted by Sasaki reached the emperor, the sovereign turned to Itō Hirobumi for his views. Itō unsurprisingly opposed the proposal, flatly denying its feasibility and signaling the need to maintain the religious settlement even in the face of impending parliamentary politics; Yamaguchi, *Meiji kokka*, 183.

27. In the 1872 the Ministry of Divinities (Jingishō) was dismantled, and rites associated with the imperial institution were moved into the palace while all else, shrines and priests included, was placed under the jurisdiction of the Ministry of Doctrine. Sasaki's memorial envisioned an Institute of Divinities (Jingiin) that would supervise the rites, ceremonies, and festivals of the state, large and small shrines, and the *daijōsai* ascension rites, as well as the oaths of civil and military officers and members of the Imperial Diet. "Sasaki sūmitsu komonkan hoka rokumei kengi jingiin setchi ni kansuru ken," *Kōbunzassan* 2A-13-纂193; partially reprinted in *NKST: STK*, 98–102.

28. "Those already fixed expenditures based by the Constitution upon the powers appertaining to the Emperor, and such expenditures as may have arisen by the effect of law, or that appertain to the legal obligations of the Government, shall be neither rejected nor reduced by the Imperial Diet, without the concurrence of the Government"; http://www.ndl.go.jp/constitution/e/etc/c02.html.

29. Preservation funds distributed to imperial and national shrines were to be divided into three parts, a shared repair fund (15 percent), administration and maintenance funds (50 percent), and an endowment fund (35 percent). In principle, shrines were to use no more than half of the preservation funds for administration and maintenance, while the remainder was to be pooled as an endowment for eventual fiscal independence. Under the revised scheme, shrines would in effect lose 15 percent of the funds designated for their endowments, significantly undermining the

possibility of eventual fiscal independence. "Kankokuheisha hozonkin haifu nengen zōka no ken," in *Kōbunruisan* 2A-011-00-類004881.

30. "Hōseikyoku shinsasho," included within "Sasaki sūmitsu komonkan hoka rokumei kengi jingiin setchi ni kansuru ken," in *Kōbunzassan* 2A-13-纂193. Inoue's personal appraisal of the proposed creation of an independent Department of Divinities was more measured, and betrayed a degree of disdain. Rather than create a department that would link the imperial palace to all shrines great and small, Inoue proposed creating a section within the Imperial Household Ministry for the sake of a few prominent shrines intimately associated with the imperial institution, such as "Ise, Atsuta, and Kamo," while all other shrines would remain outside the palace under the continued supervision of the Home Ministry; Inoue Kowashi denki hensan iinkai, *Inoue Kowashi den Shiryō hen* 2: 280–82. In a separate letter to Yamagata, Inoue sarcastically noted that Nishino Buntarō, Mori Arinori's assassin, would be pleased to see that so many in the cabinet supported reviving the Department of Divinities; quoted in Saito, *Inoue Kowashi to shūkyō*, 132.

31. "Hōseikyoku shinsasho," in *Kōbunzassan* 2A-13-纂193.

32. Ibid.

33. The Agriculture and Commerce Ministry argued that removing parcels formally held by shrines and temples from state-owned lands would undermine forestry management in general. As a compromise, the ministry suggested a program that would allow temples and shrines to lease all or part of the forestland confiscated from shrines and temples for free, thus allowing them to access the products of that property while sidestepping the fundamental question of transferring ownership. This was, in substance, a renewed version of an 1884 internal directive that allowed the free lease of forestlands to temples and shrines, a directive that had not been functioning well enough to provide significant economic relief; "Kanyū shinrin genya oyobi sanbutsu tokubetsu shobun kisoku chū tsuikasu," in *Kōbunruisan* 2A-11-類488.

34. One Buddhist journal reported that the undersecretary (*jikan*) in the Home Ministry opposed any move to increase the state's support for shrines, out of fear that it would only lead to conflict down the road; "Jingikan," *Dentō* no. 12 (December 1890): 36–37.

35. "Hōseikyoku shinsasho." One memorial submitted on November 28 merely requested that a position (*jingishoku*) be created within the Imperial Household Ministry, in effect accepting the limited scope of the recommendation that Inoue Kowashi's Cabinet Legislation Bureau had made to the cabinet; "Sūmitsu komonkan hakushaku Sasaki Takayuki hoka nimei rensho kengi jingishoku settchi no ken," in *Kōbunzassan* 2A-013-00 • 纂00193100.

36. *Kanpō Meiji-hen* 4 (11): 337.

37. A point demonstrated by the more than 600 memorials and petitions submitted by shrine priests seeking a revived Department of Divinities prior to the commencement of constitutional rule; Gluck, *Japan's Modern Myths*, 140.

38. The Diet did not possess the authority to dictate the executive structure of the state; instead, the constitution granted only the right to pass formal memorials to the throne, under Article 49, or recommendations to the government, under Article 40, both of which exerted only moral force on the government; it was left to the discretion

of the throne and the cabinet, respectively, to adopt, amend, or reject any memorials or recommendations.

39. Both Motoda Nagazane and Yoshii Tomozane died in early 1891, followed by Yamada Akiyoshi the next year. Maruyama Sakura left the government to join the House of Peers, and Sasaki, the lone Shinto supporter remaining in the government, focused his energies on educating the emperor's daughters.

40. "Shūkyō jōrei no jinja ni kakawaru fūsetu," *Kaitsū zasshi* (April 1890): 148.

41. The petition stood on the principle that all shrines, regardless of formal rank, conducted rites of the state, and complained that "religious [*shūkyōshugi*] Shinto or Shinto consisting prayer and fortune-telling practiced in vulgar society [*zokuken*] is being mistaken for the true path of Shinto." "The ceremonies of our rites," the petition explained, "are definitely not based on religious beliefs [*shukyoteki shinnen*], but on national feelings [*kokkateki kansō*]." The creation of a Department of Divinities would allow "such things as religion" to be dealt with by "creating a section for religion within the Home Ministry"; "Shinkan yūshi jingikan settchi chinjōsho," *NKST: STK*, 103–109.

42. Suzuki Ryōan, "Teikoku gikai to shūkyō mondai," *Dentō* no. 11 (November 1890): 15.

43. To underscore their concerns, some Buddhist commentators invoked the specter of Unitarianism and Islam (Kaikyō) proselytizing with impunity; "Kōninkyō jōrei seitei kenpaku shui," *Yomiuri shinbun*, October 11, 1889, 2.

44. Uchimura Kanzō (1861–1930) was accused of disrespecting a signed copy of the Imperial Rescript in a ceremony held in January 1891 at the elite First Higher School in Tokyo. A year later, a Christian faculty member at the private Kumamoto English School, Okumura Teijirō, gave a speech proclaiming altruism (*hakuaishugi*) rather than nationalism to be the aim of the school's education. An outcry of criticism, fanned by a conservative press, prompted the governor of Kumamoto to order school officials to fire Okumura. A detailed account of the events and controversy surrounding Uchimura's actions can be found in Suzuki, *Uchimura Kanzō nichiroku*. For a nuanced analysis of the Okumura case, see Ono Masaaki, "Kumamoto eigakkō jiken no tenmatsu," and Shigeru, "Kumamoto eigakkō jiken."

45. Kuga, *Kuga Katsunan zenshū*, 4: 229–37. Other complaints included a women's school that did not advertise the fact that its faculty members were fervent Christians intent on influencing the students, as well as the infiltration of Christians into public elementary schools. Christian missions were also criticized for taking advantage of poor students who could access higher education only through schools subsidized by foreign missionary organizations; "Yasokyōsha no kōkatsu to kokuteki," *Dentō* no. 9 (September 1890): 36–37; "Monbudaijin to yasokyōto no mondō," *Yomiuri shinbun*, October 6, 1892, 1; "Seifu to yasokyō," *Bukkyō* no. 70 (June 1893): 41.

46. One Buddhist commentator, for example, warned that though the 1,883 students taught by the twenty schools affiliated with the American Board and Congregational churches might appear small, their influence on Japanese customs would be exponential; "Nihon no kirisutokyō," *Bukkyō* no. 51 (August 1892): 44–46.

47. A prominent lay leader in the Kumiai (Congregational) Church, Yuasa pushed antiprostitution legislation through the Gunma prefectural assembly before serving two terms in the House of Representatives.

48. The *Yomiuri* newspaper, for instance, carried the story of a police officer in Shiga prefecture who preached Christianity while still in uniform; *Yomiuri shinbun*, March 9, 1893, 3.

49. "Hōkyōrei," *Yomiuri shinbun*, August 25, 1890, 1; "Shūkyō jōrei sōtei dan," *Bukkyō* no. 68 (May 1893).

50. "Shūkyō seiji kyōiku no gensoku," *Dentō* no. 53 (April 1893): 4–7; "Shūkyō seiji kyōiku no gensoku (shōzen)," *Dentō* no. 54 (May 1893): 3–6; "Seikyō no kankei," *Dentō* no. 41 (February 1893): 1–4. "Seikyō no kankei (kōhen)," *Dentō* no. 42 (March 1893): 1–5; Oyama Tennen, "Kenpō shūkyōkajō ni tsuite," *Dentō* no. 18 (June 1891): 26.

51. By "secular press," I mean the major newspapers and magazines that addressed a generic, public audience, in contrast to the "sectarian press," which addressed explicitly defined constituencies.

52. The editorial suggested that Shinto should evolve into a proper religion; "Nihon no shūkyō," *Yomiuri shinbun*, July 16, 1891, 1; "Nihon no shūkyō (chū)," *Yomiuri shinbun*, July 17, 1891; "Nihon no shūkyō (ge)," *Yomiuri shinbun*, July 18, 1891, 1; "Nihon no shūkyō (ge zoku)," *Yomiuri shinbun*, July 19, 1891, 1.

53. "Kōninkyō jōrei seitei kenpaku shui," *Yomiuri shinbun*, October 11, 1889, 2; "Kōninkyō (sakujitsu no tsuzuki)," *Yomiuri shinbun*, November 29, 1889, 2.

54. *SKG*, 2: 194–95; Inada, *Meiji kenpō*, 2: 1103, 1109.

55. "Shūgiin giin no kaisen ni saishi kyōshi sōryo ni kunyu seshimu," in *Kōbunruisan* 2A-11-00 • 類 00712100.

56. *NKST: STK*, 487–88. See also "Shinkan hōmu kisoku no ken," *Yomiuri shinbun*, July 9, 1891, 1; "Shinkan hōmu kisoku to shinkan no jiyū," *Yomiuri shinbun*, July 11, 1891, 1.

57. Letter to Inoue Kaoru from Aoki Shūzō, April 8, 1893, in *Inoue Kaoru kankei monjo* 219-3.

58. Yamaguchi, *Meiji kokka*, 208.

59. The Freedom and People's Rights Movement had broadly disseminated the principle that those who paid taxes and were subject to conscription possessed a right to representation. For a recent discussion of the Freedom and People's Rights Movement and the political modes it inaugurated, see Kim, *Age of Visions and Arguments*, 101–36.

60. "Sōryo wa hisenkyoken wo motomuru yorimo fukyō ni nesshin nare," *Yomiuri shinbun*, June 5, 1889, 1; "Sakujitsu no ronsetsu," *Yomiuri shinbun*, June 7, 1889, 1; "Sakujitsu no ronsetsu (sōryo no hisenkyoken)," *Yomiuri shinbun*, June 8, 1889, 1.

61. For a brief introduction to *Reichikai zasshi*, see Tanigawa Yutaka, "Meiji chūki ni okeru bukkyōsha no zokujin kyōiku," 39.

62. "Kanzoku shūgiin giin shokun ni hitokoto su," *Reichikai zasshi* no. 76 (July 1893): 1–4.

63. Maruyama and Iwashita were both long-standing advocates of reviving the Department of Divinities. Maruyama had been a member of the Hirata school of Kokugaku, and Iwashita had served as vice superintendent of the Bureau of Shinto Affairs in the wake of the Pantheon Dispute.

64. Though he lost his seat in the second general election owing to government interference, Ōtsu returned to the Imperial Diet in 1894 and remained a member of

the lower house until 1927, when he was appointed to the House of Peers; Ichimura, *Ibaraki no kokkai giin*, 57–63.

65. For a definition of the government's "transcendentalism," see Toriumi Yasushi, "Hanbatsu tai mintō," 76–78.

66. Ōtsu belonged to the Constitutional Reform Party (Rikken kaishintō), Hayakawa to the National Association (Kokumin kyōkai), and Maruyama Sakura played a part in organizing the Imperial Constitutional Government Party (Rikken teiseitō).

67. For an overview of the first four sessions of the Imperial Diet, see Toriumi, "Hanbatsu tai mintō," 61–140.

68. Shinto priests involved themselves in the general election that followed the dissolution of the second Diet, for example, supporting candidates sympathetic to their cause; "Daigishi kaisen ni tsuki shinkan no moyō," *Kannagara* no. 194 (February 1892): 22–23.

69. The infamous public controversy surrounding Kume Kunitake's essay describing Shinto as the remnant of the archaic practice of sun worship, for example, had the appearance of Shinto priests and conservatives attacking the secular disposition of the oligarchic leadership, with whom Kume was closely identified. For an overview of the controversy, see Kano and Imai, "Nihon kindai shisōshi no nakano no Kume jiken."

70. *TGSGS*, 6: 731.

71. A public incensed by leaked reports of the negotiations and the infamous Normanton Incident of 1886 had scuttled Inoue Kaoru's negotiations with the treaty powers in 1887. In October 1886 a British commercial vessel sank off the coast of Wakayama. The majority of the British crew and European passengers survived, while all Japanese passengers drowned. The press decried the incident as yet another example of Western racism. The British consular court sentenced the captain of the ship to three months' incarceration—only after significant public outrage following an initial finding of innocence. For the role treaty revision played in shaping domestic politics in the early 1890s, see Komiya, *Jōyaku kaisei to kokunai seiji*.

72. A new round of negotiations to revise the unequal treaties that commenced under Foreign Ministry Aoki Shūzō in 1891 was cut short by an attack on the visiting Russian crown prince, but resumed the following year under the second Itō Hirobumi cabinet. Those negotiations resulted in a revised series of treaties in 1894 that promised an end to extraterritoriality and the beginning of mixed residence in the summer of 1899.

73. *TGSGS*, vol. 7, Fifth Imperial Diet, 195.

74. Komiya, "Naichi zakkyo kōkyūkai," 64–65, 69–70; Uno, "Mintō no tankan to Nisshin sengo keiei"; for a broad overview of the role of treaty revision in shaping domestic politics during this period, see Sakada, *Kindai nihon ni okeru taigaikō undō*.

75. Naimusho kunrei no. 5 and no. 6, February 6, 1894, in *Kanpō Meiji-hen* 6 (2): 54. See also "Naimudaijin no kunrei," *Yomiuri shinbun*, February 7, 1894, 2.

76. Sasaki Takashi, *Hanbatsu seifu to rikken seiji*, 361–64.

77. Clashes between political parties in the lower house, which tended to represent the interests of landholders seeking lower tax rates, and so-called transcendent

cabinets seeking to safeguard state prerogatives had produced near paralysis. Another draft memorial to the throne submitted to the sixth Diet, just prior to the Sino-Japanese War, for example, failed to reach the floor due to a successful vote of no confidence against the government; *TGSGS*, 7: 378.

78. Uno, "Mintō no tankan to Nisshin sengo keiei," 167–76.

79. Draft recommendations and bills calling on the government to return significant portions of forestry property confiscated from shrines and temples had been submitted to the fifth and sixth Diets without reaching the floor. The eighth Diet debated a forestry bill on January 15, 1895. Opposition from the Agriculture and Commerce Ministry in committee forced the shelving of the question of property rights in favor of focusing on providing financial relief to the shrines and temples; the committee produced a draft bill on the custody (*hokan*) of shrine and temple forestry land that was ultimately voted own on February 13; *TGSGS*, vol. 7, Fifth Diet Session, 227–29; *TGSGS*, vol. 7, Sixth Diet Session, 3–4; *TGSGS*, vol. 8, Eighth Diet Session, 112–16; *TGSGS*, vol. 9, 442–48, 506–11.

80. "Kokuyū tochi shinrin genya sagemodoshi hō wo sadamu," in *Kōbunruiju* 2A-011-00 • 類00866100; "Shaji hokanrin kisoku wo sadamu," in *Kōbunruiju* 2A-011-00 • 類00866100. See also *SKG*, 7: 325–55.

81. Hatoyama was a lawyer, educated in the United States at Columbia and Yale, whose descendants include two postwar prime ministers, Hatoyama Ichirō and Hatoyama Yukio.

82. See, for example, "Ōtaniha hoganji matsuin no jūshoku ga zōhan," *Yomiuri shinbun*, July 29, 1888, and "Shasetsu: Sōtōshū no fungi," *Asahi shinbun*, November 23, 1889; "Sōtōshū shinnin mondai," *Yomiuri shinbun*, November 18, 1889, 3; Honganji Matsuin no jūshoku ga zōhan," *Yomiuri shinbun*, July 29, 1888, 3; "Sōtōshū no funsō," *Yomiuri shinbun*, November 15, 1889, 2.

83. The historic rivalry between the two head temples (*honzan*) within the sect, Sōjiji and Eiheiji, came to a head when the validity of the election of Eiheiji's abbot (*kanju*) was called into question. When the Sōjiji faction moved to break away and form another sect, the Eiheiji faction blocked this by appealing to the bylaws governing the sect (*shusei*) drawn up under the 1884 ordinance from the Home Ministry. The ministry, which retained the prerogative to authorize (*ninka*) the superintendents and bylaws governing the sects, had attempted to "admonish" the parties of the dispute but had been unable to resolve the matter. Inoue Kaoru, as home minister, directed the Shrine and Temple Bureau to take provisional control of the sect (*jimu toriatsukai*) through a proxy superintendent's office to resolve the matter; *Segai Inouekō den*, 4: 357–80.

84. *TGSGS*, vol. 7, Fifth Imperial Diet, 87–90.

85. *TGSGS*, vol. 8, Eighth Imperial Diet, 234–35. Some Buddhist sects had complained that the Home Ministry did not grant superintendents enough authority to prevent schisms within sects; "Naimu daijin ni nozomu," *Dentō* no. 22 (October 1891): 1–6.

86. *TGSGS*, 9: 603–8.

87. Ibid., 376–79.

88. See, for example, *TGSGS*, 11: 466–67.

89. *TGSGS*, 8: 376.

90. Ibid., 377.

91. To be sure, some did assail the anachronism of the memorial; Kusanagi Chikaaki, for example, observed that it was strange to see so many draft memorials and bills associated with Shinto and Buddhist interests come before the Diet just as Japan was fighting the benighted Qing dynasty in order to bring progress to Asia: "I cannot but be surprised by the appearance of phenomena directly opposed to the yearly progress of our realm"; *TGSGS*, 9: 604.

92. *TGSGS*, 8: 378–79.

93. *TGSGS*, 11: 466–68. It seems reasonable to believe that the less aggressive "recommendation" (*kengi*) to the cabinet, as opposed to a "memorial" (*jōsō*), helped to secure increased support.

94. *TGSGS*, 11: 467–68, 476–78.

95. Closed balloting may have kept the vote much closer and produced a different outcome; *TGKGS*, 11: 658–59.

96. *TGSGS*, vol. 8, Eighth Imperial Diet, 379–80; 9: 695–99. The Home Ministry began a survey of all historical shrines and temples in April 1895, which it followed with a standardized procedure for requesting conservation funds. Shrines and temples established prior to 1486 (*bunmei* 18) were eligible for conservation, and exceptions could be made for those established prior to 1703 (*genroku* 16) with ties to prominent historical persons. The Home Ministry also doubled the conservation fund from 20,000 to 50,000 yen in its 1896 budget request; *Kanpō Meiji-hen* 6 (18): 51; 6 (21): 153.

97. *TGKGS*, 10: 93–96; *TGSGS*, 10: 386–87.

98. The total amount of preservation funds was capped at 150,000 to 200,000 yen; any change in the amount required statutory amendments passed by the Diet. "Koshaji hozonho wo sadamu" in *Kōbunruiju* 2A-11-類796. See also *TGKGS*, 11: 13–14.

99. The clarity of this distinction was stressed by questioners in the House of Peers; *TGKGS*, 1: 16.

100. *TGKGS*, 11: 12–13.

101. As a result, concerns about the discriminatory scope of the preservation law were raised from the beginning; representatives of the Home Ministry were repeatedly asked what the designation "ancient" meant, and could provide only vague assurances that artistic, historical, and cultural significance would be weighed by experts on the committee. *TGKGS*, 11: 17–18; *TGSGS*, 9: 698.

102. "Shaji ni kansuru hōritsu-an," *Taiyō* no. 4 (February 20, 1897): 237.

103. Ōtsu, *Dainihon kenseishi*, 9: 303–8.

104. *TGSGS*, 12: 582–83, 614–15. A similar response was sent to the House of Peers; *TGKGS*, 12: 431. Shimizu Tōru, reflecting on his role in drafting the government's response as a secretary within the Shrine and Temple Bureau, claims that the head of the Home Ministry Shrine and Temple Bureau showed little interest in realizing the recommendations passed by the Imperial Diet; Jingiin and Zenkoku shinshokukai, *Jinjakyoku jidai wo kataru*, 32. While the government sat on the recommendations, the Imperial Diet moved to debate the Shrine Preservation Fund, the substance of fiscal support for shrines being the remaining issue. Kitada Nobutsuna and four others submitted a draft recommendation to the tenth Diet, demanding

the state treasury support the rites and maintenance of imperial and national shrines. *TGSGS*, 12: 613.

105. Sakada, *Kindai nihon ni okeru taigaikō undō no kenkyū*, 164–81; Uno, "Mintō no tankan to Nisshin sengo keiei," 232–36.

106. "Jingikan ni kansuru Itagakihaku no iken," *Kaitsū zasshi* no. 3 (February 1894); "Ōkumahaku no iken," *Kaitsū zasshi* no. 4 (March 1891); "Shintō yūshi sōdai Ōkuma shushō toku," *Yomiuri shinbun*, July 26, 1898, 2.

107. "Naimusho kansei," *Kōbunruiju* 2A-11-類813; "Jinjakyoku no shinsetsu," *Yomiuri shinbun*, October 4, 1898, 1.

108. The governing coalition dissolved over a dispute involving the appointment of Hoshi Tōru as foreign minister; Kuga Katsunan, "Sakkon no shūkyō mondai," *Nihon*, October 18, 1898, reprinted in Kuga, *Kuga Katsunan zenshū*, 6: 144–45.

109. Its three other goals continued what the priests had been seeking since the 1880s, namely, reestablishing a Department of Divinities, restoring permanent funding to imperial and national shrines, and returning confiscated shrine lands; Zenkoku shinshokukai, *Zenkoku shishokukai enkaku shiyō*, 9–12.

110. Ōtsu Jun'ichirō had already submitted a new draft recommendation to the House of Representatives in January 1898; *TGSGS*, 14: 244, 252–54; *TGKGS*, 15: 255–56.

111. Hanawa, *Kokkai kaisetsu*, 96–103.

112. Ibid., 82–85. This is not to suggest that all were convinced that the priests' movement transcended sectarian self-interest. When the magazine *Taiyō* addressed the recommendations, for example, it invoked the lessons of the Ministry of Doctrine to call into question what a revived Department of Divinities could hope to accomplish; "Kokkyō-ronja ni hitokotosu," *Taiyō* 4, no. 5 (March 5, 1898): 57–58.

113. Ibid., 96–103. With no movement from the government as the Diet session wound down, interested members of the Diet submitted a formal query to the government on February 25; *TGSGS*, 15: 540–42.

114. "Shūgiin kengi jingi ni kansuru tokubetu kanga setchi no ken," in *Kōbunzassan* 2A-013-00 • 纂00493100.

115. *Kanpō Meiji-hen* 7 (3): 4; 8 (6): 26.

116. I will return to this point later in the chapter.

117. *TGSGS*, 15: 765.

118. *TGKGS*, 15: 735. To further express their frustration with the government, a recommendation to provide permanent funding to imperial and national shrines was passed by the House of Representatives on the last day of the thirteenth Diet session; *TGSGS*, 15: 761–62.

119. An office dedicated to the administration of the shrine, the Jingū shichō, was created in 1896, and the Imperial Diet approved, with no debate, an outlay of more than 110,000 yen when fires destroyed Ise in May 1898. This drew attention to the funding of Ise and the fact that the 27,000 yen annually paid from the treasury did not cover the shrines' operating expenses. The political parties competed to demand increases in that support, with the result that it was nearly doubled to 50,000 yen in 1900; *TGSGS*, vol. 13, Twelfth Diet Session, 147–49, 229; *TGSGS*, 10: 23, 39; *TGKGS*, vol. 13, Eleventh and Twelfth Diet Sessions, 110–11, 190; Yamaguchi, *Meiji kokka*, 248.

120. Inoo, *Naichi zakkyoron shiryō shūsei*, 1: 1–11.

121. "Naichi zakkyo to chihō kyōiku kaigi," *Taiyō* 4, no. 5 (March 5, 1898): 256–58; diagram on 257.

122. One article estimated a total of 113,000 Christians in Japan, with more than sixty private Christian schools that educated male and female students at the middle-school level and above; Itō Shūji, "Naichi zakkyo-go ni okeru yasokyō kakuha no kanri to kyōkai gakkōno shobun hō," *Taiyō* 4, no. 5 (March 5, 1898): 5–11.

123. Quoted in Ogawara, "Meiji-ki ni okeru naichi zakkyo mondai," 123–24.

124. Itō Shūji, "Naichi zakkyo-go ni okeru yasokyō kakuha no kanri to kyōkai gakkōno shobun hō," *Taiyō* 4, no. 5 (March 5, 1898): 5–11.

125. One form of "taming" proposed involved removing all sectarian particulars from religious education; in the opinion of *Taiyō*'s editors, for example, education reform that transposed sectarian interests and content into universal humanitarian and ethical expressions would suffice to prevent Christian schools from transforming Japanese students into foreigners within their own country; "Kyōiku shūkyō bunri no zengo," *Taiyō* 5, no. 24 (1899): 66.

126. The perception that the government was intent on favoring Christianity over Buddhism in prison chaplaincies provided one flashpoint for Buddhist protests. The Sugamo prison chaplain controversy, in which Shin-sect Buddhist chaplains were replaced with Protestant Christian chaplains by a reform-minded prison official in 1898, coincided with the anticipation of a religion bill. "Kangoku kyōkaishi mondai," *Taiyō* 4, no. 21 (October 20, 1898): 50–54.

127. "Kokkyō mondai," *Dentō* no. 163 (April 13, 1898): 30.

128. "Shūkyō hōan kyokugaikan," *Yorozu chōhō*, January 19, 1900, 1; "Shūkyō hōan zatsubun," *Yomiuri shinbun*, December 20, 1899, 1; Saeki, "Meiji sanjūninen ni okeru jōyaku kaisei," 46–47.

129. "Naichi zakkyo ni tsuite," *Dentō* no. 57 (November 1893): 20–22; "Naichi zakkyo ni taisuru kyōka no kakugo ikan," *Dentō* no. 109 (January 1896): 4–8; "Naichi zakkyo ni taisuru kyōka no kakugo ikan (ge)," *Dentō* no. 110 (January 1896): 4–8. For prominent examples of this reformist perspective, see Nakanishi Ushirō, *Naichi zakkyo to bukkyō no kankei*, and Inoue Enryo, *Kyōikuka shūkyōka no naichi zakkyo junbi ni taisuru kokoroe*.

130. "Shūkyōka no shizen tōta (naichi zakkyo go no sōzō)," *Dentō* no. 150 (September 1897): 1–5.

131. "Kōninkyō-ron wo tonaeru bukkyōto" *Taiyō* 5, no. 5 (May 1899): 65–66; "Kangoku kyōkaishi mondai," *Taiyō* 4, no. 21 (October 20, 1898): 50–54.

132. "Masse no buppō," *Jiji shinpō*, September 10, 1899, 3.

133. "Iwayuru kōninkyō ronja to wa nanzoya," *Taiyō* 5, no. 2 (February 1899): 65–67.

134. "Seikyō mondai to bukkyō kakushū no tokusei," *Taiyō* 5, no. 24 (1899): 65–66; "Kōninkyō no undō ni tsuite," *Jiji shinpō*, November 18, 1899, 2; "Bukkyō kyōsei no setsu ni tsuite," *Jiji shinpō*, September 20, 1899, 2; "Seifu no shūkyō ni taisuru taido wo ronjite bunri mondai ni oyobu," *Dentō* no. 154 (November 28, 1897): 3.

135. "Wagahō no seitō to shūkyō," *Dentō* no. 187 (April 13, 1899): 2: 「同一国民の中に不和敵視する者を生ずる」and 「万民を同一視」.

136. Adjustments included amending the requirement for a signature stamp (*inkan*) on business contracts, since foreigners were unlikely to possess such stamps; Kobayashi, "Meiji nijūnananen chōin no kaisei jōyaku."

137. "Jōyaku jisshi junbi no tame hōrei no seitei matawa kaisei wo yōshi sono hoka gyōseijō shori wo yōsuru monowa jōyaku jisshi yōkō ni junshi torisute hōsoku shi an wo gushite jōyaku junbi iinkai ni teishustu seshimu," in *Kōbunruisan* 2A-11-類785; "Jōyaku jisshi no tame aratani hōritsu wo seitei shi mata ha kaisei wo kuwayuru wo yōsubeki jikō," in *Kōbunzassan* 2A-013-00 纂00446100.

138. "Shinbutsudō igai no shūkyō ni taishi naimushōrei wo motte torishimarihō wo mōku," in *Kōbunruisan* 2A-11-00 類00868100-002. The draft ordinance was first submitted to the cabinet by Saigō Tsugumichi in June 1898; it was then reviewed by the Legal Codes Research Committee (headed by Yamagata Aritomo and including Hozumi Yatsuka, Ozaki Saburō, Aoki Shuzō, and Mitsukuri Rinshō) before being presented to the cabinet. The recommendation took the form of Yamagata, as head of the committee, recommending to himself, as prime minister, the issuance of ministerial directives in anticipation of legislation.

139. The Legal Codes Research Committee was created under the second Itō cabinet (1892–96) in 1893, primarily to study the Civil Code; Hōten chōsakai, *Hōten chōsakai jin'in meibo.*

140. The ordinance otherwise introduced detailed provisions for the supervision of religious facilities (churches, shrines, and temples) and for the registration of professional clerics. In a memorandum submitted to Yamagata, Aoki rehearsed for his colleagues the precedents set by constitutional governments in Europe, which generally adopted a passive stance toward churches (*jiin*) and only actively intervened in matters vital to public stability. The Home Ministry's draft ordinance, Aoki warned, contained provisions that strayed from the important precedent of European experience; "*Shinbutsudō igai no shūkyō ni taishi naimushōrei wo motte torishimarihō wo mōku,*" in *Kōbunruisan* 2A-11-00 類00868100-002.

141. Such as, for example, the 1890 Assembly and Political Association Law (Shūkai oyobi seisha hō).

142. This was issued as Home Ministry Ordinance 41 on July 27, 1899; *Kanpō Meiji-hen* 8 (19): 445–46.

143. In the eyes of conservative commentators, following mixed residence "foreigners will be allowed rights to schools that belong to the legitimate system of national education [*kokumin kyōiku*] consisting of elementary, middle, higher, and women's schools. In the future, a segment of the nation of our great Japanese Empire will have their character molded by foreigners whose *kokutai* [and] national sentiments differ from ours." "Zassō," *Seikyō jihō*, September 1, 1899, 245.

144. Dohi, "1890-nendai no dōshisha (1)."

145. Hisaki Yukio, "Kunrei 12 gō no shisō to genjitsu 1," "Kunrei 12 gō no shisō to genjitsu 2," and "Kunrei 12 gō no shisō to genjitsu 3."

146. Discussions of the ordinance, initiated under the Ōkuma-Itagaki government, focused on whether foreigners would be allowed to establish schools; Hisaki, "Kunrei 12 gō no shisō to genjitsu 1."

147. The British and U.S. ambassadors protested these provisions as a flagrant violation of the freedom of missionaries. Kuga Katsunan reported, however, that the

foreign envoys were unable to protest very strongly; "Shiritsu gakkōrei (gaikoku senkyōshira no undō ni tsuite)," *Nihon*, May 4, 1899, 2.

148. It required instructors to demonstrate only language proficiency, and gave the minister of education the right to rescind accreditation if principals or instructors were found to be deficient.

149. Dohi, "1890-nendai no dōshisha (2)," 104–5. The Privy Council, when deliberating the Private School Ordinance, expressed concern that the ordinance would not sufficiently regulate the religious education in private Christian schools, and pointed to the so-called Jules Ferry laws enacted during the 1880s in France; Saeki, "Meiji sanjūninen ni okeru jōyaku kaisei," 63.

150. "Shiritsu gakkōrei," *Tokyo nichi nichi shinbun*, August 3, 1899, 2.

151. "Monbusho kunrei to aoyama gakuin," *Nihon*, September 5, 1899, 2.

152. They resolved to maintain Christian principles in their schools while they sought to regain state accreditation; "Shiritsu gakkōrei happu ni kanshi roku shiritsu gakkō daihyōsha no kaisho," *Kirisutokyō shinbun*, September 1, 1899, 8; "Monbushō kunrei to kirisutokyō gakkō no kesshin," *Jiji shinpō*, September 2, 1899, 4.

153. "Kyōiku shūkyō kankeiron," *Rikugō zasshi* no. 321 (May 15, 1899): 62–65.

154. Although some suggested that missionaries should establish a university so that graduates of Christian secondary schools could advance without state accreditation, most got around the directive by creating formal distinctions between the schools and their religious components by registering school chapels as independent churches. Christian elementary schools, however, were most directly affected, and many chose to close rather than comply with the directive. In Tokyo, where public elementary schools were unable to educate all students, the closure of Christian elementary schools caused a dramatic classroom shortage that necessitated converting Buddhist temples into elementary schools, an irony that did not escape commentary; "Daigakkō to senkyōshi," *Rikugō zasshi* no. 325 (September 19, 1899): 1–8; "Kirisutokyōshugi no chūgakkō ni tsuite," *Nōnin shinpō*, September 11, 1899, 3. Some periodicals, like the *Rikugō zasshi*, argued that complying with the letter but not the spirit of the directive merely underscored its unconstitutionality; "Monbushō kunrei to shūkyō gakkō," *Rikugō zasshi* no. 325 (September 19, 1899): 63–64; "Shiritsu gakkōrei to Tokyo-shi," *Seikyō jihyō*, September 15, 1899, 10–11.

155. Okada made the same point when the ordinance was debated within the government. Asked if the directive prohibited the "spirit" of religious instruction or just the formal content (i.e., reading the Bible), he responded that the intent was to prohibit the spirit of religious instruction, saying that students must never be prevented from entering a school because of its religious character; he invoked the example of a Christian school that effectively prevented Buddhist students from enrolling because of its religious instruction; Hisaki, "Kunrei 12gō no shisō to genjitsu 1," 12.

156. "Shiritsu gakkōrei ni tsuite," *Seikyō shinpō*, October 1, 1899, 24–25.

157. "Shūkyō kyōiku kinshi no riyū," *Fukuin shinpō*, January 17, 1900, 14.

158. According to one editorial, the language of removing religion in general from the classroom betrayed the need to avoid incensing Shinto and Buddhist elements by validating the use of the Christian Bible in accredited curriculums while at the same time sidestepping the potential for diplomatic protest; "Kirisutokyō gakkō

no shobun," *Nōnin shinpō* no. 586 (April 10, 1899): 4. See also "Monbushō gantoshite shūkyō gakkō ni tokuten wo ataezu," *Tokyo nichi nichi shinbun*, July 6, 1899, 32.

159. "Monbushō kunrei ni taisuru shūkyō-shugi no gakkō," *Nihon* no. 3605 (September 10, 1899): 2.

160. "Shiritsu gakkōrei to gaikoku senkyōshi," *Nihon* no. 3470 (April 28, 1899): 2; "Gakkō to tokuiku," *Nihon* no. 3482 (May 9, 1899): 1.

161. "Shiritsu gakkōrei no hihan (1) Kamata Eikichi-shi no danwa," *Mainichi shinbun*, August 5, 1899, 2; "Shiritsu gakkōrei no hihan (2) Kamata Eikichi-shi no danwa," *Mainichi shinbun*, August 6, 1899, 2.

162. The editor went so far as to suggest the Ministry of Education should appoint clergy as teachers in primary schools; "Seifu tai kyōiku to shūkyō," *Dentō* no. 163 (April 13, 1898): 3.

163. "Kyōkai genkon no ichidai mondai (hōnin ka kōninka)," *Dentō* no. 179 (December 1898): 1–5.

164. "Kyōikukai no shūkyō mondai," *Tsūzoku bukkyō shinbun* no. 293 (January 10, 1900): 13.

165. The Shrine and Temple Bureau was reorganized as part of a larger government reform in October 1893. In addition to the shrine and temple sections, the third section dedicated to sectarian affairs (*kyōmuka*) was created. The third section removed overtly religious functions from the shrine and temple sections (such as authorizing bylaws of Buddhist and Shinto sects and supervising clerical qualifications) and created a third administrative category that was most likely intended to pave the way for introducing Christianity to the regulatory portfolio of the Home Ministry. The sectarian affairs section was officially charged with overseeing Shinto and Buddhist sects as well as generic "religion" (October 31, 1893, Edict 127 "Naimusho kansei"; section designations are listed in *Kanpo* no. 3110 [November 9, 1893], in *Kanpō Meiji-hen*, vol. 5). By divorcing matters relating to sectarian Shinto from the shrine section, this tripartite division of the smallest bureau of the Home Ministry prepared the way for moving the bureaucratic administration of shrines and shrine priests to a separate office; Yamaguchi, *Meiji kokka*, 249 n. 52.

166. Shimizu Tōru, who served as secretary in the Home Ministry Shrine and Temple Bureau, recounts that three bills were drafted between 1897 and 1898: a shrine bill, a temple bill, and a religion bill; Jingiin and Zenkoku shinshokukai, *Jinjakyoku jidai wo kataru*, 33.

167. "Naimusho kansei zojingushicho kansei kotokan kantobokyureichu wo kaiseisu," in *Kōbunruisan* 2A-11-類876; "Kankokuheisha hi ni kansuru ken wo sadamuru," in *Kōbunruisan* 2A-11-類868.

168. Yamaguchi, *Meiji kokka*, 255 n. 72.

169. It was widely understood that any bill would place Buddhism, Christianity, and sectarian Shinto under a single statute and that it would carefully avoid language that addressed the specific content of religions; "Jiinhō oyobi jinja hōan," *Yomiuri shinbun*, August 24, 1898, 1; "Jinja hōan oyobi jiinhō," *Yomiuri shinbun*, October 20, 1898, 1; "Shūkyō hōan kōmoku ni tsuite," *Yomiuri shinbun*, October 27, 1899, 1; "Shajikyoku no teian," *Zenkoku shinshokukai kaihō* 2 (September 1899).

170. "Sakujitsu no kizokuin," *Yomiuri shinbun*, December 15, 1899, 1.

171. Kojima, "Meiji sanjūninen shūkyō hōanron"; *TGKIS*, 9: 343.

172. Ibid.

173. *TGKGS*, 16: 107–8.

174. The attention devoted to the Religion Bill was significant, as attested by the publication of *Shūkyō hōan zassan*, a collection of press reports and statements by prominent figures; Watanabe, *Shūkyō hōan zassan*. See also Noma, *Shūkyō hōan no tenmatsu*.

175. "Shūkyō hōan no teishutsu," *Yorozu chōhō* no. 2222 (December 10, 1899): 2.

176. Hara Takashi, *Hara Takashi zenshū*, 2: 536–37.

177. "Shūkyō hōan wo shite tsūka seshimeyo," *Taiyō* 6, no. 1 (January 1900): 36.

178. Even the conservative Kuga believed the bill should be passed with only partial amendments; Kuga, *Kuga Katsunan zenshū*, 6: 397–402.

179. "Shūkyō hōan wa shūsei wo yōsu," *Yorozu chōhō*, December 16, 1899, 1; "Shūkyō hōan wa shūsei wo yōsu (chū)," *Yorozu chōhō*, December 17, 1899, 1; "Shūkyō hōan wa shūsei wo yōsu (ge)," *Yorozu chōhō*, December 18, 1899, 1.

180. In its editorial view, religions would criticize and attack each other as a matter of course, and any attempt to legislate the natural propensity to compete was meaningless; "Shūkyō hōan," *Jiji shinpō*, December 15, 1899, 2.

181. "Shintō kakukyō teishutsu shūkyō hōan shūseian," *Zenkoku shinshokukai kaihō* no. 8 (March 1900). Some minor adjustments to Articles 2, 8, 12, 13, 16, 17, 29, 32, and 46 were proposed in early 1900; Saeki, "Meiji sanjūninen ni okeru jōyaku kaisei," 57–58.

182. "Kirisutokyo to koninkyo," *Yomiuri shinbun*, June 27, 1899, 1.

183. Watanabe, *Shūkyō hōan zassan*, 202–3,

184. Saeki, "Meiji sanjūninen ni okeru jōyaku kaisei," 58–59.

185. Quoted in Sugii, "Ozawa Saburō-hen Nihon purotesutantoshi shiryō (5)," 198.

186. Yamaguchi, *Meiji kokka*, 108–19.

187. "Shūkyō hōan zatsubun," *Yomiuri shinbun*, December 20, 1899, 1; Saeki, "Meiji sanjūninen ni okeru jōyaku kaisei," 46–47.

188. Reprinted in "Bukkyō hōan," *Zenkoku shinshokukai kaihō* no. 1 (August 1899): 40–43; see also "Kakushū kanchō kaigi," *Yomiuri shinbun*, June 9, 1899, 4; *Yomiuri shinbun*, October 27, 1899, 1; Saeki, "Meiji sanjūninen ni okeru jōyaku kaisei," 48–49.

189. "Shūkyō hōan no teishitsu ni tsuite," *Dentō* no. 177 (November 1898): 1.

190. *Yomiuri shinbun*, December 12, 1899, 1; *Yomiuri shinbun*, December 14, 1899, 1.

191. "Shūkyō hōan wo higisu," *Dentō* no. 204 (December 28, 1899): 4.

192. "Shūkyō hōan no seiron," *Mitsugon kyōhō* no. 247 (January 12, 1900): 22, 29–30; "Shūkyō hōan hantaisha taikai," *Yomiuri shinbun*, January 22, 1900, 1; *TGKGS*, 17: 603.

193. "Shūkyō hōan hantai undō," *Yomiuri shinbun*, December 12, 1899, 1; "Bukkyō kakushū iin no kaigō," *Yomiuri shinbun*, December 17, 1899, 1; "Shūkyō hōan zatsubun," *Yomiuri shinbun*, December 26, 1899, 1; "Shūkyō hōan ni tsuite," *Dentō* no. 206 (January 1900): 1–2.

194. *TGKGS*, 17: 580–81. Kobayashi Kazuyuki observes that the House of Peers was in general reluctant to take up petitions concerning "religion"; Kobayashi, "Meijiki no kizokuin to seigan," 259, 262, 264.

195. Dai nihon bukkyōto dōmeikai, *Shūkyō hōan hantai iken*, 1–2.

196. Ibid., 12–18, 60.

197. "Kōninkyō," *Yomiuri shinbun*, November 27, 28, and 29, 1899, 2; "Kōninkyō seitei no kenpaku," *Yomiuri shinbun*, October 1, 1899, 2; "Kōninkyō jōrei seitei kenpakku shui," *Yomiuri shinbun*, October 11, 1899, 2; Kobayashi, "Dai niji Yamagata naikaku 'shūkyō hōan' wo meguru shosō."

198. "Bukkyō dōmei dantai no jōin undō," *Asahi shinbun*, December 15, 1899, 1; "Shūkyō hōan kyokugaikan (futatabi)," *Yorozu chōhō*, 24 January 1900, 1.

199. The corollary was that religion could never be allowed to control the state; "Shūkyō jiyū shugi," *Asahi shinbun*, December 13, 1899, 2.

200. "Senkyo to shūkyōka," *Taiyō* 4, no. 4 (February 29, 1898): 247–48; "Shūkyō hōan zatsubun," *Yomiuri shinbun*, January 10, 1900, 1; "Shūkyō hōan zatsubun," *Yomiuri shinbun*, January 15, 1900, 1; "Sōryo no undō," *Jiji Shinpō*, January 20, 1900, 2.

201. "Shūkyō hōan to shūgiin," *Mitsugon kyōhō* no. 249 (February 12, 1900): 33–34; "Bukkyōto taikai, *Taiyō* 6, no. 2 (January 1900): 32–35; "Shūkyō hōan no seiron," *Mitsugon kyōhō* no. 247 (January 12, 1900): 21–22.

202. "Naze ni waga bukkyōto wa sara ni ichidai funki wo kokoromizaruka," *Mitsugon kyōhō* no. 248 (January 26, 1900): 1–4.

203. The four Christian members of the Constitutional Government (Kenseitō) Party considered the bill fair, while the rest of the party remained divided. The Imperial (Teikokutō) Party called for the separation of state and religion in its party platform, but its members were rumored to be interested in ties with Buddhist sects. The True Constitutional Government Party (Kensei hontō) had yet to express a position; "Shūkyō hōan to kakutō," *Yomiuri shinbun*, December 12, 1899, 1; "Teikokutō no ikō," *Yomiuri shinbun*, December 14, 1899, 1; "Shūkyō hōan zatsubun," *Yomiuri shinbun*, December 21, 1899, 1.

204. The initial members of the group numbered twenty-seven Diet members representing the House of Peers, the Progressive Party (Shinpotō), the Liberal Party (Jiyūtō), the Imperial Party, and the Giin kurabu; "Shūkyō kenkyūkai no hokki," *Yomiuri shinbun*, December 14, 1899, 1; "Shūkyō hōan kenkyūkai," *Yomiuri shinbun*, December 19, 1899, 1. The mayor of Gifu, Horigushi Yūichi, and a former Diet member from Aichi, Aoyama Rō, attempted to organize an adherents' club (*shinto kurabu*); "Shūkyō hōan zatsubun," *Yomiuri shinbun*, December 21, 1899, 1.

205. No resolution was put forward by the party, however; "Kenseitō to shūkyō hōan," *Yomiuri shinbun*, January 17, 1900, 1; see also "Shūkyō hōan zatsubun," *Yomiuri shinbun*, January 7, 1900, 1.

206. "Kōninkyō ippa iyoiyo zasetsu su," *Yorozu chōhō*, January 7, 1900, 2.

207. "Tani shōgun no shūkyōhō dan," *Mitsugon kyōhō* no. 247 (January 12, 1900): 22.

208. "Kinō no kizokuin," *Yomiuri shinbun*, December 15, 1899, 1.

209. *TGKIS*, 9: 257.

210. In fact, the only meaningful differentiation between temples and churches was the provision allowing churches to incorporate as either associations or foundations.

211. "Shūkyō hōan hiketsu no ken," in *Kōbunzassan* 2A-13-纂512.

212. As much as 61 percent of land occupied by temples and monasteries had been placed under state ownership, and temples were allowed tax-exempt use of the land.

213. *TGKIS*, 9: 299, 357.

214. "Shūkyō hōan zatsubun," *Yomiuri shinbun*, December 20, 1899, 1; "Tani shōgun no shūkyōhō dan," *Mitsugon kyōhō* no. 247 (January 12, 1900): 22.

215. *TGKIS*, 9: 410

216. Ibid., 333, 447–51; *TGKGS*, 16: 107.

217. The editors of *Taiyō* wondered what message such an exemption would send about military service. To suggest killing in war was inappropriate for religious clerics appeared tantamount to admitting that war was evil in the eyes of religion; "Shūkyō kyōshi no heieki," *Taiyō* 6, no. 1 (January 1900): 37.

218. *TGKIS*, 9: 409.

219. *Yomiuri* reported in late December that of the fifteen members of the special committee tasked with revising the bill, six were reported in favor, while six were against; "Shūkyō hōan zatsubun," *Yomiuri shinbun*, December 21, 1899, 1.

220. Soga was a retired army general, Matsuoka was a state jurist, and Kikkawa was a diplomat.

221. Hozumi, chief protagonist in the debates over the Civil Code, was serving his first year as an appointed member of the House of Peers.

222. *TGKIS*, 9: 349, and 339; ibid., 345–47.

223. Tsuzuki complained that the government bill did not adequately supervise Catholic Christianity and attempted to include provisions aimed at limiting the Vatican's role in governing the Catholic Church in Japan; *TGKIS*, 9: 373–76.

224. Ibid., 357–57; for specific revisions see also 352–53.

225. Reaching back to Shimaji Mokurai's movement to undermine the Ministry of Doctrine in the early 1870s, the Chōshū clique had maintained close ties with the Nishi-Honganji, and Yamagata made good use of his direct line of communication to Ōtani Kōson (1850–1903), the chief abbot. Yamagata personally sought Ōtani's understanding and support during a visit to Kyoto; Tokutomi, *Kōshaku Yamagata Aritomo den*, 2: 380; see also "Shūkyō hōan," *Yomiuri shinbun*, December 15, 1899, 1; "Shūkyō hōan zatsubun," *Yomiuri shinbun*, January 6, 1900, 1; Watanabe, *Shūkyō hōan zassan*, 201–2, 210–11.

226. Tokutomi, *Kōshaku Yamagata Aritomo den*, 2: 383–84. See also *TGSGS*, 16: 662, 678–80.

227. "Shūkyō hōan zatsubun," *Yomiuri shinbun*, December 26, 1899, 1; "Shūkyō hōan zatsubun," *Yomiuri shinbun*, January 5, 1900, 1.

228. Officials from the Imperial Household Ministry were also summoned to admonish him; "Seifu higashi honganji wo ikaku su," *Yorozu chōhō*, January 9, 1900, 2.

229. Konoe, *Konoe Atsumaro nikki*, 3: 60.

230. Tokutomi, *Kōshaku Yamagata Aritomo den*, 3: 385: 「何分直接には迫り立候譯にも参り兼関節に頻りに提促為致申候」.

231. Kobayashi, *Meiji rikken seiji to kizokuin*, 219–45.

232. Ozaki, *Ozaki Saburō nikki*, 3: 247.

233. *TGKGS*, 17: 571–84.

234. Ibid., 584–93.

235. Ibid., 593–604.

236. After some debate over the method of voting, the vote was taken by signed ballots; *TGKGS*, 17: 607.

237. Ozaki, *Ozaki Saburō nikki*, 3: 108.

238. "Senge chiji no kesshin sukoburu katashi," *Yomiuri shinbun*, February 22, 1900, 1; *Yomiuri shinbun*, February 24, 1900, 2.

239. Letter of February 20, 1900, reprinted in Shōyū kurabu, *Yamagata Aritomo kankei monjo*, 2: 151–52.

240. "Bukkyō no kontei," *Jiji shinpō*, February 23, 1900, 2; "Shūkyō hōan no hiketsu," *Yorozu chōhō*, February 19, 1900, 1; "Shūkyō hōan no hiketsu," *Dentō* no. 208 (February 28, 1900): 29.

241. See Kitamura, *Tsūzoku shūkyō hōan shakugi*.

242. In special committee, committee chairman Okabe Nagamoto (1855–1925) demanded that the police law explicitly prohibit clergy from joining political associations because the Religion Bill, which had contained that language, did not pass; *TGKIS*, 10: 423–36.

243. *TGKIS*, 10: 426; *TGKGS*, 17: 696.

244. Quoted in Ogawara, "Meiji-ki ni okeru naichi zakkyo mondai to kirisutokō taisaku," 131.

245. The original law of 1889 simply stated that "Priests, Monks and Instructors of various sects may not stand as candidates," but the new law expanded the exclusion to read, "Shrine priests, priests, monks and other religious instructions and elementary school instructors do not possess the right to stand for election."

246. There is evidence indicating the Home Ministry grew much more cautious in authorizing the establishment or movement of Christian churches and institutions from 1900 onward; Ogawara, "Meiji-ki ni okeru naichi zakkyo mondai to kirisutokō taisaku," 134–35; Inoo, "Bukkyōto gawa no naichi zakkyo hantai undō to sono shiryō ni tsuite."

247. The focus of the movement turned to the government's budget request following the adoption of a second set of recommendations in the Imperial Diet, and the Home Ministry's request to create a Shrine Bureau. Ōtsu Jun'ichirō petitioned Yamagata and his cabinet to fund a Shrine Bureau as early as September 1899; "Kanga setchi ni tsuki daigishi no kenpaku," *Zenkoku shinshokukai kaihō* no. 2 (September 1899). Fearful their demands might be forgotten amid the attention to the Religion Bill, members of the National Shrine Priests Association, at their national convention held in November 1899, openly discussed the option of submitting a memorial to the throne if the budget did not fund a Shrine Bureau; "Zenkoku shinshoku taikai kiji," *Zenkoku shinsokukai kaihō* no. 4 (November 1899); "Nanizo sumiyaka ni tokubetsu kanga wo setchi sezaru," ibid. Ōtsu and Hayakawa attended the convention and declared that the Diet had done all it could; "Zenkoku shinshoku taikai sekijō ni okeru san daigishi no enzetsu taiyō," *Zenkoku shinshokukai kaihō* no. 5 (December 1899). When the budget submitted by the government to the House of Representatives on November 24 did not fund a new bureau, Hirata Tōsuke (1849–1925), the head of the Cabinet Legislation Bureau, assured the priesthood that a supplemental budget request would be made. "Shajikyoku bunri no kibō," *Asahi shinbun*, January 24, 1900, 1; "Rikkyoku ni taisuru undō tenmatsu," *Zenkoku shinshokukai kaihō* no. 7 (February 1900).

248. To justify the supplemental request, Home Ministry officials described the sad state of shrine administration within the Shrine and Temple Bureau, which had only one dedicated bureaucrat; *TGSIG*, 14: 199; the request was approved by the lower house on February 21 and the upper house on February 23.

249. Quoted in Sakamoto Koremaru, *Kokka shintō keisei*, 306–7.

250. In its formal request for reorganization, the Home Ministry advanced the rationale that shrines and religion "each are of a different character," and that with the addition of Christianity to the Shrine and Temple Bureau's duties, its workload had grown; "Naimushō kansei zōjingushichō kansei kōtōkan kantō bōkyūrei chū wo kaiseisu," in *Kōbunruisan* 2A-11-類876.

251. Soeda, *Naimushō no shakaishi*, 291–92.

252. In fact, the Shrine Bureau was initially so insecure that the Katsura government in 1905 considered recombining it with the Religion Bureau as part of an attempt to reduce the state budget; Yamaguchi, *Meiji kokka*, 278–79.

253. *TGSIG*, 37: 358.

254. "Jingū hōsankai no ninka," *Zenkoku shishokukai kaihō* no. 1 (August 1899): 25; Jinja shinpōsha, *Zōho kaitei Kindai jinja shintōshi*, 121.

255. "Jinjakyoku to jinja," *Taiyō* 6, no. 7 (March 1900): 33–34.

256. Sakamoto Koremaru, "The Structure of State Shinto"; Fridell, *Japanese Shrine Mergers*.

257. Quoted in Saeki, "Meiji sanjūninen ni okeru jōyaku kaisei," 63.

258. A point made with surprising clarity in an editorial in the *Tōhoku* newspaper: "Shūkyō mondai no jōsei," *Tōhoku shinbun*, May 21, 1899, 6.

259. Sakamoto Koremaru, *Kokka shintō keisei*, 305–11.

Conclusion

1. Prime Minister Saionji Kinmochi was supposed to attend as well but could not, owing to illness; Motoda Sakunoshin, *Sankyō kaidō to kirisutokyō*, 3–10.

2. Gordon, *Labor and Imperial Democracy*.

3. Kōtoku, *Kirisuto massatsuron*.

4. Motoda Sakunoshin, *Sankyō kaidō to kirisutokyō*, 16: 「我等は各其教義を発揮し、皇運を翼賛し国民道徳の振興を図らんことを期す。我等は当局者が宗教を尊重し、政治宗教及教育の間を融和し、国運の伸長に資せられんことを望む」.

5. The three religions had already voluntarily come together during the Russo-Japanese War to declare that religious difference had no bearing on the conflict. Kozaki Hiromichi, representing Protestant Christianity, argued that the war pitted Russia, which represented the civilization of the sixteenth century without even the basic guarantee of religious freedom, against Japan, which represented the civilization of the twentieth century; Dai nihon shūkyōka taikai jimusho, *Shūkyōka taikai ihō*, 23, 54.

6. "Osekkyō no nake he hitokoto demo watashi no i wo," *Asahi shinbun*, May 25, 1919, 7.

7. "Higashi honganji ha wa hantai," *Asahi shinbun*, May 25, 1919, 7.

8. The fact that the assembly appeared to treat Christianity equally was an irritant to many Buddhist commentators, who otherwise appreciated the affirmation

of religion's role in educating the nation; see, for example, Maeda Eun, "Jitsujyō ni utoshi," *Chūō kōron* 27, no. 3 (March 1912): 65–67.

9. Hatano Seiichi, "Shūkyōshin no baiyō ni todomaru nara sansei," *Chūō kōron* 27, no. 3 (March 1912): 52.

10. To be sure, the method of comparative religious studies did not function only to equalize religions; it was just as capable of creating a hierarchical classification based on evolutionary schemas. In the late-Meiji context, however, comparative religious studies provided a useful means to defuse the language of direct competition between Christianity and Buddhism, in particular, and replace it with a discourse concerned with a universal religiosity. Yamaguchi, *Meiji kokka*, 170–76.

11. Anesaki Masaharu, "Seiji to shūkyō ni missetsu no kankei ari," *Chūō kōron* 27, no. 3 (March 1912): 58–62; see also Fukasawa, "Anesaki Masaharu to kindai no 'shūkyō mondai,'" 175–80; Hiyane, *Nihon shūkyōshi*, 402; Isomae, *Kindai nihon no shūkyō gensetsu*, 125–26.

12. Two more assemblies were held, one in 1914 when the Religion Bureau was moved from the Home Ministry into the Education Ministry, and one in 1924.

13. Tokonami Takejirō, "Sankyō kaidō ni tsuite," *Chūō kōron* 27, no. 3 (March 1912): 49.

14. Ketelaar, *Of Heretics and Martyrs*, 219.

15. For a classic articulation of this narrative of victimization, see Ashizu, *Kokka shintō to wa nanndatta no ka*.

16. It is important to note, too, that the apparent increase in state funding for shrines, especially at the prefectural level and below, was uneven because it was often left to the discretion of local governments; Hardacre, *Shinto and the State*, 96–97; Yamaguchi, *Meiji kokka*, 315.

17. Sakamoto Koremaru, "The Structure of State Shinto," 275. It also placed considerable pressure on priests to improve themselves through education and training.

18. Hardacre, *Shinto and the State*, 98; Fridell, *Japanese Shrine Mergers*. In essence, the demand that the public character of shrines be affirmed by the receipt of state funds generated the logical requirement of reducing the number of shrines to make that funding fiscally feasible; Yamaguchi, *Meiji kokka*, 292–93, 312–15.

19. See, for example, Nakamura Keijirō's questions posed in the House of Representatives in 1910; *TGSGS*, 24: 481–84, 487–89.

20. For a discussion of the internal stratification of the shrine priesthood, see Hardacre, *Shinto and the State*, 61–63, 68–70.

21. The public controversy surrounding Kume Kunitake's infamous 1891 essay in which he described Shinto as the remnant of the archaic practice of sun worship led Shinto priests and conservatives to attack the secular disposition of the oligarchic leadership, with whom Kume was closely identified. For an overview of the controversy, see Kano and Imai, "Nihon kindai shisōshi no nakano no Kume jiken."

22. Katō Genchi, *Jinja mondai no saikentō*, 39–40, 253–61. See also Yamaguchi, *Meiji kokka*, 174–75.

23. Miyaji Izuo, "Jingi to shūkyō," *Jinja kyōkai zasshi* no. 20 (October 1903): 8–14, and "Jingi to shūkyō (shōzen)," *Jinja kyōkai zasshi* no. 22 (December 1903): 20–28.

24. Shimazono, "State Shinto in the Lives of the People." For a fuller treatment of Shimazono's "broad definition" of State Shinto, see Shimazono, *Kokka shintō to nihonjin.*

25. Hardacre, *Shinto and the State*, 91–92; Sakamoto, "The Structure of State Shinto," 274.

26. That Yasukuni continues to draw on this logic is reflected in the fact that Asō Tarō, a Catholic prime minister, found little tension in visiting the shrine.

27. A point amply demonstrated in the Ministry of Education's postwar study of the problems attending the definition of religion; Monbushō, *Shūkyō no teigi wo meguru shomondai.*

28. See Inoue Egyō, *Shūkyō hōjinhō no kisoteki kenkyū.*

29. Critics such as the Ōtani Shin-sect cleric Chikazumi Jōkan consistently lobbied against any attempts to artificially equalize the treatment of Buddhism and Christianity; Chikazumi, *Shūkyū hōan hantai raireki.*

30. Minobe Tatsukichi, "Jinja no seishitsu to shinkyō no jiyū," *Chūgai nippō*, May 20 and 21, 1930. See also Minobe, *Chikujō kenpō seigi*, 403.

31. Inoue Egyō, *Shūkyō hōjinhō no kisoteki kenkyū*, 43.

32. Delmar Brown, http://sunsite.berkeley.edu/jhti/Meiji%20Horei.html, last accessed August 28, 2013.

33. Asad, *Formations of the Secular*, 25.

34. Derrida, "Faith and Knowledge," 18.

Bibliography

Archival Sources

Asahi shinbun. National Diet Library and Center for Modern Japanese Legal and Political Documents, University of Tokyo.

Bukkyō. Center for Modern Japanese Legal and Political Documents, University of Tokyo.

Chūgai nippō. Center for Modern Japanese Legal and Political Documents, University of Tokyo.

Chūō kōron. National Diet Library and Center for Modern Japanese Legal and Political Documents, University of Tokyo.

Chōya shinbun. Center for Modern Japanese Legal and Political Documents, University of Tokyo.

Dentō. Center for Modern Japanese Legal and Political Documents, University of Tokyo.

Fukuin shinpō. Center for Modern Japanese Legal and Political Documents, University of Tokyo.

Gaikokugata. *Urakami sonmin ikyō ikken*. N.p., 1867. University of Tokyo Library.

Inoue Kaoru. "Meiji jūnana-nen shichi-gatsu Inoue gaimukyō yori naikaku he no kengi." In *Meiji gannen itaru Meiji nijūrokunen jōyaku kaisei mondai ikken: Inoue gaimu daijin jidai jōyaku kaisei mondai*, vol. 2, no. 2.5.1.–2.5.8. Diplomatic Archives of the Ministry of Foreign Affairs of Japan.

Inoue Kaoru kankei monjo. Modern Japanese Political History Materials Room, National Diet Library.

Iwakura Tomomi kankei monjo. Modern Japanese Political History Materials Room, National Diet Library.

Japan Weekly Mail. University of Tokyo Library.

Jiji shinpō. Center for Modern Japanese Legal and Political Documents, University of Tokyo.

Jinja kyōkai zasshi. National Diet Library and Center for Modern Japanese Legal and Political Documents, University of Tokyo.

Kaichi shinbun. Center for Modern Japanese Legal and Political Documents, University of Tokyo.

Kaitsū zasshi. Center for Modern Japanese Legal and Political Documents, University of Tokyo.

Kannagara. National Diet Library and Center for Modern Japanese Legal and Political Documents, University of Tokyo.

Kirisutokyō shinbun. Center for Modern Japanese Legal and Political Documents, University of Tokyo.

Kirokuzairyō. National Archives of Japan.

Kōbunbetsuroku. National Archives of Japan.

Kōbunroku. National Archives of Japan.

Kōbunruisan. National Archives of Japan.

Kōbunzassan. National Archives of Japan.

Kōtenkōkyūjo kōen. National Diet Library and Center for Modern Japanese Legal and Political Documents, University of Tokyo.

Mainichi shinbun. Center for Modern Japanese Legal and Political Documents, University of Tokyo.

Meiji nippō. National Diet Library and Center for Modern Japanese Legal and Political Documents, University of Tokyo.

Mitsugon kyōhō. Center for Modern Japanese Legal and Political Document, University of Tokyo.

Motoda Nagazane monjo. Modern Japanese Political History Materials Room, National Diet Library.

Nihon. Center for Modern Japanese Legal and Political Documents, University of Tokyo.

Nōnin shinpō. Center for Modern Japanese Legal and Political Documents, University of Tokyo.

Reichikai zasshi. Center for Modern Japanese Legal and Political Documents, University of Tokyo.

Rikugō zasshi. National Diet Library and Center for Modern Japanese Legal and Political Documents, University of Tokyo.

Sanjō-ke monjo. Modern Japanese Political History Materials Room, National Diet Library.

Seikyō jihō. Center for Modern Japanese Legal and Political Documents, University of Tokyo.

Taiyō. National Diet Library and Center for Modern Japanese Legal and Political Documents, University of Tokyo.

Tankōsho. National Archives of Japan.

Tōhoku shinbun. Center for Modern Japanese Legal and Political Documents, University of Tokyo.

Tokyo nichinichi shinbun. Center for Modern Japanese Legal and Political Documents, University of Tokyo.

Tokyo-Yokohama mainichi shinbun. Center for Modern Japanese Legal and Political Documents, University of Tokyo.

Tsūzoku bukkyō shinbun. Center for Modern Japanese Legal and Political Documents, University of Tokyo.

Yomiuri shinbun. National Diet Library and Center for Modern Japanese Legal and Political Documents, University of Tokyo.

Yorozu chōhō. Center for Modern Japanese Legal and Political Documents, University of Tokyo.

Yūbin hōchi shinbun. Center for Modern Japanese Legal and Political Documents, University of Tokyo.

Zenkoku shinshokukai kaihō. National Diet Library and Center for Modern Japanese Legal and Political Documents, University of Tokyo.

Books and Articles

Abe Yoshiya. "From Prohibition to Toleration: Japanese Government Views regarding Christianity, 1854–73." *Japanese Journal of Religious Studies* 5, no. 2 (June–September 1978): 107–38.

Aihara Ichirōsuke. "Yakugo 'shūkyō' no seiritsu." *Shūkyōgaku kiyō* 5 (1938): 1–6.

Aizawa Seishisai. *Shinron*. In *NST: MG*, 49–160.

Akita, George. *Foundations of Constitutional Government in Modern Japan, 1868–1900*. Cambridge, MA: Harvard University Press, 1967.

Anderson, Kenneth Mark. "The Foreign Relations of the Family State: The Empire of Ethics, Aesthetics, and Evolution in Meiji Japan." Ph.D. diss., Cornell University, 1999.

Antoni, Klaus. "Introduction." In *Religious and National Identity in the Japanese Context*, ed. Hiroshi Kubota et al. Münster: Lit, 2002.

———. "The 'Separation of Gods and Buddhas' at Ōmiwa Shrine in Meiji Japan," *Japanese Journal of Religious Studies* 22, no. 1–2 (1995): 139–59.

Aoki Shūzō. *Aoki Shūzō jiden*. Tokyo: Heibonsha, 1970.

Asad, Talal. *Formations of the Secular: Christianity, Islam, Modernity*. Stanford: Stanford University Press, 2003.

———. *Genealogies of Religion: Discipline of Reason and Power in Christianity and Islam*. Baltimore: John Hopkins University Press, 1993.

Ashizu Uzuhiko. *Kokka shintō to wa nanndatta no ka*, rev. ed. Tokyo: Jinja shinposha, 2006.

Aston, W. G., trans. *Nihongi: Chronicles of Japan from Earliest Times to A.D. 697*. Boston: Tuttle, 1975.

Auslin, Michael. *Negotiating with Imperialism: the Unequal Treaties and the Culture of Japanese Diplomacy*. Cambridge, MA: Harvard University Press, 2004.

Beasley, W. B. "The Foreign Threat and the Opening of the Ports." In *The Cambridge History of Japan*, vol. 5: *The Nineteenth Century*, ed. Marius Jansen, 259–307. Cambridge: Cambridge University Press, 1989.

Becker, Carl. *The Heavenly City of the Eighteenth-Century Philosophers*. New Haven: Yale University Press, 1932.

Bernstein, Andrew. *Modern Passings: Death Rites, Politics, and Social Change in Imperial Japan*. Honolulu: University of Hawai'i Press, 2006.

Breen, John. "Beyond the Prohibition: Christianity in Restoration Japan." In *Japan and Christianity: Impacts and Responses*, ed. John Breen and Mark Williams, 75–93. New York: St. Martin's Press, 1996.

———. "'Earnest Desires': The Iwakura Embassy and Japanese Religious Policy." *Japan Forum* 10, no. 2 (1998): 151–65.

———. "Heretics in Nagasaki: 1790–1796." In *Japan's Hidden Christians 1549–1999*, vol. 2, ed. Stephen Turnbull, 10–16. Surrey, UK: Japan Library and Edition Synapse, 2000.

———. "Ideologues, Bureaucrats and Priests: On 'Shinto' and 'Buddhism' in Early Meiji Japan." In *Shinto in History: Ways of the Kami*, ed. John Breen and Mark Teeuwen, 230–51. Honolulu: University of Hawai'i Press, 2000.

———. "The Imperial Oath of April 1868: Ritual, Politics and Power in the Restoration." *Monumenta Nipponica* 52 no. 4 (1996): 407–29.

———. "Shintoists in Restoration Japan: Towards a Reassessment." *Modern Asian Studies* 24, no. 3 (1990): 579–602.

Breen, John, and Mark Teeuwen, eds. *A New History of Shinto*. Chichester, UK: Wiley-Blackwell, 2010.

———, eds. *Shinto in History: Ways of the Kami*. Honolulu: University of Hawai'i Press, 2000.

Bunkacho. *Meiji iko shukyo seido hyakunenshi*. Tokyo: Bunkacho bunka-bu shumuka, 1970.

Burns, Susan. *Before the Nation: Kokugaku and the Imagining of Community in Early Modern Japan*. Durham: Duke University Press, 2003.

Chamberlain, Basil Hall. *The Invention of a New Religion*. London: Watts & Co., 1912.

Chikazumi Jōkan. *Shūkyū hōan hantai raireki*. Tokyo: Chikazumi Jōkan, 1929.

Cox, Jeffrey. "Religion and Imperial Power in Nineteenth-Century Britain." In *Freedom and Religion in the Nineteenth Century*, ed. Richard Helmstadter, 339–74. Stanford: Stanford University Press, 1997.

Dai nihon bukkyōto dōmeikai. *Shūkyō hōan hantai iken*. Tokyo: Dai nihon bukkyōto dōmeikai, 1900.

Dai nihon shūkyōka taikai jimusho. *Shūkyōka taikai ihō jikyoku ni taisuru shūkyōka no taido*. Tokyo: Kinkodo, 1904.

Dajōkan honyakukyoku. "Kyōkai ritsuryō." In *Meiji seifu honyaku sōkō ruisan*, vol. 12, 327–82. Tokyo: Yumani shobo, 1986.

De Bary, Wm. Theodore, et al., comp. *Sources of Japanese Tradition*. 2 vols. New York: Columbia University Press, 2001–2005.

Derrida, Jacques. "Faith and Knowledge: The Two Sources of 'Religion' at the Limits of Reason Alone." In *Religion*, ed. Jacques Derrida and Gianni Vattimo, 1–78. Stanford: Stanford University Press, 1996.

Doak, Kevin. "A Naked Public Square? Religion and Politics in Imperial Japan." In *Politics and Religion in Modern Japan: Red Sun, White Lotus*, ed. Roy Starrs, 185–215. Houndmills, Basingstoke, UK: Palgrave Macmillan, 2011.

———. "A Religious Perspective on the Yasukuni Controversy." In *Yasukuni, the War Dead, and the Struggle for Japan's Past*, ed. John Breen, 47–69. New York: Columbia University Press, 2008.

Dohi Akio. "1890-nendai no dōshisha (1)." *Kirisutokyō shakai mondai kenkyū* 40, no. 1 (August 1976): 140–60.

———. "1890-nendai no dōshisha (2)." *Kirisutokyō shakai mondai kenkyū* 40, no. 2 (April 1977): 166–96.

Elison, George. *Deus Destroyed: The Image of Christianity in Early Modern Japan*. Cambridge, MA: Harvard University Press, 1973.

Figal, Gerald. *Civilization and Monsters: Spirits of Modernity in Meiji Japan*. Durham, NC: Duke University Press, 1999.

Fitzgerald, Timothy. *The Ideology of Religious Studies*. New York: Oxford University Press, 2000.

Foucault, Michel. "Governmentality." In *The Foucault Effect: Studies in Governmentality*, ed. G. Burchell, C. Gordon, and P. Miller, 87–104. London: Harvester Wheatsheaf, 1991.

———. *The Order of Things: An Archaeology of the Human Sciences*. New York: Vintage Books, 1994.

———. "Technologies of the Self." In *Technologies of the Self: A Seminar with Michel Foucault*, ed. Michel Foucault et al., 16–49. Amherst: University of Massachusetts Press, 1988.

Fridell, Wilbur M. "The Establishment of Shrine Shinto in Meiji Japan." *Japanese Journal of Religious Studies* 2, no. 2–3 (1975): 137–68.

———. *Japanese Shrine Mergers, 1906–1912: State Shinto Moves to the Grassroots*. Tokyo: Sophia University Press, 1973.

Fujii Sadafumi. *Edo kokugaku tenseishi no kenkyū*. Tokyo: Yoshikawa kobunkan, 1987.

———. *Kaikokuki kirisutokyō no kenkyū*. Tokyo: Kokusho Kankokai, 1986.

———. *Meiji kokugaku hasseishi no kenkyū*. Tokyo: Yoshikawa kobunkan, 1987.

———. "Senkyōshi ni okeru kyōgi kakuritsu no mondai." *Shintōgaku* 51 (November 1966): 1–16.

———. "Senkyōshi no kenkyū: Jō." *Kokugakuin zasshi* 49, no. 5 (1943): 2–29.

———. "Senkyōshi to Nagasaki kaikō." *Kokushigaku* 44 (1942): 15–29.

———. "Shimane-kenka ni okeru kyōdōshoku no katsudō." *Shintōgaku* 111 (1981): 1–23.

———. "Shiryō shōkai: 'Shinkon taishi' zakkō." *Shintōgaku* 55 (November 1967): 58–60.

Fujii Takashi. "Shinzoku nitai-ron ni okeru shintō no henka: Shimaji Mokurai no seikyō-ron no motarashitamono." In *Nihongata seikyō kankei no tanjō*, ed. Inoue Nobutaka and Sakamoto Koremaru, 199–244. Tokyo: Daiichi shobo, 1987.

Fujii Takeshi. "Nationalism and Japanese Buddhism in the Late Tokugawa Period and Early Meiji." In *Religious and National Identity in the Japanese Context*, ed. Klaud Antoni et al., 107–17. Münster: Lit, 2002.

Fujita Hiromasa. *Kindai kokugaku no kenkyū*. Tokyo: Kobundo, 2007.

Fujita Yūkoku, *Seimeiron*, in *NST: MG*, 9–14.

Fujitani, Takashi. *Splendid Monarchy: Power and Pageantry in Modern Japan*. Berkeley: University of California Press, 1996.

Fujitani Toshio. "Kokka shintō no seiritsu." In *Nihon shūkyōshi kōza*, vol. 1, ed. Kawasaki Yasuyuki, 213–90. Kyoto: Sanichi shobo, 1959.

———. *Shintō shinkō to minshū, tennōsei*. Kyoto: Horitsu bunkasha, 1980.

Fujiwara Masanobu. "Kokka shintō taisei to jōdo shinshū." In *Nihon no shūkyō to seiji*, ed. Kokugakuin daigaku nihon bunka kenkyūjo, 121–49. Tokyo: Seibunsha, 2001.

———. "Kyōbushō-gyōseika no minshū to 'bunmei kaika." In *Fukuma kōchō sensei kanreki kinen shinshūshi ronsō*, ed. Fukuma kōchō sensei kanreki kinenkai, 717–32. Kyoto: Nagata bunshodo, 1993.

———. "Kyōdōshokusei to kyōinsei." *Ryūkoku shidan* 15, no. 99–100 (1992): 463–78.

Fukasawa Hidetaka. "Anesaki Masaharu to kindai no 'shūkyō mondai: Anesaki no shūkyō riron to sono kontekusto." In *Kindai nihon ni okeru chishikijin to shūkyō*, ed. Isomae Jun'ichi and Fukasawa Hidetaka, 145–235. Tokyo: Tokyodo shuppan, 2002.

Fukushima Kanryū, ed. *Jinja mondai to shinshū*. Kyoto: Nagata Bunshodo, 1977.

———. "Shintō kokkyō seisakuka no shinshū." *Nihonshi kenkyū* 115 (1970): 83–104.

Fukuzawa Yukichi. *Bunmeiron no gairyaku*. Tokyo: Iwanami shoten, 1995.

———. "Gakumon no susume." In *Fukuzawa Yukichi zenshū*, vol. 3, 21–144. Tokyo: Iwanami shoten, 1959.

Furuya Tetsuo. "Teikoku gikai no seiritsu." In *Nihon gikai shiroku*, vol. 1, ed. Uchida Kenzō, Kanehara Samon, and Furuya Tetsuo, 1–58. Tokyo: Daiichi hoki shuppan, 1990.

Garon, Sheldon. *Molding Japanese Minds: The State in Everyday Life*. Princeton: Princeton University Press, 1997.

Gluck, Carol. *Japan's Modern Myths: Ideology in the Late-Meiji Period*. Princeton: Princeton University Press, 1985.

Gordon, Andrew. *Labor and Imperial Democracy in Prewar Japan*. Berkeley: University of California Press, 1991.

Grapard, Allan G. "Japan's Ignored Cultural Revolution: The Separation of Shinto and Buddhist Divinities in Meiji ('Shinbutsu Bunri') and a Case Study: Tonomine." *History of Religions* 23, no. 3 (February 1984): 240–65.

Griffis, William E. *Verbeck of Japan: A Citizen of No Country*. New York: Fleming H. Revell, 1900.

Gunma kenshi hensan iinkai, ed. *Gunma kenshi tsūshi-hen*, vol. 9: *Kindai gendai* 3. Maebashi: Gunma ken, 1990.

Haga Shōji. *Meiji ishin to shūkyō*. Tokyo: Chikuma shobo, 1994.

———. "Shintō kokkyōsei no keisei: senkyōshi to tennō kyōken." *Nihonshi kenkyū* 264 (1984): 1–31.

Hall, Ivan Parker. *Mori Arinori*. Cambridge, MA: Harvard University Press, 1973.

Hamaguchi Kiyoshi. "Meiji-zenki no tennōsei." *Jōkyō tokubetsugō* (July 1975): 13–29.

Hanawa Mizuhiko. *Kokkai kaisetsu zengo ni okeru jingikan kyōfuku undō*. Kazama-cho, Ibaraki: Kazama inari jinja shamujo, 1941.

Hara Takashi zenshū kankōkai, ed. *Hara Takashi zenshū*. 2 vols. Tokyo: Hara shobo, 1969.

Hara Takeshi. *"Izumo" to iu shisō: Kindai Nihon no massatsu sareta kamigami*. Tokyo: Kojinsha, 1996.

Hardacre, Helen. "Creating State Shinto: The Great Promulgation Campaign and New Religions." *Journal of Japanese Studies* 12, no. 1 (1986): 29–63.

———. *Religion and Society in Nineteenth-Century Japan*: A Study of the Southern Kantō Region, Using Late Edo and Early Meiji Gazetteers. Ann Arbor: Center for Japanese Studies, University of Michigan, 2002.

———. *Shinto and the State, 1868–1988*. Princeton: Princeton University Press, 1989.

———. "The Shinto Priesthood in Early Meiji Japan: A Preliminary Inquiry." *History of Religions* 27, no. 3 (1988): 294–320.

Harootunian, H. D. *Things Seen and Unseen: Discourse and Ideology in Tokugawa Nativism.* Chicago: University of Chicago Press, 1988.

Harris, Townsend. *The Complete Journal of Townsend Harris: The First American Consul and Minister to Japan.* Rutland, VT: Charles E. Tuttle Co., 1959.

Hayashi Makoto. "Shūmon kara shūkyō he: 'Shūkyō to rinri' zenshi." In *Iwanami kōza Shūkyō*, vol. 1: *Shūkyō to wa nanika*, ed. Ikegami Yoshimasa et al., 169–89. Tokyo: Iwanami shoten, 2003.

Hirano Takeshi. *Meiji kenpō seitei to sono shūhen.* Kyoto: Koyo shobo, 2004.

Hisaki Yukio. "Kunrei 12gō no shisō to genjitsu 1." *Yokohama kokuritsu daigaku kyōiku kiyō* 13 (1973): 1–23.

———. "Kunrei 12gō no shisō to genjitsu 2." *Yokohama kokuritsu daigaku kyōiku kiyō* 14 (1974): 34–49.

———. "Kunrei 12gō no shisō to genjitsu 3." *Yokohama kokuritsu daigaku kyōiku kiyō* 16 (1976): 69–90.

Hiyane Antei. *Nihon shūkyōshi.* Tokyo: Kyobunkan, 1951.

Hoare, J. E. *Japan's Treaty Ports and Foreign Settlements: The Uninvited Guests 1858–1899.* Folkstone, Kent, UK: Japan Library, 1994.

Holtom, D. C. *Modern Japan and Shinto Nationalism: A Study of Present-day Trends in Japanese Religions.* Chicago: University of Chicago Press, 1943.

Hoshino Mitsushige. "Bakumatsu ishinki ni okeru saisei itchi-kan: Aizawa Seishisai to kokugakusha wo megutte." In *Kokka shintō saikō: Saisei itchi kokka no keisei to tenkai*, ed. Sakamoto Koremaru, 93–119. Tokyo: Kobundo, 2006.

Hōten chōsakai. *Hōten chōsakai jin'in meibo.* Manuscript, Waseda University Library, n.d.

Howland, Douglas. *Translating the West: Language and Political Reason in Nineteenth-Century Japan.* Honolulu: University of Hawai'i Press, 2002.

Hur, Nam-lim. *Death and Social Order in Tokugawa Japan: Buddhism, Anti-Christianity, and the Danka System.* Cambridge, MA: Harvard University Asia Center, 2007.

Ichimura Shinichi. *Ibaraki no kokkai giin retsuden.* Ishioka-shi, Ibaraki: Ron shobo, 1990.

Iechika Yoshiki. *Urakami kirishitan ryūhai jiken: Kirisutokyō kaikin he no michi.* Tokyo: Yoshikawa kobunkan, 1998.

Inada Masatsugu. *Kyōiku chokugo seiritsu katei no kenkyū.* Tokyo: Kodansha, 1971.

———. *Meiji kenpō seiritsushi.* 2 vols. Tokyo: Yuhikaku, 1960–62.

Inoo Tentarō. "Bukkyōto gawa no naichi zakkyo hantai undō to sono shiryō ni tsuite." *Chūō daigaku bungakubu kiyō* 9 (September 1957): 35–50.

———, ed. *Naichi zakkyoron shiryō shūsei.* 6 vols. Tokyo: Hara shobo, 1992.

Inoue Egyō. *Shūkyō hōjinhō no kisoteki kenkyū.* Tokyo: Daiichi shobo, 1995.

Inoue Enryo. *Kyōikuka shūkyōka no naichi zakkyo junbi ni taisuru kokoroe.* Tokyo: Goto Kanjiro, 1897.

Inoue Kaoru kō denki hensankai, ed. *Segai Inoue kō den.* 5 vols. Tokyo: Hara shobo, 1968.

Inoue Katsuo. *Shirizu nihon kingendaishi*, vol. 1: *Bakumatsu-ishin.* Tokyo: Iwanami shoten, 2006.

Inoue Kowashi denki hensan iinkai, ed. *Inoue Kowashi den Shiryō-hen*. 6 vols. Tokyo: Kokugakuin daigaku toshokan, 1966–77.

Inoue Mizue, ed. *Ishin zengo tsuwanohanshi hōkō jiseki*. Tokyo: Aoyama Seikichi, 1900.

Inoue Nobutaka. *Kyōha shintō no keisei*. Tokyo: Kobundo, 1991.

Inoue Nobutaka and Sakamoto Koremaru, eds. *Nihongata seikyō kankei no tanjō*. Tokyo: Daiichi shobo, 1987.

Isomae Junichi. *Kindai nihon no shūkyō gensetsu to sono keifu: Shūkyō, kokka, shintō*. Tokyo: Iwanami shoten, 2003.

———. "Kindai ni okeru 'shūkyō' gainen no keisei katei." In *Iwanami kōza kindai nihon no bunkashi*, vol. 3: *Kindai chi no seiritsu*, ed. Komori Yōichi et al., 161–96. Tokyo: Iwanami shoten, 2002.

Itō Hirobumi. *Teikoku kenpō gikai*. Tokyo: Kokka gakkai, 1889.

Itō Yahiko. *Meiji ishin to jinshin*. Tokyo: Tokyo daigaku shuppankai, 1999.

Jaffe, Richard. "The Buddhist Cleric as Japanese Subject: Buddhism and the Household Registration System." In *New Directions in the Study of Meiji Japan*, ed. Helen Hardacre and Adam L. Kern, 506–30. Leiden: Brill, 1997.

———. "Meiji Religious Policy, Sōtō Zen, and the Clerical Marriage Problem." *Japanese Journal of Religious Studies* 25, no. 1–2 (1998): 45–85.

Jingiin and Zenkoku shinshokukai. *Jinjakyoku jidai wo kataru, Zenkoku shinshokukai enkaku shiyō*. Tokyo: Jinja Honcho kyogaku kenkyujo, 2004.

Jinja shinpōsha, ed. *Zōho kaitei Kindai jinja shintōshi*. Tokyo: Jinja shinposha, 1986.

Junshin joshi tanki daigaku nagasaki chihō bunkashi kenkyūjo, ed. *Puchijan shikyō shokanshū*. Nagasaki: Nagasaki joshi tankidaigaku, 1986.

———. *Yasokyō ni kansuru shorui*. Nagasaki: Seibo no kishisha, 1991.

Kamei Katsuichirō. "Giji shūkyō kokka." *Chūō kōron* 71, no. 10 (September 1956): 248–62.

Kano Masanao and Imai Osamu. "Nihon kindai shisōshi no nakano no Kume jiken." In *Kume Kunitake no kenkyū*, ed. Ōkubo Toshiaki, 201–316. Tokyo: Yoshikawa kobunkan, 1991.

Kanpō Meiji-hen. 24 vols. Tokyo: Ryūkei shosha, 1984–92.

Kashiwabara Yūsen. "Kinsei shinshū ni okeru jingi he no taiō." *Ryūkoku shidan* 73–74 (1978): 95–114.

Kataoka Yakichi. "Nakano Takeaki no kōchi junshi to Okumiya Zōsai no kirishitan kyōyu ni tsuite." *Kirishitan Kenkyū* no. 6 (1959): 151–83.

———. "Nihon kindai kokka kesei katei ni okeru imari-ken (Fukahori) ishūto isō jiken." *Kirishitan kenkyū* 4 (1957): 117–37.

———. *Nihon kirishitan junkyōshi*. Tokyo: Jiji tsushinsha, 1979.

———. *Urakami yoban kuzure: Meiji seifu no kirishitan danatsu*. Tokyo: Chikuma shobo, 1991.

Katō Genchi. *Jinja mondai no saikentō*. Tokyo: Yuzankaku shuppan, 1933.

———, ed. *Jinja tai shūkyō*. Tokyo: Meiji seitoku kinen gakkai, 1921.

Katō Hiroyuki. *Kokutai shinron*. In *Meiji shishōshū*, vol. 1, ed. Matsumoto Sannosuke, 76–94. Tokyo: Chikuma shobo, 1976.

Katsurajima Nobuhiro. *Bakumatsu minshū shisō no kenkyū: Bakumatsu kokugaku to minshū shūkyō*. Tokyo: Bunrikaku, 1992.

———. "Kai shisō no kaitai to jitaninshiki no henyō: Jyūhasseiki makki-jyūkyū seiki shotō wo chūshin ni." In *Kosumorojii no kinsei*, ed. Komori Yōichi et al., 237–72. Tokyo: Iwanami shoten, 2001.

———. "Kindai tennōsei ideologii no shisō katei." In *Tennō to ōken wo kangaeru*, vol. 5: *Shūkyō to ken'i*, ed. Amino Yoshihiko et al., 217–46. Tokyo: Iwanami shoten, 2002.

———. "Kyōha shintō no seiritsu: 'Shūkyō' to iu manazashi no seiritsu to konkōkyō." *Edo no shisō* 7 (1997): 7–28.

———. *Shisōshi no jyūkyūseiki: Tasha to shite no "Edo."* Tokyo: Perikansha, 1999.

Kawasaki Fumiaki. "Kaishū: Genroku, kyōhōki no minshū to shūkyō ishiki." In *Nihon bunkashi*, ed. Haga Kōshiro sensei koki kinen ronbunshū henshū iinkai, 221–43. Tokyo: Sasama shoin, 1980.

Ketelaar, James. *Of Heretics and Martyrs in Meiji Japan: Buddhism and Its Persecution.* Princeton: Princeton University Press, 1990.

Kido Takayoshi. *The Diary of Kido Takayoshi Volume I: 1868–1871.* Trans. Sidney Devere Brown and Akiko Hirota. Tokyo: University of Tokyo Press, 1983.

Kim, Kyu Hyun. *The Age of Visions and Arguments: Parliamentarianism and the National Public Sphere in Early Meiji Japan.* Cambridge, MA: Harvard University Asia Center, 2007.

Kino Kazue. *Inoue Kowashi kenkyū.* Tokyo: Zoku gunsho ruiju kanseikai, 1995.

Kinoshita Masahiro. *Ishin kyūbaku hikaku-ron.* Tokyo: Iwanami shoten, 1993.

Kitamura Keiichirō. *Tsūzoku shūkyō hōan shakugi.* Kyoto: Hozokan, 1900.

Kitsunezuka Yūko. "Kyōbushō no setchi to Etō Shinpei." In *Meiji nihon no seijika gunzō*, ed. Fukuchi Atsushi and Asaki Takashi, 138–70. Tokyo: Yoshikawa kobunkan, 1993.

Kleinen, Peter. "Nishi Hongan-ji and National Identity in Bakumatsu and Early Meiji Japan." In *Religious and National Identity in the Japanese Context*, ed. Klaus Antoni et al., 87–105. Münster: Lit, 2002.

Kobayashi Kazuyuki. "Dai niji Yamagata naikaku 'shūkyō hōan' wo meguru shosō." *Aoyama gakuindaigaku bungakubu kiyō* 29 (January 1987): 17–35.

———. "Meijiki no kizokuin to seigan." In *Nihon kindaishi no saikōchiku*, ed. Itō Takashi, 247–73. Tokyo: Degawa shuppansha, 1993.

———. "Meiji nijūnananen chōin no kaisei jōyaku jisshi junbi ni tsuite." *Nihon rekishi* 509 (October 1990): 58–75.

———. *Meiji rikken seiji to kizokuin.* Tokyo: Yoshikawa kobunkan, 2002.

Kojima Nobuyuki. "Meiji sanjūninen shūkyō hōanron no saikentō: 'Kyōkai,' 'tera,' 'kyōha,' 'shūha,' kitei no hōteki seikaku." *Shūkyō to shakai* 4 (1998): 25–47.

Kokugakuin daigaku nihon bunka kenkyūjo, ed. *Shaji torishirabe ruisan.* Tokyo: Kokugakuin daigaku nihon bunka kenkyujo, 1990.

Komiya Kazuo. *Jōyaku kaisei to kokunai seiji.* Tokyo: Yoshikawa kobunkan, 2001.

———. "Naichi zakkyo kōkyūkai to jōyaku kaisei mondai." *Nihon rekishi* 547 (December 1993): 59–74.

Konoe Atsumaro nikki kankōkai, ed. *Konoe Atsumaro nikki.* 6 vols. Tokyo: Kashima kenkyujo shuppankai, 1968–69.

Koschmann, J. Victor. *The Mito Ideology: Discourse, Reform, and Insurrection in Late Tokugawa Japan, 1790–1864.* Berkeley: University of California Press, 1987.

Kōtoku Shūsui. *Kirisuto massatsuron*. Tokyo: Heigo shuppan, 1911.

Kuga Katsunan. *Kuga Katsunan zenshū*. 10 vols. Tokyo: Misuzu shobo, 1968–85.

Kume Kunitake, comp. *The Iwakura Embassy, 1871–73: A True Account of the Ambassador Extraordinary & Plenipotentiary's Journal of Observation through the United States of America and Europe*. 5 vols. Ed. Graham Healy and Chushichi Tsuzuki. Chiba, Japan: Japan Documents. Distributed in North America by Princeton University Press, 2002.

———. "Shintō no hanashi." In *Kume Kunitake rekishi chosakushū*, vol. 3, 319–36. Tokyo: Yoshikawa kobunkan, 1990.

Kuroda Toshio. *Kuroda Toshio chosakushū*. 8 vols. Kyoto: Hozokan, 1994–95.

———. "Shinto in the History of Japanese Religion." *Journal of Japanese Studies* 7, no. 1 (1981): 1–21.

Kusumoto Masataka. *Jyūniken oazukari ishūto junshi gairyaku*. In *Yasokyō ni kansuru shorui*, ed. Junshin joshi tankidaigaku nagasaki chihō bunka kenkyūjo, 9–128. Nagasaki: Seibo no kishisha, 1991.

"Kyōbushō setchi ni tsuki sain kengi," in *NKST: STK*, 23–30.

Kyōgi shinbun. Repr. in *Meiji bukkyō shisō shiryō shūsei bekkan*, ed. Meiji bukkyō shisō shiryō shūsei henshū iinkai. Kyoto: Domeisha shuppan, 1982.

Lehmann, Jean-Pierre. "French Catholic Missionaries in Japan in the Bakumatsu and Early-Meiji Periods." *Modern Asian Studies* 13, no. 3 (1979): 377–400.

———. "Leon Roches—Diplomat Extraordinary in the Bakumatsu Era: An Assessment of His Personality and Policy." *Modern Asian Studies* 14, no. 2 (1980): 273–307.

Makihara Norio. *Meiji sichinen no daironsō: kenpakusho kara mita kindai kokka to minshū*. Tokyo: Nihon keizai hyoronsha, 1990.

Marnas, Francisque. *La "Religion de Jésus" (Iaso Ja-kyo) Ressuscitée au Japon dans la seconde moitié du XIXe siècle*. 2 vols. Paris: Delhomme et Briguet, 1896.

———. *Nihon kirisutokyō fukkatsushi*. Trans. Kuno Keiichirō. Tokyo: Misuzu shobo, 1985.

Matsumoto Takashi. "Kinsei ni okeru saisei itchi shisō no tenkai: Suika shintō yori mitogaku he." In *Kokka shintō saikō: Saisei itchi no keisei to tenkai*, ed. Sakamoto Koremaru, 39–64. Tokyo: Kobundo, 2006.

Matsuo Masato. "Meiji shoki dajōkan seido to sain." *Chuō shigaku* 4 (March 1981): 13–35.

Matsuzawa Hiroaki. "'Saigoku risshihen' to 'Jiyū no ri' no sekai." In *Nihon ni okeru seiyō seiji shisō*, ed. Nihon seiji gakkai, 9–53. Tokyo: Iwanami shoten, 1976.

Mayo, Marlene J. "A Catechism of Western Diplomacy: The Japanese and Hamilton Fish, 1872." *Journal of Asian Studies* 26, 3 (May 1967): 389–410.

McLeod, Hugh. "Protestantism and British National Identity, 1815–1945." In *Nation and Religion: Perspectives on Europe and Asia*, ed. Peter van der Veer and Hartmut Lehmann, 44–70. Princeton: Princeton University Press, 1999.

McNally, Mark. "The *Sandaikō* Debate: The Issue of Orthodoxy in Late Tokugawa Nativism." *Japanese Journal of Religious Studies* 29, no. 3–4 (2002): 359–78.

Meiji seijishi kenkyūkai, ed. *Kenpō kaishaku shiryō*. Tokyo: Nauka-sha, 1936.

Mimura Masashi. "Kōginin no sonzai keitei to kōgisho ni okeru 'giron': Mita-han wo jirei ni." *Rekishigaku kenkyū* 842 (July 2008): 33–44.

Minobe Tatsukichi. *Chikujō kenpō seigi.* Tokyo: Yuhikaku, 1927.

Mitsumata Shunji. *Kanazawa, daishōji, toyama ni nagasareta urakami kirishitan.* Nagasaki: Seibo no kishisha, 2000.

Miyachi Masato. *Kindai tennōsei no seijishiteki kenkyū.* Tokyo: Koso shobo, 1981.

———. "Kokka shintō keisei katei no mondaiten," in *NKST: STK*, 565–93.

Monbushō chōsakyoku, ed. *Shūkyō no teigi wo meguru shomondai.* Tokyo: Monbusho chosakyoku shumuka, 1961.

Mōri Yū. "Meiji ishin to shinshū shisō: minshū no negai to kyōdan kyōgaku." *Shinshūgaku* 51 (1974): 56–73.

Motoda Nagazane (Eifu). *Motoda Nagazane monjo.* 3 vols. Tokyo: Motoda monjo kenkyukai, 1969–70.

Motoda Sakunoshin. *Sankyō kaidō to kirisutokyō.* Kuwanachō, Mie: Torakuto kankokai, 1912.

Murakami Senjō, Tsuji Zennosuke, and Washio Junkei, eds. *Meiji ishin shinbutsu bunri shiryō.* 5 vols. Tokyo: Meicho Shuppan, 1970.

Murakami Shigeyoshi. *Kokka shintō.* Tokyo: Iwanami shoten, 1970.

———. *Kokka shintō to minshū shūkyō.* Tokyo: Yoshikawa kobunkan, 1982.

———. *Tennōsei kokka to shūkyō.* Tokyo: Nihon hyoronsha, 1986.

Murata Kakuzan. "Meiji shonen no tai yasokyō seisaku kō." In *Ōkura Kunihiko sensei kintei ronbunshū Kokushi ronsan*, ed. Ōkura Kunihiko sensei kintei ronbunshū hensan iinkai, 201–56. Yokohama: Kyukokai, 1942.

Murata Yasuo. *Shinbutsu bunri no chihōteki tenkai.* Tokyo: Yoshikawa Kobunkan, 1999.

Nakajima Michio. "Dai nihon teikoku kenpō dai nijūhachi-jō 'shinkō jiyū' kitei seiritsu no zenshi." *Nihonshi kenkyū* no. 168 (1976): 1–32.

———. "'Dai nihon teikoku kenpō' dai 28-jō 'shinkō jiyū' kitei no seiritsu katei." *Nara daigaku kiyō* 6 (1977): 127–39.

———. "'Meiji kenpō taisei' no kakuritsu to kokka no ideologii seisaku: Kokka shintō taisei no kakuritsu katei." *Nihonshi kenkyū* 176 (1977): 166–91.

———. "Meiji kokka to shūkyō: Inoue Kowashi no shūkyōkan, shūkyō seisaku no bunseki." *Rekishigaku kenkyū* 413 (1974): 34–5.

———. "Taikyō senpu undō to saijin ronsō: Kokka shintō taisei no kakuritsu to kindai tennōsei kokka no shihai ideologii." *Nihonshi kenkyū* 126 (1972): 45–57.

Nakamura Akira. "Kokugakusha ni okeru kyoka shiso no shoso: Urakami kirishitan mondai to 'kyo' no kanosei." In *Kokka shinto saikō: Saisei itchi kokka no keisei to tenkai*, ed. Sakamoto Koremaru, 121–54. Tokyo: Kobundo, 2006.

Nakamura Hiromu. *Senkyō to jyuyō: Meijiki kirisutokyō no kisoteki kenkyū.* Tokyo: Shibunkaku shuppan, 2000.

Nakamura Keiu. "Taiseijin no jōsho ni gisu," in *MBZ: SH*, 225–28.

Nakanishi Masayuki. *Ise no miyabito.* Tokyo: Kokusho kankokai, 1998.

Nakanishi Ushirō. *Naichi zakkyo to bukkyō no kankei.* Osaka: Shinshindo, 1894.

Nakano Takeaki. "Tokushima, Takamatsu, Matsuyama, Kōchi, Kagoshima junshi gairyaku." In *Yasokyō ni kansuru shorui*, ed. Junshin joshi tankidaigaku nagasaki chihō bunka kenkyūjo, 131–90. Nagasaki: Seibo no kishisha, 1991.

Nakanome Tōru. "Mori Arinori ni okeru 'bunmei' to shūkyō." *Nihon shūkyōshi kenkyū nenpō* 7 (1986): 18–41.

Nihon shiseki kyōkai, ed. *Iwakura Tomomi kankei monjo.* 8 vols. Tokyo: Tokyo daigaku shuppankai, 1983.

———, ed. *Kido Takayoshi monjo.* 8 vols. Tokyo: Tokyo daigaku shuppankai, 1971.

Nishida Nagao. *Nihon shintōshi kenkyū.* 10 vols. Tokyo: Kodansha, 1978–79.

Nishikawa Junji. "Meiji shonen ni okeru kyōkai kōsha no tenkai ni tsuite." *Shintō kenkyū* 4, no. 2–3 (1943): 129–45.

Nishikawa Makoto. "Meiji shonen no Aoki Shūzō: Meiji nananen zengo Kido-ha no kokka kōsō." In *Meiji kokka no seisaku to shisō*, ed. Inuzuka Takaaki, 33–57. Tokyo: Yoshikawa kobunkan, 2005.

Nitta Hitoshi. "Kindai seikyō kankei ni tsuite no ichi shiron." *Kōgakkan ronsō* 31, no. 1 (1998): 2–32.

———. "'Kokka shintō'-ron no keifu." *Kōgakkan ronsō* 32, no. 1 (February 1999): 1–36.

———. "'Kokka shintō'-ron no keifu." *Kōgakkan ronsō* 32, no. 2 (April 1999): 23–59.

———. "Meiji jūnana-nen no kōninkyō seido no saiyō ni kansuru ichi kōsatsu." *Kōgakkan daigaku shintō kenkyūjo kiyō* 7 (1991): 125–43.

———. "Meiji kenpō seiteiki no seikyō kankei: Inoue Kowashi no kōsō to naimushō no seisaku wo chūshin ni." In *Nihongata seikyō kankei no tanjō*, ed. Inoue Nobutaka and Sakamoto Koremaru, 145–98. Tokyo: Daiichi shobo, 1987.

———. "Shinto as a 'Non-religion': The Origins and Development of an Idea." In *Shinto in History: Ways of the Kami*, ed. John Breen and Mark Teeuwen, 252–69. Honolulu: University of Hawai'i Press, 2000.

Noma Ryōkū, ed. *Shūkyō hōan no tenmatsu: Dai jyūyon gikai.* Kyoto: Tsuge Shozaburo, 1900.

Nosco, Peter. "Keeping the Faith: *Bakuhan* Policy towards Religions in the Seventeenth-Century Japan." In *Religion in Japan: Arrows to Heaven and Earth*, ed. Peter Kornicki and James McMullen, 135–97. Cambridge: Cambridge University Press, 1996.

Ogawara Masamichi. "Meiji-ki ni okeru naichi zakkyo mondai to kirisutokō taisaku." In *Senzen nihon no seiji to shimin ishiki*, ed. Terasaki Osamu and Tamai Kiyoshi, 115–43. Tokyo: Keio gijiku daigaku shuppankai, 2005.

Okada Tsunesaburō, ed. *Shikyaku Nishino Buntarō no den.* Tokyo: Shoseki gyoshosha, 1889.

Ōkubo Toshiaki. *Iwakura shisetsu no kenkyū.* Tokyo: Munetaka shobo, 1976.

———. *Meirokusha.* Tokyo: Kodansha, 2007.

Ōkubo Toshimichi. "Osaka sento kenpakusho," in *NKST: TK*, 6–8.

Ōkuni Takamasa. "Shin-shinkōhōron," in *NST: HA*, 494–517.

———. "Shinto kyōsei ni tsuki ikensho," in *NKST: STK*, 7–10.

———. "Urakami mondai ni tsuki ikensho," in *NKST: STK*, 5–6.

Ono Masaaki. "Kumamoto eigakkō jiken no tenmatsu to kyōikukai." *Kyōikugaku zasshi* 28 (1994): 175–90.

Ono Nobuzane. *Shinkyō yōshi.* In *Shintō shisō meicho shūsei, chūkan, kokugakusha no shintō-hen*, vol. 2, ed. Ono Motonori, 469–70. Tokyo: Kokugakuin daigaku nihon bunka kenkyujo, 1972.

Ōta Yoshiko. "Senkyōshi no saitorai to kirisutokyō: Bakumatsu no urakami kirishitan Mondai." In *Kindai nihon no keisei to shūkyō mondai: Kaiteiban*, ed. Chūō daigaku jinbun kagaku kenkyūjo, 3–47. Tokyo: Chuo daigaku shuppanbu, 1992.

Ōtsu Jun'ichirō. *Dainihon kenseishi*. 10 vols. Tokyo: Hobunkan, 1927–28.

Ozaki Saburō. *Ozaki Saburō nikki*. 3 vols. Tokyo: Chuo koronsha, 1991–92.

Ozawa Osamu. "Minshū shūkyō to kokka." In *Kokken to minken no sōkoku*, ed. Emura Eiichi and Nakamura Masanori, 69–114. Tokyo: Sanshodo, 1974.

Pak Chinu. "Tenno junkyō kara mita tennō sūhai to minshū." In *Bakumatsu ishin no bunka*, ed. Haga Shoji, 321–55. Tokyo: Yoshikawa kobunkan, 2001.

Paolino, Ernest N. *The Foundations of the American Empire: William Henry Seward and U.S. Foreign Policy*. Ithaca: Cornell University Press, 1973.

Paramore, Kiri. *Ideology and Christianity in Japan*. Abingdon, UK: Routledge, 2009.

Pittau, Joseph. *Political Thought in Early Meiji Japan, 1868–1889*. Cambridge, MA: Harvard University Press, 1967.

Pye, Michael. "East Asian Rationality in the Exploration of Religion." In *Rationality and the Study of Religion*, ed. J. S. Jensen and L. H. Martin, 65–77. Aarhus, Denmark: Aarhus University Press, 1997.

Rogers, Minor L., and Ann T. Rogers. "The Honganji: Guardian of the State (1868–1945)." *Japanese Journal of Religious Studies* 17, no. 1 (1990): 3–28.

Ross, Ronald J. "The Kulturkampf: Restrictions and Controls on the Practice of Religion in Bismarck's Germany." In *Freedom and Religion in the Nineteenth Century*, ed. Richard Helmstadter, 172–95. Stanford: Stanford University Press, 1997.

Ruddy, Francis Stephen. *International Law in the Enlightenment: The Background of Emmerich de Vattel's Le Droit des Gens*. Dobbs Ferry, NY: Oceana Publications, 1975.

Ruxton, Ian. "Britain, 17 August–16 December 1872: The Missions' Aims, Objectives and Results." In *The Iwakura Mission in America and Europe: A New Assessment*, ed. Ian Nish, 54–68. Surrey, UK: Japan Library, 1998.

Saeki Tomohiro. "Meiji sanjūninen ni okeru jōyaku kaisei rongi to daiichiji shūkyō hōan." *Nihon bukkyō kyōiku kenkyū* 9 (March 2001): 33–64.

Saito Tomoo. *Inoue Kowashi to shūkyō: Meiji kokka keisei to sezoku shugi*. Tokyo: Kobundo, 2006.

Sakada Masatoshi. *Kindai nihon ni okeru taigaikō undō no kenkyū*. Tokyo: Tokyo daigaku shuppankai, 1978.

Sakaguchi Mitsuhiro. "Bakumatsu ishinki no haiyaron." *Kirisutokyo shakai mondai kenkyu* 37 (1989): 133–52.

Sakai Naoki. *Voices of the Past: The Status of Language in Eighteenth-Century Japanese Discourse*. Ithaca: Cornell University Press, 1991.

Sakamoto Kenichi. "Meiji Ishin to Tsuwano Hongaku." *Kokugakuin zasshi* 49, no. 4 (April 1943): 2–18.

———. *Meiji shintōshi no kenkyū*. Tokyo: Kokusho kankokai, 1983.

Sakamoto Koremaru. *Kindai no jinja shintō*. Tokyo: Kobundo, 2005.

———. *Kinsei kindai shintō ronkō*. Tokyo: Kobundo, 2007.

———. *Kokka shintō keisei katei no kenkyū*. Tokyo: Iwanami shoten, 1994.

———, ed. *Kokka shintoō saikō: Saisei itchi kokka no keisei to tenkai*. Tokyo: Kobundo, 2006.

———. "Kyōbushō setchi ni kansuru ichi kōsatsu: Shintō kokkyōka seisaku wo chūshin ni." *Kokugakuin daigaku nihon bunka kenkyujo kiyō* 44 (September 1979): 89–140.

———. "Meiji hachinen sain no kyōbushō shobunan." *Kokugakuin zasshi* 84, no. 11 (November 1983): 159–68.

———. *Meiji ishin to kokugakusha*. Tokyo: Taimeido, 1993.

———. "Meiji zenki no seikyō kankei to Inoue Kowashi: Kirisutokyō, bukkyō no shobun wo megutte." In *Meiji kokka keisei to Inoue Kowashi*, ed. Kokugakuin daigaku goin bunko kenkyukai, 159–202. Tokyo: Bokutakusha, 1992.

———. "Nihongata seikyōkankei no keisei katei." In *Nihongata seikyō kankei no tanjō*, ed. Inoue Nobutaka and Sakamoto Koremaru, 5–82. Tokyo: Daiichi shobo, 1987.

———. "The Structure of State Shinto: Its Creation, Development and Demise." In *Shinto in History: Ways of the Kami*, ed. John Breen and Mark Teeuwen, 272–92. Honolulu: University of Hawai'i Press, 2000.

Sakurai Masashi. *Meiji shūkyōshi kenkyū*. Tokyo: Shunjusha, 1971.

Sasaki Kiyoshi. "Shintō hishūkyō kara jinja hishūkyō he." *Nihon daigaku seishinbunka kenkyūjo kyōiku seido kenkyūjo kiyō* 16 (1986): 89–96.

Sasaki Takashi. *Hanbatsu seifu to rikken seiji*. Tokyo: Yoshikawa kobunkan, 1992.

Sasaki Takayuki. *Hogohiroi: Sasaki Takayuki nikki*. 9 vols. Tokyo: Tokyo daigaku shuppankai, 1970–79.

Satow, Ernest M. *A Diplomat in Japan*. Philadelphia: Lippincott, 1921.

Sawada, Janine Tasca. *Practical Pursuits: Religion, Politics, Personal Cultivation in Nineteenth-Century Japan*. Honolulu: University of Hawai'i Press, 2004.

Shigaraki Takamaro. "Kindai Shinshū Kyōgaku ni okeru shinzoku nitai-ron no shosetsu." In *Kindai shinshū shisōshi kenkyū*, ed. Shigaraki Takamaro, 7–88. Kyoto: Hozokan, 1988.

———. "Shinshū ni okeru shinzoku nitai-ron no kenkyū." *Ryūkoku daigaku ronshū* 418 (1981): 44–67.

Shigeru Yoshiki. "Kumamoto eigakkō jiken wo megutte." *Kirisutokyō shakaimondai kenkyū* 37 (1989): 153–67.

Shimazono Susumu. *Kokka shintō to nihonjin*. Tokyo: Iwanami shoten, 2010.

———. "'Shūkyō' to 'Religion.'" *Yūkyū* 87 (2001): 51–62.

———. "State Shinto in the Lives of the People: The Establishment of Emperor Worship, Modern Nationalism, and Shrine Shinto in Late Meiji." *Japanese Journal of Religious Studies* 36, no. 1 (2009): 93–124.

Shimizu Hirokazu. "Nagasaki saibansho no urakami kyōto shobunan wo megutte." In *Kindai nihon no keisei to shūkyō mondai*, ed. Chuo daigaku jinbunkagaku kenkyujo, 49–87. Tokyo: Chuo daigaku shuppanbu, 1993.

Shimizu Isao. *Meiji manga uūransen*. Tokyo: Bungei shunju, 1980.

Shimizu Shin. *Meiji kenpō seiteishi*, vol. 1. Tokyo: Hara shobo, 1971.

Shōyū kurabu Yamagata Aritomo kankei monjo hensan iinkai, ed. *Yamagata Aritomo kankei monjo*. 3 vols. Tokyo: Shoyu kurabu, 2004–.

Shunpokō tsuishōkai, ed. *Itō Hirobumi-den*. 3 vols. Tokyo: Toseisha, 1944.

Sims, Richard. *Japanese Political History since the Meiji Renovation, 1868–2000*. London: Hurst and Co., 2000.

Smith, Helmut Walser. *German Nationalism and Religious Conflict: Culture, Ideology, Politics, 1870–1914*. Princeton: Princeton University Press, 1995.

Soeda Yoshiya. *Naimushō no shakaishi*. Tokyo: Tokyo daigaku shuppankai, 2005.

Sugii Rokurō. "Ozawa Saburō-hen Nihon purotesutantoshi shiryō (5) 'monbushō kunrei dai jyūnigō' to sono hankyō (kan)." *Kirisutokyō shakai mondai kenkyū* 24 (March 1976): 174–259.

Suzue Eiichi. *Kirisutokyō kaikin izen: Kirishitan kinsei kōsatsu tekkyo no shiryōron*. Tokyo: Iwata shoin, 2000.

Suzuki Norihisa. *Meiji shūkyō shichō no kenkyū: Shūkyōgaku kotohajime*. Tokyo: Tokyo daigaku shuppankai, 1979.

———. *Uchimura Kanzō nichoroku: Ichikō fukei jiken*. Tokyo: Kyobunkan, 1993.

Takagi Hiroshi. "Shintō kokkyōka seisaku hōkaikatei no seijishiteki kōsatsu." *Hisutoria* 104 (1984): 38–60.

Takagi Kazuo. *Meiji katorikku kyōkaishi kenkyū*. 3 vols. Tokyo: Kirishitan bunka kenkyūkai, 1978–80.

Takechi Masaaki. "Meiji shonen no Nagasaki ni okeru taikyō senpu undō ni tsuite: Nishikawa Yoshisuke nikki no bunseki kara." *Nihon shisōshi kenkyūkai kaihō* 20 (2003): 236–49.

Takeda Hideaki. *Ishinki tennō saishi no kenkyū*. Tokyo: Taimeido, 1996.

Tamamuro Taijō and Morioka Kiyomi. "Meiji ishin to bukkyō." In *Nihon bukkyōshi*, vol. 3, ed. Tamamuro Taijō et al. Kyoto: Hozokan, 1967.

Tanaka Fujimaro. *Riji kōtei*. Tokyo: Monbusho, 1874.

Tanigawa Yutaka. "Meiji chūki ni okeru bukkyōsha no zokujin kyōiku." *Jinbun gakuhō* 94 (2007): 37–76.

———. *Meiji zenki no kyōiku, kyōka, bukkyō*. Kyoto: Shibunkaku, 2008.

Thal, Sarah. *Rearranging the Landscape of the Gods: The Politics of a Pilgrimage Site in Japan, 1573–1912*. Chicago: University of Chicago Press, 2005.

Tokoyo Nagatane. *Shinkyō soshiki monogatari*, in *NKST: STK*, 361–422.

Tokushige Asakichi. *Ishin seiji shūkyōshi kenkyū*. Tokyo: Rekishi toshosha, 1974.

Tokutomi Iichirō, ed. *Kōshaku Yamagata Aritomo den*. 3 vols. Tokyo: Yamagata Aritomo ko kinen jigyokai, 1933.

Tomes, Robert. *The Americans in Japan: An Abridgement of the Government Narrative of the U.S. Expedition to Japan under Commodore Perry*. Wilmington, DE: Scholarly Resources, 1873.

Toriumi Yasushi. "Hanbatsu tai mintō." In *Nihon gikai shiroku*, vol. 1, ed. Uchida Kenzō, Kanehara Samon, and Furuya Tetsuo, 61–140. Tokyo: Daiichi hoki shuppan, 1990.

Toyoda Takeshi. *Shūkyō seidoshi*. Tokyo: Yoshikawa Kobunkan, 1982.

Tozawa Yukio. *Meirokusha no hitobito*. Tokyo: Tsukiji shokan, 1991.

Tsang, Carol Richmond. *War and Faith: Ikkō Ikki in Late Muromachi Japan*. Cambridge, MA: Harvard University Asia Center, 2007.

Tsuda Shigemaro. *Meiji seijō to shin Takayuki*. Tokyo: Hara shobo, 1970.

Tsuji Zennosuke. *Meiji bukkyōshi no mondai*. Tokyo: Ritsubun shoin, 1949.

Uchida Kenzō, Kanehara Samon, and Furuya Tetsuo, eds. *Nihon gikai shiroku*, vol. 1. Tokyo: Daiichi hoki shuppan, 1990.

Ueda Kenji. "Ōkuni Takamasa no shisōtaikei to sono kihonseikaku: Jo." *Shinto shūkyō*, 7 (1954): 36–55.

Ukai Shin'ichi. *Chōya shinbun no kenkyū*. Tokyo: Misuzu shobo, 1985.

Umeda Yoshihiko. *Kaitei zōho nihon shūkyō seido-shi*. 4 vols. Tokyo: Tosen Shuppan, 1971–72.

Umegaki, Michio. *After the Restoration: The Beginning of Japan's Modern State*. New York: New York University Press, 1988.

Uno Shunichi. "Mintō no tankan to Nisshin sengo keiei." In *Nihon gikai shiroku*, vol. 1, ed. Uchida Kenzō, Kanehara Samon, and Furuya Tetsuo, 143–45. Tokyo: Daiichi hoki shuppan, 1990.

Urakawa Wasaburō. *Kirishitan no fukkatsu*, 2 vols. Tokyo: Kokusho kankōkai, 1979.

Van Hecken, Joseph L. *The Catholic Church in Japan since 1859*. Tokyo: Herder Agency, 1963.

Veer, Peter van der, ed. *Conversion to Modernities: The Globalization of Christianity*. New York: Routledge, 1996.

Veer, Peter van der, and Hartmut Lehmann. *Nation and Religion: Perspectives on Europe and Asia*. Princeton: Princeton University Press, 1999.

Viswanathan, Gauri. *Outside the Fold: Modernity, Conversion, and Belief*. Princeton: Princeton University Press, 1998.

Wakabayashi, Bob Tadashi. *Anti-Foreignism and Western Learning: The New Theses of 1825*. Cambridge, MA: Council on East Asian Studies, Harvard University, 1986.

Walthall, Anne. *The Weak Body of a Useless Woman: Matsuo Taseko and the Meiji Restoration*. Chicago: University of Chicago Press, 1998.

Watanabe Heikichi. *Shūkyō hōan zassan*. Tokyo: Rikugokan, 1900.

Wattenberg, Ulrich. "Germany: 7–28 March, 15–17 April, 1–8 May 1873." In *The Iwakura Mission in America and Europe: A New Assessment*, ed. Ian Nish, 71–79. Surrey, UK: Japan Library, 1998.

Webb, R. K. "The Limits of Religious Liberty: Theology and Criticism in Nineteenth-Century England." In *Freedom and Religion in the Nineteenth Century*, ed. Richard Helmstadter, 120–49. Stanford: Stanford University Press, 1997.

Werf, Arjan van der. "Deliberate Non-Communication: The Influence of the Religious Issue on the Diplomatic Talks during the Visit of the Iwakura Delegation to Belgium." In *Turning Points in Japanese History*, ed. Bert Edström, 57–70. Richmond: Japan Library, 2002.

Yamada Toshizō and Ōsumi Toyojirō. *Kinsei jijō*. 13 vols. Tokyo: Yamada Toshizō, 1873–76.

Yamagata Aritomo kankei monjo. Kensei shiryōshitsu, Kokuritsu kokkai toshokan.

Yamaguchi Teruomi. *Meiji kokka to shūkyō*. Tokyo: Tokyo daigaku shuppankai, 1999.

Yamane Seiji. "Meiji-zenki shūkyō seisaku ni tsuite no ichi kōsatsu." *Konkō kyōgaku* 21 (1981): 104–7.

Yamazaki Minako. *Iwakura shisetsudan ni okeru shūkyō mondai*. Kyoto: Shibunkaku, 2006.

———. "Iwakura shisetsudan to shinkō jiyū mondai," *Nihon rekishi* 391 (1980): 53–70.

———. "Kume Kunitake to kirisutokyō." In *Kume Kunitake no kenkyū*, ed. Ōkubo Toshiaki, 159–200. Tokyo: Yoshikawa kobunkan, 1991.

Yamazaki Yūkō. "'Kōgi' chūshutsu kikō no keisei to hōkai: Kōgisho to shūgiin." In *Nihon kindaishi no saikōchiku*, ed. Itō Takashi, 50–76. Tokyo: Degawa shuppansha, 1993.

Yasumaru Yoshio. *Ikki, kangoku, kosumologii: Shūensei no rekishigaku.* Tokyo: Asahi shinbunsha, 1999.

———. *Kamigami no meiji ishin: Shinbutsu bunri to haibutsu kishaku.* Tokyo: Iwanami shoten, 1979.

———. "Kindai tenkanki ni okeru shūkyō to kokka," in *NKST: STK,* 490–564.

———. *Kindai tennōzō no keisei.* Tokyo: Iwanami Shoten, 2001.

———. "Minshū shūkyō to 'kindai' to iu keiken." In *Bunmeika no keiken: kindai tenkanki no Nihon,* 337–62. Tokyo: Iwanami shoten, 2007.

Yasuoka Akio. "Iwakura shisetsu to shūkyō mondai." In *Kindai nihon no keisei to shūkyō mondai,* ed. Chuo daigaku jinbunkagaku kenkyujo, 235–68. Tokyo: Chuo daigaku shuppanbu, 1993.

Yoshida Kyūichi. *Nihon kindai bukkyōshi kenkyū.* Tokyo: Kawajima shoten, 1992.

Yūki Ryōgo et al., eds. *Saigo no hakugai.* Kobe: Rokkō shuppan, 1999.

Zenkoku shinshokukai, ed. *Zenkoku shinshokukai enkaku shiyō.* Tokyo: Zenkoku shinshokukai, 1935.

Index

Italic page numbers refer to figures.

Harvard East Asian Monographs
(titles now in print)

7. Chao Kuo-chün, *Economic Planning and Organization in Mainland China: A Documentary Study, 1949–1957*
13. S. M. Meng, *The Tsungli Yamen: Its Organization and Functions*
31. Madeleine Chi, *China Diplomacy, 1914–1918*
36. Peter Frost, *The Bakumatsu Currency Crisis*
38. Robert R. Campbell, *James Duncan Campbell: A Memoir by His Son*
39. Jerome Alan Cohen, ed., *The Dynamics of China's Foreign Relations*
40. V. V. Vishnyakova-Akimova, *Two Years in Revolutionary China, 1925–1927*, trans. Steven L. Levine
41. Meron Medzini, *French Policy in Japan during the Closing Years of the Tokugawa Regime*
46. W. P. J. Hall, *A Bibliographical Guide to Japanese Research on the Chinese Economy, 1958–1970*
47. Jack J. Gerson, *Horatio Nelson Lay and Sino-British Relations, 1854–1864*
48. Paul Richard Bohr, *Famine and the Missionary: Timothy Richard as Relief Administrator and Advocate of National Reform*
50. Britten Dean, *China and Great Britain: The Diplomacy of Commercial Relations, 1860–1864*
51. Ellsworth C. Carlson, *The Foochow Missionaries, 1847–1880*
53. Richard M. Pfeffer, *Understanding Business Contracts in China, 1949–1963*
55. Ranbir Vohra, *Lao She and the Chinese Revolution*
60. Noriko Kamachi, John K. Fairbank, and Chūzō Ichiko, *Japanese Studies of Modern China Since 1953: A Bibliographical Guide to Historical and Social-Science Research on the Nineteenth and Twentieth Centuries, Supplementary Volume for 1953–1969*
61. Donald A. Gibbs and Yun-chen Li, *A Bibliography of Studies and Translations of Modern Chinese Literature, 1918–1942*
62. Robert H. Silin, *Leadership and Values: The Organization of Large-Scale Taiwanese Enterprises*
63. David Pong, *A Critical Guide to the Kwangtung Provincial Archives Deposited at the Public Record Office of London*

69. Eric Widmer, *The Russian Ecclesiastical Mission in Peking during the Eighteenth Century*
73. Jon Sigurdson, *Rural Industrialism in China*
74. Kang Chao, *The Development of Cotton Textile Production in China*
75. Valentin Rabe, *The Home Base of American China Missions, 1880–1920*
78. Meishi Tsai, *Contemporary Chinese Novels and Short Stories, 1949–1974: An Annotated Bibliography*
80. Endymion Wilkinson, *Landlord and Labor in Late Imperial China: Case Studies from Shandong by Jing Su and Luo Lun*
84. J. W. Dower, *Empire and Aftermath: Yoshida Shigeru and the Japanese Experience, 1878–1954*
85. Martin Collcutt, *Five Mountains: The Rinzai Zen Monastic Institution in Medieval Japan*
86. Kwang Suk Kim and Michael Roemer, *Growth and Structural Transformation*
89. Sung Hwan Ban, Pal Yong Moon, and Dwight H. Perkins, *Rural Development*
92. Edward S. Mason, Dwight H. Perkins, Kwang Suk Kim, David C. Cole, Mahn Je Kim et al., *The Economic and Social Modernization of the Republic of Korea*
93. Robert Repetto, Tai Hwan Kwon, Son-Ung Kim, Dae Young Kim, John E. Sloboda, and Peter J. Donaldson, *Economic Development, Population Policy, and Demographic Transition in the Republic of Korea*
94. Parks M. Coble, Jr., *The Shanghai Capitalists and the Nationalist Government, 1927–1937*
96. Richard Wich, *Sino-Soviet Crisis Politics: A Study of Political Change and Communication*
97. Lillian M. Li, *China's Silk Trade: Traditional Industry in the Modern World, 1842–1937*
98. R. David Arkush, *Fei Xiaotong and Sociology in Revolutionary China*
100. James Reeve Pusey, *China and Charles Darwin*
101. Hoyt Cleveland Tillman, *Utilitarian Confucianism: Chen Liang's Challenge to Chu Hsi*
102. Thomas A. Stanley, *Ōsugi Sakae, Anarchist in Taishō Japan: The Creativity of the Ego*
103. Jonathan K. Ocko, *Bureaucratic Reform in Provincial China: Ting Jih-ch'ang in Restoration Kiangsu, 1867–1870*
104. James Reed, *The Missionary Mind and American East Asia Policy, 1911–1915*
105. Neil L. Waters, *Japan's Local Pragmatists: The Transition from Bakumatsu to Meiji in the Kawasaki Region*
106. David C. Cole and Yung Chul Park, *Financial Development in Korea, 1945–1978*
107. Roy Bahl, Chuk Kyo Kim, and Chong Kee Park, *Public Finances during the Korean Modernization Process*
108. William D. Wray, *Mitsubishi and the N.Y.K., 1870–1914: Business Strategy in the Japanese Shipping Industry*
109. Ralph William Huenemann, *The Dragon and the Iron Horse: The Economics of Railroads in China, 1876–1937*
111. Jane Kate Leonard, *Wei Yüan and China's Rediscovery of the Maritime World*
117. Andrew Gordon, *The Evolution of Labor Relations in Japan: Heavy Industry, 1853–1955*

119. Christine Guth Kanda, *Shinzō: Hachiman Imagery and Its Development*
121. Chang-tai Hung, *Going to the People: Chinese Intellectual and Folk Literature, 1918–1937*
123. Richard von Glahn, *The Country of Streams and Grottoes: Expansion, Settlement, and the Civilizing of the Sichuan Frontier in Song Times*
124. Steven D. Carter, *The Road to Komatsubara: A Classical Reading of the Renga Hyakuin*
126. Bob Tadashi Wakabayashi, *Anti-Foreignism and Western Learning in Early-Modern Japan: The "New Theses" of 1825*
127. Atsuko Hirai, *Individualism and Socialism: The Life and Thought of Kawai Eijirō (1891–1944)*
129. R. Kent Guy, *The Emperor's Four Treasuries: Scholars and the State in the Late Chien-lung Era*
130. Peter C. Perdue, *Exhausting the Earth: State and Peasant in Hunan, 1500–1850*
131. Susan Chan Egan, *A Latterday Confucian: Reminiscences of William Hung (1893–1980)*
132. James T. C. Liu, *China Turning Inward: Intellectual-Political Changes in the Early Twelfth Century*
134. Kate Wildman Nakai, *Shogunal Politics: Arai Hakuseki and the Premises of Tokugawa Rule*
137. Susan Downing Videen, *Tales of Heichū*
138. Heinz Morioka and Miyoko Sasaki, *Rakugo: The Popular Narrative Art of Japan*
139. Joshua A. Fogel, *Nakae Ushikichi in China: The Mourning of Spirit*
140. Alexander Barton Woodside, *Vietnam and the Chinese Model: A Comparative Study of Vietnamese and Chinese Government in the First Half of the Nineteenth Century*
141. George Elison, *Deus Destroyed: The Image of Christianity in Early Modern Japan*
144. Marie Anchordoguy, *Computers, Inc.: Japan's Challenge to IBM*
146. Mary Elizabeth Berry, *Hideyoshi*
147. Laura E. Hein, *Fueling Growth: The Energy Revolution and Economic Policy in Postwar Japan*
148. Wen-hsin Yeh, *The Alienated Academy: Culture and Politics in Republican China, 1919–1937*
149. Dru C. Gladney, *Muslim Chinese: Ethnic Nationalism in the People's Republic*
150. Merle Goldman and Paul A. Cohen, eds., *Ideas Across Cultures: Essays on Chinese Thought in Honor of Benjamin L Schwartz*
151. James M. Polachek, *The Inner Opium War*
152. Gail Lee Bernstein, *Japanese Marxist: A Portrait of Kawakami Hajime, 1879–1946*
154. Mark Mason, *American Multinationals and Japan: The Political Economy of Japanese Capital Controls, 1899–1980*
155. Richard J. Smith, John K. Fairbank, and Katherine F. Bruner, *Robert Hart and China's Early Modernization: His Journals, 1863–1866*
157. William Wayne Farris, *Heavenly Warriors: The Evolution of Japan's Military, 500–1300*
159. James B. Palais, *Politics and Policy in Traditional Korea*
161. Roger R. Thompson, *China's Local Councils in the Age of Constitutional Reform, 1898–1911*

162. William Johnston, *The Modern Epidemic: History of Tuberculosis in Japan*
163. Constantine Nomikos Vaporis, *Breaking Barriers: Travel and the State in Early Modern Japan*
164. Irmela Hijiya-Kirschnereit, *Rituals of Self-Revelation: Shishōsetsu as Literary Genre and Socio-Cultural Phenomenon*
165. James C. Baxter, *The Meiji Unification through the Lens of Ishikawa Prefecture*
166. Thomas R. H. Havens, *Architects of Affluence: The Tsutsumi Family and the Seibu-Saison Enterprises in Twentieth-Century Japan*
167. Anthony Hood Chambers, *The Secret Window: Ideal Worlds in Tanizaki's Fiction*
168. Steven J. Ericson, *The Sound of the Whistle: Railroads and the State in Meiji Japan*
169. Andrew Edmund Goble, *Kenmu: Go-Daigo's Revolution*
170. Denise Potrzeba Lett, *In Pursuit of Status: The Making of South Korea's "New" Urban Middle Class*
171. Mimi Hall Yiengpruksawan, *Hiraizumi: Buddhist Art and Regional Politics in Twelfth-Century Japan*
173. Aviad E. Raz, *Riding the Black Ship: Japan and Tokyo Disneyland*
174. Deborah J. Milly, *Poverty, Equality, and Growth: The Politics of Economic Need in Postwar Japan*
175. See Heng Teow, *Japan's Cultural Policy toward China, 1918–1931: A Comparative Perspective*
176. Michael A. Fuller, *An Introduction to Literary Chinese*
177. Frederick R. Dickinson, *War and National Reinvention: Japan in the Great War, 1914–1919*
178. John Solt, *Shredding the Tapestry of Meaning: The Poetry and Poetics of Kitasono Katue (1902–1978)*
179. Edward Pratt, *Japan's Protoindustrial Elite: The Economic Foundations of the Gōnō*
180. Atsuko Sakaki, *Recontextualizing Texts: Narrative Performance in Modern Japanese Fiction*
181. Soon-Won Park, *Colonial Industrialization and Labor in Korea: The Onoda Cement Factory*
182. JaHyun Kim Haboush and Martina Deuchler, *Culture and the State in Late Chosŏn Korea*
183. John W. Chaffee, *Branches of Heaven: A History of the Imperial Clan of Sung China*
184. Gi-Wook Shin and Michael Robinson, eds., *Colonial Modernity in Korea*
185. Nam-lin Hur, *Prayer and Play in Late Tokugawa Japan: Asakusa Sensōji and Edo Society*
186. Kristin Stapleton, *Civilizing Chengdu: Chinese Urban Reform, 1895–1937*
187. Hyung Il Pai, *Constructing "Korean" Origins: A Critical Review of Archaeology, Historiography, and Racial Myth in Korean State-Formation Theories*
188. Brian D. Ruppert, *Jewel in the Ashes: Buddha Relics and Power in Early Medieval Japan*
189. Susan Daruvala, *Zhou Zuoren and an Alternative Chinese Response to Modernity*
191. Kerry Smith, *A Time of Crisis: Japan, the Great Depression, and Rural Revitalization*
192. Michael Lewis, *Becoming Apart: National Power and Local Politics in Toyama, 1868–1945*

193. William C. Kirby, Man-houng Lin, James Chin Shih, and David A. Pietz, eds., *State and Economy in Republican China: A Handbook for Scholars*
194. Timothy S. George, *Minamata: Pollution and the Struggle for Democracy in Postwar Japan*
195. Billy K. L. So, *Prosperity, Region, and Institutions in Maritime China: The South Fukien Pattern, 946–1368*
196. Yoshihisa Tak Matsusaka, *The Making of Japanese Manchuria, 1904–1932*
197. Maram Epstein, *Competing Discourses: Orthodoxy, Authenticity, and Engendered Meanings in Late Imperial Chinese Fiction*
199. Haruo Iguchi, *Unfinished Business: Ayukawa Yoshisuke and U.S.-Japan Relations, 1937–1952*
200. Scott Pearce, Audrey Spiro, and Patricia Ebrey, *Culture and Power in the Reconstitution of the Chinese Realm, 200–600*
201. Terry Kawashima, *Writing Margins: The Textual Construction of Gender in Heian and Kamakura Japan*
202. Martin W. Huang, *Desire and Fictional Narrative in Late Imperial China*
203. Robert S. Ross and Jiang Changbin, eds., *Re-examining the Cold War: U.S.-China Diplomacy, 1954–1973*
204. Guanhua Wang, *In Search of Justice: The 1905–1906 Chinese Anti-American Boycott*
205. David Schaberg, *A Patterned Past: Form and Thought in Early Chinese Historiography*
206. Christine Yano, *Tears of Longing: Nostalgia and the Nation in Japanese Popular Song*
207. Milena Doleželová-Velingerová and Oldřich Král, with Graham Sanders, eds., *The Appropriation of Cultural Capital: China's May Fourth Project*
208. Robert N. Huey, *The Making of 'Shinkokinshū'*
209. Lee Butler, *Emperor and Aristocracy in Japan, 1467–1680: Resilience and Renewal*
210. Suzanne Ogden, *Inklings of Democracy in China*
211. Kenneth J. Ruoff, *The People's Emperor: Democracy and the Japanese Monarchy, 1945–1995*
212. Haun Saussy, *Great Walls of Discourse and Other Adventures in Cultural China*
213. Aviad E. Raz, *Emotions at Work: Normative Control, Organizations, and Culture in Japan and America*
214. Rebecca E. Karl and Peter Zarrow, eds., *Rethinking the 1898 Reform Period: Political and Cultural Change in Late Qing China*
215. Kevin O'Rourke, *The Book of Korean Shijo*
216. Ezra F. Vogel, ed., *The Golden Age of the U.S.-China-Japan Triangle, 1972–1989*
217. Thomas A. Wilson, ed., *On Sacred Grounds: Culture, Society, Politics, and the Formation of the Cult of Confucius*
218. Donald S. Sutton, *Steps of Perfection: Exorcistic Performers and Chinese Religion in Twentieth-Century Taiwan*
219. Daqing Yang, *Technology of Empire: Telecommunications and Japanese Expansionism in Asia, 1883–1945*
220. Qianshen Bai, *Fu Shan's World: The Transformation of Chinese Calligraphy in the Seventeenth Century*

221. Paul Jakov Smith and Richard von Glahn, eds., *The Song-Yuan-Ming Transition in Chinese History*
222. Rania Huntington, *Alien Kind: Foxes and Late Imperial Chinese Narrative*
223. Jordan Sand, *House and Home in Modern Japan: Architecture, Domestic Space, and Bourgeois Culture, 1880–1930*
224. Karl Gerth, *China Made: Consumer Culture and the Creation of the Nation*
225. Xiaoshan Yang, *Metamorphosis of the Private Sphere: Gardens and Objects in Tang-Song Poetry*
226. Barbara Mittler, *A Newspaper for China? Power, Identity, and Change in Shanghai's News Media, 1872–1912*
227. Joyce A. Madancy, *The Troublesome Legacy of Commissioner Lin: The Opium Trade and Opium Suppression in Fujian Province, 1820s to 1920s*
228. John Makeham, *Transmitters and Creators: Chinese Commentators and Commentaries on the Analects*
229. Elisabeth Köll, *From Cotton Mill to Business Empire: The Emergence of Regional Enterprises in Modern China*
230. Emma Teng, *Taiwan's Imagined Geography: Chinese Colonial Travel Writing and Pictures, 1683–1895*
231. Wilt Idema and Beata Grant, *The Red Brush: Writing Women of Imperial China*
232. Eric C. Rath, *The Ethos of Noh: Actors and Their Art*
233. Elizabeth Remick, *Building Local States: China during the Republican and Post-Mao Eras*
234. Lynn Struve, ed., *The Qing Formation in World-Historical Time*
235. D. Max Moerman, *Localizing Paradise: Kumano Pilgrimage and the Religious Landscape of Premodern Japan*
236. Antonia Finnane, *Speaking of Yangzhou: A Chinese City, 1550–1850*
237. Brian Platt, *Burning and Building: Schooling and State Formation in Japan, 1750–1890*
238. Gail Bernstein, Andrew Gordon, and Kate Wildman Nakai, eds., *Public Spheres, Private Lives in Modern Japan, 1600–1950: Essays in Honor of Albert Craig*
239. Wu Hung and Katherine R. Tsiang, *Body and Face in Chinese Visual Culture*
240. Stephen Dodd, *Writing Home: Representations of the Native Place in Modern Japanese Literature*
241. David Anthony Bello, *Opium and the Limits of Empire: Drug Prohibition in the Chinese Interior, 1729–1850*
242. Hosea Hirata, *Discourses of Seduction: History, Evil, Desire, and Modern Japanese Literature*
243. Kyung Moon Hwang, *Beyond Birth: Social Status in the Emergence of Modern Korea*
244. Brian R. Dott, *Identity Reflections: Pilgrimages to Mount Tai in Late Imperial China*
245. Mark McNally, *Proving the Way: Conflict and Practice in the History of Japanese Nativism*
246. Yongping Wu, *A Political Explanation of Economic Growth: State Survival, Bureaucratic Politics, and Private Enterprises in the Making of Taiwan's Economy, 1950–1985*
247. Kyu Hyun Kim, *The Age of Visions and Arguments: Parliamentarianism and the National Public Sphere in Early Meiji Japan*

248. Zvi Ben-Dor Benite, *The Dao of Muhammad: A Cultural History of Muslims in Late Imperial China*
249. David Der-wei Wang and Shang Wei, eds., *Dynastic Crisis and Cultural Innovation: From the Late Ming to the Late Qing and Beyond*
250. Wilt L. Idema, Wai-yee Li, and Ellen Widmer, eds., *Trauma and Transcendence in Early Qing Literature*
251. Barbara Molony and Kathleen Uno, eds., *Gendering Modern Japanese History*
252. Hiroshi Aoyagi, *Islands of Eight Million Smiles: Idol Performance and Symbolic Production in Contemporary Japan*
253. Wai-yee Li, *The Readability of the Past in Early Chinese Historiography*
254. William C. Kirby, Robert S. Ross, and Gong Li, eds., *Normalization of U.S.-China Relations: An International History*
255. Ellen Gardner Nakamura, *Practical Pursuits: Takano Chōei, Takahashi Keisaku, and Western Medicine in Nineteenth-Century Japan*
256. Jonathan W. Best, *A History of the Early Korean Kingdom of Paekche, together with an annotated translation of* The Paekche Annals *of the* Samguk sagi
257. Liang Pan, *The United Nations in Japan's Foreign and Security Policymaking, 1945–1992: National Security, Party Politics, and International Status*
258. Richard Belsky, *Localities at the Center: Native Place, Space, and Power in Late Imperial Beijing*
259. Zwia Lipkin, "*Useless to the State*": *"Social Problems" and Social Engineering in Nationalist Nanjing, 1927–1937*
260. William O. Gardner, *Advertising Tower: Japanese Modernism and Modernity in the 1920s*
261. Stephen Owen, *The Making of Early Chinese Classical Poetry*
262. Martin J. Powers, *Pattern and Person: Ornament, Society, and Self in Classical China*
263. Anna M. Shields, *Crafting a Collection: The Cultural Contexts and Poetic Practice of the* Huajian ji 花間集 (*Collection from among the Flowers*)
264. Stephen Owen, *The Late Tang: Chinese Poetry of the Mid-Ninth Century (827–860)*
265. Sara L. Friedman, *Intimate Politics: Marriage, the Market, and State Power in Southeastern China*
266. Patricia Buckley Ebrey and Maggie Bickford, *Emperor Huizong and Late Northern Song China: The Politics of Culture and the Culture of Politics*
267. Sophie Volpp, *Worldly Stage: Theatricality in Seventeenth-Century China*
268. Ellen Widmer, *The Beauty and the Book: Women and Fiction in Nineteenth-Century China*
269. Steven B. Miles, *The Sea of Learning: Mobility and Identity in Nineteenth-Century Guangzhou*
270. Man-houng Lin, *China Upside Down: Currency, Society, and Ideologies, 1808–1856*
271. Ronald Egan, *The Problem of Beauty: Aesthetic Thought and Pursuits in Northern Song Dynasty China*
272. Mark Halperin, *Out of the Cloister: Literati Perspectives on Buddhism in Sung China, 960–1279*

299. Yuma Totani, *The Tokyo War Crimes Trial: The Pursuit of Justice in the Wake of World War II*
301. David M. Robinson, ed., *Culture, Courtiers, and Competition: The Ming Court (1368–1644)*
302. Calvin Chen, *Some Assembly Required: Work, Community, and Politics in China's Rural Enterprises*
303. Sem Vermeersch, *The Power of the Buddhas: The Politics of Buddhism During the Koryŏ Dynasty* (918–1392)
304. Tina Lu, *Accidental Incest, Filial Cannibalism, and Other Peculiar Encounters in Late Imperial Chinese Literature*
305. Chang Woei Ong, *Men of Letters Within the Passes: Guanzhong Literati in Chinese History, 907–1911*
306. Wendy Swartz, *Reading Tao Yuanming: Shifting Paradigms of Historical Reception (427–1900)*
307. Peter K. Bol, *Neo-Confucianism in History*
308. Carlos Rojas, *The Naked Gaze: Reflections on Chinese Modernity*
309. Kelly H. Chong, *Deliverance and Submission: Evangelical Women and the Negotiation of Patriarchy in South Korea*
310. Rachel DiNitto, *Uchida Hyakken: A Critique of Modernity and Militarism in Prewar Japan*
311. Jeffrey Snyder-Reinke, *Dry Spells: State Rainmaking and Local Governance in Late Imperial China*
312. Jay Dautcher, *Down a Narrow Road: Identity and Masculinity in a Uyghur Community in Xinjiang China*
313. Xun Liu, *Daoist Modern: Innovation, Lay Practice, and the Community of Inner Alchemy in Republican Shanghai*
314. Jacob Eyferth, *Eating Rice from Bamboo Roots: The Social History of a Community of Handicraft Papermakers in Rural Sichuan, 1920–2000*
315. David Johnson, *Spectacle and Sacrifice: The Ritual Foundations of Village Life in North China*
316. James Robson, *Power of Place: The Religious Landscape of the Southern Sacred Peak (Nanyue 南嶽) in Medieval China*
317. Lori Watt, *When Empire Comes Home: Repatriation and Reintegration in Postwar Japan*
318. James Dorsey, *Critical Aesthetics: Kobayashi Hideo, Modernity, and Wartime Japan*
319. Christopher Bolton, *Sublime Voices: The Fictional Science and Scientific Fiction of Abe Kōbō*
320. Si-yen Fei, *Negotiating Urban Space: Urbanization and Late Ming Nanjing*
321. Christopher Gerteis, *Gender Struggles: Wage-Earning Women and Male-Dominated Unions in Postwar Japan*
322. Rebecca Nedostup, *Superstitious Regimes: Religion and the Politics of Chinese Modernity*
323. Lucien Bianco, *Wretched Rebels: Rural Disturbances on the Eve of the Chinese Revolution*
324. Cathryn H. Clayton, *Sovereignty at the Edge: Macau and the Question of Chineseness*
325. Micah S. Muscolino, *Fishing Wars and Environmental Change in Late Imperial and Modern China*

326. Robert I. Hellyer, *Defining Engagement: Japan and Global Contexts, 1750–1868*
327. Robert Ashmore, *The Transport of Reading: Text and Understanding in the World of Tao Qian (365–427)*
328. Mark A. Jones, *Children as Treasures: Childhood and the Middle Class in Early Twentieth Century Japan*
329. Miryam Sas, *Experimental Arts in Postwar Japan: Moments of Encounter, Engagement, and Imagined Return*
330. H. Mack Horton, *Traversing the Frontier: The* Man'yōshū *Account of a Japanese Mission to Silla in 736–737*
331. Dennis J. Frost, *Seeing Stars: Sports Celebrity, Identity, and Body Culture in Modern Japan*
332. Marnie S. Anderson, *A Place in Public: Women's Rights in Meiji Japan*
333. Peter Mauch, *Sailor Diplomat: Nomura Kichisaburō and the Japanese-American War*
334. Ethan Isaac Segal, *Coins, Trade, and the State: Economic Growth in Early Medieval Japan*
335. David B. Lurie, *Realms of Literacy: Early Japan and the History of Writing*
336. Lillian Lan-ying Tseng, *Picturing Heaven in Early China*
337. Jun Uchida, *Brokers of Empire: Japanese Settler Colonialism in Korea, 1876–1945*
338. Patricia L. Maclachlan, *The People's Post Office: The History and Politics of the Japanese Postal System, 1871–2010*
339. Michael Schiltz, *The Money Doctors from Japan: Finance, Imperialism, and the Building of the Yen Bloc, 1895–1937*
340. Daqing Yang, Jie Liu, Hiroshi Mitani, and Andrew Gordon, eds., *Toward a History beyond Borders: Contentious Issues in Sino-Japanese Relations*
341. Sonia Ryang, *Reading North Korea: An Ethnological Inquiry*
342. Susan Huang, *Picturing the True Form: Daoist Visual Culture in Traditional China*
343. Barbara Mittler, *A Continuous Revolution: Making Sense of Cultural Revolution Culture*
344. Hwansoo Ilmee Kim, *Empire of the Dharma: Korean and Japanese Buddhism, 1877–1912*
345. Satoru Saito, *Detective Fiction and the Rise of the Japanese Novel, 1880–1930*
346. Jung-Sun N. Han, *An Imperial Path to Modernity: Yoshino Sakuzō and a New Liberal Order in East Asia, 1905–1937*
347. Atsuko Hirai, *Government by Mourning: Death and Political Integration in Japan, 1603–1912*
348. Darryl E. Flaherty, *Public Law, Private Practice: Politics, Profit, and the Legal Profession in Nineteenth-Century Japan*
349. Jeffrey Paul Bayliss, *On the Margins of Empire: Buraku and Korean Identity in Prewar and Wartime Japan*
350. Barry Eichengreen, Dwight H. Perkins, and Kwanho Shin, *From Miracle to Maturity: The Growth of the Korean Economy*
351. Michel Mohr, *Buddhism, Unitarianism, and the Meiji Competition for Universality*
352. J. Keith Vincent, *Two-Timing Modernity: Homosocial Narrative in Modern Japanese Fiction*

353. Suzanne G. O'Brien, *Customizing Daily Life: Representing and Reforming Customs in Nineteenth-Century Japan*
354. Chong-Bum An and Barry Bosworth, *Income Inequality in Korea: An Analysis of Trends, Causes, and Answers*
355. Jamie L. Newhard, *Knowing the Amorous Man: A History of Scholarship on* Tales of Ise
356. Sho Konishi, *Anarchist Modernity: Cooperatism and Japanese-Russian Intellectual Relations in Modern Japan*
357. Christopher P. Hanscom, *The Real Modern: Literary Modernism and the Crisis of Representation in Colonial Korea*
358. Michael Wert, *Meiji Restoration Losers: Memory and Tokugawa Supporters in Modern Japan*
359. Garret P. S. Olberding, ed., *Facing the Monarch: Modes of Advice in the Early Chinese Court*
360. Xiaojue Wang, *Modernity with a Cold War Face: Reimagining the Nation in Chinese Literature Across the 1949 Divide*
361. David Spafford, *A Sense of Place: The Political Landscape in Late Medieval Japan*
362. Jongryn Mo and Barry Weingast, *Korean Political and Economic Development: Crisis, Security, and Economic Rebalancing*
363. Melek Ortabasi, *The Undiscovered Country: Text, Translation, and Modernity in the Work of Yanagita Kunio*
364. Hiraku Shimoda, *Lost and Found: Recovering Regional Identity in Imperial Japan*
365. Trent E. Maxey, *The "Greatest Problem": Religion and State Formation in Meiji Japan*
366. Gina Cogan, *The Princess Nun: Bunchi, Buddhist Reform, and Gender in Early Edo Japan*
367. Eric C. Han, *Rise of a Japanese Chinatown: Yokohama, 1894–1972*
368. Natasha Heller, *Illusory Abiding: The Cultural Construction of the Chan Monk Zhongfeng Mingben* 中峰明本 *(1263-1323)*
369. Paize Keulemans, *"Sound Rising from the Paper": Nineteenth-Century Martial Arts Fiction and the Chinese Acoustic Imagination*
370. Simon James Bytheway, *Investing Japan: Foreign Capital, Monetary Standards, and Economic Development, 1859-2011*
371. Sukhee Lee, *Negotiated Power: The State, Elites, and Local Governance in Twelfth-Fourteenth China*
372. Ping Foong, *The Efficacious Landscape: On the Authorities of Painting at the Northern Song Court*
373. Catherine L. Phipps, *Empires on the Waterfront: Japan's Ports and Power, 1858-1899*
374. Sunyoung Park, *The Proletarian Wave: Literature and Leftist Culture in Colonial Korea, 1910–1945*
375. Barry Eichengreen, Wonhyuk Lim, Yung Chul Park, and Dwight H. Perkins, *The Korean Economy: From a Miraculous Past to a Sustainable Future*
376. Heather Blair, *Real and Imagined: The Peak of Gold in Heian Japan*